3.11

3.11

*Disaster and
Change in Japan*

RICHARD J. SAMUELS

Cornell University Press

Ithaca and London

First published 2013 by Cornell University Press

Printed in the United States of America

Library of Congress Cataloging-in-Publication Data

Samuels, Richard J.
   3.11 : disaster and change in Japan / by Richard J. Samuels.
      p. cm.
   Includes bibliographical references and index.
   ISBN 978-0-8014-5200-0 (cloth : alk. paper)
   1. Disaster relief—Political aspects–Japan.   2. Tohoku Earthquake and Tsunami, Japan, 2011—Political aspects.   3. Fukushima Nuclear Disaster, Japan, 2011—Political aspects.   4. Japan—Politics and government–21st century.   I. Title.   II. Title: Three eleven.
   HV555.J3S26 2013
   363.34'9480952090512—dc23
   2012037621

Cornell University Press strives to use environmentally responsible suppliers and materials to the fullest extent possible in the publishing of its books. Such materials include vegetable-based, low-VOC inks and acid-free papers that are recycled, totally chlorine-free, or partly composed of nonwood fibers. For further information, visit our website at www.cornellpress.cornell.edu.

Cloth printing   10 9 8 7 6 5 4 3 2 1

To the people of Tohoku.

Contents

Preface

Fall down seven times, get up eight.

—Edo Era aphorism

On 11 March 2011, Japan moved eight feet closer to North America, the earth's axis shifted, and the world turned upside down for 128 million Japanese. Each of us watched in horror as twenty thousand people were washed away by a devastating tsunami just minutes after a 9.0-magnitude earthquake shifted the seafloor off the Sanriku coast in the Tohoku region of northeastern Japan. And then, in slower motion, we witnessed the meltdown of the Fukushima Daiichi nuclear reactor, the displacement of 110,000 residents, and the spread of an invisible radioactive terror (real, even if only imagined) across the archipelago. This quake, tsunami, and meltdown—a triple catastrophe with no precedent—formally called the Great Eastern Japan Disaster (*Higashi Nihon Daishinsai*) soon became known simply as "3.11."

But 3.11 was hardly the first earthquake to shake Japan. The antiquarian booksellers of Jimbōchō in downtown Tokyo bulge with evidence of previous disasters and how they were characterized in the popular media of their day. In one of my favorite haunts, there is a cache of several thousand photo postcards in a crate labeled simply "*shinsai*" (disasters). Most of them are photos of the Great Kanto Earthquake of 1923. They include views from the hills above Ueno of the flattened plain below, photos of smoldering buildings in the Ginza and Ōtemachi, and a powerfully symbolic image of the gate of the mighty Finance Ministry with nothing left standing behind it. Photos of citizens streaming away from the fires, of officials organizing relief supplies, of the young crown prince (later the emperor Hirohito) surveying the damage with municipal officials and military officers, and of charred corpses are all available. They provide horrifying parallels—literal and metaphorical—to the most recent crisis.

The modern bookstores nearby offer a contemporary version of much the same story. For months after 3.11, each had a *"shinsai* corner" just off the main entrance—often draped by banners with the ubiquitous rallying cry *"Ganbarō Nippon!"* (Let's hang in there together, Japan!)—filled with photo collections rushed to print by major publishing houses like Mainichi, Nikkei, and Yomiuri. In addition to magazine-style photo essays there were volumes devoted to the rescue and relief efforts of the Self-Defense Forces (SDF) and hastily produced *manga* (comics) depicting heroic feats by ordinary citizens. The *shinsai* corners were also stocked with emergency food guides, instructions on how to conserve energy, and "anywhere lights" (*do-kodemo raito*) for emergency use.

As in the United States, where 9/11 had framed every corner of the national discourse a decade earlier, 3.11 and its consequences refocused a long-standing national debate on the future of Japan. Political entrepreneurs with ideas about where Japan should go and how it should get there now armed themselves with a new tool. Those with the most compelling account of what happened—including the most convincing villains and heroes—stood the best chance of seizing the political initiative. Long before 3.11, Japan's political discourse had been dominated by a long list of concerns, with failed leadership, uncertain security, unraveling community, and desired changes atop it. After the disaster struck, elites began to refashion their arguments, incorporating lessons from 3.11 that bolstered their particular cause. The national conversation became a rhetoric of crisis and took on greater urgency. What had been a discussion about the *slow* devastation wrought by debilitating demographic and economic forces now became a pressing set of demands about how to respond to *sudden* devastation.[1] Language that had been dormant or discredited for decades—including references to "national crisis" (*kokunan*), last used a century earlier—itself became the object of debate.

Japan's elites were arguing about much more than language, of course, and were engaged in much more than a conversation. Like opinion leaders everywhere, they knew they could be empowered by control of national rhetoric, the "sweet talk" that frames public choices and enables "unforced persuasion."[2] They would use 3.11 to shape national interests (and possibly even national identity) and try to tilt the balance of history in the direction of their own choosing. There were many choices available. For some, 3.11 was a warning for Japan to "put it in gear" and go in a new direction. Japan's national interests would be achieved only by moving forward vigorously, beyond dependence on the United States or on nuclear power. For those who had more to lose from change, the catastrophe was a once-in-a-millennium "black swan," so Japan should "stay the course." It was in Japan's interest to continue to do what it had been doing—but do it better. A change in direction would be counterproductive. Still others declared that 3.11 taught the clear lesson that Japan must return to an idealized past and rebuild what had been lost to modernity and globalization. Japan's interests could be realized only by returning to the country's basic values and rediscovering its essential identity.

For a time, 3.11 seemed like an endless national nightmare. The Japanese public became familiar with units of measure and materials—microsieverts and becquerels, cesium and strontium—that were freighted with anxiety. Nor were policymakers, soldiers, or utility executives any more comfortable with the language and components of the disaster. Over time, however, the crisis would become a part of normal politics. Some became convinced, others grew worried, and some were relieved to think that "the Tohoku problem" might recede from public memory. In separate interviews less than a year after the catastrophe, a deputy mayor of Yokohama said that opponents of change were stalling, waiting for the public to lose its fervor, and a Diet member declared that the death of twenty thousand was not enough to tip national politics one way or another. If they are right, then 3.11 will prove useless as a political tool, and all that talk will have only cheapened the human pain of the disaster.

It is still too early to know if 3.11 will be a punctuation mark or merely a historical parenthesis. But we do know that however complex it was, 3.11 changed few minds within Japan's chattering classes. Opinion leaders were firm in their belief that by distilling the proper lessons of 3.11 they could lead opinions more effectively than ever. So they recrafted their arguments—adding new heroes and villains, compiling new reports and analyses—to convince citizens that there are optimal ways (their preferred ways) for Japan to pick up the shards after 3.11's devastation. It is therefore no surprise that what was optimal for partisans after 3.11 was what had been optimal for them before 3.11. They apparently assumed that the preferences of the general public are always malleable. With enough persuasion and incentive—either in the searing heat of political struggle or in its absence—a largely indifferent public can be brought to support one vision or another. Generating explanations and prescriptions, nudging preferences, and realigning policy after tragedies is a core business of democratic politics everywhere. So Japan's prolonged, intense post-3.11 engagement of government with citizens and ideas—what I call in this book its "dueling narratives"—is many things, not least evidence of a robust democracy at work. Just how the discourse works and whether the catastrophe will empower change or inertia (or neither) are my topics.

I take up these questions in three policy areas: national security, energy, and local governance. The first two choices seem self-evident. The events of 3.11 delivered to each an unprecedented reversal of fortune. A once-marginalized military found itself on center stage, achieving new levels of national esteem, while the periodically maligned military alliance with the United States performed to similar accolades. In the energy case, however, a previously confident and powerful business community became the target of sustained national opprobrium. As a result, it stood on the precipice of massive reform, one that might yet produce the most extensive sectoral re-alignment in postwar Japanese history. Finally, the reasons why local government deserves a privileged place in this analysis may be less obvious, but they are equally compelling, not least because the performance of local governments after 3.11 was so rich in clues about the future of Japanese public administration. Most notably, the crisis illuminated weaknesses in the central government and strengths in the regional and local ones that had been hidden from view. In addition, the post-3.11 visions of the most affected prefectural governments—Miyagi, Iwate, and Fukushima—revealed fundamental differences about local preferences. And 3.11 has pushed the Tohoku region, with its aging population and hollowed industries, some ten years ahead of the rest of a fretful nation. So, getting Tohoku reconstruction right ought to provide clues about national reconstruction in the years ahead.

"Getting it right" in each of these three critical policy areas could mean changes in the deliberative processes through which decisions are made. Might those largely corporatist and opaque processes become more transparent, more participatory? Or could "getting it right" mean changes in the institutions themselves? Perhaps a more robust set of policy checks and balances or a reduction in jurisdictional competition is in the offing. And perhaps we will see if new policy communities are forming. Is a new command structure readying to make consequential decisions in any of these policy areas? Are there imminent shifts in the balances of power between politician and bureaucrat, soldier and statesman, business and government, center and locality? If so, were they caused by 3.11? Did 3.11 abet them in any way? Or was 3.11 just one more event on a path of irresistible change? And if nothing comes of 3.11, why was so great a catastrophe irrelevant after all the *Sturm und Drang*?

We expect a lot from crises—perhaps too much. The Lisbon earthquake on All Saints' Day in 1755, for example, has been credited as having inspired Enlightenment philosophy. Others believe that the 2004 Indian Ocean tsunami was a "wave of peace" that washed away a protracted and bloody civil war in Indonesia. Political analysts, and I include myself, can be particularly credulous when facing events of this magnitude. Indeed, 3.11 spawned no shortage of hyperbole in Japan and abroad. Some claimed a new era was at hand—3.11 would be the grease beneath the skids of economic change, technological innovation, and political transformation; it was a turning point, a hinge, a rebirth; Japan would have its new deal, its escape from malaise, its renewal. A new generation of Japanese, the "3.11 Generation," would find a fresh motivation and stimulate a new national resolve. Their shared, awful experience would define a cohort for which national reconstruction is the new national anthem.

These outsized expectations and claims—some of which I confess to having uttered—were not specific to this event. Social and political theories uniformly hold that exogenous shocks such as war and natural disaster contain within them the seeds for structural and institutional change. And historians often remind us that traumatic events can provide particularly clear windows on political and social dynamics. While appreciating the possibility that it is simply too soon to be certain of 3.11's effects, this book explores all these claims. But I note at the start that six months into my field research, as I became less certain of the imminence of large-scale change, I revised my working title from *Rebirth of a Nation?* to *The Rhetoric of Crisis.* This was about the same time it occurred to me that the ubiquitous but unofficial rallying cry of "*Ganbarō Nippon!*"—which surfaced 23 million Google hits six months after 3.11—was, like the Edo epigram that frames this preface, a call for recovery, not for change.

This is another way of suggesting that narratives take hold in many different ways, of authors as well as the general public. Several months into field research, I realized that I had accepted without question the dominant, uncontested story line that privileged the suffering of the residents in just three prefectures. Miyagi, Iwate, and Fukushima had been hardest hit, of course, and its governors sat prominently on the various reconstruction councils, but they should not have been alone. The rest of Tohoku also suffered, as did parts of Kanto (the densely populated capital district) and the rest of the nation. Moreover, the very term 3.11 is like 9/11, a framing that deserves interrogation. Does it limit political discourse by focusing on specific policy areas or, by virtue of the fact that everyone had a 3.11 experience, does it widen the aperture too much by putting every national issue in play?

By Friday morning, 11 March 2011, I had been working for four years on a book about how political captivity distorts democratic institutions and, having already worked through Japanese, South Korean, and Israeli cases, I was readying to do research on Colombia, Italy, and the United States. But over the next weeks, the dimensions of the 3.11 disaster became clearer, and so too, it seemed to me, did the responsibilities of analysts of Japan. Many of us came to suspect this would be the most dislocating event in our professional lives. I put the still undrafted *Kidnapping Politics* on the shelf and began imagining the rebirth of the Japanese nation.

This book was a project of discovery and rediscovery; of connection and reconnection. It was an unexpected culmination of a lifetime of research and writing on the very policy issues most affected by 3.11: my earlier books on local government, energy policy, the political economy of technology, military security, and political leadership all inform this study. Indeed, they converged on the topic with a force I could not have anticipated. Even my very first publication, an edited volume on political generations, helped me think about the task facing the Japanese nation. I was delighted to spend time again with colleagues of decades' standing, some of whom were interlocutors when I was still a graduate student and with whom I had regrettably lost touch.

And so I thank them and the many new colleagues and friends I made during an intense year in the field. This includes some seventy municipal, prefectural, and central Japanese government officials—military and civilian, elected and career—as well as more than a dozen U.S. government officials who provided time, data, and insights about 3.11 and its aftermath. Dozens of senior officials from the U.S. Embassy (Tokyo); U.S. Forces Japan; the Japanese Ministry of Defense; Japan Self-Defense Forces; the Cabinet Office; Tokyo Electric Power Company; Ministry of Economy, Trade and Industry; and the Ministry of Internal Affairs and Communications requested anonymity in exchange for frank and very helpful interviews.

Among those I can—and am delighted to—thank here are: Abe Tomoko, Akasaka Norio, Michael Cucek, Alexis Dudden, Fujiwara Michitaka, Lance Gatling, Andrew Gordon, Ido Toshizō, Iida Tetsunari, Iokibe Makoto, Ishikawa Makiko, Iwama Yoshihito, Shun Kanda, Kanemoto Toshinori, Kawamura Takashi, Kimizuka Eichi, Kitaoji Nobusato, Kōno Tarō, Paul Midford, Mikuriya Tadashi, Nishikawa Masashi, Okamoto Yukio, Ōnishi Takashi, Joel Rheuben, Sasaki Atsushi, Seguchi Kiyoyuki, Shimizu Isao, Suzuki Tatsujirō, Takamizawa Nobushige, Tasso Takuya, Toichi Tsutomu, and Jim Zumwalt. In addition to providing helpful advice along the way, Andrew DeWit, Christopher Hughes, Jeff Kingston, Michishita Narushige, Muramatsu Michio, and Paul Scalise each took the time and trouble to read draft chapters and save me from mistakes I should never have been so ready to make. (Any remaining errors, of course, are entirely my own.) I am especially grateful to David Leheny, who read the entire manuscript and helped me understand its argument and architecture in a new way. Suzanne Berger also provided very welcome comments on early draft chapters. Shiraishi Takashi allowed me to spend several months at the National Graduate Institute for Policy Studies, and Nakamura Yoshio, Nakayama Hiroshi, Aburaki Kiyoaki, and Handa Akemi supported me at Keidanren's Keizai Kōhō Center in Tokyo. I am also grateful to Giovanni Orsina and Alessandro Orsini, who hosted me at LUISS University in Rome for two months, where I wrote a large part of this manuscript in splendid isolation. Fernando Scaduto, a Roman friend of thirty-five years' standing who insisted I come up for air from time to time, was also characteristically generous and gracious. Verena Blechinger and her talented colleagues at the Free University of Berlin were warm hosts to this peripatetic scholar.

I also wish to acknowledge the support of MIT's Department of Political Science, Security Studies Program, and Japan Program, without which the project could not have been undertaken so soon after 3.11.

Christopher Clary, Fukushima Mayumi, Tobias Harris, and Joseph Torigian were reliable research assistants as I tried to get my footing in the immediate wake of the catastrophe, and Yumi Shimabukuro helped by correcting some of my Japanese spelling just before the book went to press.

Finally—but only because last place is the convention—I thank Laurie Scheffler, who again held down the fort for me in Cambridge while I was away on sabbatical, and Roger Haydon, my longtime friend and editor at Cornell University Press, whose enthusiasm for the project kept me (and it) going. Both are consummate professionals with whom it is a privilege to work. I apologize to both for creating so much of it for them.

And speaking of enthusiasm, no one has more of mine than my wife, Debbie. It was a special thrill to be able to celebrate the publication of her wonderful Japanese cookbook, our elder son's wedding, our younger son's engagement, and our own fortieth anniversary while this book was being formed. Without the love in which those events bathed us, it would not have been possible to keep the catastrophe of 3.11 in proper focus, or our lives in balance.

3.11

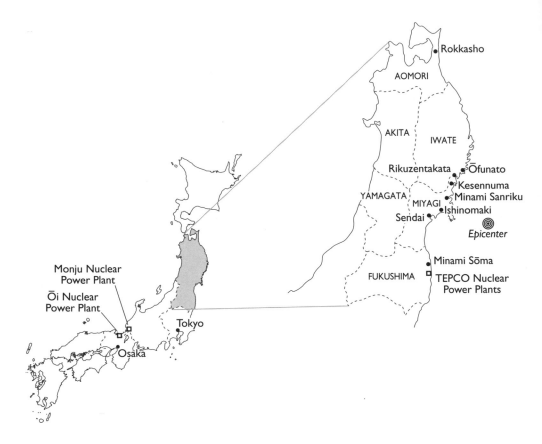

The Status Quo Ante and 3.11

What the hell is going on?
> —Prime Minister Kan Naoto to Tokyo Electric Power Company
> officials, 15 March 2011

I am truly disappointed at how Japan has been providing information over the last few days.
> —U.S. Ambassador John Roos to Chief Cabinet Secretary Edano,
> mid-March 2011

The Great Eastern Japan Disaster, now known simply as "3.11," could not have come at a worse time for Japan. Or, if one believes in the cathartic power of natural disasters, perhaps it could not have come at a better time. A generation ago, in the late 1970s–early 1990s, Japan was the envy of the world. Ezra Vogel's *Japan as Number One* captured the awe and admiration—and dread—that Japanese economic successes inspired. It was a model for how to run an economy and how to manage a society, even how to govern a nation.[1]

Forty years later, such claims seem preposterous. After the policy-induced asset bubble burst in the early 1990s, Japan's economic performance turned lackluster. Between 1990 and 2009, real gross domestic product (GDP) growth was only 1.1 percent per year, less than half the U.S. rate, and barely one-eighth the combined performance of Brazil, Russia, India, and China—the so-called BRICs that had been attracting much of the world's attention and investment. Low growth is preferable to no growth at all, but the list of Japanese economic ills during these "lost decades" defines a vicious circle of contagion. Japanese stock markets and real estate prices plunged 70 percent from their 1980s peak, banks found themselves loaded with bad debt requiring massive restructuring, and deflation gripped the economy. Public debt soared to the highest level in the world. Japanese investors became risk averse, and industry responded by setting up shop abroad, "hollowing" domestic manufacturing. By 2009, nearly a fifth of Japanese industrial production—including more than half of all automobile manufacturing—was done elsewhere.[2] Income inequality in Japan was above the Organization for Economic Cooperation and Development (OECD) average, and the number of Japanese citizens receiving public assistance was approaching early postwar levels. In fact, after transfers and taxes, Japan's relative poverty rate had increased by 24 percent from the 1980s to the 2000s, and became the second highest in the developed world, behind only the United States.[3] In March 2011, fewer workers had lifetime employment and fewer college graduates received job offers than ever before. The latter development was connected to a 250 percent rise in suicides by unemployed college graduates between 2007 and 2011, in a country where suicide had already reached epidemic proportions.[4] In a 2012 study of the competitiveness of world cities by Citigroup and the *Economist*, Tokyo—by far the most prosperous metropolitan area in Japan—was the only Japanese city among the top forty. Osaka and Nagoya, the only other Japanese cities among the world's top sixty, were judged to be less than 78 percent of Tokyo's strength.[5] It was hard to avoid the consensus view that the sun was setting on the Japanese system.[6]

Keidanren, the guardian of Japanese business and industry, blamed Japan's political leadership: "Japan's presence in the international society has diminished in recent years. In particular, its internal business environment has consistently deteriorated. The fundamental problem is that the government lacks a sense of crisis, a commitment to action, and a futuristic vision."[7] And the government accepted responsibility. The opening sentence of its "New Growth Strategy," launched less than a year before 3.11, articulated Japan's long-standing economic and social malaise: "The Japanese economy has continued to stagnate for nearly 20 years . . . [and] the Japanese people have lost their confidence and have been demoralized."[8]

The government's willingness to confront these problems would have been more encouraging had the very term "political leadership" not acquired an oxymoronic quality long before the center-right Liberal Democratic Party (LDP) surrendered power to the center-left Democratic Party of Japan (DPJ) in 2009. With the exception of the popular Koizumi Junichirō, who governed effectively for six years from 2001 through 2006, the prime minister's office had to be fitted with a revolving door. Thirteen of Japan's fifteen other prime ministers have held office for less than two years since the long-running administration of Nakasone Yasuhiro ended in 1987. From the day Koizumi left office, in September 2006, until 3.11—a period of less than four and a half years—Japan had five prime ministers. None generated sustained public support and none gained any policy traction. Meanwhile, some two dozen political parties—most of which came and went without causing so much as a ripple in the national pond—had been formed since the end of LDP hegemony in 1993. By 3.11, the level of public confidence in Japan's political class was near a postwar low, and dissatisfaction was widespread. More than three-quarters of those surveyed before the quake reported they were "dissatisfied with the way things are going in our country today."[9]

There was plenty of blame to go around, and politicians busied themselves by pointing fingers at one another. Channeling many of the rightists' criticisms of early twentieth-century Japanese politicians, Tokyo governor Ishihara Shintarō insists that Japan and its leaders had lost their way in the months and years before 3.11. He and his conservative allies argued that as national values became more materialistic, Japan's leaders became excessively populist; they competed more to deliver welfare benefits than to build a greater nation.[10] The once-vaunted bureaucracy, famously credited by Chalmers Johnson with "ruling while the LDP reigned," had long since been discredited.[11] Virtually every ministry and agency of the central Japanese government had been rocked by scandal—including lax regulation that led to infected blood supplies, fifty million lost pension records, and failed economic policies—at one time or another during the previous quarter century. It was therefore no surprise that one of the most popular promises of the DPJ was its pledge to end "bureaucracy's control of public administration."[12] The 3.11 catastrophe tested this promise on a daily basis. It also seemed to enhance the prospects for significant change.

The Costs of 3.11

HUMAN COSTS

But change, if it were to come at all, would arrive at immense human, economic, and political cost.[13] The 3.5- to 9.3-meter tsunami that washed over the settled coast of northeastern Japan claimed the lives of nearly twenty thousand residents.[14] Entire communities were obliterated. By the time the waters that covered an area equivalent to 90 percent of central Tokyo receded and the rescue effort was in full swing, a 500 km stretch of coastline had been destroyed, seventy thousand homes were washed away, and 160,000 people were moved to temporary shelters. More than three hundred hospitals, nursing homes, public health centers, and other medical institutions had to shut down and could not serve a suffering public.[15] More than half of those who died were over sixty-five years old, but the dead also included some five hundred schoolchildren and the parents of 240 others who were suddenly orphaned—many because their teachers whisked them to the safety of higher ground that their parents could not reach. Life insurance payouts may ultimately top $2.5 billion.[16]

The tsunami was only part of the story, however. Never have so many localities been decapitated at the same time. At just the moment when they were most needed, mayors, vice mayors, and other senior administrators,

Rikuzentakata City Hall, where one-third of the city's public officials perished. September 2011. Photo by the author.

along with forty city halls and other public buildings, all disappeared in the same instant.[17] Nor was Tohoku particularly robust to begin with. Its six prefectures were already on track to lose 15–20 percent of their populations by 2025. Even Miyagi Prefecture, where depopulation was slowest, was slated to lose that proportion by 2035. Population losses that would have taken twenty years suddenly would take only five to ten years. In Miyagi, for example, Minami Sanriku lost nearly 7 percent of its population in an instant, and Rikuzentakata in Iwate lost one-third of its municipal officials. Planning under these unexpected changes—and at a time of unprecedented social need—could now be undertaken by local officials only with considerable outside assistance.[18]

There was also the invisible—and therefore especially terrifying—shroud of radioactivity. Fewer than two thousand people died from the tsunami in Fukushima Prefecture.[19] Still, cities and towns that had ceased to function in neighboring Miyagi and Iwate began to return to a semblance of normalcy in the months after the disaster, but the meltdown of the three nuclear reactors at the Fukushima Daiichi complex of the Tokyo Electric Power Company

Debris in Ōfunato. 15 March 2011. U.S. Navy photo by Matthew M. Bradley.

(TEPCO) bathed the immediate area in crippling radiation.[20] Few of the 110,000 residents of the neighboring towns and villages who were evacuated can expect to ever return to homes that could sicken them on contact.[21] In June 2011, the government acknowledged that the amount of radiation released was double what it had earlier reported. And by August, the government estimated that nearly 170 times more cesium 137 and more than twice the strontium were released in Fukushima than by the bomb that had leveled the city of Hiroshima in August 1945.[22] In December, the Environment Ministry designated more than one hundred localities as eligible for decontamination subsidies—a mixed blessing because the designation brands as suspect even uncontaminated products from those localities.[23]

Most specialists became less concerned about the direct health effects of irradiation once they were able to assess the dosage level and determined that these levels were not especially worrisome.[24] But a drumbeat of news reports of radiation—in day-care centers; on playgrounds; in the Tokyo water supply; in the breast milk of mothers; in baby formula; in lake smelt caught hundreds of kilometers from the reactor site; in beef, green tea, and the rest of the general food supply—kept the population on edge.[25] It did not help when, in November 2011, the Ministry of Education, Culture, Sports, Science and Technology (MEXT) confirmed that radioactive cesium had been found in every prefecture in Japan—including Okinawa, 1,700 kilometers away.[26] Nearly half the children in Fukushima had tested positively for internal radiation in August 2011, and by December, Fukushima governor Satō Yūhei had to apologize to consumers of his prefecture's rice when it was discovered to contain excessive levels of radioactive cesium just two months after he had declared that the year's crop was safe.[27] Making matters worse, many Fukushima residents who lost access to their property also faced discrimination when public hostelries refused them accommodations.[28] The concurrent psychological effects likewise remained to be measured, let alone ameliorated. Suicides by residents who had lost families and/or livelihoods spiked—in May 2011, there were 151 in Iwate, Fukushima, and Miyagi, the three most affected prefectures.[29] Six months later, nearly half the disaster victims were suffering from sleep disorders, depression, and stress.[30] As Rikuzentakata mayor Toba Futoshi, whose own wife and children were washed away on 3.11, pointed out: "Disaster victims are disaster victims 24 hours a day."[31]

ECONOMIC COSTS

The official estimate of the physical cost of this disaster was put at 16.9 trillion yen—more than 10 trillion yen in buildings and nearly 4 trillion yen in power, communications, and transport infrastructure.[32] Standard & Poor's, however, estimated that 20–50 trillion yen was more accurate.[33] And these estimates do not include damage, cleanup, and decommissioning expenses from the reactor accident. Near-term economic effects were easier to observe. First there was the disruption of the global supply chain. Little more than a week after 3.11, the *Nihon Keizai Shimbun* published a comprehensive sampling of Japanese manufacturers who were affected by the disaster, the product lines that were disrupted, and the efforts being made to resume operation. Many of these firms were global leaders, with more than 90 percent market share in some cases.[34] In a nationwide survey by the *Yomiuri Shimbun* in May 2011, half of enterprises reported adverse effects from 3.11. Most suffered interruptions in the supply of components and materials, a decline in consumer confidence, and reduced production due to the interruption of electric power.[35] Toyota was forced to suspend auto production in the United States and Europe, and its 2011 sales declined by 31 percent.[36] In the first two months after the disaster, the Nikkei index of shares traded on the Tokyo Stock Exchange had fallen more than 6 percent and domestic motor vehicle output plunged 60 percent. Foreign residents left Japan, and tourists canceled visits. The number of foreign visitors to Japan fell 24 percent in 2011, the largest drop in sixty-one years.[37] Fully one-fourth of Tokyo's foreign residents returned home temporarily after 3.11.[38] But it was not only foreigners who fled. The population of the Tokyo metropolitan area dropped by four thousand in the summer of 2011—normally a period of population increase.[39] Firms began openly contemplating disaster-induced moves offshore.[40]

There were fiscal effects as well. By mid-July, even before securing its second and third supplementary FY 2011 budgets, the highly leveraged Japanese government had already spent 6 trillion yen in affected areas, twice the amount allocated after the last major disaster (the Kobe earthquake in 1995).[41] Citing weak growth prospects and massive debt, Moody's and other firms cut their ratings of Japan's long-term sovereign debt to "negative," adding considerable costs to what was already the world's largest sovereign debt.[42] In the event, Japan's economy shrank 3.7 percent in the first quarter of 2011 and another 1.3 percent in the second quarter.

Trade was especially hard hit, as many of Japan's trading partners restricted Japanese food imports, rerouted container ships away from Japanese ports, and began testing radiation levels of containers. Former prime minister Nakasone Yasuhiro spoke for many when he fretted about the deleterious effect of 3.11 on "the Japanese brand."[43] By 15 April, the Japan Chamber of Commerce and Industry had issued more than one thousand "radiation-free" certificates for Japanese industrial goods, but to little effect. The next day, the European Union, which already had imposed restrictions on Japanese products, set radiation thresholds for ships from Japan. With import restrictions in place in more than forty countries and regions as late as February 2012, Japanese food exports declined by 8.3 percent in 2011.[44] Japan recorded its first trade deficit since 1980, the result of a "perfect storm" of lost production and closed agricultural markets, a historically strong yen, a eurozone financial crisis, and increased fossil fuel imports to compensate for downed nuclear capacity.

The Tohoku regional economy was hardest hit of all, of course. Sendai and two other regional airports were swamped by tsunami waters, fourteen international ports were shut or washed away, and 260 smaller fishing harbors were destroyed. More than 5 percent of the region's agricultural land was rendered useless.[45] In the first nine months after 3.11, the unemployment rate in the three hardest hit Tohoku prefectures—Miyagi, Fukushima, and Iwate—increased by 60 percent.[46] Public fears of contamination, combined with measurable levels of radioactivity, decimated primary product sales. Demand for the region's beef was down 50 percent—even after it was declared safe by authorities. Japan's largest national retail food chain announced it would use imported rice, dealing a particularly sharp blow to Fukushima, which had been Japan's fourth-largest rice producer before 3.11.[47] Iwate lost 14,000 fishing boats and the use of 108 of its 111 fishing port facilities.[48]

Notwithstanding efforts by the government and nongovernmental organizations (NGOs) to reassure consumers that the region's agricultural and maritime products were safe, the bottom fell out of Tohoku's primary product markets. Mushroom shipments from Fukushima were banned, and all 525 members of the prefectural fishing cooperative had to suspend operations after 15 March. Before the end of the month, 58,000 people in 4,800 workplaces within the 30 km exclusion zone lost their jobs in Fukushima.[49] The prefecture estimates that losses due to just the earthquake and tsunami were more than 950 billion yen.[50] Ironically, Fukushima Prefecture—the source of fully 14 percent of the nation's electric power before 3.11—had to forego nearly 5 billion yen in FY 2011 revenues it would have received from TEPCO in the form of a "nuclear fuel tax" for hosting its power plants.[51] Trying to put the best face on a desperate situation, Miyagi governor Murai Yoshihiro suggested that 13 trillion yen of stimulus for the local economy would provide a great business opportunity, enabling reconstruction of 150,000 homes in Miyagi and relocation of whole communities from the shore to the hills.[52]

The governor's figure was surely inflated, but the region began to grope its way back to health. By the end of April, high-speed rail service had been restored to the region, Toyota resumed production at all eighteen of its domestic factories, the volume of commerce at Tokyo's central fish market (Tsukiji) had returned to pre-3.11 levels, and, after an extraordinary effort by the Self-Defense Forces (SDF) and the U.S. military, even the Sendai Airport was reopened for commercial flights. Cargo soon was moving smoothly in and out of Tohoku—and even the morning market was reopened in Kesennuma, a particularly hard-hit coastal city in Miyagi. And in news celebrated by many observers, by the end of the year, shipments of Tohoku sake and other spirits were up 7–28 percent in Miyagi alone.[53]

Even so, the larger wheels of reconstruction turned slowly. Seven months after the disaster, less than two-thirds of the temporary housing for the displaced had been built, and nearly a full year later, only 5 percent of the voluminous debris left by the tsunami had been removed. More than half of the funds allocated for rebuilding Tohoku were still unspent.[54] A Great Eastern Japan Earthquake Disaster Relief and Revitalization Law, first introduced by the DPJ in late March 2011 to create a "super agency" to oversee the region's recovery as a "one stop shop" for land-use projects and central assistance, was not passed by the Diet until June. And, due to political infighting, the Reconstruction Agency (Fukkōchō) that it authorized did not begin operations for nearly a year. On the first anniversary of the disaster, only seven businesses had received restart loans from the fund.[55] Newspapers were puzzled that it took so long, and one editorialized that the new agency looked like a "ploy" to perpetuate central control of local development.[56]

Other critics were skeptical that any government organ could overcome "the evils of vertical administration" (*tatewari gyōsei no heigai*), the Japanese term for the chronic lack of coordination and debilitating jurisdictional competition among central government ministries and agencies. Although the Reconstruction Agency was established as a "control tower" to help local governments draw up plans and slice through the welter of central government regulations and competing authority, some observers questioned whether any of the central ministries were prepared to cede even an inch of jurisdiction.[57] Reconstruction Design Council chairman Iokibe Makoto was frustrated to learn that the plan to move residents' homes to higher ground fell under the jurisdiction of the Land, Infrastructure, and Construction Ministry, whereas responsibility for relocating hospitals was the job of the Ministry of Health and Welfare, and moving schools belonged to the portfolio of MEXT: "We needed to end this, and did in this particular instance. But I am afraid that the government will revert to vertical administration as usual after Tohoku recovers."[58] One leading urban planner complained that "there were five ministries and forty projects involved in the supplementary budget. It was entirely a matter of vertical administration." But she added hopefully: "If the new Recovery Agency can put an end to this, it could be the major innovation to come out of 3.11."[59] Positive and negative, skeptical and hopeful, public attention was focused closely on the crisis management skills of the Kan administration.

Crisis Management

We expect missteps during crises. Governments perform best when the situations they confront are consistent with what they were designed to do.[60] "Routine emergencies" like house fires and traffic accidents are familiar, and responses to them are adequately scripted and often practiced. But there are also "novel emergencies," unexpectedly destructive and rare events for which scripts may not have been written. In both kinds of emergencies, government responses across key functions—communications, coordination, and resources allocation—will depend on the stakes, the levels of uncertainty, the novelty, and the leaders' response under stress. Novel emergencies demand "adaptive leadership" if they are to be met with effective countermeasures.[61]

Japan met 3.11 with an untested but nominally fortified crisis management system and, even if not always successful, its leadership was clearly adaptive. After the Kobe quake in 1995 had revealed the government's primitive level of emergency preparedness, dozens of laws were passed to enable a more coordinated and effective response.[62] The centerpiece of these reforms was the creation of a unit attached to the prime minister's office, headed by a deputy chief cabinet secretary for crisis management. Still, many felt that the absence of a national agency like the Federal Emergency Management Agency (FEMA), the lack of a comprehensive national disaster response plan, the inability and unwillingness of ministries to share their agency-specific plans, and the limited resources and size of the crisis management office were evidence of "systematic shortfalls" that may have hampered adaptability after 3.11.[63]

Still, the Japanese government moved with dispatch on learning of the quake. Within minutes of the 2:46 p.m. temblor, the largest earthquake ever recorded in Japan, a Crisis Management Center and Disaster Countermeasures Headquarters was stood up in the Cabinet Office and prefectural governors requested mobilization of the SDF.[64] Similar headquarters were established nearly simultaneously in the Ministry of Economy, Trade and Industry (METI), the agency with responsibility for nuclear power plants, and in the Ministry of Defense (MOD). In less than an hour after the highest recorded tsunami in Japanese history washed inland over a vulnerable landscape to distances of up to 10 kilometers, Prime Minister Kan ordered the SDF mobilized "to the maximum level," and the region was designated a large-scale disaster. By 7:00 p.m., after it was clear that a large number of local governments had ceased to function, the government declared a nuclear emergency, and the first rescues had already been made by Air Self-Defense Force personnel. Within three days, more than 100,000 Japanese troops—nearly half of the nation's total military—had been mobilized for search and rescue in the largest-ever mobilization of the SDF. Months later, a team of experts from the International Atomic Energy Agency (IAEA) praised the government's response to the nuclear plant crisis as "exemplary."[65]

This evaluation came as a surprise, for as one of the principals on the government's crisis management team described it, 3.11 touched off "a management crisis of crisis management."[66] Another senior government official who participated in post-3.11 search-and-rescue operations explained that he felt as if he was "watching small children play soccer—always clustering around the ball."[67] Much of this aspect of the problem was attributed to Prime Minister Kan's distrust of the bureaucracy and his tendency to micromanage.[68] His DPJ had declared war on the bureaucrats in its manifesto, and on taking power in 2009, the new administration had moved vigorously to strip them of many of their prerogatives. A retired Defense Ministry official insisted that the DPJ had gone about its business "making enemies of the bureaucrats as if this were Stalin's purge of the Red Army."[69]

It was not surprising, therefore, that when Prime Minister Kan moved to establish emergency task forces, he "sidestepped" the career civil servants and placed elected politicians in charge—often himself and Edano Yukio, his chief cabinet secretary. In the view of some, he was "test-driving a new way of governing Japan."[70] The chairman of the Reconstruction Design Council, a Kan appointee, was straightforward on the matter, stating that "Prime Minister Kan did not trust the bureaucracy and this was a problem for us," but he also insisted that the prime minister "made it clear to the bureaucrats that they were there to listen, and not to talk."[71] Another member of the council applauded this, saying that the council was "exceptional because it was not set up to ratify the plans of bureaucrats."[72] Still, the lack of bureaucratic ballast produced widespread criticism.[73]

So did the political naiveté of the council. When Chairman Iokibe announced at the council's inaugural meeting that he favored tax hikes to pay for reconstruction, he was swiftly and firmly slapped down by Iwate governor Tasso Takuya, DPJ secretary general Okada Katsuya, and more than one hundred of Kan's nominal allies on the DPJ backbench who opposed "reconstruction taxes."[74] In the end, the council left the question for the politicians to sort out. Problems derived from the politician-bureaucrat divide were ameliorated a bit when Kan brought back Sengoku Yoshito as deputy chief cabinet secretary before the crisis was even a week old.[75] Sengoku, who for a senior DPJ politician enjoyed relatively good relations with the bureaucracy, immediately assembled a secretariat of twelve senior officials seconded from across government ministries to staff a new Headquarters for Special Measures to Assist the Lives of Disaster Victims.

The proliferation of new organizations like this headquarters and the Recovery Agency—what some might have seen as evidence of adaptability, but others saw as "dueling headquarters"—was the heart of the problem for many critics of the government's approach.[76] Indeed, the roles and missions of some two dozen new headquarters, councils, working groups, and task forces, many with similar names and memberships, were not always clear. In the first week after the disaster, Prime Minister Kan personally chaired twelve meetings of the Emergency Disaster Countermeasures Headquarters, ten meetings of the Nuclear Power Disaster Countermeasures Headquarters, and one meeting of the DPJ's Committee on Earthquake Countermeasures, and established an Electric Power Supply Emergency Countermeasures Headquarters chaired by Edano.[77] Along the way, he also took a personal interest in the Headquarters for Reconstruction, the Reconstruction Design Council, and many more issues.[78]

In a well-publicized personal intervention during the reactor accident, Prime Minister Kan browbeat TEPCO for suggesting they might withdraw their staff from the three wounded reactors at Fukushima Daiichi. He was widely ridiculed for this, and TEPCO insisted it had never had such an intention, a finding confirmed by a special commission established by the Diet to investigate the accident.[79] But a private investigative commission found that the prime minister's intervention may have prevented an even more catastrophic nuclear accident. Rather than a confused and incoherent crisis manager, the report found that Kan had excellent situational awareness. It praised him for recognizing that neither TEPCO nor his own Nuclear and Industrial Safety Agency had coherent plans for dealing with the meltdown, and concluded that he may have prevented "massive radioactive fallout that could have contaminated the whole of eastern Japan, including even Tokyo."[80] Kan also personally authorized the SDF to douse the smoldering reactor with water in an utterly ineffectual effort that reportedly was staged to demonstrate his seriousness of purpose to the Japanese and to President Obama.[81]

In other circumstances, the direct engagement of a chief executive officer in a crisis of this magnitude and his efforts to create a Weberian rational set of institutions might be more widely applauded, but in the poisoned political atmosphere of post-3.11 Japan, Kan attracted more rebukes than support.

Milder critics claimed that his approach was counterproductive; it would compound the problems of vertical administration by dispersing legal power across headquarters, councils, working groups, and task forces in a maze of understaffed, competing, and ill-conceived new organizations.[82] One critic remarked that Kan's effort "to bypass the mandarins" resulted in a "confused chain of command."[83] Not surprisingly, an unscientific survey of eighty-three Japanese government officials conducted by the monthly *Bungei Shunjū* found that they judge the Kan administration's response to 3.11 to be "reckless," "incompetent," "feckless," and "naïve."[84] It was odd to many that the prime minister never convened the National Security Council and did not include senior military officers in his emergency management team, even though he had mobilized half the nation's armed forces.[85]

Notwithstanding the IAEA report noted earlier, most domestic criticism of the Kan government's crisis management was reserved for its response to the meltdown at Fukushima Daiichi. Difficulties with the world's largest private utility began almost immediately after the quake when the company's president, Shimizu Masataka, in Nara on business, was cleared by the cabinet to use a military plane to return to Tokyo only to be forced off by Defense Minister Kitazawa, who commandeered the C-130 for emergency supplies and medical professionals.[86] On 14 March, TEPCO reportedly told the Cabinet Office that it was going to abandon the site. Edano immediately pushed back, demanding to know if TEPCO was also planning to abandon the Japanese people. At 4:00 a.m. the next morning, after a delay in learning of the hydrogen explosion at the Fukushima Daiichi reactor, Prime Minister Kan called the TEPCO president to the Cabinet Office and seized control of the utility. Kan established another emergency headquarters, this time in TEPCO's corporate offices staffed by his own aides.[87]

At the root of Kan's pique was his sense that TEPCO was holding back information, a complaint that he was hearing from the media and foreign embassies about his own performance. On 13 March, the nation's largest daily decried a five-hour delay in announcing the explosion in the Number One reactor and blasted the prime minister's office for its "weak sense of crisis" (*kantei wa kikikan usui*).[88] The U.S. Embassy pressed especially hard on the Japanese government for information and, not getting timely or sufficient answers, began preparing for evacuation of its nationals. U.S. Nuclear Regulatory Commission (NRC) officials felt they were "dying in a sea of silence," and in the absence of reliable information, recommended an 80 km evacuation zone around the stricken plants—a radius far wider than that set by an embarrassed Japanese government.[89] Meanwhile, the French and other governments chartered airplanes to evacuate their citizens, and the German government moved its embassy functions to Osaka. Foreign governments were operating with an "abundance of caution," and the Japanese government was concerned that following suit would set off a panic among its citizens.[90]

The Kan government had yet another problem with TEPCO—how to make sure the company compensated the victims. A 1961 Japanese law suspends corporate liability in the event of a "grave natural disaster."[91] It was natural, therefore, for TEPCO to insist that it had limited liability at best, just as it was natural for the government to insist that the meltdown was a man-made disaster. It was, of course, both.[92] Kan acknowledged that a government that promoted nuclear power also shared responsibility, but insisted that TEPCO be responsible for compensation payments as "the number one principle of the Atomic Power Compensation Law."[93] Chief Cabinet Secretary Edano insisted that TEPCO had unlimited liability because it had not taken sufficient precautions to avoid the catastrophe. TEPCO responded by reminding the government that when the law was enacted, the then Science and Technology Agency director general (and future prime minister) Nakasone Yasuhiro told the Diet that firms would be exempted from liability in the event of disasters three times the size of the 1923 Great Kanto earthquake.[94] Tohoku was far larger—so large, if fact, that TEPCO insisted it could not have been anticipated. With Keidanren chairman Yonekura on its side, TEPCO also asserted that it had followed all extant regulatory guidelines.[95]

Whether the company's liability would be limited or unlimited, the challenge for the government was to keep TEPCO alive long enough to pay compensation. As one nuclear expert pointed out, "If TEPCO goes under, there will be no cash for the victims and some of Japan's largest financial institutions will collapse."[96] So, yet another new government office was created—the Nuclear Generator Accident Economic Damages Response Office—before which a variety of schemes were floated by a range of interested parties, including TEPCO, its bondholders, banks, the major parties, several government ministries, and others: temporary loans (*karibarai*), obligating the other utilities, injecting public funds, raising the consumption tax, nationalizing TEPCO, power rate hikes, and debt forgiveness were all on the table.[97] TEPCO began paying compensation in May, to fishermen and farmers. By November it had received its first injection of public funds, and by February 2012, it surrendered management control to the state. TEPCO was required to pay nearly $13 billion to accident victims, of which nearly 12 percent was to come from the government.[98] The once-vaunted firm received a one trillion yen bailout ($12.5 billion)—the partial cost of its nationalization—and still faced liabilities of 4.5 trillion yen in just the first two years after 3.11.[99]

The disaster also created battalions of unofficial but often reliable sources of information, connected through social media, who acted as truth squads pressing TEPCO and the government to reveal more information more quickly.[100] Citizens armed with Facebook and Twitter informed one another about radiation levels and other features of the crisis ahead of official sources. They helped locate displaced and deceased friends and family members. On 3.11, the number of uploaded tweets increased by 80 percent, and an elevated level of messages and videos continued for months.[101] Occasional misinformation created problems for the relief effort, and by April 2011, a battle erupted with civil liberties groups when the Ministry of Internal Affairs and Communications (MIAC) tried to remove posts with what officials considered alarming information that "could not be confirmed."[102]

Meanwhile, more authoritative antinuclear power activists and scientists found a new voice. Many blamed the government as much as TEPCO for failures to keep the public informed. Based on the limited data available on 12 March, Koide Hiroaki, a dissident nuclear physicist of long standing, and other antinuclear power scientists recognized that the nuclear accident would be larger than the "level four" estimate of the Nuclear and Industrial Safety Agency (NISA). Koide and his colleagues insisted that it would be at least a much more severe "level six," and decried the significant understatement of the risks to local residents.[103] NISA raised its evaluation to "level five," but the IAEA assessed the event as a "level seven" disaster—the highest possible. Other nongovernment experts knew of and criticized MEXT for failing to use its "System for the Prediction of Environmental Emergency Dose Information"—the so-called SPEEDI simulation data system that was able to predict the airborne flow of radiation and thereby warn residents of danger. MEXT bureaucrats responded that they had not wanted to create a panic, but the interim report of the government's official investigation commission included this in a list of government failures to provide full, accurate, and timely information about radiation leaks and health risks to the public.[104] The government was not entirely at fault. It learned only months after the accident that the feared "total meltdown" of the Fukushima reactors had occurred just three days after the earthquake and tsunami.[105] Nor did it help that Kan's handpicked independent nuclear expert, Tokyo University professor Kosako Toshisō, resigned in frustration when he encountered what he considered sustained incompetence in the prime minister's office. On Kosako's account, Kan's impromptu and nonstrategic approach to crisis management was akin to playing "whack-a-mole."[106]

While a lack of reliable information and questions about the competence of the crisis managers had everyone on edge, the government was also making efforts to balance science-based concerns for nuclear safety against the political costs of panicking the nation. It was learned well after the event that in the early days after the meltdown—when information was scarce and panic could have easily overwhelmed the populace—the Kan administration had secretly considered ordering the evacuation of Tokyo.[107] When pressed by a group of DPJ lawmakers who insisted on an expanded, U.S.-scale 80 km evacuation zone, Prime Minister Kan reportedly refused, insisting he did not wish "to jolt the entire nation."[108] But the nation was already jolted—in some cases by literally not knowing which way to turn. When the government finally decided to expand the evacuation zone, some local governments were not informed whether they were included. According to the *Asahi Shimbun*, "the information residents most wanted was not provided."[109] And when some localities were informed of their inclusion, they insisted that the evacuation perimeter was too large. Minami Sōma, for example, is a city whose southern third lies within the 20 km "Restricted Zone." Its middle third lies within the 30 km "Evacuation-Prepared Area in Case of an Emergency," and its northern third is undesignated. Making administration even more complicated, seven of its western districts outside the 20 km radius were designated "Specific Spots Recommended for Evacuation."[110] After first posting a personal appeal for relief supplies on YouTube that earned him global attention, the mayor expressed his frustration and pleaded for greater clarity and guidance vis-à-vis evacuating his citizens.

Getting to an acceptable level of clarity was nightmarishly difficult for officials and residents alike. Deputy Chief Cabinet Secretary Fukuyama Tetsurō apologized to residents of one village for failing to include them in the hastily drawn evacuation zone, whereas his boss had the opposite task: Edano had to plead publicly with mayors to secure their support for evacuation of their towns.[111] Meanwhile, the government repeatedly changed safety advisories, raising the allowable level of contamination in school yards by twenty times and by one hundred times for power plant workers.[112] Officials kept busy with public apologies for the lack of clarity and sudden policy reversals.

In the most dramatic reversal of all, Prime Minister Kan suddenly announced in May 2011 that Japan should reduce dependence on nuclear power with the ultimate goal of eliminating it altogether. He had not informed his closest political allies or the cabinet, and Chief Cabinet Secretary Edano was obliged to reinterpret the statement as "the prime minister's personal opinion."[113] In July, he announced the need for additional "stress tests" for off-line reactors, again without consulting his advisers. In this case, his declaration came just one day after a mayor in Saga Prefecture had given his approval for a restart of the Genkai reactor based on the METI minister's assurances that it was safe to do so. The minister, Kaieda Banri, indicated that he would resign to take responsibility for the lapse in communications.[114]

Sometimes, though, officials had to apologize for their arrogance. After being appointed the first minister for reconstruction by Prime Minister Kan, Matsumoto Ryū visited the governors of Miyagi and Iwate prefectures, where he was caught on camera lecturing them not to expect handouts unless they generated their own recovery plans. He also berated Miyagi governor Murai for making him wait.[115] Overwhelmed by howls from the press and public for his resignation, Matsumoto lasted only one week in office. Nor did it get better after the government changed in September 2011. Less than a week after Noda Yoshihiko became prime minister, his METI minister, Hachiro Yoshio, was forced to resign for insensitive remarks about a "ghost town" near the reactor site and for making light of the radiation threat.[116]

Support for the prime minister and his reconstruction program quickly softened. The public complied with exhortations to reduce energy consumption, and the trade unions complied with calls for restraint in wage demands; but overall public opinion was hardly satisfied with the quality of the government's ministrations. One unnamed "top bureaucrat" told the *Yomiuri Shimbun* that "the Prime Minister's office only issues good news, while the residents are in a state of confusion."[117] Despite a raft of limited palliatives, such as two dozen press conferences by the prime minister and chief cabinet secretary in the first five days after 3.11, site visits by senior politicians (three by Kan in the first month alone), a tranche of emergency spending released to localities on 18 March, long-term zero-interest loans to small businesses affected by the disaster, ambitious new legislative initiatives, the creation of new jobs for displaced workers, and even an evaluation from the IAEA calling the overall response "exemplary," support for Kan's government rapidly eroded.[118]

Playing Politics with 3.11

Kan had teetered on the edge of a no-confidence vote before 3.11, saved only by a "rally 'round the flag" effect immediately after the catastrophe. The weakness of his government—partly because of his precarious hold on power within the DPJ itself—was evident from the start. His primary adversary was DPJ party boss and Tohoku native Ozawa Ichirō, who held sway over dozens of fellow party members. In his first public appearance after 3.11, Ozawa openly criticized Kan for failing to lead.[119] Then, just a month after the quake, during the first electoral test of the DPJ's response in nationwide local elections, its candidates did poorly—losing seats in prefectural and municipal assemblies and gaining no ground in the governors' races.[120]

Head counts began to compete with body counts for the attention of the Japanese public. Ozawa was joined by a Greek chorus of DPJ members, including former prime minister Hatoyama Yukio, Kan's former chief cabinet secretary Sengoku Yoshito, and the deputy minister of finance Sakurai Mitsuru in declaring that Kan's response to 3.11 was "too little, too late" and that the voters had issued him a warning.[121] Ozawa charged Kan with "invisible leadership" and heading an "irresponsible cabinet."[122] In what editorialists called an "ethical transgression," even the president of the House of Councilors (HOC), Nishioka Takeo, criticized Kan's crisis leadership and called on him to resign.[123] A battle erupted over how to pay for Tohoku reconstruction. Ozawa and his allies argued for bond issues and the purchase of national debt by the Bank of Japan. But the public largely supported Kan's preference for a reconstruction tax, so it is likely that this conflict rehearsed deeper splits within the DPJ and between the DPJ and the LDP.[124] By the end of April, when sixty of Ozawa's DPJ allies met to discuss Kan's ouster as head of the party and prime minister, the cabinet's approval rating was already sinking, particularly with regard to its handling of the nuclear accident.[125]

The LDP had waited impatiently for an end to the 3.11-induced truce, and used the DPJ intraparty rebellion as a signal that hostilities could now resume. Typically, without consulting his party, Kan had earlier offered to form a suprapartisan, "grand coalition" government.[126] But despite strong public support for such a move—even from some within the LDP—party leader Tanigaki Sadakazu preferred to watch Kan fail. Offered the post of minister for reconstruction, he rejected the idea outright.[127] The LDP refused to approve new taxes to pay for reconstruction unless Kan agreed to abandon his "big spending" policies in other areas, such as highway toll reductions and child allowances. Editorialists and business leaders protested that a crisis was no time to discuss Kan's tenure, but the die was cast.[128] As the vice chair of the Reconstruction Design Council aptly put it, the LDP now was pursuing "a strategy of destruction, not construction."[129] One result was legislative gridlock—no new bond program could be passed.[130] Another was a deep public disaffection for both parties and for politics as usual.[131]

Although Prime Minister Kan survived a vote of no confidence in the Diet in early June 2011, when only two in his own party actually pulled the trigger on him, he was forced to promise that he would resign by August. His pledge was dependent on three conditions: (1) that the Diet would provide supplemental reconstruction funding, (2) that bonds would be issued to pay for it, and (3) that an innovative and therefore hotly contested policy to subsidize renewable energy development would be enacted.[132] He left office on 2 September 2011, less than six months after the disaster, with all three conditions fulfilled. But memories of delays, missteps, and insufficiencies in the government's response to the crisis lingered. During Kan's months as a lame duck, his cabinet passed two relatively small supplementary budgets in May and July, totaling only 6 trillion yen. Then, while the municipalities in the affected area and their residents waited, a third, much larger supplementary budget of 12.1 trillion yen was held up in the Diet until October.

Still, There Were Successes

Fortunately for the people of Tohoku, heavy-handed administrative responses to the tragedy and dysfunctional politics were balanced by an outpouring of international support and volunteerism. Tokyo welcomed offers of outside assistance. There were 163 countries and 43 international organizations that extended help to Japan in the wake of 3.11. Twenty-nine sent rescue teams and medical personnel during the first weeks.[133] This included China, which acknowledged Japan's aid after its own Sichuan earthquake in 2008 and sent a fifteen-member rescue team along with a pledge of $4.5 million in humanitarian assistance.[134] The Republic of Korea also moved quickly to provide relief supplies, and the media there stimulated widespread and generous charity—the Korean Red Cross collected

$19 million in two weeks for Tohoku victims. Taiwanese charities alone provided $175 million in aid.[135]

Meanwhile, Japan's own vibrant civil society had never been more effectual than after 3.11. Despite Tohoku's remote location and despite the devastation, nearly 150,000 volunteers made their way to the affected areas in April alone. In May, the number spiked to nearly 170,000.[136] The number of volunteers continued to grow. Within the year following the catastrophe, more than 935,000 volunteers had found their way to Fukushima, Iwate, and Miyagi.[137] Overnight buses filled with volunteers left Ikebukuro (Tokyo's northern rail terminus) and other locations delivering workers to Volunteer Centers established by each of the affected municipalities—and staffed by NGOs—where tasks were assigned and coordinated. These centers had already become primary institutions for coordinating disaster relief across Japan—often ahead of and always a welcomed supplement to the government. Connected to municipal Disaster Headquarters, to local business organizations, and to social welfare NGOs, these centers were among the first to provide needs assessments, to assemble and assign volunteers, to evaluate their work, and to provide information to the rest of the nation and world. Before 3.11 there were just twenty-four registered NGOs in Iwate Prefecture; six months later, there were 360.[138] In one survey by the Keizai Kōhō Center, 90 percent of its members reported making donations to disaster victims and 77 percent said that their firm/workplace organized an effective response to the disaster, such as dispatching volunteers, collecting funds, and distributing goods.[139] In another survey, more than 60 percent reported that they had performed volunteer activities.[140] The Japanese business community reports that it collected 122.4 billion yen in disaster relief funding and provided paid leave, transportation costs, insurance coverage, and other facilitations to employees who wished to do volunteer work in Tohoku.[141] The justice minister even announced that more than 20 million yen was donated to the victims by nearly three thousand inmates in Japan's prisons.[142] In an unprecedented outpouring of generosity, more than 5.7 trillion yen in contributions were received by affected localities within the first year.[143]

As discussed in chapter 3, volunteerism came of age after the earthquake that ravaged Kobe in 1995. But this time—in part due to legal changes in the status of nonprofit organizations—the volunteers and their organizations were more experienced, better prepared, and more widely accepted as professional actors by the government and the victims.[144] In fact, after many of these individuals and groups had cut their teeth in Kobe, they gained further experience and built deeper networks by providing disaster relief services around the world, sometimes in cooperation with official Japanese aid organizations.[145] Many of these groups—such as the Rescue Stockyard, Peace Boat, and the Nippon Volunteer Network Active in Disaster—started out with markedly antiestablishment orientations, including environmental and peace activism; some were even transformed motorcycle gangs.[146]

But as the former president of the Japan International Cooperation Agency, Ogata Sadako, has said, "relief experience is fungible," and by 3.11, the government and the business community were eager to work with them—and vice versa.[147] Indeed, cooperation on the ground between Peace Boat, a leading pacifist organization, and the Ground Self-Defense Forces attracted special notice.[148]

When Peace Boat exhorted the business community to declare 2011 "Year One of Corporate Social Responsibility [CSR]," it was pushing on an open door.[149] CSR offices had already been widely diffused within corporate Japan, and a "gentlemen's agreement" among Keidanren members required that 1 percent of corporate profits be allocated to charities. With this so-called One Percent Club already in place, the relationship between business and the NGO sector had "evolved considerably" well before 3.11.[150] After the disaster struck, most large firms provided "volunteer leave" for employees who wished to help in Tohoku, and the business community was a key source of relief supplies, funds, logistical support, and NGO volunteers. As a further measure of the elevated status of civil society, Tsujimoto Kiyomi, a founder of Peace Boat, was appointed director of the Cabinet Secretariat's Volunteers Coordination Office by the former civic activist, Prime Minister Kan. As "volunteer czar," Tsujimoto worked closely with the One Percent Club to generate funds and volunteers. Still, the volunteer professionals never completely abandoned their antiestablishment past. Despite new levels of cooperation with the military and the state, they used social network technology, particularly as a means "to compensate for, or move in alternative directions to, official statements and the mainstream media."[151]

Considerable support came from the United States. Within hours of the quake, President Obama declared the alliance "unshakable" and promised to "stand with the people of Japan."[152] On the same day, C-130 aircraft from the III Marine Expeditionary Force arrived in the affected region with supplies and troops to begin rescue operations. Within forty-eight hours, a United States Agency for International Development (USAID) Disaster Assistance Response Team (DART) arrived with staff from the NRC and several search-and-rescue teams—144 personnel overall. At its peak, there were 145 additional U.S. government personnel from the State Department, USAID, the Department of Energy, the NRC, and the Department of Health and Human Services working on disaster response and relief under the umbrella of the U.S. Embassy in Tokyo.[153] In addition, the Japan Center for International Exchange estimated that U.S. civic groups provided more than $630 million of aid to the disaster victims, the highest ever for relief to a developed country.[154]

But the U.S. military played the most prominent role. The USS *Ronald Reagan*, an aircraft carrier that had been exercising with the navy of the Republic of Korea on 3.11, was immediately redeployed; it arrived off the Tohoku coast on 13 March to begin refueling support and transport for

Gotō Yumiko's store/warehouse in Kesennuma. 2011. Photo courtesy of Jennifer Robertson.

Japan's SDF troops.[155] Within days, nearly 20,000 U.S. troops, using 140 aircraft and 20 ships—many from politically sensitive bases in Okinawa—were supporting the search-and-rescue and relief operations of the Japanese ground forces. The U.S. military moved supplies, troops, and equipment for the SDF and trained Japanese soldiers. Using Japanese commercial airfields for the first time, they also provided radiation-immune robots and unmanned aerial vehicles that could safely assess the damage at Fukushima Daiichi.[156] In short order, U.S. forces flew nearly two thousand sorties, using nearly two hundred aircraft of every size and capability from transport to helicopter.[157] According to one senior diplomat, the division of labor was simple: "Japan handled the retail and the U.S. handled the wholesale" operations.[158]

Almost immediately, several U.S. liaison officers joined a command post within Japan's MOD and others were deployed aboard the JS *Hyūga*, one of the newest and most advanced ships in the Maritime SDF. For their part, Japanese liaison officers were posted to the USS *Ronald Reagan*. Throughout the effort, soon labeled "Operation *Tomodachi*" (friendship), the U.S. military positioned itself as a "joint *support* force" rather than as a "joint *task* force" out of consideration for the need to keep attention focused on the SDF.[159]

The U.S. Forces Japan (USFJ) commander, General Burton Field, and other U.S. military leaders clearly were sensitive to how the 3.11 narrative would be written. Admiral Robert F. Willard, commander of the U.S. Pacific Command (PACOM), and his troops stood in the background as the Sendai Airport reopened; credit went to Japanese troops, despite the central role of U.S. troops in cleaning the airport. As one U.S. army officer explained, "We couldn't be seen as guys with pearl handled revolvers."[160] The U.S. military even removed signs on portable toilets that had read "for use of U.S. Forces only." Even more important than the choice of "support force" over "task force" was the fact that after decades of joint military *exercises*, 3.11 gave birth to the first joint military *operation* in the half century of the Japan-U.S. alliance.

Operation Tomodachi—and the effort to coordinate U.S. and Japanese responses—were not without their glitches, however. For starters, the U.S. side had to sort out its own command structure. When the USFJ, which was not an operational command, was superseded by PACOM, it created temporary operational problems and, apparently, some resentment.[161] And, for its part, the ever-conservative Japanese side had to get used to the idea of having U.S. boots on the Japanese ground far from their bases. According to one MOD official, "At first we were not sure that U.S. troops would be welcomed in Tohoku. . . . We remembered the opposition there to the establishment of

Prime Minister Kan Naoto visits U.S. fleet commander Patrick M. Walsh (left) and Joint Disaster Response Task Force commander general Eiji Kimizuka (right) at Camp Sendai during Operation Tomodachi. April 2011. U.S. Navy photo by Tiffany Dusterhoft.

new X-band radar facilities in 2005. But when the 31 Marine Expeditionary Unit arrived in Kesennuma, it was warmly received."[162] Within little more than a month, Defense Minister Kitazawa remarked that "we are seeing the full fruit of the efforts made over a half century to deepen the alliance through untiring joint exercises and sharing of bases."[163]

Minister Kitazawa could make that claim only after serious problems of communication between the U.S. and Japanese governments and between the U.S. Embassy and U.S. citizens in Japan had been sorted out. In the case of the former, some on the Japanese side complained of excessive pressure from the U.S. embassy for information and access to Japanese government decision making.[164] In addition, decades of bilateral collaboration had been channeled through the fragmented and competitive administrative environment in Japan, the "*tatewari gyōsei*" described above. As one government official explained, "individual offices within the Embassy and in Washington tended to put forward the views expressed by the Japanese counterparts with whom they most regularly interact. . . . We had become advocates for our counterparts."[165] This sort of "*tatewari* coordination" seemed to clog the flow of information to the decision makers who most needed it.[166] On 14 March, U.S. Ambassador John Roos, concerned by the scarcity of accurate and timely information about the radiological event to the Northeast, asked Edano to allow U.S. experts to sit inside the prime minister's office (*kantei*) "to obtain information for U.S. citizens."[167] The chief cabinet secretary, feeling Japan's prestige was at stake, rejected the request.

But U.S. concerns were heightening. In addition to exercising what it called "an abundance of caution" with its 80 km evacuation zone for U.S. citizens, the embassy also began issuing "warden notices"—informational missives— to the American community that some say were more frightening than reassuring.[168] Some contained conflicting and misinformation about potassium iodide and, in one particularly alarming example, mention was made of a "limited number of seats available" for voluntary evacuation to "safe haven locations in Asia."[169] On 16 March, the day after the USS *Ronald Reagan* and its Carrier Strike Group moved upwind from Fukushima due to radiological concerns, a joint Japan Self-Defense Forces (SDF)/U.S. military helicopter operation to pour water over the damaged Fukushima nuclear plants was canceled due to the growing radiation hazard. Meanwhile, unsure of their safety, thousands of Americans—and other foreign nationals—left Japan.

The "slow trickle" of information frustrated U.S. officials as much as it alarmed U.S. nationals, and Ambassador Roos pressed ever harder.[170] General Kimizuka Eiji, commander of the joint task force, attributed the initial problems to not knowing what the Americans could and could not do to help, and not having the time to sort it out while under pressure to respond to immediate needs.[171] But the DPJ politician tasked with helping to ameliorate the tension explained that "the Prime Minister insisted that we speak to the Americans with a single voice and eliminate the problems of administrative silos."[172] He noted that "the frustration was so serious that mutual trust between the U.S. and Japan was endangered."[173]

This "*tatewari* coordination" now had everyone's attention, and Ambassador Roos met with the prime minister on 19 March to fix it and demand a better "dialogue framework."[174] Kan assigned the task to Defense Minister Kitazawa, who handed it off in turn to Hosono Gōshi, a rising star in the DPJ firmament. By 21 March, senior U.S. and Japanese government officials were meeting formally on a daily basis and in order to fix the problem from the bottom up, so were all of the Japanese government stakeholders. What came to be known as "the Hosono Group" became the key institutional problem solver and solution coordinator that had been missing in the first weeks.[175] In Hosono's own words, it was "the highest decision-making body for Japan-U.S. cooperation."[176] As alliance managers acknowledge, this was not exactly the formal "Bilateral Coordination Mechanism" that the Japan-U.S. alliance guidelines called for, but it was close enough.[177]

Ambassador Roos was also rewarded with permission to install U.S. NRC officials inside the Cabinet Office, a move that did not meet with uniform enthusiasm in the Japanese government or with the public, where there was a growing sense of enfeeblement.[178] But with senior U.S. military officers and NRC officials embedded in Japanese military command centers and in the prime minister's office, and with Japanese flag officers now in U.S. military command centers, bilateral cooperation proceeded more smoothly. For all that, not every problem of jurisdictional competition or siloed communication had been fixed. According to one participant, the Foreign Ministry was largely sidelined once the U.S. and Japanese militaries took center stage. A participant in the Hosono Group explained: "Defense Minister Kitazawa [Toshimi], sensing the confusion, personally took the lead, knowing he had influence with Prime Minister Kan. MOD was not afraid to assert itself. . . . [As a result] the U.S. government stopped using the Ministry of Foreign Affairs [MOFA] as its interface after the first two weeks. By the end, MOFA was so marginalized, they were sitting behind U.S. government representatives at the meetings."[179] As another principal explained, "MOFA is still struggling to keep MOD down, but it is natural and inevitable that MOFA should accept a MOD policy role."[180]

The short and intense period of tension between Washington and Tokyo on how to conduct Operation Tomodachi was soon overtaken by the successful deployment of the SDF and the achievements of the joint operation with U.S. forces—including the truly innovative idea of embedding senior Japanese officials in U.S. command headquarters and vice versa. Indeed, this new level of alliance coordination may be among the most enduring accomplishments of the Kan team's response to 3.11. This possibility is explored in chapter 4. First, though, we turn to an examination of how the 3.11 narratives were constructed and how to evaluate their importance for political change in historical and comparative perspectives.

Never Waste a Good Crisis

Bad people did it.

—Deirdre Nansen McCloskey, 2011

Cataclysmic events do not always deliver large-scale change, but much of social theory predicts—and many practitioners proclaim—that they are likely to do so. Social science has focused on "critical junctures"—so-called moments of "punctuated equilibria"—when constraints on choice "soften" or "relax" for short periods due to power shifts in the course of normal domestic politics or to exogenous shocks such as war, ideological collapse, depression, or natural disasters.[1] Leaders at such moments of crisis are thought to enjoy a greater range of choices than those who operated before the constraints lifted.[2] Their choices, moreover, are presumed to be more consequential than choices made before the crisis because now they may set society on a new course that will foreclose other future options. The new structures and institutions that emerge can be dislodged in turn only by shocks of equal or greater magnitude.

These ideas about change are consistent with the notion of "paradigm shift" that has found its way into our conventional wisdom. We presume that significant adjustments follow sudden, major challenges to a previously stable system. We therefore speak confidently of a post–World War II world that operated under different rules (as set by the superpower confrontation) and with different institutions (e.g., those of Bretton Woods) than the prewar world. Revolutionary ideas, such as communism or Keynesianism, have had the same transformative effect.[3] Similarly, technological innovations—in transportation, communication, and other elements of infrastructure—can also provide dramatic "punctuation" of a stable order.[4] Entrepreneurs had different expectations of markets before the Industrial Revolution than they did later, before the diffusion of railways or telephones than afterward, and prior to the introduction of just-in-time production than they do today. Microelectronics and, even more recently, the Internet and social media have transformed business models designed to generate wealth and profit. New technologies, like crises, have famously led to the redistribution of economic and political power. New products, like a new world order, can transform what we believe are the "normal" social, political, and economic conditions within which we make choices.

This focus on epochal moments, crises, turning points, and revolutionary innovation has another lineage in our political and sociological imagination. Karl Mannheim suggested in 1928 that political values formed by disjunctive historical experiences become the enduring part of a generation's intellectual orientation.[5] Similarly aged individuals forge a political identity when they are "endowed . . . with a common location in the historical dimension of the social process"—that is, when they experience the same historical events, what Mannheim refers to as "crystallizing agents."[6] We have ever since spoken with confidence about the Depression generation and the Vietnam generation in the United States. The Japanese similarly refer to the *ampo* generation that came of age during the political struggles over renewal of the Japan-U.S. Mutual Security Treaty or, earlier (and with greater pride), the postwar generation that rebuilt the nation from ashes. In post-3.11 Japan, many are asking whether their grandchildren will be motivated to sacrifice and dedicate themselves to national reconstruction, thereby becoming Japan's second "greatest generation."[7] While presiding over the first six months of the national trauma, Prime Minister Kan Naoto spoke of how the Japanese people "stood up bravely and achieved a reconstruction that amazed the world," and he challenged the nation to "renew the determination that we had in the post WWII reconstruction period."[8] It will be some time before we know if his exhortation will be matched by action. We cannot yet know if 3.11 will catalyze the energy of Japan's youth or if they will carry on unaffected by the disaster.

But crises routinely provoke the demand for and supply of more immediate solutions. They are, after all, by definition the largest and most urgent of problems. But what else are they, and why do crises offer such potential for (or at least expectation of) change in the near term? Colin Hay offers us a provocative—and deliberately contradictory—compendium of their features: "Crises may be singular, exceptional, recurrent, or periodic; momentary, ephemeral, enduring, or eternal; linear or cyclical; destructive or creative; underdetermined or over-determined; inevitable or contingent; pathological or regenerative; organic or inorganic; paralyzing or liberating; immanent, latent, or manifest. They may be appealed to as mechanisms, processes, properties, or conditions; failures, contradictions, ruptures, or catastrophes; endings, beginnings, or transitions."[9]

Of course, crises cannot be all these things at once; but they may be even more, including tools, as in this study. I focus on their instrumental features for two reasons. First, there is the matter of emotions. Like politics itself, crises are affective and very often cathartic. Their capacity to transform is greatest when large populations suddenly feel deprivation or suffer injustice firsthand. As Baumgartner and Jones suggest, the roots of policy change lie in the "emotional architectures of people."[10] But if the window of opportunity for change—this highly emotional moment—is not seized by attentive political entrepreneurs and social engineers, it may close prematurely. Political fervor may recede, and briefly relaxed constraints may recongeal; the most acute phases of the crisis will pass with little lasting effect.[11] This is why, as Rahm Emanuel famously put it when he was President Barack Obama's first White House chief of staff in 2008, political leaders should "never waste a good crisis."[12]

In this sense, crises are by their nature incubators for contending ideas about the past and future that contain what Hart has described as "multiple realities" and "conflicting cognitions."[13] Crises provide the stage on which groups battle to define the situation and so to control it. In the competition for control of how the crisis is to be understood, populations can be made anxious or they can be calmed. In either state, they can be led in new directions.

There is an unlimited range of crisis outcomes, but after catastrophes there are three directions in which prescriptive narratives are most likely to point. The first calls for acceleration away from the trauma and the immediate past that led to it. Such a "put-it-in-gear" narrative is an exhortation to go forward, farther, and faster in a new direction. Putting it in gear will take survivors of a catastrophe to a newer, better, safer place. It is an argument of quality (new), not quantity (more). The second is a "stay-the-course" narrative, whose advocates insist that the crisis is overblown and little adjustment is necessary. Indeed, much as Albert Hirschman anticipates in his classic *The Rhetoric of Reaction*, large-scale adjustment would likely be futile or, worse, could have perverse consequences that jeopardize previous gains.[14] The natural remedy for a catastrophe that reinforces and validates—or at least fails to negate—extant wisdom is to keep on track and improve. Staying the course, then, is the most likely route to a secure and prosperous future. Its prescriptions are quantitative, not qualitative; that is, any change in this account is likely one in which more or less of the same is in order. The nation is advised to adjust and improve, but not to do things differently. Rather than accelerate toward uncharted territory or sustain the status quo, the third narrative response to a crisis calls for undoing what had led to the catastrophe by returning to better and, possibly, simpler times. Advocates of this "reverse-course" narrative are convinced that the lesson of the catastrophe is that we have come too far in the wrong direction; it instructs us to turn back. Undoing the damage requires more than building something new or reinforcing what was—indeed, either of these choices would invite repeated catastrophe. It requires that we undo the structures and assumptions about progress that led to the catastrophe in the first place.

Crises are constructed and manipulated by stakeholders and are constituted in and through such narratives.[15] Narratives are temporally ordered and causally linked stories that are told (and repeated) by advocates. Their rhetorical structure is simple: "A says X happened because of Y and will lead to Z."[16] They have beginnings, middles, and ends, and are organized around protagonists whose actions transmit moral lessons. It is in the re-telling and broadcasting and retransmission by advocates—sometimes in "discourse coalitions" with others—that these narratives assume political significance.[17] Political objectives that include the reordering of public under-standing and preferences are embedded within them. Gregory Clancey suggests that the emergence of competing narratives can be especially rele-vant after natural disasters that "are culturally and politically quite mallea-ble, resembling holes in a fabric over which much feverish stitching takes place. Nature kills some number of people in a sudden and shocking fash-ion, and survivors are tasked with drawing lessons and carrying on. But exactly what lessons are drawn, and by whom, is [variable]."[18]

Those who can best define the problem will get to prescribe the solution. Along the way they also assign blame—often to political opponents of long standing. McCloskey calls this "the master narrative of journalism" and suggests this is because people want to be told that "bad people did it."[19] Although 3.11 also worked the other way, by legitimating the Self-Defense Forces (SDF) and the Japan-U.S. alliance, crisis narratives are commonly used to challenge the competence of national guardians and delegitimize the claims to authority of those who were governing when the disaster struck.[20]

In a world in which there is only one truth and in which people are as-sumed to be rational and well informed, politically inspired narratives do not matter. But we do not live in such a world. We know that citizens in demo-cratic states are often exceptionally uninformed and that their attitudes to-ward politics depend on a host of factors that are often distant from the policy issue at hand.[21] Thus, the way they learn about the world—who tells them the "right" story, how these stories are constructed (and for whose benefit)—is of critical importance in the analysis of political change. So, therefore, is an understanding of why some public narratives are more effective than others as citizens struggle to interpret their environment.

Effective narratives are marked by several features. First, as noted, is their moral appeal; they are used to identify good and evil—those who have been harmed and those who have caused harm.[22] Second, the ideas and language of powerful narrative packages must "resonate with larger cultural themes."[23] People are more likely to accept ideas, like other products, that seem famil-iar and legitimate. Third, they are sticky. Once narratives are accepted in the discourse, they are hard to replace. Citizens tend to ignore the existence of information if it does not fit with a familiar causal structure, even if new information is provided multiple times. Instead, a new causal story must be provided for conflicting information to register—or else a new shock must displace old discourse with new.[24] Fourth, to be effective, narratives must depend on the credibility of the deliverer. We know that "those to whom

"*He's* the bad guy!"
(1945)

"*He's* the bad guy." Cartoon by Yutaka Asō, 1945, courtesy of Jun Asō.

society has already allocated a special protective or interpretive role" are more likely to prevail.[25]

There is an extensive interdisciplinary literature on the political effects of narratives and the framing of events.[26] The consensus is that, as Joseph Gusfield pointed out years ago, politics and social situations are not understood objectively because "'objective conditions' are seldom so compelling and so clear in their form that they spontaneously generate a 'true' consciousness."[27] Narratives become important in the process of interpretation because they pick and pack the facts to achieve a desired end.[28] It is not surprising, then, that the rhetoric of crisis is so often an exercise in excess, prone to overvilification and overglorification. Japan's post-3.11 discourse is no exception and, as we discuss herein, may serve as an archetype of excess.

The most important mechanism by which narratives may shape interests is framing, the selection of "some aspects of a perceived reality and [making] them more salient . . . in such a way as to promote a particular problem definition, causal interpretation, moral evaluation, and/or treatment recommendation."[29] Of course, "interpretation" borders on manipulation. Frames organize reality by providing meaning—often meaning that simultaneously promotes the vision of the framers and appeals to core values and priorities of the public.[30] They are designed to portray something as problematic, find causes for that problem, introduce a moral element, and suggest solutions. There are, moreover, first-mover advantages for especially prompt storytellers because as already noted, first impressions may be difficult to dislodge.[31]

I have elsewhere emphasized the importance of leaders in the development of narratives, through a mechanism called "bricolage."[32] I focus on elites because not all political actors have equal abilities to influence policy. Nor do they have equal capabilities to define reality for others.[33] That being said, we know that elites are often divided and "wage a war of frames because they know that if their frame becomes the dominant way of thinking about a particular problem, then the battle for public opinion has been won."[34] In an era of social networking and independent platforms for spreading information, it is striking that citizens still seem to place so much faith in elites. Or do they? How much does framing and narrative construction by elites still dominate the discourse and the formation of preferences? As we discuss in this book, Japan's 3.11 narratives may have been more difficult for elites to control because they were generated in such a highly distributed and interactive context.[35]

To whatever extent leaders matter, political change is never a simple case of the elite telling a particular story and imposing their preferred narrative. "Receiver characteristics," such as the political sophistication of citizens, levels of trust in government, the proliferation of stories, and the distribution of ideological preferences are all important factors in how people react to public messages.[36] We do not know whether citizens exposed to multiple frames revert to underlying values to sort through the claims, or whether these values can accommodate multiple interpretations and are better understood as more plastic than fixed.[37] Either way, the development of new narratives is always contested. Activists' challenges invite counterframing by targeted opponents, bystanders, or the media, which joins in by evaluating claims and reporting on disputes about the best frame to use.[38] Such competition and disputes may even negate framing effects because citizens often know their own values and can discover (or shop for) the elites they want to believe.[39] We can anticipate that the most influential post-3.11 narrators in Japan were also the most influential political commentators before the crisis, and that their stories about 3.11 were crafted to be consistent with their extant preferences.

The response to 3.11 also illustrates how narratives multiply and can be particularly influential when politics and society are in flux. It is a perfect setting to understand Thomas Rochon's suggestion that "public recognition of a crisis generates demand for a political response; it represents an opportunity for bureaucratic agencies and policy advocates to put forward their cherished proposals. Crisis divides old allies and makes possible new coalitions. For political leaders, crisis loosens the normal constraints on action by creating expectations of the kind of leadership that is normally hemmed in by constitutional routines."[40]

Crises serve as focusing events that can help shape the political agenda by creating openings for policy advocacy. Sudden events that simultaneously focus the attention of elites and mass publics can generate media coverage on a problem that earlier would have required a great deal of mobilization by groups in favor of change or else would have gone unattended.[41] Catastrophes like Japan's 3.11 seem to have special power. Kent Jennings connects our focus on the instrumental rhetoric of crisis with Mannheim's longer-term concern for political generations: "Some pain and loss events are so epochal that they become entrenched in their nation's collective memories, exerting their influence long after the events themselves have transpired. These events become part of the cultural stock that conditions the public's response to political issues and provide activists with a repertoire of images and symbols that can be invoked on behalf of a cause."[42]

In precisely this way, 3.11 provides the potential disjuncture many social scientists believe is necessary for substantive political, economic, and social change in a nation that has become accustomed to questioning its own vitality. In the case of post-3.11 Japan, it has generated the three prescriptions for change outlined earlier, each with its own causal energy and its own villains and heroes.

Change and the 3.11 Narratives

The weeks and months after 3.11 were certainly filled with calls for (or anticipation of) wholesale change across a very broad institutional horizon. Google searches in Japanese more than nine months after 3.11 that paired "Rebirth" (*saisei*) with "Great Eastern Japan Disaster" (*Higashi Nippon Daishinsai*) generated nearly twenty-seven million hits. Substituting "Change" (*kaikaku*) for "Rebirth" yielded ten times more (261 million) hits, suggesting that a deep yearning for (or at least a heightened expectation of) change undergirded the national conversation. And, indeed, there emerged a widespread optimism on both the Left and the Right that a stagnant nation had experienced a sort of Schumpeterian moment of "creative destruction."

Japan would "put it in gear," and 3.11 would be the trigger for a long-sought national recovery. On the right, a retired defense official said there would be a reawakening of Japanese hearts after a period of excessive materialism, and predicted that "the 3.11 disaster will be seen as a big shock that led a declining Japan to revival."[43] Conservative Tokyo governor Ishihara Shintarō went him one better, arguing that 3.11 was an opportunity to "wash away the greed" that had become central to Japanese national identity.[44] On the left, a group of activist scientists and engineers insisted that 3.11 marked "the beginning of a new chapter in Japanese history," one that would be more transparent and that would put an end to the "spell of deceit" engineered by elites in Tokyo.[45] Abe Tomoko, the Policy Committee chair of the Democratic Socialist Party, insisted that "all of Japan, not just Tohoku—needs a recovery."[46] In the center, a former prime minister spoke of 3.11 as an opportunity for Tohoku to become the model for twenty-first-century Japan, insisting that "unless we resolve to reset and be reborn, we will never recover"; a senior member of the Iokibe Commission spoke of the "geriatric diseases" afflicting Japanese institutions and expressed hope that 3.11 would "generate a new nation."[47] Some of the discourse was not so much hopeful as openly hyperbolic—as in the statement by one veteran political journalist who insisted that 3.11 "changed everything" by creating "a new political paradigm."[48] Professor Wada Akira of the Tokyo Institute of Technology saw 3.11 as "an opportunity to change our thinking, our civilization."[49] Even the otherwise analytical Mikuriya Takashi, vice chair of the Iokibe Commission, proclaimed in the first sentence of his memoir that "3.11 will change Japan and the world."[50]

After they had caught their breath, however, most analysts agreed with Taggart Murphy that 3.11 would be understood as a historical punctuation mark, a "hinge of history" after which "something both irrevocable and transforming ha[d] occurred."[51] Professor Mikuriya captured this idea in his widely embraced neologism: 3.11 marked the end of the long (and long dysfunctional) "postwar" (*sengo*) and the transition to a "postdisaster" (*saigo*) in which salutary change would be possible "at last."[52] Former prime minister Nakasone Yasuhiro, Nippon Steel chairman Mimura Akio, and Tokyo University professor Kitaoka Shinichi issued a plan for post-3.11 national reconstruction that included a reexamination of land-use plans to avoid excessive urban concentration, recommitment to Japan as a technology-based nation, nurturance of a civic-spirited nation, opening Japan to freer trade, and promotion of fiscal reform.[53] Channeling their inner Mannheim, analysts across the board predicted that younger Japanese would become more public spirited and Japan's neighbors would perceive Japan as less threatening.[54] The ubiquitous postrecovery national slogan, "Hang Tough, Japan!" (*Ganbarō Nippon!*) would be supplanted by the more forward-leaning "Let's do it this way, Japan!" (*Kōshiyō Nippon!*).[55] Japan should, in short, "put it in gear."

That being said, not all discussion of change after 3.11 was painted on a teleological canvas. The expected range of discourse—from accelerating to sustaining to returning to better days past—was all actively in play. Powerful arguments for "staying the course" emerged from both the energy sector and national security experts. In the former, energy analysts and stakeholders insisted that "if we change too fast, the situation will become more chaotic. We need to be prudent."[56] Japan must not write off the enormous sunk costs of its nuclear power program, for doing so would increase energy costs, destroy jobs, slow growth, result in power shortages, pollute the environment, and result in higher taxes. Japan would be worse off than before.[57] With regard to national security, the exceptional performance of the Japanese military and of the U.S.-Japan alliance demonstrated the importance of both. These institutions proved their value and should be reinforced and enhanced, but not transformed. Arguments for "less troops and less equipment" should be put to rest at last.[58]

There were also voices arguing to go "back to the future." Perhaps the most distinguished advocate of this (decidedly minority) position was Kyoto University philosopher (and Tohoku-born) Umehara Takeshi. Umehara, who served as a special adviser to the Iokibe Commission, is widely known as a proponent of Japanese essentialism—the much maligned *nihonjinron*.[59] He has long extolled (and has long advocated a return to) the values of *jōmon* culture, based on ecological harmony. He labeled 3.11 a "civilizational disaster" (*bunmeisai*), interpreting it as a signal that Enlightenment thinking and modernity—malicious western imports—have reached their limits and that Japan should "return to coexistence with nature" (*kyōzon ni kaerō*).[60] Umehara prescribes that the Japanese rediscover their spirituality based in Buddhist values and reject the materialism they imported from the West. Wasteful consumption and "arrogant" aggression against nature must be replaced by a renewed, spiritually grounded civilization built upon respect for the natural world. These views were echoed by an activist "eco-priest" Naitō Kanpū, founder of a nonprofit organization (NPO) called the "Simple Life Diffusion Center," who blogged a list of 3.11 lessons that included the need to turn away from materialism and reduce the demands that humans make on nature.[61]

This notion of a return to simpler, more harmonious times, with its anti-growth tilt, was not the sole preserve of conservatives such as Umehara or Buddhist intellectuals and activists. Philosophers on the left, such as Uchiyama Takashi, offered a different but parallel critique of the "failure of modernity."[62] For Uchiyama, modern history is a tale in which production systems grew larger and larger while individuals' powers shrank. He suggests that 3.11 demonstrated the limits of modern technology and showed us that "we live in an age where we can witness the deterioration and contradictions of capitalism, the nation state, and civil society."[63] "Simple lifers" on the left support renewable energy but express reservations because alternatives to nuclear power have their own technical flaws. As humans continue to despoil the planet, the way forward is as fraught as the status quo.

Change, or resistance to it, was the principal motif of 3.11; it was more contested and applied more widely than any other. But it was only one of four elements that came to dominate the postdisaster discourse. Change was joined in a crowded and confused rhetorical landscape by leadership, risk, and community. We examine each of these other tropes—and their villains and heroes—in turn.

The Expanded Rhetoric of Crisis

LEADERSHIP

It is difficult to find many observers who were satisfied with the quality of Japanese leadership after the crisis. Japan's leadership deficit—long recognized as a serious shortcoming—was widely viewed as the single greatest impediment to an effective response to 3.11, let alone some sort of transformation of Japan.[64] In early April 2011, an *Asahi Shimbun* editorial writer, Soga Takeshi, declared that "our political leaders have yet to offer a single convincing statement about the disaster that strikes an emotional chord in the hearts of the people." Instead, he said, politicians and bureaucrats fight among themselves, while "our nation is waiting to hear the voice of a great orator."[65] This view was widely embraced in the Japanese media across the ideological spectrum. *Jiji Press*, for example, opined in late March that the prime minister "has not given sufficient explanation to dispel the people's fears nor has he displayed leadership."[66] Three days earlier, the *Yomiuri Shimbun* insisted that "the prime minister is not showing vital leadership," and a few days later, the *Nihon Keizai Shimbun* reported that "criticism is mounting" over Kan's "unseen face."[67] There was a widespread yearning for a contemporary Gotō Shinpei, the visionary mayor of Tokyo who had moved vigorously to rebuild the capital after the Great Kanto Earthquake in 1923.[68]

Plenty of shots (cheap and otherwise) were fired at Prime Minister Kan by opponents both within and outside the Democratic Party of Japan (DPJ).[69] But the larger problems of leadership were expressed with particular gravity by those who most depended on it. A great many local public officials declared the government to be insensitive to the victims. Mayor Toba Futoshi of Rikuzentakata, for example, threw up his hands in frustration, declaring that nothing changes for the people on the periphery. Local victims, he said, are treated as distant objects by politicians, none of whom made sufficient efforts to assess their needs or to appreciate how those needs evolve.[70] His colleague Fukushima Kenji, mayor of Rokkasho Mura in nearby Aomori Prefecture, asked incredulously: "Does the premier know the hardship that we at the site are going through?"[71] As we discuss in chapter 6, it was the localities' frustration with ineffective responses from the central authorities that led to some of the most immediate—and likely consequential—policy innovations after 3.11.

As problems of leadership moved front and center, a motif of leadership villainy evolved in which the center-left government of Kan Naoto became the lead rogue. On this account, the DPJ was a group of "amateurs" who were insufficiently aggressive in implementing the changes they had promised in their 2009 party manifesto and too slow to respond to the crisis itself.[72] Prime Minister Kan, who went to Fukushima the day after the quake and tsunami, was roundly criticized for trying to micromanage rescue and relief operations, thereby delaying an effective response.[73] He had no command authority, in part because he had neutered the bureaucracy on which crisis management had to depend.[74] As a result, it was said, "the government's move was always one step behind . . . caus[ing] the damage to spread."[75] His creation of multiple task forces and councils was roundly criticized for unnecessarily snarling the chain of command.[76] The term "*donkan*" (thick-headedness or excessive insensitivity) was an easy pun on the prime minister's name, and came to be applied routinely to him as the personification of failed leadership.[77]

A tale of grossly incompetent leadership was being spun, and the same villain was in everyone's crosshairs. In what took on the characteristics of an echo chamber, Kan—and the public—began hearing the same criticisms from every corner. According to some, Kan was an antiprofessional who governed the nation as if it were a citizens' movement; to others, like former prime minister Nakasone and Keidanren chairman Yonekura Hiromasa, Kan lacked crisis management skills.[78] Even Abe Shinzō, whose own premiership had crashed and burned just four years earlier, wrote an article entitled "If It Were Me, This Is What I'd Do," in which he declared that Kan was an emperor with no clothes.[79] A deputy news editor of the *Yomiuri Shimbun* asked rhetorically: "Is Kan going to be the worst premier in history?"[80] A weekly magazine spoke of "Kan's meltdown" and "slapstick theater" at the prime minister's office.[81] Even the judicious public servant Ogata Sadako, who was president of the Japan International Cooperation Agency during 3.11, has said that the prime minister "did not understand what he was doing. The people were good, but their leaders were poor. It was clear that people in the most responsible positions were simply not capable."[82]

The critiques of government were inconsistent: too much or too little consultation, too much on-site presence versus too much distance, too much or too little elite direction, too much or too little political control of the bureaucrats, too much or too little "presidentialism," too much micromanagement versus too much detachment, too much speed versus too much lethargy, too many snap decisions versus too much caution. But they were relentless, and the Japanese public accepted them. Although the prime minister's support seemed to increase when he acted presidentially, he did so too rarely and saw his public support ebb away.[83] Poll results varied, but it soon became clear that the criticisms were eating away at what remained of Kan's popularity. Although he enjoyed some support in general terms a month after the disaster, the public came to be overwhelmingly dissatisfied with his handling of the nuclear disaster. Nearly three-quarters of respondents in one poll found the disclosure of information regarding the nuclear crisis to be "unsatisfactory," and fully 70 percent said they did not support the prime minister because "he has no leadership capability."[84] Within a month, more than three-quarters of the public reported that Kan was "not exercising leadership."[85] Leadership, the holy grail of Japanese governance and the equal of any post 3.11 national concern, requires trust. For Kan, trust became a rapidly wasting asset. But there was another emerging theme competing for space in the public imagination, one centered on vulnerability and risk that identified an even more imposing villain—the Tokyo Electric Power Company (TEPCO).

RISK

The risk motif was officially introduced by the Reconstruction Design Council at the beginning of its June 2011 report: "The disaster revealed in one fell swoop the inherent vulnerability of modern civilization."[86] Vulnerability, a hoary trope in Japanese discourse, is often captured in the "small island nation" (*shimaguniron*) explanation for contemporary life that many Japanese invoke to remind themselves that they are an endangered people in a fragile land.[87] So it is no surprise that this fragility became a leading element of national discourse after 3.11. As one senior Defense Ministry official explained with reference to the themes of change and leadership introduced earlier: "The quake highlighted the country risk of Japan. Without leadership and a better political system, Japan will not be good at managing crises—and there is more danger ahead."[88] Anticipation of future danger was everywhere after 3.11. On the four-month anniversary of the disaster, Japan's leading booksellers displayed titles such as: *The Meltdown of Japan*; *Japan's Third Defeat*; *What Will Happen to the Japanese Economy after the Disaster?*; *Japan's Nuclear Crisis Zone*; and *A Manual to Deal with Nuclear Power Accidents*. And on the six-month anniversary, the pairing of the term *fuan* (insecurity or anxiety) with "3.11" in a Japanese Google search surfaced 131 million hits, while *anzen* (safety) with "3.11" yielded 524 million.

There are a great many ways to express concerns about risk and vulnerability in Japanese, including a term borrowed from English: *risuku*. But the one that came to dominate the post-3.11 national discourse along with change, leadership, and community was the slightly more oblique—and, as it turned out, the far more incendiary—term "unimaginable" (*sōteigai*). *Sōteigai* cannot be translated directly as either risk or vulnerability, but perhaps because the greatest threats to a people are the ones that are unanticipated, its use by government and TEPCO as an explanation for their failure to prepare for a 3.11-scale disaster evoked both, and soon dominated the national discourse. A search for the paired terms *sōteigai* and "3.11" five months after the catastrophe surfaced more than seven million hits on Japanese blogs and Web pages. The first dozens of hits included scalding denunciations of the very idea that the tsunami and resulting reactor meltdown may have been unimaginable. The notion of failed imagination in the face of assumed vulnerability seems to have attained a special purchase in the Japanese discourse for, by comparison, a search for "unimaginable" and "9/11" surfaced only 2.5 million hits a full decade after the U.S. tragedy.

Sōteigai is used both by those who advocate putting Japan in gear and by those who insist that Japan should stay the course. For the latter, it is often used as a masking argument, a common rhetorical device that shifts responsibility for a performance failure.[89] TEPCO vice president Fujimoto Takashi, for example, insisted that it was not TEPCO's failure to anticipate such a calamitous natural event, but the *nation's*: "To what extent can we burden ratepayers to prepare for disasters that occur only every several hundred years and that considerably exceed in scale what the nation has foreseen?"[90] He was joined by a TEPCO general manager who insisted that "the accident at Fukushima Daiichi was caused by a tsunami far beyond the design basis." It was, he said, an "unforeseeable accident."[91] Former TEPCO vice president and influential member of the House of Councilors Kanō Tokio rejected the idea that the nuclear power industry might have been too complaisant about risk, and further widened the circle of responsibility for 3.11: "It is a shame, but it was not only TEPCO and the nuclear power industry that found it convenient not to imagine these possibilities. [The failure to foresee] emerged from a democratic debate and from government established safety standards. It was on these standards that nuclear power plants were built and operated."[92] These stakeholders were joined by an occasionally sympathetic media. The *Yomiuri Shimbun*, for example, reminded readers that the Jōgan earthquake, the last temblor and tsunami on this scale, occurred in the year 869 and asked a now familiar question: "How do we prepare for something that happens once in 1,000 years?"[93]

For those who deployed *sōteigai* as a call to action, the discussion of unimaginable and unanticipated events was merely a useful foil against which to argue for better preparation, larger budgets, better government, and stronger leadership—that is, improvements across the board.[94] They echo Nakagawa Kazuyuki who, after the 1999 nuclear accident at Tokai Mura, insisted: "It is time to get moving! We must reduce the situations we are unprepared to imagine and prepare ourselves for the unimaginable. Nuclear accidents and earthquakes present the same problems for crisis management."[95]

Indeed, like Nakagawa before them and much like the general public after 3.11, few experts accepted TEPCO's *sōteigai* defense. To the contrary, many protested what they considered the misappropriation of the term by the nuclear power industry and its allies in business and government. Even the head of the Nuclear Safety Commission testified before a special Diet panel and excoriated his own staff and utility officials for their insouciance vis-à-vis safety. He suggested that they ignored international guidelines, and were instead "spending their time finding excuses" for not taking adequate safety measures.[96] One critic asked: "If I . . . was able to foresee this and the nuclear power specialists from TEPCO and from the government's nuclear related agencies were not, then for what do they exist?"[97] Others argue that use of the *sōteigai* defense is irresponsible and reckless—a "trap" that Japanese should have been able to avoid.[98] Hatamura Yōtarō, a Tokyo

University professor specializing in what he calls "dangerology" (*kikengaku*) and "failureology" (*shippaigaku*), criticized nuclear experts for using the term *sōteigai* too casually, maintaining that "imagining disasters is the responsibility of experts."[99] Professor Nakabayashi Itsuki of Meiji University distinguished different kinds of accidental events—those that are fully within human imagination and can be mitigated by prior planning (*sōteinai*) and those that are imaginable but cannot be fully mitigated ahead of time (*sōtei ijō*). For truly unimaginable events, he considered "resilience" the only response available, and suggested that 3.11 was not in this category.[100] At first invoked to defend, the *sōteigai* trope was soon used to shift blame and assign villainy; rather than protecting its promulgators, it turned them into villains and emboldened their critics.

There was certainly no shortage of critics. If Kan became the whipping boy in the discourse on leadership, TEPCO became the consensus villain with regard to risk and vulnerability. It was an easy target.[101] TEPCO has a long history of falsifying safety reports and covering up violations, and in this instance, its managers reportedly withheld information from the public and hesitated to cool the crippled Fukushima Daiichi reactors with seawater in order to avoid compromising its capital investment.[102] TEPCO's alleged deceits were captured most luridly in a nine-story compendium in an early April issue of a major Japanese weekly with the headline: "TEPCO's Crimes and Punishment."[103] The August 2011 issue of *Sekai*, a leading progressive monthly, contained an article titled "TEPCO as a Social Problem." Prime Minister Kan was among the first to demonize TEPCO, demanding that its executives tell him "what the hell is going on" in the first days after the accident at the Fukushima Daiichi reactors.[104] Satō Yūhei, the governor of Fukushima Prefecture, joined the chorus of TEPCO critics and refused to accept a personal apology from TEPCO president, Shimizu Masataka. After being taunted by lawmakers on the floor of the Diet, Shimizu was hospitalized before resigning to take responsibility for "bring[ing] much grief and fear to society."[105] Arguing that "people would be arrested if gas tanks explode or if a fire breaks out in a department store," Saitama governor Ueda Kiyoshi insisted that TEPCO officials should be held criminally responsible for the nuclear crisis.[106] The patriotic textbook activist Nishio Kanji blasted those whose imagination failed the nation. But Japan was supposed to be a technological superpower. So where were the robots that could have secured the reactor sooner? Where were the water pumps that might have cooled it and prevented a meltdown? Where was the radioactivity protection gear? Why was so much left unplanned for and unimagined? "Japan's utilities had an accident plan that presumed there would not be an accident," an indignant Nishio declared.[107]

The demonizing critique had even sharper teeth when it came from Fukushima itself. Sakurai Katsunobu, the mayor of Minami Sōma who lost more than 650 of his neighbors and who became internationally known for his plea for assistance on YouTube, called out TEPCO as the chief villain of 3.11.[108] He insisted that the utility reverted to old patterns of lying and falsifying data in its interactions with victims. Residents who were forced from their homes near the crippled reactors left their evacuation centers and came to Tokyo to protest in front of TEPCO's corporate offices and demand compensation.[109] Even before the end of March, just twenty days after the accident, TEPCO actually submitted plans to add two more reactors to the Fukushima Daiichi complex—an act of hubris that was not lost on the general public.[110] The public finally learned in late May—more than two months after the disaster—that TEPCO had known that three of its four reactors had melted down within days of the tsunami. One foreign columnist captured the mood by referring to TEPCO's "shameful mismanagement of the meltdown" and suggesting that all of Japan is undergoing a "TEPCO-ization" of its once lofty reputation for quality and efficiency. He added: "TEPCO is the poster child of Japan's culture of corporate complicity."[111]

TEPCO was the arch villain here, but government regulators—many of whom were in line to enjoy a postretirement sinecure in the electric power industry—were cast in the roles of abettors and attendants.[112] The system overestimated safety and underestimated risk because the regulators and the regulated had been in a conspiratorial embrace for decades. The press was full of accounts of Ministry of Economy, Trade and Industry (METI) regulators allowing TEPCO to draft their regulations and, more salaciously, of officials demanding compensation in the form of entertainment.[113] The two are often joined at the hip in accounts of 3.11 that routinely touch on "slipshod" regulation and cover-ups and record tampering after previous accidents.[114] Former Fukushima governor Satō Eisaku, for example, decried TEPCO's and METI's "malign concealment" of past mishaps. A wounded veteran of Japan's nuclear power politics, Satō referred to METI as the "root of all evil" and concluded that 3.11 was a "man-made crime of omission by the government and TEPCO"—a "betrayal" of the people of Fukushima.[115] The public concurred. In May 2011, nearly three-quarters of those surveyed by the *Asahi Shimbun* said that they "cannot trust TEPCO" for information about the nuclear crisis.[116]

It should be noted that *sōteigai* has been used to construct heroes as well as villains. On the three-month anniversary of 3.11, for example, the *Mainichi Shimbun* issued a collection of three hundred photos to celebrate the rescue and relief services performed by the SDF. An opening two-page spread shows the drowned wreckage of a doomed coastal town, its land flooded and its fuel depot afire. Above the photo is the headline "There Is No Word for 'Unimaginable,'" and below the photo is an explanation: "The SDF has no word for 'unimaginable.' It is an organization that must immediately confront any nation or entity that attacks Japan's sovereignty. There is no 'unimaginable' condition. At 2:46pm on March 11, 2011, at the very moment of the disaster, the Northeast army, very near the epicenter, set up a command headquarters. . . . From that moment, the SDF began its battle to protect the lives and properties of the people in response to every kind of condition."[117] The more conservative *Yomiuri Shimbun* reinforced this message by pointing out that when there is a crisis, the nation does not hesitate to mobilize the SDF, adding that "when the existence of the nation is at stake, we cannot put up with excuses about 'unimagined' [threats]."[118]

COMMUNITY

If the national sense of failed leadership and the overwhelming (and understandable) sense of vulnerability generated more villains than heroes in post-3.11 Japan, the crisis also generated a lively discourse about community and, thereby, about heroism. Social solidarity is hardly a new tile in the mosaic of Japanese national identity—it is impossible to read a primer on Japanese society that does not emphasize the collectivity, or one on Japanese politics that fails to mention consensus decision making.[119] But social solidarity is always tested and, if it passes, it is always reinforced in a crisis. After the Hanshin/Awaji disaster in 1995, Kobe's municipal restoration project was designed to promote "community creation by working together." The planners envisioned "a kind and gentle community built through close cooperation among its people," and postdisaster evaluations routinely celebrated the ways in which "residents overcame innumerable trials and tribulations by helping and encouraging each other."[120]

It was no different after 3.11. The people of Tohoku were repeatedly (and by all accounts deservedly) applauded for their selflessness and resolve. They were widely admired—almost to the point of essentialist caricature—for their patient and persevering nature (*gaman zuyoi*) and for their acceptance of what had befallen them. Japan and the world were told that the displaced residents of Tohoku did not loot and that rather than covet their neighbors' belongings, they shared what they had with those in need.[121] As the discourse evolved, the people of Tohoku suffered, but they suffered *together*. It was from that social fabric that they would rebuild their communities (*machizukuri*) and their region (*kōikizukuri*), and in so doing, that they would lead the way in the rebuilding of the nation (*kunizukuri*). An article in the *Nihon Keizai Shimbun* connects two motifs: change and community. Under the headline "Toward a New Japan: The Recovery Is Nation Building," the editors devoted a half page to analysis of how community building in Tohoku would lead to "an entire national regeneration."[122]

On this account, the people of Tohoku embodied what it meant to be Japanese—they formed a community (*komyunitei*) connected (*tsunagu*) by bonds (*kizuna*) and human contact (*fureai*) that sustains solidarity (*renkei*) through common struggle (*Ganbarō Nippon!*). Each of these terms was familiar—some stirringly so—and each enjoyed a renaissance after 3.11. Virtually overnight, the exhortation to persevere together embodied in

"*Ganbarō Nippon!*" could be found on posters, social media, advertisements, bumper stickers, and handwritten missives of every kind. A Google search for the Japanese expression yielded eighteen million hits in March 2012, a number that surely understates its ubiquity.[123] Paired Google searches in Japanese for "connection" and "Great Eastern Japan Disaster" surfaced nearly four million hits in December 2011. Substituting "bonds" for "connection" generated more than three times that many, and the borrowed term *komyunitei* paired with the disaster generated nearly forty-two million hits. Nor was social solidarity limited to the people of Tohoku. The entire nation applauded itself (again deservedly) for the outpouring of material and human support for displaced and distraught neighbors to the northeast.

Still, one of the most intractable problems for post-3.11 reconstruction—and for the discourse on community—was the shallowness of local identities. Many of the region's municipalities were of recent vintage, created during a wave of administrative consolidation in the early 2000s, when more than 3,200 municipalities were reduced to just over 1,700 nationwide.[124] The city of Ishinomaki, for example, was created out of seven towns and villages in 2005. Minami Sōma was created in 2006 through the amalgamation of three separate towns. The idea was to rationalize the provision of public services, but some of these new cities were so sprawling—Minami Sōma, 20 km from north to south, is a good example—that some residents found themselves cut off from first responders on 3.11.[125] The consolidation seems to have weakened the capacity of localities to respond to citizens at just the moment when they were in greatest need. Just as important, few residents felt allegiance to the newly constructed localities. Instead, they were connected to their original villages and counties, communities that were difficult to reconstruct in temporary shelters. Reports of distrust among the new neighbors were reflected in choices of temporary shelters and undercut the ideals of community that were being spun by political leaders and editorialists.[126]

Just as the Reconstruction Design Council officially validated the vulnerability and risk motif, so did it sanctify community as a key element for postdisaster Japan. The word *kizuna* appears a dozen times—and in every chapter—in the council's short report. The companion term *tsunagu* (connection) appears thirty-six times, usually in brackets for emphasis. In addition, the report uses the borrowed word *komyunitei* thirty-five times. In all, there are eighty-three references to social solidarity in just thirty-nine pages.[127] The report was the handiwork of Vice-Chair Mikuriya Takashi, who invoked poetry in his appeal to fellow council members: "People connect to people, regions connect to regions, firms connect to firms, and municipalities connect to prefectures and to the central government. Regional communities connect within and without, Eastern Japan connects to Western Japan, and nations connect to one another. Whether they are big or small, we have

"Ganbarō Nippon" (Let's hang in there together, Japan). Message displayed on the Tokyo Tower. 15 April 2011. Photo by YUTAKA/NipponNews.

discovered that connections (*tsunagu*) are the means by which support becomes reality and the means by which light will shine on recovery."[128]

The first of seven fundamental principles articulated in the Basic Law for Recovery from the Great Eastern Japan Disaster was that the recovery should honor the loss of lives and learn lessons from 3.11. Three others focused on community and social solidarity: the second principle called for "restoration of the essence of regional community," the fourth addressed the need "to continue protecting the strong bonds of regional society," and the seventh identified "citizens' solidarity" as a requisite for recovery.[129] Likewise, each of the affected prefectures emphasized community building in official postdisaster planning documents. The first of eight points in the ten-year Miyagi recovery plan called for "promotion of community building." The Iwate plan was based on nine special zones, the sixth of which called for "community building" to replace the more than 47 percent of capital stock lost in the tsunami. Fukushima's "recovery vision" was the product of the region's most exhausted and paralyzed prefecture. It seemed to contain more bromides than hope, but called prominently for "the rebirth of solidarity."[130]

No doubt because it evokes practical next steps, the term "community building" (*machizukuri*) was invoked by government officials and planners more than any other reference to the postdisaster collectivity. But the metaphorically richer term *kizuna* was also prominent in the broader post-3.11 discourse. *Kizuna* was already a familiar, and therefore easily embraced, social referent. Used in the titles of songs, anime, manga, and video games, *kizuna* was ubiquitous in Japanese popular culture well before 3.11. It was even the nickname given to the high-speed Internet communications satellite launched by the government in 2008.

Kizuna was formally consecrated as the representation of postdisaster solidarity twice. The first instance was official: one month after 3.11, Prime Minister Kan issued a statement entitled "*Kizuna:* The Bonds of Friendship," thanking the world for its generosity and its outpouring of concern for the people of Tohoku.[131] The Japanese people may be forgiven for missing this missive to the international community, but *kizuna* became the most prominent representation of postdisaster community when it was celebrated in an annual ceremony at the Kiyomizu Temple in Kyoto in December 2011. In autumn and early winter each year, just prior to the New Year holiday, the Buddhist priests of Kiyomizu invite the Japanese public to submit their choice of the single Chinese character that best captures the mood of the previous year. While sometimes celebratory ("love" in 2005 and "life" in 2006), the zeitgeist is represented more often by expressions of concern and anxiety: "war" in 2001, "return" (of kidnapped youth) in 2002. The character had been inspired by disasters twice before: "quake" (*shin*) in 1995 after Kobe, and "disaster" (*sai*) after the Chūetsu quake in 2004. This time, after sorting through more than sixty thousand entries, Chief Priest Mori Seihan wielded a long brush

揮毫 清水寺 森 清範 貫主

漢検 **2011年「今年の漢字」**Ⓡ

主催 財団法人 日本漢字能力検定協会

Mori Seihan, chief abbot at Kiyomizu Buddhist Temple, Kyoto, writes *"kizuna"* (bond), chosen as the kanji character of the year for 2011. 12 December 2011. Photo by Akihiro Sugimoto/NipponNews.

dabbed in black ink and inscribed the more forward-oriented and celebratory *kizuna* before a national audience.[132]

Kizuna was appropriated broadly as a metaphor for social solidarity. The Japan Graphic Design Association created a striking Web-based *"Kizuna Japan Project"* that captured the cultural, spiritual, and ethical climate of a nation determined to connect to itself and its future. In a bit more than six minutes, more than five dozen separate graphic images flow one into another, evoking a national family that is reconnecting and recovering. The rising sun is represented variously as a knot of red silk, a heart, a backdrop for the character *kizuna*, and in multiple messages of solidarity with the people of Tohoku. The disaster victims are reminded they are "never alone." They are exhorted to "take each others' hands" and to "connect everyone's thoughts and feelings."[133] Fund-raising events across the nation used the *kizuna* symbol—often in combination with other metaphors for connection—as in Hyōgo Prefecture, where the Kadokawa Music Festival was organized around the theme of "Connecting the Bonds!"[134]

Politicians and private firms were not far behind in the appropriation of newly fortified metaphors for national solidarity. In January 2012, nine dissident DPJ Diet members, all allies of Ozawa Ichirō, left the party to form the "New Party *Kizuna*."[135] The irony, of course, was that in doing so they slashed their "bonds" with the DPJ. The Japanese Trade Union Confederation (Rengō) campaigned for members yearning for community. Union membership, according to one subway poster, would "build a society (*shakai-zukuri*) with hope and peace of mind" and promised to "connect Japan."[136] Meanwhile, a sake brewer issued a new brand labeled *"Tohoku no Kizuna"* (The Bonds of Tohoku), promising that 2 percent of the proceeds from sales would support disaster victims.[137] For its part, the giant telecommunications firm NTT issued a polished forty-page brochure entitled "The Path of Active Recovery from the Great Eastern Japan Disaster," above which was affixed the exhortation: "Let's Connect to Tomorrow" (*asu tsunageyō e*).

Heroes are much easier to find in this corner of the national discourse, as they come directly from the affected communities. They were the municipal mayors, like Minami Sōma's Sakurai Katsunobu, who stood by his post and issued a quickly famous "YouTube SOS" on behalf of eight thousand displaced residents in forty shelters within city limits, and Rikuzen-takata's mayor, Toba Futoshi, who continued to supervise rescue and relief efforts even after his wife, children, and sixty-eight employees were swept into the sea. They included rank-and-file local officials like the twenty-two police officers who died while on duty, and emergency workers like Endō Miki, the twenty-four-year-old woman who broadcast repeated tsunami warnings until she herself was washed away from her post in Minami San-riku's crisis management center. Ms. Endō is credited with saving seven hundred lives, and is memorialized on dozens of YouTube videos and on hundreds of blogs. Her "determination to fulfill a public duty in the midst of a crisis" was recognized by Prime Minister Noda Yoshihiko in his first Diet speech in September 2011. She also was celebrated by Kobayashi Yoshinori, the right-wing cartoonist.[138] In what amounts to a deep split in the celebration of community solidarity, however, victims' groups began to form in Tohoku to press claims that the safety of their relatives was not adequately protected by municipal officials. The first civil suit to result in a police investigation was brought against Ms. Endō's boss, Mayor Satō Jin, in August 2012. Satō had been a widely acclaimed hero after the disaster.[139]

There were others who were also ambiguously heroic, however. The first to come to the attention of the global media were plant workers who, ignoring their personal safety, returned to the reactor site in an effort to contain the damage. Dubbed the "Fukushima Fifty" by the foreign media, the story of these workers was too enticing for some hagiographers to ignore. A headline in the *Asahi Shimbun* declared that "The Struggles of the Fukushima Fifty Will Not End," and the newspaper reported that "bearing the burdens and uncertainty, they continue to battle an unseen enemy."[140] There were two problems with these accounts. First, there were far more than fifty workers—TEPCO said that the actual number of workers who returned to the plant was closer to seven hundred. Only small numbers could enter at one time, and only for brief periods, so they rotated through quickly. More problematic, many of these workers may not have been the "samurai salarymen" of legend or even "volunteers" at all, but low-paid and exploited contract workers who had no other employment options. One analyst asked provocatively if these men were "a committed TEPCO vanguard, or the castoffs of Japan's employment system who are being brought in for a highly paid suicide mission."[141] Indeed, in its 2010 annual report, TEPCO disclosed that fewer than 20 percent of the employees at Fukushima Daiichi were regular TEPCO staff and reports that fully 100 percent of severe injuries to plant workers were incurred by contractors in 2009, up from 89 percent in 2008.[142] A conservative vice governor of Tokyo ignored all that, focusing his account instead on how welcome it was that plant workers shattered the postwar taboo against living or dying for others.[143]

Indeed, heroes and suicide and sacrifice often pop up together in accounts of the Fukushima Daiichi disaster. When a retired Sumitomo engineer, Tamada Yasuteru, recruited three hundred volunteers between the ages of sixty and seventy to handle the reactor crisis on the assumption that radiation effects on older workers would be limited, he claimed he was creating a "skilled veterans' corps." But the media dubbed it a "suicide corps," and the METI minister extolled their virtue.[144] There was no ambiguity attached to the heroism of one TEPCO employee, however. Plant Manager Yoshida Masao is widely credited with saving the lives of workers in the plant by ignoring orders from TEPCO that he stop injecting seawater into the reactor.[145]

Like all catastrophes, 3.11 generated pain and imagination, heroes and villains. Political entrepreneurs with motivation and resources were quick to do battle for control of the event. They spun narrative explanations for the tragedy across a broad horizon of meanings and values, all conforming to their existing preferences for change tailored to what they believed would be effective with the Japanese public. Existing enemies were enemies still, but newly villainous. The stakeholders, thus rearmed, then used these narratives aggressively in an effort to shift the still unformed preferences of a general public struggling to make sense of otherwise unfathomable events. We will turn to the dynamics of these efforts in three specific cases—national security, energy, and local government—but first we need to locate them in their historical and comparative contexts.

Historical and Comparative Guidance

Following a destructive earthquake, even the ceremony of rescue is morally and politically ambiguous, as rescuers fight not against nature, but against the twisted ruins of their own design failures.
—Gregory Clancey, 2006

When the earthquake struck I knew that I had survived, and I feared for my wife and daughter, left behind in Yokohama. Almost simultaneously I felt a surge of happiness which I could not keep down. "Tokyo will be better for this!" I said to myself.
—Tanizaki Junichirō, 1923

Such genuine and cordial friendship by the Government and people of the United States . . . will further increase the intimacy of the two countries and strengthen those bonds of concord and peace that exist throughout the world.
—Prime Minister Yamamoto Gombei to President Calvin Coolidge, 1923

The list of natural disasters along the Japanese archipelago is sadly long. It is so long, in fact, that as Peter Duus has noted, over the course of two millennia there has always been a disaster that older residents can remember.[1] Indeed, they have been so frequent that the Japanese tell themselves the four most frightening things in life are (in order): earthquakes, thunderstorms, fires, and fathers.[2]

Historical Guidance from Japanese Disasters

The first recorded Japanese earthquake occurred in 416.[3] More than forty large-scale earthquakes have struck Japan since the mid-nineteenth century alone, and many of those within living memory, such as Fukui (1948), Niigata (1964 and 2007), Tokachi-Oki (1968), and Sanriku-Oki (1994), are all but footnotes in this repetitive history of tragedy. During the Edo period alone, more than 500 major fires occurred, 100 of which consumed more than 3,000 homes. One conflagration in Edo in 1657 claimed 100,000 lives, and another 25,000 were lost in 1772. The Japanese of that era were taught that no life span was complete unless it included three of these "flowers of Edo" (*Edo no hana*).[4] It is no surprise, then, that the Iwakura Mission, sent abroad after the opening of Japan to scan and absorb Western practice, made a special effort to learn how other nations controlled fires.

The most-destructive and best-documented earthquakes before 3.11 are the Ansei quakes of 1854–1855, the Nōbi quake in central Japan (1891), the Meiji-Sanriku earthquake of 1896, the Great Kanto Earthquake in 1923 that struck Tokyo and Yokohama, and the Hanshin/Awaji earthquake of 1995 in Kobe. The physical footprint and impact varied considerably: Ansei was actually three separate temblors and many dozens of fore- and aftershocks that stretched from the coast of Tokai north through Edo and Chiba and south to Kyushu within a single year. The cauldrons of fire and tsunamis of these quakes claimed more than 17,000 lives. The 8.0-magnitude Nōbi disaster claimed 7,000 lives, still the largest known inland earthquake in modern Japanese history.[5] The Meiji-Sanriku Earthquake generated two tsunamis, caused more than 22,000 deaths, and eerily prefigured 3.11. The 1923 Kanto quake was the world's largest urban natural disaster since the London fires of 1666.[6] Only 10 percent of the 140,000 who died in the quake were crushed by falling structures. Most were burned to death—including 40,000 refugees who were tightly packed in a military clothing depot at Honjō when the wind unexpectedly changed direction. Of Tokyo's 500,000 buildings, 300,000 burned to the ground. It was the reverse in 1995 in Kobe, which failed "the first really severe test for a modern city built, theoretically, to be earthquake resistant."[7] In what was the area's first recorded quake in 1,500 years, 89 percent of the 6,400 who died were crushed to death. These differences notwithstanding, the political dynamics and the explanatory narratives that each disaster stimulated reverberate in—and inform the discourse of—post-3.11 Japan.

ANSEI, 1854–1855

The political target of the Ansei quakes was the already-rickety shogunate in Edo and its local functionaries. Within two days of the December 1855 Ansei-Edo quake, hundreds of anonymous broadsheets with wood-block print images of giant catfish—the mythic creature that carried the archipelago on its back—appeared on the streets.[8] These *namazu-e* (catfish prints) depicted merchants, tradesmen, and government officials whose fortunes the catfish could undo with a swish of its tail.

Indeed, because its tantrums could convulse the earth, conscientious overseers were needed to prevent shifts in its posture. In the wood-block images, the god of merchants and commerce, Ebisu, was widely depicted

水うみろ つげゝ いのちと
たゝらりく 三分の うちふ
へもぞうきてき

地震よけの 歌

A nineteenth-century earthquake wood-block print shows Daikoku, the popular god of wealth, showering people with money, while the god Kashima restrains a catfish (*namazu*). From the National Diet Library website, courtesy of the National Diet Library.

as having failed in his duty to control the giant creature. One recurrent motif was of gold coins falling from burning skies—an indicator that the redistribution of wealth was a prominent central concern. The prints were hardly subtle. They clearly presented a class-based narrative of inequity and corruption in which incompetent officials, greedy tradesmen eager to rebuild (presumably at extortionate rates), and prostitutes were set against the suffering masses who had lost everything. They offered a barely veiled critique of the sour and pessimistic mood of late-Edo Japan. One social historian of the period says that their reflection of popular "fear, disgust, and anger" was a "direct attack on the heart of the *bakufu* [government]."[9] The teetering shogunate certainly saw them as a dangerous source of criticism, and moved quickly to ban them. A decade later, the 250-year military regime collapsed. Its officials could not have been missed by those who had lost so much from the quakes and resultant fires.

NŌBI, 1891

If the Ansei disaster generated a class-based critique of a weakened government, the Nōbi disaster—coming three decades later, when Japan was newly open to global commerce and preparing a catch-up imperialism of its own—was used to cast foreigners in the villain's role. The very pattern of the destruction, in which some (mostly Western) buildings were heavily damaged and others (mostly Japanese) survived, triggered a vigorous public debate over the value of Western science and modernity. Even though most victims died in wooden homes of indigenous design and construction, the collapsed brick-and-mortar buildings—mostly public offices and icons of Western technology such as railway stations—that had connoted modernity soon came to represent the disastrous, slavish, debased path toward Western models of development. "Modernity had seemingly made the new regime not stronger than its predecessors, but weaker."[10] Post-Nōbi politics, like the politics after Ansei, were fought through the medium of wood-block prints; some called attention to failed Western structures, while others portrayed the collapse of traditional-style Buddhist temples. This time, there were few catfish: "a discourse formerly about class and state-subject relations becomes one about civilizations."[11] Why were foreigners allowed to build without sufficient regulatory oversight? Should Japanese believe in their superiority after all? Clancey captures this brilliantly: "An unmistakable impression left by these woodblock prints . . . was of the fragility and danger of the new western-style landscape. . . . [T]he prints neatly reversed the colonizing tropes so common in Meiji discourse over the previous two decades, which had located fragility exclusively in the 'feudal' landscape and volatility in Japanese nature."[12]

A nationalizing narrative emerged from the Nōbi disaster, in part because for the first time there were foreigners to blame, and in part because this was the first large-scale disaster to receive sustained nationwide news coverage. The localized self-criticism that emerged after Ansei would not suffice. Now many Japanese expected and demanded a national response. Once media reports reached the provinces, charity flowed to the disaster site from across the country. But no response after the Restoration could be national without the invocation of the Meiji emperor, the deployment of the military, or discussion of scientific progress. As in most matters, the Meiji oligarchs were quick to deploy the imperial family.[13] "Ceremonies of [imperial] consolation" were held frequently in the affected areas to portray the imperial family in national media as empathetic and actively involved in relief efforts.[14] But they were more than just available for display. Clancey explains that they were elements in the construction of a "much different Japanese government than the one that lived in mysterious seclusion in Kyoto or Edo," and describes how the imperial family and government officials were frequently depicted as moved by the plight of the victims to the point of tears.[15] This no doubt helped shield the young regime when it called on the military to suppress riots that erupted in Gifu after angry residents with nothing left to lose protested the dilatory response of the government. Science and technology also were not ignored. Each modern disaster has provoked actions to mitigate future damage, and in the wake of Nōbi, the Japanese government established its first interdisciplinary research institute to investigate a quake and its consequences.[16]

KANTO, 1923

The Great Kanto Earthquake, on 1 September 1923, was a greater disaster-induced test of state capacity. The authority of the Japanese state had long since been consolidated, and once again the state would prevail and shut the window on transformative change. The suppression of reluctant feudal domains and then two foreign wars—one against a decrepit China, the other against a decrepit, but Western, imperial Russia—had proved to most observers the rectitude of Japan's path toward Western-style industrialization. Still, this was an inopportune time for the Japanese government to have to confront a major disaster; 1923 was a time of domestic political disarray. Parties governed, but not effectively, and the military was flirting with political power. Like March 2011, it was a time of frequent cabinet shifts, weak parties, economic malaise, nationalist posturing, the incipient rise of civil society, massive disaster diplomacy, and the fear of terrorism.[17]

The confusion started at the top. Katō Tomosaburō, the viscount and admiral who had become prime minister a year earlier, died just days before the quake, and—as in the weeks after 3.11—an overture to create a nonparty, grand coalition government was summarily rejected by the largest party, the Seiyūkai.[18] When the new prime minister, Admiral Yamamoto Gombei, convened his first cabinet meeting the day after the quake, six ministers were absent, making it easy for the Home Ministry to introduce martial law.[19] The army assumed full and direct control of the capital district, and within one week, thirty-five thousand troops were mobilized to preserve order in four prefectures. This proved largely unnecessary. On most accounts, despite their deprivations, the populace was orderly and compliant. One eyewitness anticipated observations that would reemerge ninety years later from visitors to Tohoku: "In the course of my long wanderings throughout the devastated area . . . I saw or heard of no instance of profiteering among the common people. . . . One admired their stoicism."[20] Another added that "the earthquake brought to the fore some of the finest traits of the Japanese character."[21]

It was not only the rhetoric of 1923 that echoed after 3.11. As in Tohoku, the military immediately mobilized for rescue and infrastructure repair. Within a week, the streetlights of the capital had been relit and its trams and postal system were operating; soon thereafter, Imperial Army engineers had built or repaired forty-five bridges.[22] Viscount Gotō Shinpei, a former colonial administrator and Tokyo mayor who was named home minister in Yamamoto's "earthquake" cabinet, became the recovery czar. No one had grander ambitions for change than Gotō, who insisted that the imperial capital reflect the grandeur of the empire itself. He would not rebuild Tokyo along its old contours, but would redefine the urban landscape. Gotō's Tokyo was to be an "awe-inspiring" place of urban renewal, great boulevards, green zones, civic centers, sustainable development, and social progress.[23]

With the assistance of the American political historian and urban planner Charles A. Beard, Gotō pushed forward with his grandiose plan, thought by many to be unrealistic and excessive. The government would purchase the burned-out areas and redevelop them with a modern transport and sewer infrastructure. In its initial rendering, Gotō would have spent upwards of 4 billion yen, well beyond the state's fiscal capacity—and well beyond its political capacity to declare eminent domain. Just as many wondered nearly ninety years later in Tohoku, Beard reflected: "Will the Japanese seize this opportunity to correct ancient errors and lay out a modern city well defended against the recurrence of another holocaust, or will they follow the example set by London and San Francisco and rebuild substantially along the lines of the old street network?"[24]

The answer was not long in coming. Enthusiasm for Gotō's vision was not shared by bureaucratic colleagues who fretted about costs and doubted that local officials would spend central funds honestly.[25] There were also political objections. On Beard's account, many of Gotō's colleagues were allied with political parties loaded with "slogans, prejudices, and hatreds."[26] Jealously guarding the prerogatives of their individual ministries, they relied on the Imperial Capital Recovery Advisory Council (*Teito Fukkō Shingikai*), a commission convened by Prime Minister Yamamoto in September to advise him on reconstruction, to undercut the initiatives of the central plan-ning apparatus. The Advisory Council attacked Gotō for opportunism—namely, introducing long-desired projects into his reconstruction plan—and nearly killed his plan. In a move that would be replayed after 3.11, Gotō responded by trying to create a superministry that would concentrate re-sources in a single entity with powers beyond the existing ministries and urban planning apparatus. As it turned out, however, the Finance Ministry, led by the imposing Inuoue Junnosuke, bewailed "extravagance" and cut back reconstruction funding from 4 billion to 500 million yen, a figure Beard called "practically nothing."[27] The organization that was eventually created, the Imperial Capital Reconstruction Office (*Teito Fukkō In*), was headed by Gotō but was tasked with assisting other agencies involved in reconstruction rather than with developing and implementing a plan independently.[28] Gotō also met strong opposition from landowners who had the ear of the politi-cal class. The deputy head of the 3.11 Reconstruction Design Council has described Gotō's plan as "a technological success and political failure."[29]

Indeed, the debate over reconstruction—much like the discourse after 3.11—foundered on existing political, administrative, and social schisms. The reconstruction bill was further watered down by the Diet before being replaced entirely after the Yamamoto government collapsed. Gotō's plan

Downtown Tokyo after the Great Kanto Earthquake. 1923. Contemporary postcard from the author's collection.

Survivors in a devastated Tokyo after the Great Kanto Earthquake. 1923. Contemporary postcard from the author's collection.

was undone by a national politics characterized by excessively diffused power guarded tenaciously within narrow policy silos.[30] Beard, who saw in Gotō's failure the fundamental pathologies of an immature democracy, concluded that the solution resided in democratic reform, including the extension of suffrage: "[The government] is conservative at a time when nothing but radical courage can prevent Tokyo from rebuilding . . . another fire trap . . . It remains to be seen whether in an age when the people have a voice in affairs there can be effected a concert of powers sufficiently potent to carry out a comprehensive scheme of city planning in the face of organized, short sighted private interests and political ineptitude."[31] Notwithstanding Gotō's ambitions, when the recovery of Tokyo was declared complete in a "rebuilding festival" in March 1930, it had been rebuilt largely as it had been before the disaster.

First, though, there were ominously antidemocratic developments. Security officers used the cover of martial law to persecute political radicals and Asian foreigners in the days after the catastrophe.[32] They fed a hungry media with provocative stories of sedition and deceit. On 2 September 1923, for example, the *Tokyo Nichinichi Shimbun* reported that "Koreans and socialists were planning a rebellious and treacherous plot. We urge the citizens to cooperate with the military and the police to guard against Koreans."[33] At the same moment that the government was creating its Earthquake Relief Executive Bureau, fifty naval vessels, including battleships and destroyers were dispatched to the Korean coast.[34]

The persecution of Koreans continued with state acquiescence for days after the disaster.[35] According to one eyewitness, "wild rumors swept through the city and a reign of terror followed that the police, exhausted with their efforts, were powerless to control."[36] These rumors that Korean immigrants had fanned the earthquake's fires, had formed a militia of their own, were in cahoots with anarchists, were looting, and were poisoning Tokyo's water supply led to "wanton attacks" in which vigilante bands and soldiers hunted Koreans and Bolsheviks, dispatching thousands of such "enemies" with summary justice.[37] By 4 September, the Korean scare had subsided, and Japanese authorities could arrange a segregated evacuation facility for ten thousand Koreans outside Tokyo. On September 5, the government formally condemned the vigilantism, in part because it "would bring blemish upon our honor when reported abroad."[38] Indeed, in a transparent propaganda exercise, the government produced and distributed a film of the military's rescue of several thousand Koreans to depict their "considerate treatment."[39]

Because of the efficacy of other media, particularly wireless communication, the Great Kanto Earthquake was the first Japanese natural disaster to fully engage the international community. A spontaneous outpouring of munificence shocked contemporary observers, who reported with no little amazement that "a contest of generosity" had broken out among foreign powers and that "nations forgot boundaries and racial distinctions."[40] Washington was first off the mark with an international relief mission of unprecedented scope that prefigured Operation Tomodachi in remarkable detail. President Calvin Coolidge directed the American Red Cross to collect contributions for Japan relief. By December 1923, $12 million had been raised. Prime Minister Yamamoto telegraphed President Calvin Coolidge to thank Washington and reassure the president of Tokyo's commitment to the bilateral relationship. On the ground in Tokyo, U.S. ambassador Cyrus Woods organized an American Relief Committee, which worked primarily to shelter or evacuate American citizens left homeless by the disaster. U.S. warships anchored in Dairen set sail for Japan with relief supplies on 2 September and arrived in Yokohama on 5 September, three hours ahead of the British, who also had steamed in from China.[41] The U.S. Navy joined the Imperial Navy and private steamship companies to provide relief supplies and to ferry refugees to safety.[42] U.S. marines helped clear debris. U.S. Army personnel dispatched from the Philippines built a hospital they soon turned over to Japanese staff. Sensitive to the pride of the Japanese military and government officials, the commander of the U.S. Asiatic Fleet, Admiral Edwin Alexander Anderson, ordered U.S. Navy ships to simply drop off relief supplies dockside for the Japanese to distribute. Like Admiral Willard nine decades later, he insisted that "we were here to do all in our power to help the Japanese, but not to force any of our ideas on them."[43] U.S. secretary of state Charles Evans Hughes declared that "the traditional friendship between Japan and the United States has been further strengthened."[44]

Despite this sensitive and massive relief effort, however, U.S. disaster diplomacy ultimately failed. The two countries were incapable of turning the disaster to their mutual benefit over the longer term. The proximate reason was that even as U.S. relief aid was being distributed in Tokyo, the U.S. Congress was debating the National Origins Bill, which would ban immigration from Japan to the United States. Amid accusations that the Japanese had been insufficiently grateful for U.S. aid, President Coolidge succumbed to racist lobbying and declared "America must be kept American."[45] The so-called Japan Exclusion Act became law in July 1924 over just nine dissenting votes in the U.S. Senate and despite the protests of the Japanese government and Ambassador Woods. The day the bill passed was marked in Tokyo as National Humiliation Day. The immigration act "completely negated the goodwill" engendered by U.S. disaster relief.[46] It is not surprising, then, that while the international response was immediate and generous, it was "not entirely welcome."[47] There remained considerable suspicion—with some justification—that U.S. aid might be a cover for Washington-based plans of domination.

In fact, however, the Great Kanto Disaster paved the way for political domination by the Japanese military. In its immediate aftermath, Tokyo-based units provided much needed support to badly depleted emergency services and, supplemented by units based elsewhere in Japan, they worked for months to clean up the destruction, assist the homeless, and aid the reconstruction of the capital region. Ultimately, fifty-two thousand troops from around the country—nearly a fifth of the standing army—was deployed to restore order in Tokyo and the surrounding prefectures in a largely unnecessary show of force.[48] The contrast between the military's restoration of order and the sustained bickering among politicians over how to pay for reconstruction was stark. The use of martial rhetoric by political leaders and commentators as they discussed the disaster further enhanced the military's standing. Commentators noted that the devastation visited on the capital region was a "totalizing experience" like that experienced in the Great War. Nagata Hidejirō, Gotō's successor as Tokyo's mayor, deliberately chose to hold a memorial service for the victims of the disaster on 11 November 1923, Armistice Day.[49] The military was not spared from the spending cuts demanded in a government-wide austerity drive, but the new public appreciation for the military, and its emergence as a hero in the dominant disaster narrative, stood it in very good stead. The military had rallied a vulnerable nation under banners of leadership, social solidarity, and change that would be waved more benignly nearly a century later.

In this way, the hand of the Imperial Japanese military was strengthened after a period in which it had been waning. The rise of political parties and the growth of the political Left had forced the military to face new contenders for power in Tokyo and challenges to its reputation. In Japan, as elsewhere, World War I produced a peace movement and a belief that international relations could be managed amicably through treaties and international organizations like the League of Nations. The postwar economic downturn also led to pressure for military spending cuts. Recruitment sagged, more soldiers left the service early, and morale sank among those who remained. The military response to earthquake relief and reconstruction was a turning point for its fortunes: "Under these fortuitous circumstances the army consciously labored to recoup its position of esteem among the Japanese people, and from that time popular treatment of the army took a dramatic turn for the better, not only in the capital but throughout the country."[50]

There were surely plenty of villains to array against the heroic military. But soon after the Kanto quake, when heroes and villains were still being created, the Taisho emperor tilted the playing field by calling for the restoration of traditional values: "In recent years much progress has been made in science and human wisdom. At the same time frivolous and extravagant habits have set in. . . . If [they] are not checked now, the future of the country, we fear, is dark, the disaster that has befallen the Japanese people being severe."[51] In so doing, he unleashed every variety of critique against modernity.[52] Commentators were freed to stress the connection between the earthquake and the perception of Tokyo as a center of decadence and moral decay—a trope Tokyo governor Ishihara Shintarō would try unsuccessfully to invoke after 3.11. Many argued that the earthquake was a divine warning to Japan to change its ways. For example, Keio University economics professor Horie Kiichi viewed wasteful spending on fine food and products as especially egregious and advocated a tariff on luxury imports. He believed "heaven had done what the people of Tokyo and its leaders had failed to do: eliminate the centers of hedonist consumer culture."[53] The fact that the devastation in Tokyo centered on the entertainment districts in the east of the city reinforced the argument that it was divine punishment for impropriety: according to one Buddhist priest, "that the entertainment districts were completely destroyed must be an expression of divine will."[54] It is uncertain what God may have been thinking when the red-light district in Yoshiwara was one of the first neighborhoods to be restored to prequake prosperity.[55]

Many intellectuals and progressive (*kakushin*) bureaucrats argued that the disaster would serve as a wake-up call for the Japanese people, suggesting that controls be imposed to rectify society. But their narratives competed with prescriptions for how the state might best promote spiritual correction. Takashima Heizaburō, a child education expert, stressed that parents had to begin setting good examples for their children at home, using the experience of the earthquake to break bad habits. Fukasaku Yasubumi, a philosopher, recognized the value of self-improvement within the family, but believed that the state should embark on a program of cultural renewal, using public resources to spread "messages of sacrifice, frugality, and diligence to a wider cross-section of society."[56] As it happened, the Japanese state took up the ideological cause of spiritual renewal as a priority alongside relief and reconstruction. It thereby used the disaster to address existing concerns about civic duty.[57] Less than two months after the disaster, the Yamamoto government directed the Ministry of Education to collect still-fresh stories of sacrifice and heroism and published them in a three-volume set for nationwide distribution. These materials featured "recurring themes of loyalty to the Emperor, filial piety, benevolence, personal sacrifice, courage, and obedience which the government stressed were relevant in everyday life."[58]

Even as an official disaster narrative—replete with emphases on vulnerability, community, and state leadership—was taking shape, the Japanese political system continued to be plagued by disorder. Just three months after the disaster, the son of a Diet member who was angered by the treatment of Koreans after the earthquake fired a pistol point-blank at the prince regent— later the Showa emperor. Although it missed, the shot did enormous political damage. Prime Minister Yamamoto took responsibility and dissolved his cabinet, opening the way for an equally ineffectual nonparty "grand coalition" cabinet that lasted only six months.[59] The ensuing instability provided the military with justification for its repressive "Peace Preservation Law" a year later. Its status enhanced by the disaster, the Imperial military became more powerful than ever and, despite massive sympathy and aid from the United States, U.S.-Japan relations continued to be characterized by mistrust.

HANSHIN/AWAJI, 1995

Many of these dynamics—particularly those related to political instability and the role of the military in disaster relief—were replayed seventy-two years later, after the Hanshin/Awaji (Kobe) earthquake, in an entirely different political context. Kobe was the largest temblor in Japan since the Great Kanto Earthquake and, as in 1923, the human and economic costs were staggering. More than 6,400 persons perished, most of them elderly; one-fifth of all Kobe's office space and four-fifths of the docks at Japan's largest port were put out of commission. The affected area—twenty-five municipalities in two prefectures—suffered between 9 and 13 trillion yen in damages, an amount equal to more than 2.5 percent of Japan's gross domestic product (GDP).[60]

By 1995, Japanese democracy had long been fully consolidated and, as a result of the catastrophic Pacific War, the Japanese military had long since been returned to its barracks. While the widespread embrace of democratic norms ensured civilian control and greater transparency, however, it did not ensure better leadership or guarantee more-effective relief. The government was criticized for acting too slowly, for being insufficiently prepared for a disaster, for placing excessive confidence in the mitigating capacity of the postwar infrastructure, and, in the words of one particularly acute critic, for having an "ossified administrative structure."[61]

All this was personified in Prime Minister Murayama Tomiichi. Murayama was Japan's first Socialist prime minister since 1948, but he governed in a cabinet dominated by the conservative Liberal Democrats who had used him cynically (but successfully) to regain power after an unaccustomed nine months in opposition. If the political order was not as unstable as in 1854 or 1923, it was by no means as stable as it had been during the Liberal Democratic Party's (LDP's) first four decades in power (1955–1993). Moreover, while the military may have returned to barracks long before the crisis, its marginalization in some elite opinion is blamed for the problems of disaster response and management in Kobe.[62] Although the public likely would have welcomed Self-Defense Forces (SDF) rescue and relief teams, competing narratives grew from Kobe's ashes that reflected a disconnect between the military and civilian authorities and deep divisions about SDF legitimacy. The SDF, the prime minister, the governor of Hyogo Prefecture, and volunteers all played leading roles as villains and heroes in the drama. In any number of ways that would reverberate in the 3.11 echo chamber, the dominant post-Hanshin/Awaji narrative combined maligned leadership and bureaucratic negligence in equal measure with the importance of self-help and social solidarity.

The former was captured in Prime Minister Murayama's clumsy and belated response to the disaster and by his frequently ridiculed defense that the devastation was (in his own poorly chosen words) *sōteigai*, "beyond anyone's imagination."[63] Since the prime minister's office did not have a twenty-four-hour duty officer in 1995, Murayama's ineptitude is usually dated by a phone call from a friend who suggested he turn on the TV news.[64] By then, thousands of Kobe citizens already lay beneath the rubble of homes and offices, and the city was engulfed in flames. In an astonishing misjudgment that compounds the damage to his legacy, Murayama decided to keep his original schedule of meetings for the rest of the day.[65] Meanwhile, the National Land Agency, which nominally owned disaster management responsibilities, busied itself squabbling with other ministries and agencies for control of the policy response. As a result, it took two days to establish an Emergency Disaster Relief Headquarters in the cabinet office. After further dithering, Murayama handed off responsibility he had never really assumed to a bureaucracy that was equally ill-prepared to accept it.[66] The inability of the government to rapidly and accurately assess the situation led to delays in the mobilization of critical resources that cost lives.[67] Many communications links—mostly landlines in that era before cell phones—were broken, compounding the problem. On one account, "poor planning and abysmal lack of preparation moved Kobe from the category of tragic natural disaster to that of preventable human catastrophe."[68] Significant reputational damage to the once-vaunted Japanese bureaucracy was merely collateral damage—it paled in comparison to the human tragedy that was unfolding less than three hundred miles to the southwest.

The problems of disaster management and political leadership were multiplied by the responses of local governments. A Disaster Countermeasures Headquarters was created in the Hyogo prefectural office within an hour after the quake, but its disaster preparedness plan imagined a much less-challenging scenario.[69] While the prefectural government was quick to call on neighboring jurisdictions for police and fire services, Kobe City did not invoke the Disaster Relief Law until five days after the quake, and Kobe officials refused assistance offered by medical personnel from outside the area as well as temporary shelters proffered by Osaka City.[70] Governor Kaihara Toshitami was slow in transmitting requests to the central government for aid, and did not request the dispatch of SDF forces until several hours after the quake.[71] Worse, the military did not arrive until several days later, with only nine thousand underequipped troops.[72] When "fully mobilized," moreover, only twenty-four thousand troops were dispatched to the scene.[73] The dilatory and inadequate response of the SDF has long been central to the Hanshin/Awaji story.

But accounts differ sharply on the cause, passing blame back and forth between politicians and soldiers, and between the central government and the affected localities. Some insist that the delay was due to incompetence in Tokyo—either in the prime minister's office or in the Defense Agency.[74] Defense officials acknowledge that they arrived late and came up short, but argue that this was because the quake hit in the predawn hours and smoke covered the city, making damage assessment difficult. Some are more direct; they say that the delay was caused by the ideological rigidity of a left-wing prime minister and governor.[75] Like many opposition party politicians of that period, Governor Kaihara Toshitami was said to be reluctant to cooperate with the military.[76] An SDF flag officer who was involved in disaster management planning at that time commented: "In 1995, the Hyogo governor was the problem. We had approached him before the quake, but he refused to cooperate with us."[77] A senior U.S. military officer who has studied this event agrees. He claims that the SDF was "all ready" to mobilize, but did not get the necessary authorization from local authorities. He insists that "the bad press the SDF received was undeserved."[78] According to a United Nations (UN) study of the disaster response, the SDF responded within minutes with several hundred troops—under a legal provision allowing it to begin to act without formal invitation "when there is no time to wait."[79] But then it waited several days more.

Governor Kaihara acknowledges that he was roundly criticized for his handling of the disaster response. He says the problem was structural:

> The government of Japan had been very centralized and undemocratic until after the Pacific War. Under the Meiji Constitution, the central government

would handle all natural disasters, directing the prefectures and municipalities as necessary. That was the extent of it. When the Local Autonomy Law and the new constitution came into effect, however, there was decentralization of police and other functions. But until 1995, local capabilities were never tested. The problem was not my incompetence or that of Prime Minister Murayama, but the system itself.[80]

The system did indeed have serious problems. There was no central government ministry or agency with the authority to coordinate responses across all administrative jurisdictions. At the local level, before governors could ask the military for aid, mayors had to deliver written requests that specified what resources they required and the expected duration of the operation. Telephone and faxed requests were not permitted. Moreover, the costs of SDF operations would be charged to the prefectures. This combination of paperwork and fiscal disincentives may have slowed disaster response considerably.[81]

Governor Kaihara rejects the ideological criticism outright:

> I had no allergy to the military. I am a legal expert and I knew the law. I did not need a crisis management specialist to tell me that I had to make a formal appeal to the SDF for help (*haken yōsei*). The problems were on their end. The SDF did not anticipate such a large-scale disaster and was not ready. I issued my appeal three hours after the quake because it happened early in the morning darkness and I needed to see and assess the extent of the damage. I was not getting much information at first because no one was in the prefectural offices. The commanding general, Matsushima Yūsuke, had no experience mobilizing the sort of unit needed.[82]

Either way, General Matsushima, commander of the Ground Self-Defense Force (GSDF) Middle Army, failed to work effectively with the local authorities and was passed over for promotion; his rumored ambitions for national office were shattered. More important, the deaths and injuries of thousands of Kobe residents are blamed on the delays.

There was also considerable criticism of the government's response to the numerous, immediate offers of assistance from foreign governments, private firms, and nongovernmental organizations (NGOs). Just as in 1923, Washington offered the services of its fleet in Asia, now homeported in Yokosuka, a short sail from the affected areas. But Japanese officials refused all but seventy-eight tents and fifty thousand blankets.[83] After a two-day delay during which it rejected offers from fourteen other countries, the Foreign Ministry permitted Switzerland to send a thirty-person search-and-rescue (SAR) team with twelve sniffer dogs. But when they arrived at the airport, immigration authorities placed the rescue dogs in quarantine. When British and French SAR teams were finally invited, it was through NGO channels and over Ministry of Foreign Affairs (MOFA) objections. The Foreign Ministry also rejected multiple offers of medical teams, arguing that there was suffi-cient domestic capacity and that foreigners lacked requisite Japanese lan-guage skills. Seventy-six countries made offers to supply basic consumer goods, but these too were initially turned aside "because the Japanese gov-ernment reasoned that there were enough consumer goods in Japan."[84] It was only later, after a raft of deeply embarrassing international press reports, that the government reversed itself and accepted offers of assistance from foreigners. In the meantime, organized crime groups established themselves in Kobe as the most-efficient community servants.[85]

The greatest success of the Hanshin/Awaji experience—and the phenom-enon that ultimately came to dominate all Kobe disaster narratives—was the unexpected and unprecedented upsurge of volunteerism. Within two weeks, more than 7,200 volunteers had registered, and a far greater number arrived without registering. Volunteer centers were established in each of Kobe's wards, and volunteerism soon replaced administrative incompe-tence as the dominant story in the affected areas. Despite an "inhospitable regulatory environment" and a "rudimentary infrastructure," volunteers made their way to the disaster area in what amounted to a "quantum leap for volunteering in Japan."[86] This outpouring of support from civil society came to be known as "the birth of Japanese volunteerism" (*borantea no gan-nen*).[87] Interaction centers (*fureai sentaa*), designed to stimulate community formation in temporary shelters, were also used as bases for the unexpected and unprecedented number of volunteer activities. According to former gov-ernor Kaihara, volunteer organizations "sprouted like bamboo shoots after the spring rain" even without formal legal standing because by 1995, "we Japanese recognized that we were rich in things, but poor in heart."[88] Indeed, more than 1.2 million Japanese flooded into Kobe and the surrounding cities and towns to provide every variety of health and human services—from employment and psychological counseling to the distribution of relief sup-plies and the clearing of rubble.

These volunteers made enormous contributions to postquake Kobe. Their good works were especially critical because of the burden that rebuilding placed on local resources. Although an initial central government aid pack-age was in place within two months, Tokyo and local authorities engaged in a long-running dispute over the appropriate level of central assistance. The Finance Ministry was reluctant to set a precedent by providing relief funds directly to disaster victims, making rebuilding more difficult.[89] Hyogo Pre-fecture and Kobe City sought some 17 trillion yen in central government aid over ten years for their "Phoenix" plan; but much less central aid was forthcoming, and the reconstruction of Kobe was funded locally for the most part.[90] Kobe's utilities were restored to full service within months, and its transport network within two and a half years—the former with disaster-resistant piping, new emergency storage, and redundant transmission sys-tems. Public spaces—museums, enterprise zones, and so forth—were completed within a decade, but their connection to Kobe's urban revival has been mixed.[91] Kobe did not return to its prequake population until 2004 and, as late as 2009, its overall manufacturing base was only four-fifths of its prequake level.[92] Disaster reconstruction spending had a negligible effect on Japan's macroeconomic performance, and seemed more directed at restoring what once was than at building something new.[93] Instead, it built a crippling local debt.[94]

Once a Hanshin/Awaji narrative critical of the government's lack of crisis preparedness became dominant, sixteen new national laws were passed. One centerpiece of this national legislation was the July 1995 Special Measures Law on Earthquake Disaster Prevention that created a central government office attached to the prime minister's office and headed by a deputy chief cabinet secretary for crisis management.[95] The formation of this office, later moved to the Ministry of Education, was an effort to reestablish central accountability and begin construction of a comprehensive national disaster response policy. It was based on a reading of the crisis, which held that the problems of postquake response in Kobe lay with both local incompetence and the endemic jurisdictional overlap and competition—the so-called vertical administration that has long been a problem in Japanese governance. The new central office would be dedicated to administrative coordination and crisis management; it was tasked to establish effective protocols for disaster response, to create new crisis management manuals for the prefectures and municipalities, and to support the prime minister in making public statements in a timely fashion. As the 3.11 crisis would demonstrate sixteen years later, however, it was not clear that further centralization and the production of ready-made crisis manuals was the correct lesson.

A second prominent result was national legislation in 1998 supported by all the major parties that provided legal status to nonprofit organizations in Japan for the first time.[96] Before this legislation, NGOs had no corporate identity, and consequently had difficulty renting office space and hiring staff. Now, organizations that promote activities in health, medical care, social welfare, education, community development, culture, the environment, disaster relief, community safety, human rights, international cooperation, and gender equality, inter alia, could qualify for special legal status. As a consequence, civil society enjoyed a renaissance; active citizenship and community involvement have not flagged since. As discussed in chapter 1, NGOs that had become major contributors to the civic life of Kobe became leaders in Tohoku after 3.11.[97]

Other lessons drawn from the bureaucratic inefficiencies that dominated the disaster narratives did not require new legislation or further centralization. Perhaps the most important lesson was that effective disaster response requires cooperation across levels and branches of government.[98] Observers across the political spectrum came to agree that this cooperation, in turn, must include both military and civil authorities. Although Japanese conservatives continued to have trouble passing national emergency mobilization legislation (*yūji hōsei*), discussion of emergency response was no longer taboo and virtually everyone came to accept a role for the military in disaster relief. According to the editor of a major progressive monthly: "Both the SDF and the localities changed after 1995. The SDF, because it failed to help enough people, and the local governments because they came to realize how much they need the SDF as a disaster relief force."[99] An SDF general concurs: "If there had been no Hanshin/Awaji failure, there would have been no 3.11 success."[100] The single most important development in cooperation between the SDF and local government was the dramatic increase in—and widespread acceptance of—joint disaster management exercises with better equipment.[101]

Comparative Guidance

In order to broaden our perspective on how natural disasters become political events, it is useful to examine the experience of other countries and that of Japan abroad. We start with a domestic U.S. case that offers uncomfortable parallels to Hanshin/Awaji. After exploring several cases of U.S. disaster diplomacy, we conclude with an examination of how the Japanese government mobilized resources to assist victims in China. Taken together, these episodes raise important analytical questions for understanding how disaster narratives form and the extent to which they shape political choices going forward.

Hurricane Katrina, the horrendous natural disaster resulting in the deaths of nearly 1,500 persons in and around New Orleans in late August 2005, was notable for four reasons relevant to 3.11.[102] First, it had been anticipated as a high-consequence but low-probability event. As such, the inadequate response of civil authorities revealed worrisome deficiencies in U.S. disaster preparedness. Second, as in Tohoku after 3.11, the military—in this case, the U.S. Coast Guard and National Guard—came to be viewed as especially competent when compared to civilian officials. Third, the disaster melded with and shaped a broader narrative questioning the competence of the central government and the commander in chief. Finally, again like 3.11, the perception of Katrina varied predictably among those with different predisaster political preferences.

The public had every reason to believe that the government was well prepared to respond to a major natural disaster on the Gulf Coast. The local and national media had predicted such an occasion, and near-disaster events had occurred in the recent past. One former head of the Federal Emergency Management Agency (FEMA) repeatedly declared more than a decade earlier that his most serious concern was "that a storm surge as high as 15 to 20 feet could drive Lake Pontchartrain over its levees and submerge New

Orleans" with catastrophic results.[103] A 2001 feature article in *Scientific American* titled "Drowning New Orleans" stated simply: "New Orleans is a disaster waiting to happen."[104] And the New Orleans *Times-Picayune* ran a five-part series in 2002 that warned "flooding from even a moderate storm could kill thousands. It's just a matter of time."[105] These warnings were not ignored. Local, state, and federal officials organized a large-scale disaster management exercise in 2004 to identify the consequences and effective responses to a major hurricane hitting the New Orleans area.[106]

Despite considerable forewarning and planning, however—and despite accurate weather forecasts of the path and intensity of the storm—the dominant post-Katrina narrative portrays civil authorities as being unprepared. From the beginning, most reports held state and local officials particularly culpable. Louisiana and New Orleans were blamed for failing to order mandatory evacuations in a timely manner, and not at all in some specific areas.[107] The New Orleans Police Department's failure to maintain law and order—and indeed, criminality in its own ranks—became central to many accounts.[108]

Federal officials were also targeted. After crediting FEMA director Michael Brown with "doing a heck of a job" on 2 September 2005, even President George W. Bush became an object of criticism.[109] The next day, twin items in the *New York Times*—a news story and a blistering Maureen Dowd op-ed—questioned Brown's qualifications and competence. His most notable job prior to federal employment had been as head of the International Arabian Horse Association, a position he resigned under pressure.[110] There had been little mention of Brown's background in news reports prior to 3 September, but after the president's "heck of a job" endorsement, Brown's poor performance in both his previous post and in FEMA press conferences became prominent. This villain narrative had a long reach. FEMA was now denounced for a variety of pre- and postdisaster decisions, even in reports written at Republican-led institutions. Brown's failures and questionable qualifications made him the poster boy of federal government failures, linking him to President Bush. CBS News polls found approval of President Bush's response to Katrina sinking from 54 percent to 38 percent within a week.[111] Responsibility for search-and-rescue and recovery efforts was reassigned to U.S. Coast Guard vice admiral Thad Allen, and Brown resigned from FEMA on 12 September.

While not exempt from criticism for a slow response, the U.S. military was viewed widely as more capable than civilian administrators. The report of the U.S. House of Representatives select bipartisan committee on Katrina captures the overall tone of this trope when it concludes that "[t]he military played an invaluable role, but coordination was lacking."[112] As in Japan after 3.11, images of the military were visually compelling and widely disseminated—helicopter rescues, search-and-rescue flights, troops in camouflage, transport planes landing. Two larger-than-life military leaders—

Lieutenant General Russel Honoré and Vice Admiral Thad Allen—came to dominate their respective phases of the post-Katrina response, and anchored the post-Katrina hero narrative.

New Orleans mayor Ray Nagin's description of Honoré captures several military stereotypes in quick succession and exemplifies the narrative's civil-military competence gap: "Now, I will tell you this—and I give the president some credit on this—he sent one John Wayne dude down here that can get some stuff done, and his name is General Honoré. And he came off the doggone chopper, and he started cussing and people started moving. And he's getting some stuff done. They ought to give that guy—if they don't want to give it to me—give him full authority to get the job done, and we can save some people."[113] Even the generally critical New Orleans–based journalist Jed Horne is largely positive in his description of Honoré; again, because the contrast between military and civilian stereotypes is so apparent, it is worth quoting at length: "What the media wanted, of course, was a star—someone on whom to focus the yearning for effective leadership that seemed so sorely lacking among the many politicians jabbering, finger-pointing, and blubbering on camera. And briefly, at least—for as long as he could put up with it—the media had their man in Lt. Gen. Russell [sic] Honoré. . . . In a landscape crawling with double-talk, he was blunt, action-oriented, and, after a delayed start, capable of results."[114] In a crisis with racial overtones, the fact that the general was an African American with Louisiana roots added to Honoré's positive image.

While Thad Allen did not project the same "central casting" qualities as Honoré, press coverage of him was also admiring—in stark contrast to coverage of Mayor Nagin, Director Brown, and other flawed civilians. A sampling of headlines from the week of Allen's appointment captures the tone of the press coverage: "Brown Replacement Familiar with Challenges," "New Katrina Chief Seen as Experienced," "Bush Sends in the Coast Guard to Take the Helm of Katrina Relief," "New Katrina Recovery Chief Viewed as Smart and Incisive," "Commander Accustomed to Scrutiny and Crises."[115] In the dominant narrative, Brown was the villain, Nagin was ineffectual, and Honoré and Allen were heroes.

Katrina soon became embedded in a broader narrative about the competence of the Bush administration. The president's job approval rating had already begun a slow decline, one not evident in press coverage in the days immediately following the storm. In fact, among major news publications, the first wave of criticisms that linked the response to Katrina with general Bush incompetence came from the British and European media, where columns in the *Independent*, the *Sunday Times*, and the *Guardian* linked the Katrina response to the Iraq War and other failures. These columns featured American commentators. Camille Paglia wrote of her surprise with "the disintegration of the administration's mask of competence and confidence, as New Orleans sinks day by day into squalor and savagery, a shocking panorama of unrelieved human suffering."[116] Andrew Sullivan commented: "The seeming inability of the federal or city authorities to act swiftly or effectively to rescue survivors or maintain order posed fundamental questions about the competence of the Bush administration and local authorities."[117] Jonathan Freedland argued that "Americans expect competence from their leader as a minimum requirement. And if an image of a crashed helicopter in the Iranian desert could undo one president, surely pictures of an American city reduced to a Somali or Bangladeshi kind of chaos spell disaster for this one."[118] David Frum, a former Bush speechwriter, noted on 3 September 2005 in a Canadian newspaper that "chaos and disorder in the streets of New Orleans inevitably remind Americans of chaos and disorder in Iraq, and raise questions about whether the hand on America's tiller is as skilled and capable as it ought to be."[119]

The U.S. press soon joined the scrum, focusing on questions of presidential competence. On 8 September, the *New York Times* reported that "Democrats appear able to question the administration's competence without opening themselves to attacks on their patriotism."[120] Another Maureen Dowd column on 12 September—the same day as Brown's resignation— argued that "ever since W. was his father's loyalty enforcer, his political decisions have been shaped more by loyalty than substance or competence."[121] Liberal columnist E. J. Dionne was instrumental in articulating what would become the dominant narrative: "The Bush Era ended definitively on Sept. 2, the day Bush first toured the Gulf Coast States after Hurricane Katrina. There was no magic moment with a bullhorn. The utter failure of federal relief efforts had by then penetrated the country's consciousness. Yesterday's resignation of FEMA Director Michael Brown put an exclamation point on the failure."[122] By April 2007, this narrative was so widely embraced that even conservative writer Richard Lowry argued in the *National Review* that "Republican primary voters will be looking in 2008 for someone who doesn't run the government like George W. Bush."[123]

The case of Hurricane Katrina reminds us of the power of narrators to create heroes and villains. It suggests that leadership can be a key trope in the creation of a postdisaster narrative, that existing lenses filter evaluations of government performance, that this performance has implications for larger narratives about competence, and that even partisans can be persuaded to abandon their cause in the face of a particularly muscular counternarrative.[124] In short, strong narratives can squeeze out weak ones and gain dominance.

Disaster Diplomacy

Humanitarian Assistance and Disaster Relief (HA/DR) is commonly extended to states after devastating wars, usually by the victor and often with salutary effect. The Marshall Plan in Europe and U.S. aid to Japan are routinely credited with consolidating U.S. leadership and the postwar order, for example. A subset of postwar aid, "natural disaster diplomacy," is also a long-standing tool of statecraft. Observers ask if these operations yield diplomatic advantages. Do they induce international cooperation between competing states and beget reconciliation, do they exacerbate conflict, or do they have no lasting effects at all?[125]

This tool has often been extended to current, as opposed to former, rivals.[126] A list of major disasters—those with more than twenty thousand victims— since the end of the Cold War to which both the United States and Japan responded with assistance includes friendly and rival states alike:

Table 1 Disasters since 1989

January 2010	Haiti earthquake	Haiti
May 2008	Sichuan earthquake	China
May 2008	Cyclone Nargis	Myanmar (Burma)
October 2005	Kashmir earthquake	Pakistan
December 2004	Indian Ocean tsunami	Indonesia, India, Sri Lanka
December 2003	Bam earthquake	Iran
August 1999	İzmit earthquake	Turkey
April 1991	Bangladesh cyclone	Bangladesh
June 1990	Manjil-Rudbar earthquake	Iran

The question inevitably arises whether natural disasters can create opportunities for rapprochement or even peacemaking. What advantages accrue to states that reach out to assist rivals or rebels after a natural disaster? Does trust evolve? Do preferences or interests shift? The evidence to date is both limited and mixed. One comparative study found that disaster assistance after the 2005 Kashmir quake did not lead to the sort of rapprochement between India and Pakistan that the 1999 İzmit quake did for Turkey and Greece because long-standing enemy myths in Kashmir were particularly difficult to overcome. They sparked communal violence that became routine and undermined efforts by state leaders to use the disaster as an opportunity to reset relations. Other work has questioned the reconciliatory power of the İzmit quake as well.[127]

The end of the insurgency in Banda Aceh after the Indian Ocean tsunami is also frequently cited as an example of the pacifying effects of disaster diplomacy. When the tsunami struck Indonesia, it disproportionally affected northern Sumatra, the site of a long-running separatist conflict between the Indonesian government and the independence-seeking Free Aceh Movement. Early reports suggested that after years of fighting, rebels and government officials used the disaster as a tool for peacemaking. One community leader told the British newspaper *Guardian* that "we would not be here without the tsunami. . . . It focused the minds on all sides. It demonstrated that there has been enough suffering in Aceh." A rebel leader concurred, saying that the tsunami "opened a huge door in the deadlock that no one thought was there." The tsunami may have been a pretext for the acceleration of peace efforts on both sides, but research indicates that the disaster was only one of several factors that brought the two sides together.[128] The case confirms that disaster can facilitate and catalyze diplomacy, but is unlikely to cause reconciliation on its own.[129]

These findings seem consistent with the U.S. experience, but there have been cases in which U.S. relief efforts have had salutary diplomatic effects. U.S. assistance to Bangladesh in 1991 after Tropical Cyclone 02B (Marian) is an example. Washington had opposed Bangladeshi independence in 1971, and the hope in some quarters was that U.S. aid might "wash the stink" off U.S.-Bangladesh relations. It was also hoped that aid might highlight Washington's compassionate side in the aftermath of the 1991 Persian Gulf War, an engagement that many Bangladeshis had opposed. Bangladesh had dispatched forces to Saudi Arabia to participate in Operation Desert Shield, a decision that led to anti-American protests, including a mob that overran the American Club in Dhaka.[130]

President George H. W. Bush diverted U.S. marines returning from the Persian Gulf to help with the relief effort. The U.S. military relief operation in Bangladesh was at that point the second-largest overseas humanitarian mission undertaken by the United States since World War II, surpassed only by the simultaneous U.S. relief effort in the Kurdish areas of northern Iraq.[131] In all, U.S. Air Force planes flew nearly two hundred missions delivering more than two thousand tons of cargo to affected areas. U.S. Army Blackhawks (helicopters) and navy and marine aviation flew an additional 1,774 sorties, delivering more than 1,500 tons of relief supplies in a mission that would ultimately be called "Operation Sea Angel." U.S. medical teams dispatched to Bangladesh treated 15,000 patients.[132] General Henry Stackpole, who commanded the U.S. relief effort, somewhat grandiloquently explained in early remarks, "We went to Kuwait in the name of liberty, and we've come to Bangladesh in the name of humanity."[133]

The operation had three long-term impacts. First, it was the most substantive engagement between the U.S. and Bangladeshi militaries to that point, and came to be viewed as the beginning of U.S.-Bangladeshi military cooperation. Based on his conversations with senior Bangladesh military leaders, one Pentagon official claims that the U.S. disaster relief mission is why "the Bangladesh military holds the U.S. military in the highest esteem and looks to always partner first with [it]."[134] Second, its success led to aid and relief missions becoming a major component of U.S.-Bangladesh military training and joint exercises, with considerable improvement in the Bangladesh military's ability to respond to disasters, either alone or with the assistance of others.[135] Third, the cyclone struck one month after the end of a decade of military rule; a new democratic government had just taken power in Bangladesh.[136] Although no evidence suggests it was an objective of the mission, U.S. assistance may have helped stabilize the young democracy. As General Stackpole wrote a year after the operation, "We shored up a fledgling government that everyone had expected to fail. That produced a political fallout, a benefit that had not been anticipated."[137]

The situation (and results) were different in Myanmar (Burma) when Cyclone Nargis cut a swath of destruction along the southern coast in early May 2008. High-speed winds of up to 135 miles per hour combined with a 12-foot storm surge to kill approximately 140,000, destroy 450,000 homes, and displace 800,000 people. The delta region, the country's "rice bowl," suffered the most severe damage, but Yangon's buildings, power, transport, and communications infrastructure were also heavily affected.[138] Losses totaled about 3 percent of Myanmar's GDP.[139]

The United States, which had no diplomatic relations with the country it insisted on calling Burma, requested and received permission to begin shipping relief supplies. The first U.S. C-130 departed Utapao Air Base in Thailand and landed at Rangoon International Airport within two weeks, carrying 28,000 pounds of cargo as well as Admiral Tim Keating, the head of U.S. Pacific Command, and Henrietta Fore, the administrator of the U.S. Agency for International Development. Keating carried with him an appeal to the government of Myanmar to allow considerably greater U.S. aid and an expanded U.S. presence in the country. But permission was denied. The Myanmar government allowed flights in, but did not allow U.S. ships to dock or U.S. military personnel to come ashore. In fact, Myanmar did not allow any international aid workers into the country before a personal appeal in late May from UN secretary-general Ban Ki-Moon.[140]

Rather than mark a turning point for the relationship, this episode largely reinforced U.S. and Burmese suspicions about each other. For its part, the United States viewed obstruction by the government of Myanmar as morally indefensible. Motivated in part by the slow response of the junta, the Bush administration awarded Burmese dissident Aung San Suu Kyi a Congressional Gold Medal for her human rights work. It is perhaps no surprise, then, that the Burmese government was highly suspicious of the flotilla of U.S. (and French) military vessels that quickly deployed off its coast, offering to deliver aid, troops, and helicopters.[141] In 2011, the Obama administration achieved a diplomatic breakthrough with Burma, but it is difficult to claim that the post-Nargis experience contributed to this outcome. It is easier to argue that it may have actually slowed a thaw in relations.

If the record of U.S. disaster diplomacy with rival states is mixed, what is the record with those that are friendly? Operation Tomodachi was not the first time the U.S. military was used to provide aid to a friendly, disaster-affected country. In order to answer the question of whether U.S. aid after 3.11 strengthened relations and led to new levels of mutual commitment, I examine two cases—both in Asia, and each following one of the most devastating natural disasters in history. In both cases, the U.S. military was deployed to assist suffering people in a friendly state. As we discover, the diplomatic consequences varied in ways that are relevant for how we assess the impact of Operation Tomodachi on U.S.-Japan relations.

In December 2004, a 9.1- to 9.3-magnitude earthquake off the northern tip of Sumatra—the world's largest in four decades and third largest ever recorded—triggered a massive tsunami that raced across the Indian Ocean. The quake and resultant tsunami killed approximately 230,000 people and displaced another 1.75 million. The majority of those dead or missing and presumed dead were from Indonesia, although Sri Lanka, India, Thailand, Malaysia, the Maldives, and the Seychelles also suffered substantial deaths and damage. The massive wave even slammed into Somalia on the far side of the Indian Ocean. Fifty-four nations, led by Australia, India, Japan, and the United States, mobilized to assist these countries.[142]

Aid from the United States has been credited with improving U.S.-Indonesian relations. One observer argued that post-tsunami assistance "transformed America's image in Indonesia. Even more remarkably, it undermined support for Osama bin Laden."[143] Indeed, widely cited opinion polls indicated that U.S. post-tsunami relief had both effects.[144] Admiral Mike Mullen, then chief of naval operations and later chairman of the Joint Chiefs of Staff, referred to this polling when he wrote in 2006: "The poll found that, as a direct result of our humanitarian assistance—and for the first time ever in a Muslim nation—more people favored U.S.-led efforts to fight terrorism than opposed them (40% to 36%)."[145]

It is difficult to determine how much U.S. assistance contributed to these shifts of opinion. In 2003, Indonesians had vehemently opposed the U.S. invasion of Iraq, which was justified by a "war on terror" rhetoric that many in the world's most populous Muslim nation took to be directed at them. The United States had generally been popular in Indonesia until the Iraq War, when support sank to new lows. Even the election of President Barack Obama, who had spent part of his childhood there, was not sufficient to raise U.S. popularity in Indonesia to prewar levels.[146] The United States had a similar experience with another nominally aligned state, Pakistan, after the 2005 earthquake in Kashmir.

On 8 October 2005, a 7.6-magnitude earthquake struck outside the city of Muzaffarabad in Pakistan-administered Kashmir, killing more than 73,000 (including 18,000 schoolchildren) and wounding an additional 69,000.[147] Although Indian-administered Kashmir was not spared, casualties there were much lower: around 1,300 dead and 6,500 wounded on the Indian side of the Line of Control. The approaching onset of winter led to concerns that up to 200,000 of the several million displaced persons might die from exposure.[148]

Perceiving this as a "strategic moment" for U.S.-Pakistan ties that were critical to the U.S. war effort in Afghanistan, U.S. ambassador to Pakistan Ryan Crocker immediately concluded that the U.S. response would be "crucial to our future relationship" with Pakistan.[149] U.S. aid began arriving in Pakistan the day after the quake, and by the time the operation ended six months later, U.S. air and ground crews had conducted the largest and longest airborne relief operation since the Berlin Airlift.[150] More than eighteen million pounds of humanitarian aid and relief supplies were off-loaded, and U.S. military medical personnel treated approximately thirty-five thousand patients. Including civilian efforts, the United States provided medical care or medical supplies to eighty thousand Pakistanis.[151]

The humanitarian benefits of the aid seem clearer than the political impact, despite overwhelming evidence that Washington sought to win Pakistani "hearts and minds" through assistance.[152] One senior U.S. Marine officer who participated in the relief effort acknowledged that U.S. assistance was not purely humanitarian. Claiming that U.S. military assistance to Pakistan "provides a useful model of how humanitarian missions can contribute to political success," he explicitly compares the effort to the Berlin Airlift as an example of "how a humanitarian assistance campaign could engender lasting political success in an ideological struggle."[153]

The evidence, however, is mixed. Polls conducted by A. C. Nielsen Pakistan suggest that U.S. assistance enhanced bilateral relations.[154] They show a dramatic shift in opinions of Pakistani adults, more of whom felt that suicide bombing and other forms of violence against civilians were never justified, disapproved of Osama bin Laden, and had a favorable opinion of the United States. Fewer Pakistanis had confidence in Osama bin Laden, and the number with very unfavorable views of the United States declined considerably. Similar evidence comes from focus group discussions and interviews.[155] Researchers found "near unanimous sentiment by local respondents that [U.S.] organizations responded for humanitarian reasons rather than to promote hidden political, cultural or religious agendas." This overall sentiment is echoed in the response of one resident of Muzaffarabad, the city near the epicenter: "The international military response was perceived as humanitarian. People said farewell to the U.S. Army with flowers. They had no political agenda."[156]

However, other polling results show little or no lasting impact on Pakistani views of the United States.[157] In a Pew study, U.S. military aid did not appear to substantially or irrevocably change Pakistani perceptions of the potential threat from the United States. A shift away from support for terrorism in Pakistan did begin around the time of earthquake relief, but attitudes appear to have changed before the relief effort. A localized increase in esteem and trust of Westerners in areas where the aid was most concentrated is apparent, but it is equally clear that this trust did not spill over across Pakistan. As the U.S.-Pakistan relationship entered its most difficult period after the 2011 assassination of Bin Laden, the transitory nature of public and elite-level opinion appeared more evident than any fundamental improvement. After the relief operation, positive views of the United States in Pakistan improved only slightly—to 27 percent from 23 percent—and within two years, it would slip to just 15 percent. The Pew study concludes that "distrust of American motives and opposition to key elements of U.S. foreign policy may run too deep in Pakistan for humanitarian effort to have a significant impact over the longer term." U.S. disaster relief in Pakistan after October 2005 was a "stark example of the limits" of disaster diplomacy.[158]

What about Japanese disaster diplomacy? Japan had first authorized the international dispatch of rescue workers in 1987 and had sent its first Japan Disaster Relief (JDR) team to a frosty Iran after the Manjil-Rudbar earthquake claimed forty thousand lives there in 1990. In 1992, the enabling legislation was amended to allow dispatch of military personnel. In May 2008, less than one month after Cyclone Nargis devastated Myanmar, two months after the most violent disturbances in Tibet in twenty years, and just three months before Beijing was scheduled to host the Summer Olympic Games, an 8.0-magnitude earthquake struck Sichuan Province in western China. Japan had another opportunity to organize and dispatch a JDR team, its twelfth.

The Sichuan (or Wenchuan) earthquake was thirty times greater than the 1995 temblor in Kobe and affected a territory the size of the Republic of Korea. It claimed 90,000 lives, injured 363,000, and left millions homeless.[159] Whole mountains were shaken loose, shedding rocks and trees that covered entire valleys and the communities beneath. And in the most conspicuous tragedy of all, one thousand schoolchildren were crushed when their school buildings were pancaked by the earth's tremors. The temporal proximity to the Cyclone Nargis in Myanmar invited comparisons by observers who, by all accounts, found the Chinese response to the disaster timelier, better coordinated, and far more effective. Contrasting narratives about the two authoritarian states were quick to form: Beijing was remarkably accountable and transparent; Naypyidaw was irresponsible, opaque and "inhuman."[160]

China had responded to its most recent natural disaster, the 1976 Tangshan earthquake that had claimed three times more lives, much as Myanmar did after Nargis. This time, party and state would engineer a response that boosted its legitimacy at home and its prestige abroad. Within hours of the quake, Premier Wen Jiabao was at the site, having already mobilized 130,000 People's Liberation Army (PLA) troops for rescue and relief operations and having authorized the dispatch of local rescue teams and sniffer dogs from across the country. Invoking a model refined during the construction of the Three Gorges Dam, which relocated 840,000 people, Beijing ordered local governments to join the military on the front line of state support for the stricken province. Under the Wenchuan Disaster Recovery Pairing Support Plan, Beijing paired eighteen regions and municipalities—as well as universities—with partner localities and schools in the affected area. To continue receiving central government support, these cities and regions would have to provide three years of reconstruction assistance—planning, housing, medical support, social welfare, agricultural and industrial assistance, education, and so forth—to their partner localities at the level of at least 1 percent or their previous year's budget.[161]

The voluntary mobilization of two hundred thousand people, half of them college students, in the first week after the quake was even more striking—and likely even more consequential. The unprecedented surge of volunteers and their organization by some two hundred Chinese and foreign NGOs was heralded as a "watershed event" for China's civil society.[162] After all, these were organizations that the Chinese state had tried to contain in the past.[163] As a result, much like 1995 in Japan, 2008 in China was hailed as the "Year of the Volunteer," signaling the importance of a surprisingly vibrant associational sphere. A ballast against the state was said to have emerged stealthily.[164] Change seemed to be everywhere, as individuals and groups from all across China competed to provide funds to the region. The response was by all accounts flexible and timely.[165] Private charitable contributions amounted to $6.6 billion within a month.[166]

But China's authoritarian reflexes had not atrophied entirely. Chinese officials imposed tight security in damaged areas to prevent demonstrations by distraught parents, in one case even preventing a memorial ceremony for lost children in Dujianyan, where journalists were banned and detained.[167] Party chief Hu Jintao became so concerned with the government's initial relaxation of controls on the media—which resulted in damning reports on shoddy construction that accounted for thousands of deaths—that he called for new party guidance in the form of "construction of a new force" of journalists to lead public opinion.[168] Still, the Chinese people were rediscovering their own voice and a sense of national unity that, it was said, had been flagging.[169]

They were also discovering their appeal to the outside world. International relief agencies and disaster diplomats lined up to help, and this time—after a short delay that may have cost lives—Beijing welcomed them with open arms. More than 160 nations and international organizations expressed condolences and offered assistance.[170] To the surprise of most observers, the first on the list was Japan. The quake had occurred just after Hu Jintao's return from a state visit to Japan—the first by a Chinese leader after a decade of frayed relations. Hu was determined to maintain forward diplomatic progress, and when the Japanese Disaster Relief team arrived before dawn on 16 May, they were the first foreign rescuers to set foot on Chinese soil since the 1949 revolution. Beijing denied any political motives and attributed this to Japan's "proximity and speed." But a heavy dose of disaster diplomacy, from both sides, was clear to all observers.[171] According to a retired Japanese government official who was in Beijing at the time, the Chinese government was eager to soften public opinion vis-à-vis Japan in order to avoid an Olympic reprise of the nationalist disruptions that had marred the 2004 Asian football championships. It placed a Chinese television crew on the JDR bus to record its every effort, supervised by a Chinese diplomat who had a cell phone with a "direct line to Premier Wen Jiabo."[172] News of the Japanese rescuers was broadcast live across China for days.

Japan was ready for this moment and just as eager as China to gain diplomatic advantage from the tragedy. Preparations began immediately after news of the quake reached the Cabinet Office. Within minutes, ten Ministry of Defense (MOD) and MOFA officials were assembled to organize a JDR team for dispatch to China, and the team was ready within thirty-six hours, while Tokyo waited for Beijing's green light and felt out its willingness to allow Air Self-Defense Force (ASDF) C-130 transports to shuttle relief workers and supplies to western China.[173] The use of the Japanese military in this rescue operation had immediate appeal among politicians. One unnamed Diet member declared that "this is a good opportunity to have the Chinese understand the real mission of the SDF," and the Policy Affairs Research Council of the ruling LDP affirmed its support for the use of the ASDF.[174]

This may have delayed China's invitation to the JDR team, however; which in turn made the Japanese rescue of survivors even more difficult. Growing testy as hours dragged on into days, Foreign Minister Kōmura reminded the Chinese that "Japan is ready with trained personnel," and Chief Cabinet Secretary Machimura Nobutaka declared undiplomatically that "China is a self sufficient country that wants to do everything on its own."[175] Not having heard from Beijing, the team was recalled from Haneda Airport on 13 May.

Permission was finally granted late on 15 May 2008—a welcome development attributed by Prime Minister Fukuda to his successful summit meeting earlier in the month with General Secretary Hu.[176] The JDR was in the air in chartered aircraft within six hours, led by a foreign ministry official, Koizumi Takashi.[177] But vital time had been lost, and it turned out that two Japanese rescue teams with sixty-one trained personnel were unable to save any lives. They did, however, pull sixteen corpses from the wreckage in three locations.[178] An additional Japan International Cooperation Agency (JICA) team of twenty-three doctors and nurses provided medical assistance to survivors, and the Japanese government gave $1.7 million through the International Red Cross and Red Crescent, along with tents, food, blankets, and other supplies.[179] Group leader Koizumi pronounced his regret at not having found anyone alive in the rubble, but expressed pride in having "received high evaluations and gratitude from both the Chinese government and its citizens," adding that "although the purpose of the JDR effort was entirely humanitarian assistance, it also had a positive effect on the bilateral relationship . . . a silver lining in this dark cloud."[180] The JICA teams were followed by a more symbolic string of visits by Japanese politicians bearing supplies, and cash donations from Kansai political leaders, including Hashimoto Tōru, then governor of Osaka, as well as six months of substantive assistance from Japanese NGOs supported by the government and Keidanren.[181]

Both sides were unabashed about the diplomatic advantages they could gain from the crisis and from their unprecedented bilateral cooperation. Prime Minister Fukuda used the opportunity to call for "diplomacy for disaster management cooperation," in effect a regional agreement to cooperate on disaster relief.[182] China's ambassador to Japan, Cui Tiankai, called Japan's response "a sign of strategic, mutually beneficial relations."[183] Japanese editorialists concurred. The conservative *Sankei Shimbun* suggested that Sino-Japanese cooperation in Sichuan demonstrated that "the Chinese government viewed the earthquake as a rare opportunity to quickly promote reciprocal strategic relations."[184] The more moderate *Mainichi Shimbun* pointed out that China clearly deemed its relations with Japan to be of great importance, and said that "apparently China accepted the Japanese relief team ahead of other countries with the goal of deepening popular understanding of Hu's visit to Japan." It then quoted an unnamed Japanese diplomat who reported that "state-run TV cameras covered our relief teams from the start. One could sense the intentions of the Chinese government there."[185] A Japanese Foreign Ministry official declared that the JDR team "displayed Japan's presence and had a positive effect on Sino-Japanese relations."[186]

In China, the emerging narrative was one of new social solidarity and effective but compassionate leadership. The Chinese government won over the foreign media, which hailed its quick response and new openness.[187] Even human rights groups that had been extremely critical of the People's Republic of China (PRC) in Tibet now were acknowledging its sensitivity and concern for the people of Sichuan. China's Foreign Ministry spokesman, Qin Gang, connected Chinese relief operations to the PRC's concerns for human rights, calling the Chinese effort a "people-centered relief effort" that demonstrates how "the Chinese government respects and protects human rights."[188]

In Japan, there was also widespread self-congratulation. Much of it was leveraged off the attention given to the JICA team by the Chinese media, particularly the public broadcaster, CCTV, and Xinhua, which repeatedly reported how Japanese rescuers "worked around the clock" and "never gave up," working without regard for their own safety.[189] It was Xinhua that snapped and published a photo of Japanese rescue workers bowing before the corpses of a mother and infant they had pulled from the rubble. The incident touched Chinese hearts, and the photograph became iconic.[190]

Japanese observers fixed on the bravery of Japan's rescue workers and on the gratitude of average Chinese who, they reported, could previously have imagined uniformed Japanese only in the form of cruel, marauding invaders. Now, they said, it was clear to the average Chinese that Japan had changed. According to opinion polls—and as evidenced by the standing ovation Japanese athletes received from Chinese fans at the Olympic opening

Japanese rescue workers from the Self-Defense Forces pay respects to the bodies of a mother and child recovered after the Sichuan earthquake. 2008. Photo by Li Tao, Xinhua photographer, courtesy of Xinhua News Agency.

ceremonies—the Chinese were seeing Japan clearly for the first time.[191] Japan's relief effort would be remembered as a "turning point," a moment of deep reconciliation in Sino-Japanese relations.[192] Japanese foreign minister Kōmura crowed to reporters that a visitor to the Chongqing consulate had declared that "ill feelings toward Japan had changed," and Chief Cabinet Secretary Machimura reported a new respect and admiration now harbored by the Chinese for Japan.[193]

The collateral diplomatic benefits of this operation had their limits. Two weeks after the disaster—while Japan was still basking in the success of its JDR team—Tokyo again pressed Beijing for permission to use ASDF C-130s to shuttle relief supplies to Sichuan. At first, they seemed to be pushing on an open door; word of imminent approval of eight round-trip military relief flights was leaked to a credulous press, which spoke of a breakthrough in bilateral relations.[194] These reports touched off a backlash in China. Anti-Japanese posts began to appear on Chinese electronic bulletin boards, and the Chinese government quickly announced that the SDF "cannot be welcome [due to] the impact on the psychology of the Chinese people."[195] Military officers who welcomed the dispatch as laying the way for "a large expansion in the scope of SDF missions abroad" were now embarrassed that U.S., South Korean, and Russian military transports had been welcomed to China while they were turned away.[196] In the words of a *Yomiuri Shimbun* editorial: "Both governments apparently concluded it would be unwise to risk putting a damper on Chinese public opinion toward Japan, just as it was finally warming up."[197]

There would be one more opportunity, and it too was missed. In June, after the C-130 imbroglio had settled down, the PRC invited the destroyer JS *Sazanami* to visit Shenzen, per a 2007 arrangement made by the two nations' defense ministers and ratified by Prime Minister Fukuda and General Secretary Hu at their prequake summit in Japan. Even before the *Sazanami* arrived in Zhanjiang port—sixty-three years after the last Japanese military had left China—the Chinese government had cancelled virtually all public events, and foreign journalists were not allowed to cover the port call. The Japanese sailors off-loaded relief supplies for Sichuan as a band played to a limited audience in the military base, and they returned to Japan with little fanfare. China's English-language press ran photos of the *Sazanami* visit and the overseas *People's Daily* editorialized that the port call was a "sign of the broadmindedness and confidence of the Chinese people," but criticism at home was suppressed and anti-Japanese websites were temporarily shut down.[198] A Chinese navy admiral, Yang Yi, explained that "a port call by a warship with a Japanese flag easily calls up our painful memories."[199] It was yet another reminder of the limits of disaster diplomacy.

Conclusion

These historical and comparative cases are filled with clues for how to understand the impact of 3.11 on Japanese politics and public policy. We have seen how earthquakes and other natural disasters have served as moments for reinforcing, revising, or replacing the status quo. Optimism and pessimism always mingle in unstable suspension alongside crisis management, national mobilization, and recovery. The many domestic antecedents of the Tohoku disaster were each laden with popular dissatisfaction with national leadership, brimming with expectations for fundamental change, and debilitated by administrative competition within the state. Postdisaster politics were dominated by political actors with extant preferences who would generate and use narratives to explain what had happened and sell their prescription for how to make things better. And so each Japanese disaster engendered new building codes, new regulatory structures, new land use plans, and new promises of public safety.[200] Just as important, each unleashed new promises of change and new forms of political and social activism that challenged national policy. Each triggered contestation among political entrepreneurs who sought to impose their preferred meaning on the disaster and to take control of the recovery. Debate ensued, but so did politics—often in chaotic form—involving military, civic, bureaucratic and, after Japan opened to the outside world in the 1860s, the disaster diplomacy of foreign powers.

Nor should we forget that indeterminacy is among the many lessons to be drawn from historical and comparative material here. In addition to being struck by the constants across such a diverse array of disasters, we are also reminded of how open-ended disasters can be. It is, we see, difficult to know a priori how each catastrophe will be unwound and spun up in the narratives that follow. They serve not only as sources of guidance for the questions we ask of 3.11 and its consequences, but also warn of the susceptibility of disaster to narrative construction. History and comparison remind us that crises are as much tools for policy entrepreneurs as they are sources of pain for those who must experience and recover from them.

Recovery from each disaster occurred against a political and economic backdrop of instability and mistrust, requiring large and consequential choices under uncertain conditions. Without regard for regime type—autocratic or democratic—government officials always responded by trying to reassert central authority; and local actors pushed back with demands for greater local autonomy. Competition across bureaucratic jurisdictions at the center always slowed the response and resulted in promises that "the evils of vertical administration" would be corrected. Lofty hopes for significant change were proclaimed and then dashed. Social ills were laid bare and debated. Scapegoating was ubiquitous—at times with deadly consequences. Offers of foreign aid, even when not viewed with suspicion, were weighed against the appearance of domestic incompetence. Communication failures and the insufficiency of emergency management training were met by tightfisted central budget officials pleading fiscal constraints. Perverse and unintended consequences were never far from the postreconstruction landscapes. And there were always the same broad-brush choices to make: rebuild the devastated area as it was or use the crisis as an opportunity to invent something new. Reconstruction always hinges as much on prior political divisions as on opportunism. But above all, in each case, we observe the Japanese people responding with determination and the Japanese nation responding with resilience. At the level of regional survival, at least, we are led to wonder just what choices they really had.

Our comparison to non-Japanese cases also offers lessons for 3.11, not the least of which is that there is nothing unique about Japan's rhetoric of crisis. As President George W. Bush learned the hard way, national governance—and the public support on which it depends—hinges on an empathetic and effective response to local needs as much as it depends on abstract economic policies or foreign conquests. Hurricane Katrina generated narratives about competence and caring that were eerie precursors of those that emerged in Japan after 3.11. Prime Minister Kan's failures and the criticisms of his leadership were different in kind from President Bush's—Kan was seen as too close to the crisis and Bush as too distant—but their credibility as national leaders suffered in parallel ways and they were victims of similar political dynamics. Questions of leadership, community, vulnerability, and change are as American as they are Japanese. But the comparison also reminds us that talk of change is cheap—certainly cheaper than the lives claimed by natural disaster and the actions that states take to ameliorate the destruction.

We learn from our cases of disaster diplomacy—American, Japanese, and Chinese—that humanitarian assistance and disaster relief are no substitutes for the fundamental forces, the normal dynamics, of international politics. Whether U.S. efforts (as in Pakistan, Myanmar, and Bangladesh) were strategic or simply opportunistic, extant divisions were more likely to constrain postdisaster diplomacy than munificence was likely to transform it. States that fundamentally mistrust one another seem unlikely to reset their relationship as a result of aid, and actors that have other reasons to pursue reconciliation will find humanitarian assistance a useful tool in their efforts. This was no less true in the Sino-Japanese case, when both sides aggressively used the Sichuan disaster to further diplomatic ends, with limited results.

How do such lessons apply to 3.11, where the United States came to the immediate aid of an ally? We want to learn whether humanitarian intervention can lead to even higher levels of cooperation and trust in allied nations where public acceptance of the alliance is high. But these other cases suggest it may be best to lower our expectations. So with these historical and international comparisons in hand—and with a healthy appreciation of how indeterminate outcomes can be—we turn to a much finer grained analysis of the impact of 3.11 on policy debate in Japan. We begin with an analysis of dueling narratives in the discourse about security after 3.11—precisely the realm where domestic politics and disaster diplomacy come together most directly.

Dueling Security Narratives

100 microsieverts or 1,000 microsieverts—it doesn't matter. Our job is to protect the Japanese people.
—General Hibako Yoshifumi, Ground Self-Defense Force (GSDF) chief of staff, March 2011

Undefeated by earthquakes, undefeated by tsunami, unafraid of radiation, sound of body, unselfish, never satisfied, always silently carrying on . . . thinking only of the safety of the people and defending the nation, sweating profusely and not sleeping amid the debris, the mud, and the small graves in the ocean . . . satisfied when the people say thank you. That's the kind of soldier I want to be.
—Miyajima Shigeki, 2011

If we can cooperate successfully in humanitarian assistance and disaster relief, we can do it in the face of hostilities.
—Lt. Col. Gregg Bottemiller, U.S. Forces Japan, July 2011

There are no withdrawals from the Bank of Goodwill.
—U.S. government official, Tokyo, May 2012

For those less familiar with the history reviewed in chapter three than with the theories of change reviewed in chapter two, 3.11 ought to be the mother of all catalysts—or at least their aunt. And if the greatest benefits come to those who had the greatest success, then the Japanese military and the U.S.-Japan alliance ought to expect a "Tohoku dividend"—the institutional silver lining in the dark cloud of 3.11. Chronicles of the exploits of Japan's soldiers were on public view everywhere—on television, in bookstores, and in the social media. The Self-Defense Forces (SDF) joined civilian volunteers in the small pantheon of the nation's most celebrated heroes since the 1940s. A January 2012 cabinet poll found that 97.7 percent of the Japanese appreciated the SDF operation in Tohoku.[1] Approval of the alliance was nearly as striking: the U.S. military had never been as popular in Japan as after it was mobilized for Tohoku rescue and relief missions.[2]

Both welcomed the boost in popular esteem, but 3.11 seemed a particularly important moment for the SDF. Japan's Self-Defense Forces were formally established a decade after the end of the Pacific War, a conflict that was blamed on military intervention in politics and the loss of civilian control. From the beginning, Japan's redesigned military was the central object (and reflection) of a deeply divided polity. The Cold War Left—in permanent opposition—insisted on a strict interpretation of article 9 of the postwar constitution: the SDF was unconstitutional. And the hegemonic but pragmatic Liberal Democratic Party (LDP) conceded by inserting civilians from nondefense ministries to supervise civilian defense officials and uniformed officers, by limiting defense budgets to less than 1 percent of gross domestic product (GDP), by banning arms exports, and by adopting other measures to limit the SDF consistent with the preferences of an antipathetic public.[3] Still, the SDF had been making steady progress toward public acceptance as a necessary and legitimate arm of the Japanese state.[4] A Defense Ministry was finally established in 2007, and overseas missions under the banner of United Nations (UN) peacekeeping operations had become routine. In fact, even before 3.11, nearly four-fifths of the Japanese public approved of using the SDF for disaster relief, a higher percentage than for defense against invasion.[5]

Nonetheless, a steady 10–14 percent of the public continued to reject the legitimacy of the SDF.[6] While this minority opposition had shrunk as the SDF modernized after the end of the Cold War, the defense establishment understood that sustaining domestic support remained one of its most enduring challenges. The chief of staff of the Ground Self Defense Forces (GSDF), General Kimizuka Eiji, believes that there was no uniformly sound "foundation for cooperation" between the SDF and local governments before 3.11.[7] And according to a senior counselor in the defense minister's secretariat, neither had there been an "acknowledgment by the public or by the Emperor of [the SDF's] rightful place in Japanese society."[8]

Legitimated militaries and strengthened alliances are usually products of success in war. One of many examples of the former is the exorcism of the Vietnam debacle and the new level of popular support enjoyed by the U.S. military after the Gulf War in 1991. Examples of the latter include the enhancement of China-North Korea ties after the Korean War. There are fewer cases in which militaries were legitimated and alliances strengthened short of military campaigns. But they do exist. The Chinese military enjoyed a measure of new support after the 2008 Sichuan earthquake; the *Bundeswehr* (German military), which undertook the biggest operation in its history, enjoyed a small boost in public support after the Elbe floods in 2002.[9] A less agreeable case was that of the Japanese military after the 1923 earthquake, which it used to consolidate its political power and to snuff out a nascent democratic transformation. The key question for this chapter is whether the devastating peacetime events of March 2011—and the response by the

Japanese and U.S. militaries—will stimulate the sorts of benign institutional transformations in security affairs that leaders in both countries have long sought.

Many thought such a transformation would be automatic. Japan's post-3.11 national conversation was filled with inflated expectations. A former prime minister suggested that 3.11 was a "turning point" in the Japan-U.S. alliance.[10] This notion was echoed across the aisle by a Democratic Party of Japan (DPJ) Diet member who argued that the United States and Japan will "use this experience as a lesson and build a new cooperative strategic program."[11] A former defense minister declared that 3.11 provided an opportunity for Japan "to shed the SDF allergy" and trust its military.[12] One professor saw the disaster as "an opportunity . . . to set Japan on the path to end militarization," and another predicted that 3.11 would "bring about an overdue move for Japanese pacifism away from anti-militarism."[13] A senior Foreign Ministry official expected that "alliance security is one area where change would actually happen" and predicted that the Japanese government will "capitalize on" its experience of "working well with the Americans during the crisis."[14] Japan's largest daily, the *Yomiuri Shimbun*, editorialized that Operation Tomodachi "will take the alliance to a new level."[15] And a former commandant of the National Defense Academy even included the possibility of constitutional change: "[T]he government should seize the moment to give the force a wider and more responsible role in Japan's defense, as well as a larger budget. Giving the SDF a proper place in Japan's constitution and security policy also will strengthen the country's alliance with the United States."[16]

But a more sober GSDF chief of staff simply noted that "there are many changes being discussed for the SDF," and added a caution of contingency: "if we shrink, change will be impossible."[17]

The discussion of possible change in national security institutions and policies proceeded in accordance with the three rhetorical models outlined in chapter 2, each with its own heroes, villains, thought leaders, and policy preferences. Advocates of "putting it in gear"—mostly on the right—treated 3.11 as Japan's wake-up call, a warning that it was past time to make the military more muscular, more capable, and more independent of the United States. Most of those who would "stay the course" were centrists and alliance managers convinced that the disaster provided a welcome proof of concept, which they had insisted for decades was the right course for Japan. And those who would go "back to the future"—mostly on the left—saw 3.11 as justification for disarmament and a stricter interpretation of the original intent of article 9 of Japan's postwar constitution. All three groups lauded the SDF for its performance—though the third was just as likely to praise citizens' groups and volunteers—but their prescriptions varied considerably.

National Security and the Rhetoric of Crisis

WAKE-UP CALL

Most of those who saw 3.11 as a warning that Japan should do more had long hoped Japan would rebuild its military capabilities, usually in ways that would end Japan's infantilization by the United States. Japan had been "lulled into pacifism" by its dependence, and having lost the ability to take care of itself, was left dangerously unable to imagine war. What happened on 3.11 was "nothing other than a war in which a Japan that had forgotten war, was attacked."[18] But, the argument went, as heroic as the SDF had been, Japan's fighters still needed the U.S. military to support its relief and rescue operations. Those who could not imagine a 3.11-scale natural disaster were the same people who had allowed Japan to become dependent on the United States. They certainly could not be relied on to take care of the nation. The inability of Japanese to imagine the worst was on full display in March 2011, evidence of the extent to which the nation had grown soft and vulnerable.[19] In short, 3.11 demonstrated that Japan had been lulled into submission— the U.S. military had become "Japan's protector in a sort of Disneyland."[20]

Since Japan was not ready for 3.11, the primary lesson of the catastrophe is that the nation must put it in gear and prepare for its real enemies. According to one commentator, "This time it was a nuclear accident, but tomorrow it could be an attack by a foreign enemy. Even now we smell the smoke in the Senkaku area."[21] Another suggests that unimagined internal troubles, like natural disasters, prefigure unimagined foreign attacks. If Japan is not ready for the former it cannot be prepared for the latter.[22] The popular right-wing cartoonist Kobayashi Yoshinori reminded his readers that it is the military's responsibility not only to defend when there are no enemies but to confront real enemies wherever they exist. For Kobayashi, as for others, Japan must not let down its guard because its enemies are legion.[23] One alarmed analyst argued that "the true national crisis" (*kokunan*) was Russia's preparation to invade Hokkaido.[24] Another agreed, connecting Japan's "irresponsible approach to crisis management" to the need for enhanced protection from Russia's "obstinate anti-Japan policies."[25]

A former commander of Japan's forces in Iraq widened the aperture. Satō Masahisa, now a member of Japan's House of Councilors, pointed out that Russian forces in the north and Chinese forces in the south probed Japan's air and sea defenses during the crisis. They collected information about how Japanese forces operate with the U.S. military and, in what he bemoaned as "not a very promising situation," he said they found weaknesses everywhere.[26] The conservative national security scholar Nakanishi Terumasa used 3.11 as an occasion to point out that few Japanese government officials appreciate China's aggressive intent, and fewer still understand why North Korea developed nuclear weapons.[27] A retired National Police Agency official, referring to a territorial dispute with China that has become one of Japan's most difficult foreign and security problems, declared that 3.11 has proved "the SDF is no longer a bastard child (*shoshi*). . . . Its real job is 'national defense,' so let it defend the homeland, starting from the Senkaku Islands and including our territorial waters and airspace."[28]

An early post-3.11 analysis from the more centrist PHP think tank offered a structural justification for the wake-up call narrative. In its April newsletter, analysts supported the Japan-U.S. alliance, but argued that 3.11 occurred at a moment in which the international order was at an inflection point, when "the fundamental antagonisms among nations have not been resolved."[29] They predicted that with rising powers like China challenging the Western-centered world order, "the disaster will be used as an opportunity to adjust policies toward Japan." These adjustments are likely to be made by Russia and China—hostile countries that offered assistance just before resuming "military surveillance" of Japan. But the PHP analysis does not rule out the possibility that the United States might also find rebalancing (its own accommodation with China) attractive in the wake of 3.11.

PROOF OF CONCEPT

Others were far more confident that because both the SDF and the alliance had proved their worth following 3.11, each would receive fuller public support. In their view, this was because the two militaries had kept to the course set out for them years earlier by defense planners in both countries. Rather than view the unprecedented 3.11 mobilization as a historic deviation—and generally ignoring the considerable difficulties the alliance encountered in the first weeks—these analysts celebrated a demonstration of the natural consequence of several generations of military planning that began during the Cold War and retains its relevance today. The DPJ's Nagashima Akihisa, a defense specialist who helped convene the bilateral coordinating committee at the height of the crisis, was clear on this point: decades of joint exercises accounted for the success with which U.S. forces and the Japanese military handled 3.11. Calling the creation of the coordinating mechanism "particularly symbolic," he insisted that "we were able to demonstrate something very important about joint U.S.-Japanese decision-making."[30]

Former prime minister Nakasone Yasuhiro was also impressed that the test of solidarity with the United States produced such excellent results. After all, he reminded the Japanese, the United States was under no formal treaty obligation to come to Japan's aid in the event of a natural disaster. But it did so, and the accomplishment should be understood as "one more valuable element in the future rebuilding and deepening" of the alliance.[31] Elsewhere, Nakasone and his colleagues suggest that the support Japan received from the United States served as "important proof to the world" of the value of the alliance.[32] Another analyst built on this point by noting that since the

Japanese did not feel threatened by the movements of Russian and Chinese military near Japanese territory "when its military's hands were full," the joint operation also clearly demonstrated their confidence in the deterrent power of the alliance—a view widely shared by specialists.[33]

The SDF also proved its worth to many quite apart from the alliance framework. Just as years of U.S.-Japan joint exercises were credited with ensuring successful alliance cooperation during the crisis, years of disaster exercises with local governments proved their worth after 3.11. One Ministry of Defense (MOD) official explained that "mayors who would not meet us before 3.11 now invite us to visit and help plan for the next disaster."[34] But there had been at least some joint planning ahead of the crisis. Analysts were impressed at how, after its Hanshin/Awaji debacle, the SDF had placed retired military officers as liaison officers in local governments, and how a large-scale exercise in October 2008 involving six Tohoku prefectures, ten thousand troops, and twenty-two municipalities anticipated 3.11.[35] In a remarkable departure from decades of criticizing the SDF, the *Asahi Shimbun* praised its "constant improvement"—specifically its coordination with local governments, its ability to effect a joint command, its training with U.S. forces, and its "new level of intimacy" in helping victims. Without singling out humanitarian and disaster relief missions for special attention, the *Asahi* editorialized that there should be a "flexible increase" in the size of Japan's military because "Japan cannot neglect its responsibilities for national defense or for UN peacekeeping."[36]

The professionalism of the SDF became part of the hagiography surrounding its performance. In one best-selling chronicle of the rescue and relief operation, the SDF was characterized repeatedly in a revelatory tone, and offered "the whole story of professionals you do not know."[37] A Defense Ministry publicist, Sakurabayashi Misa, celebrated "hyper-rescue relief efforts" and reported that Japan's "earnest" and "devoted" soldiers were thrilled to be operating "on their own."[38] But the most notable accolade for the SDF's contribution came from Emperor Akihito himself. On 16 March, he delivered a message of encouragement to the people of Tohoku on national television in which he acknowledged the extended efforts of the Self-Defense Forces and other first responders, including foreigners. It did not go unnoticed—and indeed was deeply appreciated by many commentators—that the emperor thanked the SDF before thanking the others. It was the first time that an emperor had ever referred directly to the SDF in public.[39] One senior MOD official suggested that alongside the SDF and the alliance, the Imperial Household was one of the best-performing institutions during the crisis.[40]

Many analysts in this group were quick to insist that 3.11 demonstrated that the SDF needed—and deserved—the better equipment and higher numbers its supporters had long been advocating. In the words of one observer, 3.11 should put an end to the "less troops, less equipment" rhetoric popular among some politicians and the media.[41] Nakamura Shingo, a

SDF troops rescue elderly citizens. 14 March 2011. Photo courtesy of Japan Self-Defense Forces Joint Staff Office.

former GSDF officer, insisted that 3.11 demonstrated it was time to reverse the secular reduction of ground forces that had been under way since the end of the Cold War.[42] For some, 3.11 signaled the importance of amphibious capabilities, remotely operated unmanned aerial vehicles, and robots, as well as a range of lift capabilities the MOD had sought for years but that had been in short supply.[43]

DISARM

A third group agreed that 3.11 demonstrated that the SDF needs—and maybe even deserves—more equipment, but would prefer that Japan's soldiers get more shovels rather than guns. Japan should have what one leading editor referred to as "an Article Nine military that builds, not destroys things."[44] This reorientation has been framed in the language of national identity itself. Just as Japan was once mobilized to build a "Rich Nation, Strong Army" (*fukoku kyōhei*), and just as this exhortation later was supplanted by calls to become a "technology based nation" (*gijutsu rikkoku*), now there are those who call for Japan to become a "Strong Nation with Advanced Disaster Response Capabilities" (*senshin saigai kyōkoku*).[45]

For some in this camp, 3.11 was merely a reminder of the many dangers inherent in Japan's alliance with the United States and of the rectitude of antimilitarism. Waseda University professor Mizushima Asaho argued that 3.11 contributed to the "unconstitutional" integration (*ittaika*) of the U.S. and Japanese militaries and that U.S.-Japan cooperation during the crisis was "a full scale trial run" for joint operations under the National Defense Program Guidelines.[46] The lessons of 3.11 for activist Kawasaki Akira of the non-governmental organization (NGO) Peace Boat were that natural disasters and nuclear power are greater threats than foreign states and, drawing a parallel to the "safety myth" propagated by the nuclear power industry, he insists that the U.S. commitment to Japanese peace and security was little more than a "deterrence myth."[47] The Communist Party newspaper editorialized that the Fukushima meltdown is a warning "not only to residents of localities where nuclear reactors are located, but also [to those] where U.S. nuclear-powered vessels are deployed. With the myth of nuclear power plants no longer tenable, the policy of allowing the United States to deploy its nuclear ships and make port calls should also be reviewed."[48]

Most in this group acknowledged the good works of the SDF in the aftermath of 3.11, but they are more likely to connect the disaster to Hiroshima and the firebombing of Tokyo than to Russian or Chinese threats.[49] They pivot from the services performed by the SDF for the people of Tohoku to those it could perform for the rest of the world. In short, SDF's 3.11 success points the way toward a more appropriate role for Japan in world affairs. For them, there can be no connection between the 3.11 Humanitarian Assistance and Disaster Relief (HA/DR) mission and war fighting. The SDF should shift from defending the state to protecting the people of Japan and the world. According to Professor Mizushima, the chief proponent of a Japanese global Disaster Relief Force (DRF), "we should shrink the military aspect of the SDF so that in the future we can deploy it—even overseas—as a non-military, multifunctional disaster rescue force."[50]

A radical shift in the Japan-U.S. alliance should accompany the reinvention of the SDF as a nonmilitary international disaster force.[51] Its funding— and also that for the reconstruction of the Tohoku region—should come from a reduction in Host Nation Support (HNS), the controversial funds provided to Washington for everything from utilities on U.S. bases to the construction of new facilities on Guam. Some of this money—$3.3 billion in 2010—has also paid for amenities such as bowling alleys and snack bars, which have become associated with U.S. extravagance.[52] In a widely read op-ed in the *Asahi Shimbun* soon after 3.11, Professor Mizushima suggested that the crisis offered Japan the chance to reaffirm its original peaceful and productive postwar identity, which had been slipping away. He argued that if the SDF is transformed into a globally active, nonmilitary relief force that assists neighbors in times of need, "no country will any longer have reason to attack Japan" and the need for the alliance will disappear.[53]

It was no surprise that this suggestion was met with derision on the right. In his post-3.11 "Theory of National Defense," Kobayashi Yoshinori reproduced Professor Mizushima's *Asahi* op-ed in its entirety. Dismissing the idea as a joke, Kobayashi insisted that "the Self-Defense Forces must not be deodorized!"[54] The former Japanese GSDF commander in Iraq was more polite, pointing out that the SDF exists to protect the nation and must not be transformed into a relief organization per the "Democratic Socialists and the old Socialist Party types who would like to completely overturn the SDF, root and branch." He concluded that those who advocate remodeling the SDF are actually trying to weaken it and, thereby, Japan.[55]

The post-3.11 debate was consistent with existing ideological orientations across a predictable range of narrative forms. Whether they advocated putting it in gear, staying the course, or disarming Japan, policy entrepreneurs of every stripe highly valued the efforts of Japan's soldiers. They agreed on 3.11's heroes but differed on its villains—usually pointing at one another. But above all, advocates differed fundamentally on the nature of the threats facing Japan and the appropriate means by which national policy might mitigate them. Where some saw a threat from nuclear power, others saw threats from neighboring states. Where some embraced the United States, others (on both the Left and the Right) were eager to disconnect Washington from Japan's national security.

To connect these narratives to possibilities for institutional and policy change, we turn to what the government may actually have learned from the 3.11 catastrophe, keeping in mind a lesson about 3.11 success and failure noted by one senior SDF officer who served in Tohoku: "Because Hanshin/ Awaji was a failure, 3.11 was a success. But if we think of 3.11 as a success, it will become a failure."[56]

What Was Learned?

The MOD took away three broad sets of lessons from its experience during the 3.11 crisis.[57] Each was consistent with an institutional preference to stay the course, though for some, 3.11 also opened the door for enhancing SDF roles and missions. Indeed, the first and most extensive set of lessons concerned its own capabilities; the second related to its legitimacy and level of public support; and the third set of lessons concerned its partnership with the United States. For the most part, all three were positive. How might the debate we have outlined turn these lessons into long-term policy change?

SDF CAPABILITIES

The SDF impressed itself, the nation, and the world with its effectiveness. Within hours, the military was in motion; within one day, the prime minister had approved mobilization of fifty thousand troops; and within two days, that number was expanded to one hundred thousand—half the total national troop strength. In a matter of weeks, in the largest mobilization in SDF history, five times more troops were in Tohoku than had served in Kobe after the Hanshin/Awaji quake.[58] This troop level—70 percent from the GDSF—was sustained for nearly two months. Deployed on 500 aircraft and 50 ships, soldiers served 4.5 million meals, supplied more than 30,000 tons of water, cleared 500 km of roads, and collected the remains of more than 8,400 dead.[59]

The MOD was satisfied that it could mobilize with speed.[60] But as important, it also learned that its three service branches could work together. By 14 March, a joint task force headquartered at the GSDF Sendai base was created under the command of General Kimizuka. As a result, decision making was rapid and generally well coordinated within the military. But communication with the Cabinet Office and other ministries, as well as coordination with private firms, was often problematic.[61] The success of the joint command led the MOD to revisit earlier plans to strengthen the functions of the general staff and create a unified command and control function for the GSDF.

The performance of its troops under severe pressure for an extended period was another critical measure of SDF capabilities. By all accounts, the troops were deeply committed to the mission and proved to be very tough. The standard SDF practice had been to deploy Japanese soldiers near their homes. Since more than twenty thousand of Japan's total force come from Tohoku, a disproportionate number of first responders were serving their own neighbors and families under particularly difficult circumstances. Others, who were required to enter the area around the Fukushima Daiichi plant, did so with equipment that the MOD later judged insufficient. The psychological effects of dealing with corpses on a daily basis, of facing radiation with insufficient protection, and of extended separation from families were more significant than expected.[62] The MOD doubled the allowances paid to 3.11 frontline troops, raising their pay to the highest in SDF history and basing it on "the level of psychological burden placed on soldiers." At the same time, after some troops took their own lives, the MOD enhanced medical services and mental health counseling by improving convalescent centers.[63]

More had been asked of these soldiers than ever before. They and their officers remained at post long enough to reveal to the MOD that the SDF has too few specialists in some critical areas to permit timely rotation. This "short bench" problem was particularly pronounced at the senior officer level. The MOD learned that no team of top leaders can work twenty-four hours a day indefinitely. One result was an effort to create a command reserve that would include recent retirees who could be called on in a crisis.[64] Apparently, too much was asked of the regular reservists as well; 3.11 marked the first mobilization of the reserves in SDF history. There were

2,400 reserves called up on 16 March, but despite "exceptionally high levels of motivation" and "civilian experience," only 70 percent could respond "due to scheduling conflicts with employers."[65] Another lesson learned.

Overall, however, SDF collaboration with civilian partners—NGOs, commercial firms, and local governments—proved to be a source of strength. In Ishinomaki (Miyagi Prefecture) in May, the GSDF and the NGO Peace Boat worked together for the first time, distributing relief supplies to 3.11 victims at temporary shelters and breaking down long-standing barriers between the antiwar movement and the Japanese military establishment.[66] The SDF also benefited from enhanced relations with commercial firms, predominantly in the transport sector. In addition to gaining unprecedented access to commercial airfields, the SDF was able for the first time since the Pacific War to use commercial ferries to transport troops and relief supplies. Its limited number of troop transports forced the SDF to charter commercial ferries, an outsourcing model later adopted in MOD policy for future contingencies.[67]

Given the human costs of the mishandled response after the Hanshin/Awaji earthquake in 1995, the cooperation between local civilian authorities and the military on 3.11 was of great significance. The MOD and local governments had learned that standard operating procedures may not suffice when officials do not know and trust one another. In the words of one former minister of defense, crises are "not the time to exchange business cards."[68] In a determined effort to deepen and regularize relations with local governments after 1995, the MOD had made sure that the Crisis Management Offices of each prefecture were staffed with a retired military officer, some of whom (as in Iwate and Miyagi) reported directly to the governor. This helps explain why the prefectures wasted no time requesting the emergency mobilization of the military under the Self-Defense Forces Basic Law. Iwate governor Tasso Takuya was first to file a request for troops, just six minutes after the quake: "The governor of Hyogo, the Mayor of Kobe, and Prime Minister Murayama were [in 1995] all anti-military. They hesitated to ask the SDF for assistance. I reached out immediately and gave them the 11th floor of our prefectural office building for use as the military headquarters. An SDF general and I worked closely together."[69] Likewise, Miyagi governor Murai Yoshihiro, a former Air Self-Defense Forces (ASDF) officer, immediately established an operations room for civil-military cooperation.[70] Each of the other five prefectures in the region had reached out to the SDF and had set up crisis headquarters within minutes.

The problems were different at the municipal level where, in some cases, public administration itself was washed away by the tsunami. In situations where the SDF was the only administrative organization standing, it took responsibility for rescue and relief "without formalities or complaints, not even from the Socialists," according to one MOD official who found himself performing the functions of local public officials.[71] Reflecting on this, GSDF chief of staff Kimizuka acknowledged that "we need to clarify our roles when there are no civilians to exercise civilian control."[72] The military's civil intervention was welcomed and praised. One Iwate prefectural official recalled how the SDF stepped in after he could no longer coordinate with localities that had ceased to function: "We were overwhelmed trying to find places for displaced people and provide them shelters. The SDF took charge and got it done impressively. Their command structure is straight, top to bottom."[73] At times, the SDF directly provided local services. For example, the military is forbidden to protect public order without the direct command of the prime minister. So, when there were no police available for patrol duty, the SDF "traveled widely" on neighboring roads when delivering supplies in order to reassure residents of their safety.[74]

These capabilities were the result of considerable training, planning, and experience. By 2011, the SDF had accumulated experience in twelve different relief operations abroad, starting with the Honduras hurricane in 1998 and including its small 2010 relief operation in Haiti.[75] At home, the number of disaster prevention drills involving the SDF and local governments more than tripled after Hanshin/Awaji—from 177 involving 8,000 personnel in 1994 to 624 involving 12,100 personnel in 2008.[76] In the autumn of 2008, the Northeast Army conducted a large-scale "Michinoku Alert" exercise ("Michinoku" is a historical name for Tohoku), coordinated with the National Police Agency, the Coast Guard, and authorities from six prefectures and twenty-two municipalities. The exercise was premised on a 6.0-magnitude earthquake off the Miyagi coast with a subsequent tsunami. Some ten thousand troops participated.[77] There was enthusiasm among local public officials for this change. According to Nagoya mayor Kawamura Takashi, "Believe it or not, even after 1995 Nagoya did not exercise with the SDF until two years ago when I became mayor. At that time we began disaster exercises— terrorism, earthquakes—and have now conducted five of them."[78] It was propitious that a GSDF planner had just completed the draft of a manual for dealing with an ocean trench earthquake off the Sanriku coast weeks before 3.11. That manual became the initial guide for SDF deployment.[79]

The lesson from 3.11 was that, as helpful as these exercises and preparations surely were, there cannot be enough of them and they cannot be too complex.[80] As one official explains, the 3.11 mobilization may seem to have no connection to war fighting, but the SDF has the same responsibilities for natural disasters as for defense of the homeland—getting civilians out of harm's way. Doing so, he asserts, requires the same level of cooperation from prefectures and municipalities, so "we tell them to prepare for crises so that we can prepare for war."[81]

Indeed, one of the most difficult problems for the SDF was its lack of preparation for a radiological event of the sort that struck Fukushima Daiichi. A 2010 tabletop nuclear reactor crisis simulation conducted in the office of the deputy chief cabinet secretary for crisis management was "not very challenging" according to one participant, who blames the general disregard of a nuclear catastrophe on the electric power companies.[82] For years the utilities rejected offers by the SDF to conduct nuclear crisis simulations in situ out of a concern that doing so would signal to residents that they were not safe—a message that would undermine the utilities' programs and national policy. As one Tokyo Electric Power Company (TEPCO) official acknowledged: "We had a big dilemma. We should have held exercises with the SDF and police, but if the residents learned of them, it would make them very anxious. They would object [to nuclear power] and we did not want them to think we were imagining the worst case scenario."[83] The purposeful soft-pedaling of nuclear risk—including terrorist attacks, as well as accidents—was rectified immediately after 3.11.

A final lesson centered on Japan's own disaster diplomacy. Although one senior MOD official insisted that "HA/DR is a low end mission and not a top priority for the SDF," her boss, Defense Minister Kitazawa Toshimi, announced plans to create a regional HA/DR hub in Okinawa three months after 3.11.[84] He planned to preposition rescue and relief matériel for rapid response to disasters across East and Southeast Asia. Disaster relief operations have for decades formed the backbone of public support for the SDF.[85] The initiative was also consistent with both the disarmament and more conservative 3.11 narratives. It was therefore a great disappointment to some conservative editorialists when this initiative was not funded: "Just when it is said that the appreciation of the SDF activities is deepening and it attempts to take new steps forward, we have yet another illustration of the allergy [to the SDF]."[86] If the opinion polls are correct, however, the *Yomiuri* was blaming failure on an allergy that had long since been treated. This leads us to the second set of lessons that officials drew from 3.11, concerning the legitimacy of the postwar Japanese military.

SDF LEGITIMACY

Many conservatives continued to refer disparagingly to Japan's "military allergy," presumably out of a concern that the SDF would not attract public support in an emergency. After 3.11, however, this concern had a weaker foundation than ever. In April, just a month after the catastrophe, the *Mainichi Shimbun* found that 95 percent of respondents to its survey supported the actions of the SDF in Tohoku and 88 percent agreed it was appropriate for the SDF to have worked closely with the U.S. military to provide relief. These levels of support stood out dramatically against the 68 percent who did not think highly of the government's overall response to the disaster.[87] Over time, and after months of overwhelmingly positive media treatment, this support was transferred to the SDF as an institution. In December 2011, 75 percent of those surveyed by the *Yomiuri Shimbun* said that the SDF is the institution they most trust.[88] And in a Cabinet Office poll conducted one year after 3.11, public support for the SDF was at an all-time high of 91.7 percent. Nearly three-quarters of those surveyed reported they would approve of someone close to them joining the SDF—up from less than two-thirds in 2009.[89]

There was a new level of pride in the service and a higher interest on the part of the MOD to get its message out through a "centralized public information system for strategic information and reporting."[90] But there were other ways to connect with an ever more agreeable public. Soldiers who had been instructed in years past to change into mufti when leaving the base now paraded in local festivals proudly wearing their camouflage battle uniforms.[91] More important, troop deployments abroad were no longer controversial, as in the late 2011 decision to send troops to Southern Sudan. Although the number of billets did not markedly increase after the disaster, the quality of new recruits was boosted after 3.11. The number of applicants for commissions as officers actually declined slightly in the first six months after 3.11, but the number of applicants to the National Defense Academy was the highest in history and the number of applicants to the Ministry of Defense bureaucracy doubled. Likewise, the number of applicants to the Defense Medical College increased by nearly 10 percent.[92] Some recruiting stations attracted a full year's worth of applications in the six months following 3.11.[93]

The enhanced legitimacy of the SDF ought to have been reflected in the budget. Indeed, equipment became a central focus of MOD attention after 3.11. In drawing up their list of lessons learned, defense planners acknowledged that they need to take stock of the "equipment whose use was constrained in the disaster and to understand why."[94] They concluded that demands on Japan's forces will likely be greater in the future, and argued for acquisition of more equipment. Specifically, they stated the need for robots and unmanned aerial vehicles, which could be more effective than humans in radioactive theaters. They also made the case for new facilities that would be better protected from tsunamis and other sources of damage. In the first MOD budget request after 3.11, the MOD sought a modest 0.6 percent increase to 4.8 trillion yen.[95] Reaction to the budget proposals focused on line items for "remote island defense" prescribed by the National Defense Program Guidelines, but several items were explicitly justified by 3.11. One was a request for the first increase in SDF personnel in nineteen years, "to deal with the cleanup at Fukushima Daiichi." Also included was a request for 900 million yen for research on nuclear, biological, and chemical contamination and 15 billion yen for new field communications equipment "to enhance response to large scale disasters." Radioactivity shields were sought for vehicles and, as part of a special budget quota, the MOD asked for nearly 100 billion yen to enhance training to respond to nuclear disasters. The Japanese government also used 3.11 as justification for development of a new "quasi-zenith" global positioning satellite system that would free Japan from dependence on U.S. GPS and "would also serve as a disaster prevention counter measure."[96] Curiously, it decided not to make the case for additional sea- and airlift capability.[97]

This case was left for imaginative and friendly interlocutors outside the military establishment, many of whom were more comfortable putting it in gear than staying the course. SDF supporters had to walk a fine line between praising the military for accomplishing so much and arguing that they could have done better had they been better equipped.[98] Remote surveillance and transportation were the most promising areas for those who saw in 3.11 an opportunity to press for force modernization and dual-use procurement to enhance "strategic agility." Observers hoped that unmanned aerial vehicles (UAVs) and military robots could do double duty in antiterrorist operations.[99] (Many judged that dependence on U.S. remote sensing equipment was problematic.) In the case of transport, the SDF had to depend on civilian ferries and on U.S. and Australian ships for lift to the affected areas because of the limited number of Ōsumi-class transport ships, and the situation was widely labeled unacceptable.[100]

Here is where the wake-up call and proof of concept narratives met head-on. Advocates of the former grumbled about 3.11 insufficiencies and questioned whether the SDF would be able to fulfill its responsibilities under the National Defense Program Guidelines. If post-3.11 budgets were not going to deliver 3.11 dividends—and they did not—how would the SDF evacuate remote southwest islands in the event of a contingency in Okinawa? How could it respond to crises without better transport capacity?[101] The *Sankei Shimbun* reported that 3.11 had taught the MOD that it must reverse its reliance on commercial ferries and aircraft.[102] Defense Minister Kitazawa allowed that he would like to expand the Maritime Self-Defense Force (MSDF) capabilities, but he defended the use of commercial ferries, insisting that "it is not realistic to have equipment ready to respond at all times to the greatest imaginable crisis."[103] MOD Policy Bureau director general Takamizawa Nobushige concurred, saying that the viability of outsourcing transport—including freight railways—was a key lesson of 3.11.[104] And the MOD afteraction report was straightforward on this matter: 3.11 taught the importance of "integration with private firms in a crisis situation."[105] This sort of cooperation provided important lessons, of course, but integration with the U.S. military proved to be a far richer source of lessons for Japanese national security.

WORKING WITH AN ALLY

It is widely acknowledged that the U.S. and Japanese governments initially did not work well together. As noted in chapter 1, the Hosono Group was cobbled together to coordinate rescue, relief, and information sharing at the highest levels of civilian leadership. The path to civilian cooperation was bumpy, but it is often suggested that the two militaries found coordination easy. In fact, however, despite years of joint exercises, even the two militaries needed time to work out the kinks in this, their first operational relationship. It may have been because exercises rarely addressed an HA/DR contingency, but it took a considerable amount of time to find a formula that worked—one in which each military supported the other using senior "embeds" at the other's command centers in Sendai (GSDF Northeast Army), Ichigaya (MOD), and Yokota (U.S. Forces Japan).[106] The director general of the MOD Bureau of Finance and Equipment acknowledged that "for the first 48 hours the U.S. forces and the SDF could not find a meeting point."[107] It is not clear if he was speaking metaphorically or literally (or both), but the lesson for the military alliance was no different from the lesson for the SDF itself—there can never be enough practice and exercises.

Despite the bumps in the road, U.S.-Japan military cooperation was easier to achieve than cooperation between the U.S. Nuclear Regulatory Commission and TEPCO, or even cooperation across the "vertical" jurisdictional boundaries of some Japanese ministries. One participant from the U.S. side called the system of embedded personnel and commanders "a true innovation."[108] Most insist that it worked because of years of joint exercises and a limited amount of actual experience. One U.S. military public affairs officer explained that the two governments had years of "foreign consequences management exercises" and that these "established pathways paid off" during 3.11.[109]

The centerpiece was the Yama Sakura exercises that began as component exercises (that is, limited to the U.S. Army and GSDF) in the early 1980s. Over time, Yama Sakura evolved considerably, to the point where today it is the SDF's major annual exercise, involving regional and division headquarters as well as the testing of tactical- and operational-level doctrine. According to one force planner, who explained that the exercises were nearly terminated in 2004 for "lack of relevance," Yama Sakura is now designed less to provide exercise experience than to facilitate the transfer of U.S. doctrine and, in particular, to "support the formation of an expeditionary GSDF capable of operating alongside U.S. forces in global contingencies."[110] Over time, it was joined by additional component exercises and then by joint exercises, such as Keen Edge, Keen Sword, and Cope North, which involve multiple service branches from each country, civilian ministries, and even local government officials. Some were command post (tabletop) exercises; others were more elaborate field training exercises that deploy troops to train in simulated warfighting roles. By 3.11, the U.S. and Japanese militaries were annually holding two joint exercises involving thousands of troops.

Despite these exercises and even with bilateral cooperation in the 2004 Indonesian tsunami relief operation, joint HA/DR experience was limited.[111] The two militaries learned that there is a critical difference between paper-based standard operating procedures and the trust that only repeated practice

Self-Defense Forces search-and-rescue team in Wakuya, Miyagi Prefecture. 15 March 2011. U.S. Navy photo by Alexander Tidd.

Members of the 31st Marine Expeditionary Force march past a local woman on Oshima Island. 3 April 2011. Photo by Caleb Eamers, courtesy of defenseimagery.com.

and experience can provide. The "Guidelines for U.S.-Japan Defense Cooperation" issued in 1997 clearly laid out mechanisms for bilateral coordination in a crisis and, at the October 2005 U.S.-Japan Security Consultative Committee (the so-called 2+2 bilateral meeting of defense and foreign ministers), it was agreed that U.S. Forces Japan (USFJ) would establish a "bilateral and joint operations coordination center" at Yokota Air Base to "ensure constant connectivity, coordination, and interoperability among U.S. forces in Japan and the SDF."[112] But because the Japanese government judged them to be "too provocative," the Bilateral Coordination Mechanism (civilian) and Bilateral Coordination Cells (military) had never been used—despite opportunities (and requests by the U.S. military) to do so in the face of North Korean provocations.[113]

Nor, despite claims to the contrary, were they invoked even after 3.11.[114] Instead, coordination was reinvented on the fly. According to one embedded participant, "the Hosono Group was not the 'Bilateral Coordination Mechanism,'" adding that the reasons require "forensic analysis."[115] He concluded that the success of Operation Tomodachi was an "anomaly" in which "any crossover benefits were accidental" because bilateral exercises had focused on war plans, not on HA/DR.[116] Another participant explained that the U.S. side asked for implementation of the Bilateral Coordination Mechanism, but the Japanese government was too confused and "the switch was never toggled."[117] A third acknowledged that "despite lots of exercises and practice, the crisis didn't actually unfold as we thought it would." This official reported that "we did great on public relations, but in fact we were slow. We did not really get into gear until PACOM [the U.S. Pacific Command headquartered in Honolulu] came in and took over like the cavalry to the rescue."[118]

In fact, a great many saviors materialized on both sides. But just as there can be too many cooks, there can also be too many generals. One participant, a field grade officer, said that he was told there were nineteen flag officers together at Yokota, but he counted only nine, adding "that was eight too many."[119] Irony aside, 3.11 did attract the full attention of the senior leadership on both sides. In addition to the dozens of U.S. foreign area officers, functional liaison officers, and nuclear experts who were dispatched to serve in Japanese military and civilian crisis management headquarters and ships at sea, General Banshō Kōichirō went to the USFJ headquarters at Yokota and General William Crowe was embedded in SDF headquarters at Ichigaya.[120] This was jokingly referred to by the principals as an "exchange of hostages at the senior leadership level." But just as initial disconnects produced an important set of lessons for alliance management, levity could not mask the fact that 3.11 also produced the highest level of sustained cooperation the alliance had ever experienced.[121] Ten U.S. military officers worked with twenty SDF military officers at the MOD Joint Staff Office in Ichigaya, a post that was connected directly to the Joint Support Force Office in Yokota, where ten SDF officers were embedded. Ichigaya supervised and Yokota supported the headquarters of the Northeast Army headquarters in Sendai, where fifty U.S. officers were embedded. The GSDF Central Readiness Command and 140 members from the U.S. Marine Corps Chemical Biological Incident Response Force were dispatched together to respond to the radiation threat in Fukushima. Units of each military worked together in unprecedented ways and with unprecedented urgency. Cooperation was plain for all to see—including rival states—and working level embeds remained on post for months. The high level of U.S. commitment to Japan's security and Washington's respect for Japan's own responsibilities had deterrent value as well—Operation Tomodachi was a "joint *support* force," not a joint operation, and "mission accomplished" was never declared. As one analysis concluded, Operation Tomodachi "sent an important signal of alliance solidarity to the region."[122]

Prime Minister Kan, who effusively and repeatedly thanked the U.S. government for its support, was especially clear about Japan's own responsibilities during the crisis. Asked why he did not turn to the United States for help immediately after the reactor went down, Kan channeled the sensibilities of some of his greatest detractors, the wake-up call narrators: "This happened in our own country. Is our military so dependent on the United States? Should Japanese sit silently and watch American troops do the work? First we must rely on the SDF for Japanese problems. . . . We could not ask the United States for help until we Japanese first risked our lives."[123] Clearly, lessons were learned about SDF capabilities, its standing in public opinion, and its alliance capacity. But what about the impact of these lessons—indeed, of 3.11 itself—on the institutions of Japanese national security?

What Will (and Will Not) Change?

It is too soon after the catastrophe to identify lasting changes in the institutions of Japanese national security and the alliance. But it is not too early to begin assessing what might change and how these potential changes are connected to the preferences of the champions of each of the 3.11 security narratives. Potential changes can be sorted into three general categories: (1) changes in the command and force structure of the Japanese military, (2) changes in its roles and missions (including enhanced budgets and equipment), and (3) the prospects for new alliance dynamics.

CHANGES TO THE COMMAND AND FORCE STRUCTURE

If one of the most prominent lessons of 3.11 was that the SDF could act effectively in a crisis under a joint command, one of the most prominent recommendations for change was that a joint command be incorporated formally in the structure of the SDF. Endorsing this Goldwater-Nichols style reorganization, General Kimizuka pointed out: "We need to use the same brain and the same body."[124] First, though, there was the matter of consolidating command of the GSDF itself. This is part of an institutional change long sought by military commanders, by some within the civilian defense hierarchy, and even by those who saw 3.11 as a wake-up call. The MOD after-action report was explicit about this reform: "Because of the sudden increase in duties of the chief of the joint staff in carrying out the orders of the ministers and advising them from a military perspective, the functions of the general staff should be strengthened going forward. In addition, because the Ground Self Defense Force cannot function nationwide, we should consider a command and control function."[125]

The report refers here to a legacy of Japan's unhappy experience with the Imperial Army. In 1954, at the creation of the postwar military, former Interior Ministry officials led by those in the new National Police Agency worried that a unified GSDF might reproduce the power of the Imperial

Army.[126] The solution was to "divide and conquer" the GSDF. The GSDF, alone among the three service branches, was not permitted to have a strong Joint Staff Office with a chief of staff (*rikujō sōtai shireikan*) who could exercise command authority. Incremental changes to this structure had been made from time to time—in 1961, the authority of the chair of the Joint Staff Conference was increased and, in 2006, the Joint Staff Office (*tōgō bakuryō kanbu*) was created—but lack of a single commander continued to frustrate GSDF leaders. Suggestions for revision had been floated periodically inside the MOD and had been rejected most recently by former defense minister Kitazawa. Ministry officials, U.S. government officials, and analysts expect the idea to be revived with new vigor after 3.11. In their view, the crisis opened a simultaneous window of opportunity for both military "jointness" and a newly unified GSDF command structure.[127]

Plans for the creation of other new positions that would enhance the policy role of the SDF included: an assistant deputy chief cabinet secretary post in the cabinet secretariat dedicated to security affairs; a director-level defense policy planning post for coordination with the U.S. military; an SDF Reserve Office that would assemble outside personnel in an emergency; a position for a flag officer (J-3) as deputy chief for the joint staff; and a new deputy minister of defense position. All were activated immediately after 3.11.[128]

Some of these changes were already in the works. Following the 2010 National Defense Program Guidelines and the Midterm Defense Program of the same year, the MOD established a committee to promote structural reform. The committee's first report, issued after 3.11 in August 2011, was filled with recommendations it attributed to lessons learned during the crisis. In addition to recommending changes in the command and control structure of the SDF, the report proposed strengthening joint transportation control functions, changes to procurement systems, coordination with commercial transportation companies, and enhancing joint exercises.[129] Programs and projects that had stalled—including the possible creation of an amphibious force that, as noted, would be welcomed by advocates of putting it in gear—were now in motion again.

Also active once more were programs and projects where matters of national policy had already seemed to be settled. The size and shape of the GSDF came into play once again. The ground component of the national military had been flagged for reduction, as part of a shift from emphasis on defense against Russian attack in the north to Chinese attack in the south in the 2010 National Defense Program Guidelines. To maintain its budget share, the GSDF had argued for its centrality in rescue and relief activities, but MOD internal bureaus and political leadership determined that police, fire, and volunteer workers could be counted on to lead such operations. After 3.11, however, the decision began to unravel, in part under pressure from those in the "put it in gear" camp who would tolerate no force reductions.[130] As MOD Policy Bureau chief Takamizawa Nobushige pointed out:

"Some say that 3.11 showed that the SDF should return to its original levels of deployments. No. 3.11 should be used to accelerate the reforms envisioned in the National Defense Program Guidelines."[131] His successor, Nishi Masanori, concurred, explaining that "it is easy to say we need more, but we have to prepare for the future based on future needs. We need to focus on China, not on 3.11."[132] The lesson for Ichigaya was clear, and it sat on the border of the first two narratives: changes in the size and shape of the Japanese military are acceptable if they are closely related to decisions about roles and missions.

CHANGES IN ROLES AND MISSIONS

The acquisition of amphibious capabilities (a "put it in gear" favorite) was already in the works before the crisis. It was built into the U.S.-Japan Yama Sakura exercise and etched into the 2010 guidelines. The MOD took it up again in its after-action report—at least obliquely—by noting that GSDF vehicles and MSDF ships had only "restricted access" to the affected areas.[133] The report called for additional transport and left open the possibility that amphibious equipment should be acquired if Japan is to "stay the course." It was left for outside analysts to note that the lack of amphibious capability was a problem for the SDF and that acquisition would serve multiple functions, including rescue and relief missions as well as transport of expeditionary forces.[134] DPJ Diet member Nagashima Akihisa has suggested that the GSDF would use 3.11 to ask for hollow-hulled ships, formally (*tatemai*) for disaster relief but de facto as the basis for the development of a Japanese marine corps: "That way the SDF could solve both disaster response and China problems at the same time."[135] This suggestion is consistent with the observation of one U.S. military officer who worked directly with the Japanese SDF during the crisis. He said that the need to develop a joint amphibious capability was the first lesson learned by his Japanese counterparts. Had they had that capacity, he pointed out, "many lives would have been saved."[136] This field officer added his voice to many others, including the director general of the MOD Policy Bureau, who insisted on the importance of practicing joint operations with the U.S. military.[137] When the FY 2012 budget was submitted, there was no 3.11-inspired request for additional amphibious training or equipment. A request for four landing craft (at a cost of 3 billion yen) was included in the MOD's FY 2013 budget request.[138]

Potential changes to the SDF's equipment mix accompany—and enable—changes in roles and missions. Indeed, in some quarters, there were high expectations for a "Tohoku dividend," but little was forthcoming in the near term. Although one MOD official claimed that the third supplementary budget passed in late 2011 was "our reward" (*gohōbi*), funds allocated to the SDF amounted to less than 2 percent of the three supplementary budgets and less than 8 percent of the FY 2011 defense budget. SDF troops were exempted for six months from the 7.8 percent pay cut mandated for national public servants, but the FY 2012 budget actually cut the MOD by 1.3 percent.[139] The funds allocated to the military were enough to rebuild facilities damaged on 3.11 but were not sufficient for the acquisition of much new equipment.[140] Military advocates—both those who would put security policy in gear and those who would simply stay the course—saw the defense budget not only fail to increase after 3.11 but actually continue a decade-long descent, down 5 percent since its Koizumi-era peak in 2002.

Among the few programs to get a direct boost from 3.11 was remote sensing equipment. In August 2011, Prime Minister Kan approved funding to restart the unmanned aircraft program virtually cancelled the year before, after six years of research and development (R&D) that had cost 10 billion yen. The MOD was also authorized to increase R&D for robot technology. Kan was very clear: "Japan has advanced technology in robotics and radio-controlled equipment. I want the Defense Ministry to develop Japan's own unmanned vehicle."[141] The defense budget now allocates funds for depots where relief supplies and power generation equipment are prepositioned for distribution in emergencies, but Minister Kitazawa's proposal for an East Asian regional "disaster relief hub" was abandoned in the budget process. According to Iokibe Makoto, commandant of the National Defense Academy and chair of the Reconstruction Design Council, he and his council members supported these measures but decided not to include them in their recommendations because they were not directly relevant to the council's mission. Noting that the post-3.11 defense budgets do not reflect many of the lessons from the catastrophe, he remarked: "It is hard to believe (*shinjigatai*) how obstinate (*shibutoi*) the Finance Ministry has been."[142] MOD's FY 2013 budget request was nearly two percent lower than its previous year's allocation–the largest year on year defense budget decline in half a century.[143]

There was, however, one important change in roles and missions that did not require significant budgetary action: the SDF gained unrestricted access to Japan's nuclear power plants for the first time. The SDF had long focused on nuclear security and nonproliferation, its central concern being to prevent the acquisition of fissile material by unfriendly actors. But measures taken to avoid losing control of nuclear materials to terrorists are different from measures taken to protect civilians against radioactive contamination. According to one senior Japanese military officer, "the battle between pro- and anti-nuclear groups created two poles. They lost sight of reality. They were at each other's throats and no planning [for 3.11-like contingencies] could get done."[144] Fearing a loss of public confidence in their safety claims, the electric utilities had placed the "earthquake proof command centers" (*jūyō menshintō*), designed to function when all other control facilities are damaged, off-limits to the SDF and other crisis management professionals before 3.11. After 3.11 it became possible for the SDF to visit these plants and gain fuller knowledge of the facilities.[145]

ALLIANCE DYNAMICS

The largest questions about 3.11-induced change relate to the alliance and to the efficacy of U.S. "disaster diplomacy." There is no evidence that the United States moved to aid Japan in order to enhance its power in the relationship. To the contrary, the reflexive speed with which the U.S. government moved—President Obama authorized assistance within hours—suggests that the claims of Pentagon press secretary Geoff Morrell can be accepted at close to face value: "[T]here was never a doubt in our minds that we had to respond and had to respond aggressively and with as much as we could bring to bear to help the Japanese."[146]

But that is not the way that many perceived U.S. action. Despite the positive response of the general public, some Japanese analysts—particularly proponents of disarming and those in favor of putting it in gear—speculated that the United States, acting in its own interests, had calculated that Japanese gratitude would pay for repairs to the alliance. Operation Tomodachi was therefore a strategic move. In the words of one critical weekly, it was "not friendship for nothing," and the Communist Party daily insisted that there was an "ulterior motive."[147] Specific explanations for U.S. assistance included: Washington's desire to send deterrence signals to China and North Korea; its interest in establishing a precedent for use of civilian airfields in some future North Korean contingency; its hope that disaster assistance would grease the skids for the implementation of its long-sought base realignment; public relations to soften America's warlike image and appear merely a "gentle neighbor"; President Obama's commitment to the promotion of nuclear power; the desire of U.S. industry to gain contracts from Tohoku reconstruction; experience that would be useful for dealing with "dirty" radiological bombs; groundwork for future joint operations with the SDF; softening opposition to Japan's participation in the Trans-Pacific Partnership (TPP), an evolving free trade zone; and the Pentagon's desire to prop up Japan as a credible partner in its effort to maintain regional stability and contain China.[148] The *Tokyo Shimbun* challenged Washington to return Japan's HNS payment "to demonstrate its true friendship."[149] The rightwing cartoonist Kobayashi Yoshinori points out that Operation Tomodachi cost just a fraction of the 1.8 trillion yen the United States receives in HNS, and ridiculed the movement of the USS *Ronald Reagan* to safety after the Fukushima Daiichi hydrogen explosion as the action of a "heartless friend" (*hakujō na tomodachi*).[150] Nor did it help when it was revealed that U.S. forces were given data on the radioactive plumes three days after the quake, whereas the Japanese public did not learn about radiation levels until nearly two weeks later.[151]

The Okinawan press was singularly negative. The *Okinawa Times* insisted that the disaster was "put to political use" by a calculating U.S. government, and the *Ryūkyū Shimpō* expressed its "strong sense of discomfort," questioning why marines from Okinawa, who are supposed to be used for rapid response, were sent from so far away, three days after the earthquake struck.[152] In contrast, after a unit of marines arrived from Malaysia, one Okinawan critic cited the deployment as proof that U.S. Marines do not need to be based in Okinawa to protect Japan.[153] Tokyo-based media and home islands–based tweeters noticed that their Okinawan counterparts were carrying few stories about the U.S. Marines' work in Tohoku and, in a backlash of considerable intensity, began to criticize them.[154]

The majority of Japanese were overwhelmed by the U.S. response. A Pew Research Center survey found that 85 percent of Japanese held a favorable view of the United States in the weeks after 3.11, up from 66 percent a year earlier.[155] The Associated Press polled Japanese attitudes six months later and found that support for U.S. bases in Japan had increased by ten points to 57 percent.[156] Three months thereafter, in December 2011, a Japanese government poll found that the percentage of Japanese with friendly feelings toward the United States had reached an all-time high of 82 percent.[157] A *Yomiuri* poll found that 94 percent of its respondents approved of Operation Tomodachi. Even Okinawa governor Nakaima Hirokazu praised the U.S. Marines for their relief work in the weeks after 3.11.[158]

So even if a boost in relations and an enhanced alliance were not the immediate or primary objectives of Operation Tomodachi—and even if Washington was acting on its own national interests, as surely it was—one might nonetheless expect to find evidence of a "Tohoku effect" on the alliance, perhaps in the form of progress on earlier sticking points, such as basing issues and U.S. access to ports, harbors, and airfields. There was some progress in the latter area, but in fact U.S.-Japan alliance relations did not change significantly after 3.11. As if to underscore the limits to disaster diplomacy discussed in chapter 3, the anticipated "deepened alliance" did not materialize, at least not in the form of structural change or agreement on the realignment of forces.[159]

The first disappointment came after U.S. and Japanese government officials met in November 2011 to discuss the lessons learned from their bilateral response to the disaster.[160] At the top of the U.S. list was the need to review and adjust the Bilateral Coordination Mechanism (BCM) that nominally had been in place since 1997, but which—after considerable confusion and multiple missteps—had to be reinvented as the Hosono Group during the crisis. The BCM had been conceived as the "premier communication channel" in such scenarios and, on the basis of 3.11 experience, the U.S. side suggested that it be expanded from military contingencies to encompass various situations requiring the large-scale mobilization of U.S. and Japanese forces. According to one participant, "we imagined that our Tomodachi experience should have made this possible," but in the first plausible test case—the March 2012 North Korean missile launch—the Japanese side demurred, saying that the BCM should be reserved for a real war. The government was unwilling to risk sowing panic among the public. U.S. alliance managers concluded that their Japanese counterparts had "lost a chance to get the Japanese people used to the idea of high level security coordination."

Alliance managers had better luck in resolving a less difficult issue—U.S. military use of Japanese civilian facilities in the event of a crisis. Indeed, this outcome gave them hope that staying the course would provide a proof of concept that the relationship deserves to be deepened and transformed. After the Hanshin/Awaji disaster in 1995, local governments were less reluctant to cooperate with the SDF, but continued to keep their distance from the U.S. military. Military use of civilian airfields, ports, and roads in an emergency had appeared in central government planning documents since 1997 and was later enshrined in a Law on the Situation in Surrounding Areas (*Shūhen Jitai Hō*), but, like the BCM, that law had never been invoked.[161] In fact, the plans had been tested twice, both times in Niigata. After the 2004 Chūetsu earthquake, local officials denied permission for the U.S. Navy to use the harbor; in 2009, during a North Korean missile launch alert, the Harbor Bureau of the Ministry of Land, Infrastructure, Transport and Tourism (MLIT) did likewise—critics claimed that the bureau was acting on behalf of left-wing local officials.[162] During the 3.11 crisis, Defense Minister Kitazawa took no chances. He did not try to invoke the law, but instead telephoned the MILT minister and the chief cabinet secretary to make sure that the U.S. Air Force could use Yamagata Airport to land C-17s loaded with relief supplies and troops. The success of that intervention has been widely seen as a precedent for cooperation in future crises—and perhaps for more. As one pleased MOD official argued: "We do not expect to have any more 'Niigatas.' I am quite sure U.S. forces will be able to use ports, roads, and airfields in any emergency and joint mobilization will be easier going forward."[163]

The far more difficult, base-related problems—what one senior MOD official says led to a pre-3.11 "wobble in the relationship"—were not ameliorated, much less resolved.[164] Operation Tomodachi and public support for the alliance notwithstanding, bases remained an intractable problem. Like the access issue, it connects Washington to Tokyo to local government. The basing of U.S. forces in Japan is obligated by the 1960 Japan-U.S. Treaty of Mutual Cooperation and Security and operates under a Status of Forces Agreement (SOFA) that dates from the same time.[165] Few localities have sought to host U.S. forces, and many have resented their imposition. These bases are never without controversy. Indeed, even when local support for a U.S. base is high, as in Yokosuka after 3.11, where a record number of poll respondents supported the home porting of the U.S. Navy's Seventh Fleet, that number was still only one-third (34.7%) of the residents.[166]

To ameliorate such concerns and enhance interoperability, many of the military bases across Japan have come to be used jointly by U.S. and SDF troops. We might have expected such development to accelerate after 3.11. But this did not happen. Moreover, no joint bases are located in Okinawa, home to three-quarters of all U.S. forces in Japan. Far from the main centers of population, these facilities—and the Okinawans who resent having to shoulder an "unfair burden"—have hardly been out of sight, out of mind: they have been the centerpiece of base politics for decades. The need to realign U.S. forces there was declared long before 3.11. The problem has been that while the larger battle is joined between pacifists and the central government, local government officials are key players because their approval is required for construction of new facilities or for the acceptance of repositioned forces. Local officials appreciate the economic benefits that U.S. facilities provide, but they are equally aware of the social and political costs, manifest in the form of violence by U.S. troops, environmental degradation, and resulting electoral mobilization.

If 3.11 had stimulated a change in attitudes about accepting U.S. bases, it was not evident in policy change. Japan had ten governments in the first sixteen years after the original agreement in 1996 to move the controversial Marine Corps Air Station Futenma to a less crowded offshore base to be constructed in Henoko Bay, far to the north of Okinawa Island. This on-again, off-again agreement, the poster child for problems in the alliance, was off again soon after 3.11. In May, Defense Minister Kitazawa made his first post-3.11 visit to Okinawa in an effort to gain Governor Nakaima Hirokazu's support for the Henoko plan. Kitazawa reportedly promised resources for Okinawan development if Okinawa would accept the move. But his effort failed. Governor Nakaima continued to insist that Futenma be moved outside Okinawa Prefecture altogether. Although the governor took the high road, many suspected that the real problem was his concern that the demands of Tohoku reconstruction would reduce the fiscal benefits to Okinawa Prefecture.[167] Others resented the expectation that 3.11· would unfreeze more than a decade of intransigence. Ginowan mayor Iha Yōichi declared that "it would be a mistake to say U.S. forces are necessary because there was a disaster."[168] By the time the "2+2" meeting of U.S. and Japanese defense and foreign ministers was held in mid-June 2011, relations on the base issue had regressed to stalemate. Despite expectations of enhanced cooperation between the U.S. military and Japanese localities, the two governments acknowledged there would be no move to Henoko anytime soon. Prime Minister Kan was corrected by his chief cabinet secretary for using the term "burden" to characterize U.S. basing in Okinawa.[169]

In late April 2011, Minister Kitazawa had declared gamely that he did not expect 3.11 to affect plans to relocate the Futenma base, and U.S. undersecretary of defense Michelle Flournoy signaled that Washington might be willing to renegotiate Japan's 6 billion yen pledge to underwrite a facility on Guam that would accept eight thousand marines currently on Okinawa. But by the first anniversary of the 3.11 catastrophe, it had become clear that Washington's Asia strategy hinged on much more than domestic Japanese politics.[170] With Senator John McCain wondering aloud whether either country now had the resources to implement their basing agreements, the U.S. Senate unceremoniously cut funds for relocation of U.S. Marines to Guam and, in the context of a White House commitment to "pivot" toward Asia, the Pentagon announced plans to relocate an Okinawa-based Marine Corp unit to Darwin in Australia's Northern Territory.[171] There was going to be movement, and much of it would be to bases outside Okinawa. But contrary to 3.11-inflated expectations, this realignment was not going to have much input from America's Japanese ally.

Indeed, to the extent that there was Japanese input, it was negative. Tokyo and Washington returned to discussion of realignment in February 2012, after the American side unofficially sounded out the Japanese government on the possibility of transferring marines to bases on the home islands. The first reported suggestion from the U.S. side was that 1,500 marines be transferred from Okinawa to the Marine Corps Air Station Iwakuni in Yamaguchi Prefecture. It seemed like a smart move. The troops would be transferred between U.S. Marine Corp (USMC) facilities after all, and nine months earlier, Fukuda Yoshio, the mayor of Iwakuni, had presented base commander Col. James Stewart a public letter of gratitude for delivering supplies that his constituents had collected for Tohoku during the 3.11 crisis. The mayor commended the marines for "deepening ties" between the base and the city.[172] Apparently, those ties were still not deep enough. The proposed transfer of Okinawa marines to Iwakuni was summarily dismissed by the Japanese government on the basis of anticipated "local opposition."[173] Using language distinctly at odds with the spirit of U.S.-Japan military cooperation during the 3.11 crisis, Foreign Minister Genba Kōichirō explained: "We have no plans to ask for [Yamaguchi Prefecture to shoulder] any additional *burden*" in hosting U.S. forces in Japan under the mutual security treaty.[174] When agreement was later reached for the transfer of U.S. forces to Guam, the Japanese government agreed to a contribution of $3.1 billion, far less than the original U.S. request.[175] The more diplomatic U.S. alliance managers point out that this is a disappointing and suboptimal way for Japan to stay the course. Some privately suggest that Tokyo was on the wrong course altogether.[176] And there are pundits who look at the post-3.11 record and declare that "Tokyo would be foolish to stop free riding on America's exertions in Asia."[177]

Conclusion

Both the 3.11 disaster and the response were unprecedented in every respect, not least in terms of national security. The timely and effective mobilization of the Japanese military and the activation of the Japan-U.S. alliance were credited with saving innumerable lives and generated enthusiastic popular support. There would be neither a militarist consolidation of power nor a suspension of civil liberties as there were after the 1923 Kanto quake, and there would be none of the vacillation and indecision that had character-ized Japan's flawed response in Kobe in 1995. No institutions in postwar Japan, save perhaps the factories that powered its economic growth and technological development, had ever been so warmly embraced. That so many had questioned for so long the legitimacy of the SDF and the alliance made their performance all the more heroic and their supporters all the more hopeful.

As expected, the disaster stimulated a rhetoric of crisis; a vigorous national debate about the past and future of national security policy and its institu-tions ensued in which political entrepreneurs from all sides jostled for ad-vantage. As it turned out, however, 3.11 did not catalyze the changes many anticipated and some sought. For those most eager for a more muscular Japan, the nation's wake-up call was not answered. Japan would neither ex-pand nor significantly reorient its military capabilities. It would not "put it in gear" and wean itself from dependence on the United States. Nor would Japan reorient its military to confront natural disasters rather than foreign enemies. It would stay the course, and it would do so with little more than incremental tinkering. Japan took away (and implemented) lessons about the rotation of troops and commanders and the provision of support ser-vices, and made small shifts in policy toward jointness within the military command. There would be increased reliance on commercial transport com-panies, acquisition of a small number of landing craft, changes to road use laws, acquisition of minor non-war-fighting equipment, and creation of prepositioned relief supplies, but there would be few changes in plans and policy. Large-scale boosts to Japan's national security infrastructure and giant steps toward the genuine interoperability of U.S. and Japanese forces were not in the offing. The only proof of concept in evidence reaffirmed Japan's long-standing commitment to a cheap ride on U.S. security guarantees.

By all accounts, this was acceptable to Washington as well. There was some disappointment but little surprise that the 3.11 successes were not fun-gible. Efforts by U.S. alliance managers to use 3.11 to expand bilateral coor-dination were rejected. Efforts to transform new levels of alliance efficacy into alternative basing formulas were stiff-armed; and efforts to manage force realignment were met with protestations about fiscal constraints. Nor was there much forward movement in other important areas in the overall relationship. In trade, for instance, the Japanese government temporized in the face of strengthening domestic opposition to the TPP, an incipient re-gional trade agreement championed by the United States and eight other states.[178] Even nominal commitments to the TPP were reversed, first by Prime Minister Kan in May 2011 and later by Prime Minister Noda, who appointed a TPP opponent, Kano Michihiko, as minister of agriculture, forestry, and fisheries.[179] Instead, small steps were taken toward institutionalizing crisis management "coordination cells," improving the U.S. military's relations with local governments, and gaining access for the U.S. military to commercial airfields that they will need in a regional contingency.

Apart from a renewed general confidence in the SDF and in the reliability of the U.S. security partnership, in short, there was no major Tohoku dividend—either for the war-fighting capacity of Japanese troops or for the U.S.-Japan alliance. Basing problems remained intractable and difficult questions over alliance confidence in facing down North Korea and China were no closer to clarification.

Debating Energy Policy

The history of nuclear power is actually the history of postwar Japan. Nuclear energy was chosen in the name of economic growth, and risk was shifted to poor localities with weak citizens, so that city dwellers could enjoy the good life, while the real costs could be buried and a new form of discrimination evolved.

—Koide Hiroaki, 2011

We'll promote nuclear power while stepping on the brake at the same time.

—Amari Akira, 2007

[The] accident was the result of collusion between the government, the regulators and TEPCO. . . . They effectively betrayed the nation's right to be safe from nuclear accidents.

—Report of the Fukushima Nuclear Accident Independent Investigation Commission, 2012

TEPCO should not be sentenced to life imprisonment.

—Sawa Akihiro, 2011

After 3.11, discussions of change were most active—and expectations for change were most extravagant—in two policy areas: security and energy. As we have seen in the case of security, this was because its institutions succeeded and heroes abounded. In the case of energy, it was because most of the protagonists failed dramatically. In the dueling narratives about the nuclear meltdown, potential villains were everywhere and each of our four themes was in play. Elite chatter about *change* was ubiquitous; *leaders* either did not lead or else they misled; in the process, they were blamed for destroying whole *communities* and making the Japanese nation feel deeply *vulnerable*. Ironically, this state of affairs actually did represent great change, for the first half century of nuclear power in Japan was one of strong leadership, enriched communities, and repeated reassurance about risk.

The Status Quo Ante

The leadership came from politicians and business executives, starting with a petition to John Foster Dulles in 1951 from an ambitious young Diet member, the future prime minister Nakasone Yasuhiro, who wanted Japan to develop a nuclear power industry.[1] Nakasone was soon joined by two *éminences grises*—Keidanren chair Ishikawa Ichirō and Shōriki Matsutarō, the powerful publisher of the *Yomiuri Shimbun*. Working with senior Liberal Democratic Party (LDP) leaders, the electric utilities, and equipment vendors, they engineered Japan's first atomic power budget in 1954—just 250 million yen. The next decade was filled with competition for control of the pace, shape, and direction of this fledgling industry. Bureaucrats bickered among themselves over jurisdiction and with the business community over control; academics struggled to secure resources for basic research; vendors muscled one another for access to foreign technology; and utilities battled to maximize public funding and minimize public supervision. What would later be seen as one of the most tightly knit policy communities in the industrial world started out in a state of open warfare.

State leadership and a steady rise in public funding consolidated the industry. After its humble origins in 1954, nearly 10 trillion yen was spent on nuclear power by the Japanese government between 1970 and 2007, accounting for nearly a third of all public-sector energy spending, nearly 70 percent of all energy-related allocation grants, and fully 95 percent of the entire national budget for energy research and development (R&D).[2] The nuclear power budget had grown to more than a trillion yen by 1982 and by 2011, more than 2.5 trillion yen was coursing through the industry annually.[3] The industry now included forty-five thousand workers, three-quarters of whom were not employed by the utilities themselves. It had settled down to business with the government by its side.

It had come a long way on the well-traveled path of national industrial policy. Following a prewar formula, the government's Ministry of International Trade and Industry (MITI) created "public policy companies" to assist private firms with the introduction of the new technologies, socializing start-up costs. At first it was not clear which technology would prevail, so MITI and each of the major industrial groups worked out partnerships with foreign firms to bring different nuclear power technologies to the Japanese table—Toshiba with General Electric, for instance, and Mitsubishi with Westinghouse. Over the years, MITI also guided utilities, vendors, banks, construction companies, insurance companies, iron and steel manufacturers, chemical firms, shipbuilders, and trading companies to invest in public policy companies that would survey for uranium and underwrite R&D costs in waste disposal and reprocessing. With the business community and the government now fully committed to nuclear power—and given the deeply held view of Japan as a resource-poor manufacturing and trading nation—nuclear power came to dominate Japan's electric power fuel mix planning. By the mid-1980s, with the exception of Okinawa Electric Power Company, each of Japan's utilities owned and operated nuclear power plants.

Nuclear power not only promised to lower power costs for industry but also responded to both Japan's energy insecurity and its technological ambitions. Nuclear fuel recycling—an untested plan to close the nuclear fuel cycle—was stipulated as a matter of national policy as early as 1956. Japanese utilities would generate power in commercial light water reactors (LWRs) and, with government assistance, would reprocess spent fuel to produce plutonium to fuel fast breeder reactors (FBRs) that would generate more fuel than they consumed.[4] Three problems in this program would come to haunt the utilities and the government. The first concerned cost: by the early 2000s, opponents of the effort to close the nuclear fuel cycle estimated that it had cost nearly 19 trillion yen ($250 billion).[5] The second problem was disposal and storage of used fuel: by the early 1970s, Japanese reactors were already producing more spent fuel than they could reprocess, and critics argued that Japan had in effect built an expensive home without a toilet.[6] The third problem concerned plutonium, a by-product of the reprocessing:[7] not only was the industry generating more waste than it could safely dispose of, but this waste was very dangerous. Still, Japan proceeded with its breeder reactor program despite concerns from countries worried about diversion of Japan's considerable—and growing—stockpile of plutonium.[8] Interim storage solutions and reprocessed fuel shipments from European facilities involving plutonium, contrived at just the moment when foreign governments were canceling their FBR programs, were expensive and risky.[9] The reprocessing project at Rokkasho-mura in Aomori Prefecture and the Monju FBR project in Fukui Prefecture were plagued by cost overruns, serial accidents, and delays. Yet government officials as well as activists never quite succeeded in shutting them down, and Japanese reactors—including reactor unit 3 at Fukushima Daiichi—routinely used so-called Pluthermal Mixed Oxide Fuel (MOX).

The nation's ten electric utilities each enjoyed a regional monopoly in both generation and transmission. Their senior executives routinely became titular heads of regional business federations. They collaborated with one another and with vendors, in public-private partnerships to promote the industry, invest in new technologies, and develop schemes to export nuclear power plants. Prices were static, uniform, and comparatively high—by the mid-1980s, Japanese utility prices (based on reimbursable costs inflated by policy-driven siting decisions) were nearly double the Organization for Economic Cooperation and Development (OECD) average.[10] The business press reported that utility revenues in 2010 accounted for nearly one-quarter of industry revenue nationwide.[11] If ever a sector were too big to fail, this was it. Indeed, Tokyo Electric Power Company (TEPCO) qualified for this status on its own: On 3.11, it had 168 subsidiaries and was by far Japan's largest issuer of corporate debt (7% of the national total). So when concern for TEPCO's future spread after 3.11, share prices of its debt holders—many of Japan's largest banks—dropped and the prospects for some of the nation's largest pension funds sank.[12]

Industry leaders and the government had factored failure into their calculations. A 1961 Act on Compensation for Nuclear Damage held plant operators liable in the event of a nuclear accident, but excluded "case[s] where the damage is caused by a grave natural disaster . . . [or] . . . insurrection."[13] Soon thereafter, though, a series of design- or operation-related accidents began to affect the commercial industry, beginning in 1974 with radiation leakage from Japan's first nuclear-powered ship. By 2007, the utilities reported that there had been ninety-seven mishaps in nuclear power plants nationwide, including criticality accidents in 1978 and 1989 at TEPCO's Fukushima Daiichi plant.[14] The most prominent accidents were the 1995 sodium leak at the Power Reactor and Nuclear Fuel Corporation's (PNC's) Monju FBR and the twenty-hour-long criticality accident in 1999 at a plant in Tōkai-mura, in which two poorly trained workers died after exposure to massive doses of radiation.[15] Some two-thirds of Tōkai-mura residents felt "safe" or "fairly safe" before the accident, but only 15 percent felt this way afterward.[16] It did not help the industry that many of these incidents went unreported at the time or were covered up with falsified data.

Popular confidence in nuclear power safety had been purchased at a high price. After the government went all-in for nuclear power in the wake of the first oil crisis of 1973, it worked with the utilities to secure public trust by spending considerable time and money reassuring the populace.[17] This effort was especially difficult and costly because nuclear accidents in the United States and the Soviet Union captured Japan's attention. Public sentiment was shifting, and a grassroots antinuclear power movement began to gain traction.[18] Nuclear proponents responded with a sustained public relations campaign that brooked no suggestion of danger in the use of nuclear fuel. As we discuss in chapter 4, their concern about public distrust even led them to prevent first responders from conducting exercises on the premises of nuclear facilities.[19] Advertising supplements in newspapers and magazines documented nuclear safety, and animated cartoons were produced for television carrying the safety message. Most famous was the 1993 animated cartoon produced by the PNC in which a friendly "Pluto Boy" offered glasses of liquefied plutonium to his friends.[20]

Although the Japanese public accepted the prevailing wisdom about energy security, it did so with reservations about nuclear safety, especially if plants were to be built close by. So, a second prong of the strategy involved the government and utilities having sufficient resources to gain support from residents who might otherwise be uneasy about—or actively oppose— living near nuclear plants. By the early 1970s, before the Arab oil embargo

"Pluto Boy" cartoon. Screen shot captured from animated cartoon, c.1993. Online at: http://woody.com/2011/08/03/plutonium-kun/ and http://news.linktv.org/videos /anime-characters-tweet-on-fukushima-disaster.

focused the world's attention on energy, a vigorous environmental movement in Japan had begun to take notice of nuclear power, stretching the average lead time for licensing, siting, and building plants through litigation.[21] In 1974, in the immediate wake of the oil crisis, the Tanaka government passed the Three Basic Electric Power Laws, which together provided a legal basis for massive subsidies—twice the going rate for conventional thermal plants—to local governments that agreed to accept nuclear power plants. "Cooperation funds" would come from taxpayers through a special budgetary account beyond the grasp of the Finance Ministry.[22] Over time, nuclear power–related siting subsidies from the central government expanded to eleven different categories, including special funds for recycling and for R&D.[23] Localities were eligible for more than 500 billion yen in subsidies before the completion of a reactor, and once it began operations, they could qualify for more than 1 trillion yen over forty-five years.[24]

For some rural areas, like Fukui Prefecture, which hosts thirteen nuclear power plants, energy came to be very lucrative. From 1974 to 2009, its cities, towns, and villages received more than 150 billion yen in subsidies from the central government, and the prefecture received nearly 175 billion yen—some two-thirds of all central government transfers to Fukui.[25] In similarly rural Saga Prefecture, 60 percent of the budget of the town of Genkai and one-sixth of its employment is nuclear plant–related.[26] In addition to civic centers, museums, schools, hospitals, and other infrastructure, these subsidies provided trips abroad for "habituation visits" with residents of foreign communities who shared tips on how to live comfortably in the shadow of nuclear facilities.[27] Utilities and related organizations also gave host governments separate funding—some 30 billion yen between 2006 and 2011, through 650 separate "donations."[28] According to some analysts, these transfers caused an "addiction" to subsidies that led to a vicious cycle of grants, dependence, and supplication: since power plants age and fiscal transfers decline after they have hollowed out much of local industry, depopulated villages have no other options for economic vitality. The solution is to attract new nuclear facilities just to keep up, even as their "buyers' remorse" peaks.[29]

Public and utility largesse was apparently used to buy the cooperation of residents at election time.[30] Some residents, satisfied with the benefits of hosting nuclear power, simply turned out to protect their gains, of course. Others, though, had been persuaded to do so by utilities and regulatory authorities who packed public forums and got plant employees to lobby the local media in order to tilt the outcome of public debate.[31] In one instance, the pronuclear governor of Hokkaido, Takahashi Harumi—herself a former Ministry of Economy, Trade and Industry (METI) official—took a temporary pay cut to take responsibility for a prefectural employee who tried to manipulate public opinion in favor of a Pluthermal project of the Hokkaido Electric Power Company. In another case, METI punished six senior officials for manipulating public opinion during open hearings.[32] Not all residents and not all localities would be bought, however. In August 1996, for example, the voters of Maki Village in Niigata rejected a Tohoku Electric Company proposal for a nuclear plant.[33]

Power plant licensing and siting decisions, tariff rates, and fuel choices came to be regulated by the government, as were the maintenance and safety checks every thirteen months. But these utilities were among the largest private firms in Japan. Like such firms everywhere, they participated in setting the terms of their own regulation.[34] The privileging of particular fuels—coal in the 1950s, oil in the 1960s, nuclear in the 1970s—was all carefully negotiated with suppliers and with bureaucrats. MITI, today the Ministry of Economy, Trade, and Industry (METI), had at first been kept at arm's length by the private sector. But in 1974, it prevailed in a battle with the Science and Technology Agency for general jurisdiction over nuclear power, and in the 1990s, it wrested the Nuclear and Industrial Safety Agency (NISA) away from the Nuclear Safety Commission (NSC), an understaffed, academic, and largely powerless unit in the Cabinet Office. It had come to be both regulator and promoter of the industry, a one-stop shop that negotiated and coordinated policy with private firms.[35] NISA became a regulatory body located inside MITI's Agency for Natural Resources and Energy (ANRE), and MITI's Economic and Industrial Policy Bureau officials worked with utility executives to promote the industry at home and abroad. In the popular metaphor, MITI was now the driver that controlled both the accelerator and the brake.[36] Officials insisted that regulation and promotion did not interfere with each other, but after a series of scandals linked to lax oversight—and after NISA reported that the actual number of its plant inspectors had been less than 80 percent of the statutory number for years before 3.11—public opinion and analysts came to see the situation differently.[37]

Japan's fuel mix shifted several times in the decades after the Pacific War. But the shift from coal to oil in the 1960s and from oil to nuclear in the 1970s

TEPCO's Fukushima Daiichi nuclear power plant before the Great Eastern Japan Disaster of 11 March 2011. From right to left are Units 1 through 4. Taken from a helicopter in Ōkuma-machi, Fukushima Prefecture, 18 September 2010. Posted on 16 March 2011 morning edition. Photo courtesy of Yomiuri Newspaper/AFLO.

did not affect the privileges of the regional monopolies that had been created in the 1950s to promote rapid economic growth.[38] By the mid-1990s, however, fuel prices had declined, the economic bubble had burst, and a coalition emerged to support regulatory and structural reform. Consumers joined independent suppliers and industrial consumers to gain government support for lower electricity prices and regulatory change. In 1995, the Diet revised the Electric Utility Industry Law for the first time since 1964. To promote competition, it loosened licensing restrictions for suppliers, allowed more auto- and cogeneration, and spawned a new industry segment in which independent power producers (IPPs) could provide power directly to customers and sell their excess supply to the power companies. This partial deregulation had little effect on the regional monopolies because demand was declining, licenses were difficult to obtain due to public objections, and

In this 24 March 2011 aerial photo taken by a small, unmanned drone and released by Air
Photo Service, the crippled Fukushima Daiichi nuclear power plant is seen in
Ōkuma-machi, Fukushima Prefecture, northern Japan. From bottom to top are
Units 4 through 1. Photo courtesy of Air Photo Service/AFLO.

the IPPs were charged a significant fee to deposit their electrons on the
utilities' grid. A number of firms canceled plans to supply power to the
utilities—three whose bids had been accepted by TEPCO alone.[39]

In 2010, after several piecemeal revisions of the Electric Utility Industry
Law, METI settled on four objectives for a new national energy strategy.[40] Its
Basic Energy Plan would promote energy security (a euphemism for stable,
diversified supplies of fossil fuels), energy efficiency (a reference to the need
to reduce electric power prices), environmental protection (to make good on
a national commitment to reduce emission of greenhouse gasses), and economic growth. More nuclear power was the key to all four goals. The 2030
target for the share of nuclear power in the nation's power mix was set at an
ambitious 53 percent. It would require construction of nine new reactors
within a decade and fourteen or more by 2030.[41]

On the eve of 3.11, Japan had what one analyst called "an ideal fuel mix—or
at least the best one Japan had ever had."[42] In 2010, 29.2 percent of the nation's electric power was generated by nuclear power, slightly less than liquefied natural gas (29.4%) but far more than oil (7.6%), which had shrunk into

117

a welcome insignificance. Even coal, once maligned but now scrubbed and cheaper, accounted for more than 20 percent of the fuel mix for electric power.[43] But despite claims that the nuclear power sector was "too big to fail," 3.11 ended all talk of a "nuclear renaissance." The public megaphone was now open for advocates of renewable energy. Solar and wind still occupied negligible shares, but Japan's energy future was again up for grabs.[44]

The Energy Policy Change Narratives

The 3.11 catastrophe was widely seen as an "opportunity for major transition" in the domestic energy system.[45] The *Asahi Shimbun* editorialized that "there have been many efforts to reform the electric power sector in the past, but this time the unprecedented crisis provides a chance for a deep cut with a scalpel."[46] Koide Hiroaki, widely known as a rogue nuclear engineer for his career-long opposition to nuclear power, knew just where the surgery should begin: "After 3.11 the world has changed. Adults who had approved of nuclear power and those who had taken a more neutral position, now cannot. Those in society who enjoyed the benefits now will bear responsibility."[47] Koide was speaking of the "nuclear village," undoubtedly the most widely embraced metaphor in Japan's post-3.11 discourse.[48]

THE NUCLEAR VILLAGE

The "nuclear village" (*genpatsu mura* or *genshiryoku mura*) became much more than a metaphor. It was an archetypal crisis narrative invoked by those who would put Japan in high gear toward a nuclear-free energy future. It is also a classic blame narrative that touches on each of the central elements of public discourse in post-3.11 Japan. If Japan were to shift toward clean, safe energy, it would first have to acknowledge the villainy of those in industry and government who, along with facilitators in academia and the media, turned a devastating natural disaster into an even greater man-made one. The metaphor originated in a 1997 critique by Iida Tetsunari who, like Professor Koide, became an outspoken insider critic of nuclear power.[49] "Nuclear village" is shorthand for the policy community in which energy policy has been made and which "captured" the industry.[50] Although this narrative is associated with the activist Left, two of the most outspoken critics of nuclear power come from the conservative mainstream: LDP Diet representative Kōno Tarō and former Fukushima governor Satō Eisaku. Both openly deplore the failures of Japanese leadership in the face of national vulnerability and comfortably deploy the nuclear village critique.[51] Hosono Gōshi, the environment minister responsible for appointing members of a new nuclear oversight commission, declared "we will end our relationship with the electric utilities and will not select members from the nuclear village," and a special investigative commission created by the Diet was equally comfortable with this narrative. Its final report spoke of "regulatory capture" and slammed TEPCO for the way it "manipulated the cozy relationship with the regulators to take the teeth out of the regulations."[52] The more conservative *Yomiuri Shimbun* declared that "destroying the nuclear village will be no easy task."[53] Indeed, as the cover story in the 21 May 2011 issue of the business weekly *Daiyamondo* illustrates, the nuclear village is very much a mainstream narrative.[54] Even Tatsujirō Suzuki, the sitting vice-chair of the Atomic Energy Commission (AEC), has acknowledged that "Yes, I am living in the village hall."[55]

The most prominent structural features of the nuclear village are its lack of transparency and the alleged collusion of elites.[56] Widely reported cover-ups and data falsifications reinforce the image. Representative Kōno wrote after 3.11 of the difficulty his Diet committee encountered trying to acquire unredacted documents from METI when it investigated rate setting and other nuclear power–related policy decisions. He complained that the utilities and METI conspired to keep information secret.[57] According to the Diet testimony of one disgruntled NSC commissioner, the METI- and utility-dominated NISA blocked an effort to coordinate Japan's evacuation guidelines with international standards in the event of a nuclear accident on the basis that "it could trigger confusion and escalate public fear over nuclear safety."[58]

What some critics of the nuclear village call an "ethically suspicious rapport" is a prominent feature of the narrative. Iida argues that this is due to a mismatch between its influence and its size: "the village has huge influence, but few inhabitants."[59] One longtime member of METI's Energy Advisory Commission (*Sōgō Enerugī Chosakai*), Hasegawa Manabu, elaborates by noting how private-sector groups like the Japan Atomic Industrial Forum (JAIF) enable firms to hammer out congenial nuclear policies before presenting demands to the government, a situation he compares to making security policy "in the absence of civilian control."[60] One weekly magazine takes this further, personifying the entire industry in the character of a single 3.11 villain: the village is a system in which "the government and TEPCO became one and, like a bulldozer, pushed nuclear power forward."[61] However mixed their metaphors, opponents believe that this conspiratorial community trampled on prospects for alternative energy systems that might have challenged the dominance of nuclear power or the utilities' monopoly over power generation and transmission.[62]

These structural features have several behavioral corollaries. The first was the alleged co-optation of academics and the media. On this account, "kept intellectuals" acted like Meiji Era "servants of the state" (*goyō gakusha*), serving complacently inside various regulatory advisory bodies as flunkies and endlessly repeating the mantra that "nuclear power is essential for Japan."[63] Critics point to what they consider puff pieces written by journalists who allegedly received largesse from the nuclear power industry. They note that on 3.11 itself, the TEPCO chair and vice-chair were in China with senior executives from Chubu Electric Power Company, leading the latest in a decade of "China tours" for some twenty journalists from leading dailies and other media.[64] The narrative is also replete with references to the "Toyota-scale" size of TEPCO's public affairs and advertising budgets, much of which is spent in the print and broadcast media. Representative Kōno says that this is to "soften up" the media with stories of the nuclear "safety myth" (*anzen shinwa*).[65]

Academics made themselves equally easy targets, for most nuclear energy researchers had accepted funds from utilities, vendors, and/or the pronuclear bureaucracy.[66] Acknowledging this, the NSC set up a panel in 2010 on conflicts of interest, which concluded that strict rules would preclude the participation of virtually all of its more than one hundred expert advisers. The panel opted instead for voluntary disclosure and open records "to allow the public to judge conflicts of interest for itself."[67] This policy led to the disclosure that the new NSC head, Professor Madarame Haruki, had received 1 million yen in each of the four previous years from Mitsubishi Heavy Industry, and that one of his commissioners, Kyoto University professor Shiroya Seiji, had received more than 3 million yen from the JAIF for research and overseas travel.[68] Three university professors on the post-3.11 nuclear power task force reportedly received more than 18 million yen from the industry between 2005 and 2010.[69] Nuclear village narrators claim that those who could not be co-opted, like Koide, were refused promotions and marginalized.[70] One such researcher, Anzai Ikurō, a Tokyo University nuclear engineer, believes that he was "ruthlessly ejected from the village (*mura hachibu*) in the 1970s when I was identified as a dangerous critic of its policies."[71] In the view of a retired professor of seismology who had warned for years of the dangers of siting nuclear reactors on seismically active islands: "The haggling over the relative costs and risks [of placing nuclear reactors] here there and everywhere on active fault lines was an indecent (*rokotsu*) performance by electric utilities, NISA, NSC, and specialists. The specialists in particular have a grave responsibility."[72]

Nor, other critics say, is the largesse of the nuclear village limited to the scientific and technical research community. In 1981, TEPCO and other utilities established a legal think tank, the Japan Energy Law Research Institute (*Nihon Enerugii Hō Kenkyūjo*), in anticipation of suits and demands for compensation from accidents. When the post-3.11 compensation panel, the Nuclear Power Damage Compensation Dispute Investigation Board, was created in April 2011, several of the nine members were associated with this institute, a result that the *Asahi Shimbun* said "raised concerns about the board's neutrality" and that Representative Kōno called "contaminated."[73]

The co-optation of government officials is also central to this narrative. The post-3.11 critique has been filled with stories related to *amakudari* (literally, descent from heaven), the well-documented, system-wide practice by which private firms and affiliated institutions hire retiring government officials in their fifties who are thought to be at the peak of their influence. Four ex-METI bureaucrats have become deputy-presidents of TEPCO, and a fifth—a recently retired chief of ANRE who was in line for the post when he was hired in January 2011—abruptly resigned "for personal reasons" after 3.11.[74] As of August 2011, there were still more than fifty former government officials—from the Foreign Ministry, National Police Agency, Finance Ministry, and other agencies in addition to METI—working at TEPCO alone.[75] In 1980, only three of twenty-five MITI *amakudari* placements were in the electric power sector, whereas ten of twenty-two made that transition in 2010. There were fifty former METI officials in the senior ranks—including on boards of directors—of the electric utilities in May 2011.[76] High-visibility efforts by the Democratic Party of Japan (DPJ) to end *amakudari* were ridiculed as "partial measures of convenience."[77]

The political class is also singled out in this narrative. Although the electric utilities followed Keidanren's lead and suspended political contributions to politicians in 1974, much is made of their support through alternate channels. For example, it was widely reported—often with blaring headlines—that more than four hundred TEPCO executives donated nearly 60 million yen to LDP politicians from 1995 to 2009, and that more that 70 percent of political donations made to the LDP by individuals in 2009 (an additional 40 million yen) came from 153 electric utility executives.[78] This is not a significant amount of money, but critics of the nuclear village are quick to add that these figures do not include donations made by executives of TEPCO subsidiaries or by the firms themselves.[79] Moreover, for years, TEPCO had also been purchasing tickets for the campaign fund-raisers for more than fifty LDP politicians at prices just below the reportable minimum of 200,000 yen; after the regime change in 2009, it began doing so for DPJ politicians, at higher rates.[80] In addition, retired utility executives have been elected to the Diet with the generous support of the nuclear power community. The former head of TEPCO's nuclear unit, Kanō Tokio, for example, speaks of the "grass roots" support he received from the CEOs of TEPCO, Toshiba, Hitachi, and Mitsubishi Heavy Industries, adding that one of his five Diet aides was a retired TEPCO official and that each of the other four was a TEPCO employee on leave.[81] Utility employees have also been elected to local assemblies and executive posts where nuclear power plants are located.[82] In Saga Prefecture, a former employee of the Kyushu Electric Power Company was elected governor with the utility's support, and a relative of the mayor of Genkai, a nuclear power plant site in Saga, was awarded contracts for more than 5 billion yen.[83]

The nuclear village narrative rarely fails to point out that TEPCO often provided data and analysis for NISA reports and that the utilities and vendors populated NISA with their own experts.[84] This claim is substantiated by reports that by 2011, eighty utility and vendor employees had worked at NISA, and that since 2000, the utilities had dispatched one hundred employees to "de facto reserved seats" throughout the government.[85] In one particularly well-publicized example, it was reported that more than half the members of a NISA-empowered Tsunami Evaluation Subcommittee of the Japan Society of Civil Engineers had been seconded from the nuclear power industry. It was this committee that wrote guidelines on tsunami height that underestimated the size of the 3.11 tsunami by more than 150 percent and ignored pre-3.11 warnings by other experts that it had done so.[86]

The final corollary in this narrative is lax oversight and promulgation of the nuclear "safety myth." Iida invokes his own experience inside the industry and insists that safety inspections were perfunctory performances orchestrated by friendly experts: "They did not check our analyses independently and confirm if the plant was really safe. No wonder accidents happen."[87] According to one former NISA chief, efforts to introduce U.S.- or European-style oversight were "overpowered by utilities that argued against having to shoulder the extra costs of regulatory compliance."[88] This view—originating in investigative reports and whistle-blowers—often highlights the suppression of public information by electric power companies and their allies in METI.[89] The independent Diet investigative commission connected problems of regulatory capture and minimal transparency to failures by the industry to keep up with safety policies adopted abroad.[90]

Even Prime Minister Kan also came to embrace the nuclear village narrative. In April 2011, when he established an independent panel to investigate the causes of the accident at Fukushima Daiichi, he told a plenary session of the Diet that "the nuclear safety myth" had been prevalent in the thinking of government and utility officials.[91] The next month, announcing plans for a bottom-up review of Japan's Basic Energy Plan, the prime minister was again unequivocal: "There is no alternative but to start from scratch on a new national energy policy." A week later, he explained why: a system in which regulators and promoters inhabit the same agency "raises questions of independence . . . [and] we do not have a sturdy structure in this regard."[92] Seven months after the disaster, a former METI official, and veteran of (lost) fights to change the nuclear power industry, explained that "it was difficult to change energy policy before 3.11 due to the strength of the 'nuclear village,' but after 3.11 changes became possible. Over time though, it will become more difficult."[93] He was prescient: the Japanese government failed to complete its promised restructuring of nuclear regulation by the target date of 1 April 2012 due to political disagreements within the DPJ and between the DPJ and the opposition. The minister in charge, Hosono Gōshi, acknowledged that "having regulators and promoters under the same roof is not desirable." He called the delay "regrettable," and the policy debate continued.[94]

BLACK SWANS

The debate continued without resolution because the nuclear village narrative was confronted by several competing ideas about what happened on 3.11 and what ought to be done about it. If the nuclear village narrative was the archetypal explanation for putting it in gear, proponents of nuclear power responded with two narratives loaded with reasons to stay the course. Both were built on the same base—the idea introduced in chapter two that 3.11 was an exceptionally rare natural disaster beyond the imagination of any planners (sōteigai).

Business as usual. The first group, led by representatives of institutions with deep ties to the nuclear power industry, was just as determined as nuclear village narrators to spin a compelling account of 3.11. Some took umbrage at the idea that a collusive nuclear village might even exist. The LDP's Kanō, for example, insisted that the very term is "discriminatory" (sabetsuteki), and another former TEPCO executive, Masumoto Teruaki, explained that policy communities exist on the basis of shared knowledge, not collusion. If there is a community of nuclear power supporters, he suggested, it is epistemic rather than conspiratorial.[95] A leading Japanese "disasterologist," Tokyo University professor Hatamura Yōtarō, gives this view credence but ties it to the nuclear village narrative: he explains that nuclear experts invoke the sōteigai defense precisely because they live in a relatively closed community of specialists like themselves. When attacked, he says, they have tended to overstate the safety of nuclear power.[96]

Defenders of the status quo insisted that 3.11 was the consequence of special and irreproducible circumstances, so there was no reason for policy change other than perhaps an enhanced safety regime. Japan ought simply to return to nuclear normalcy. The best evidence of the confidence that nuclear power proponents had in the black swan argument was a plan announced less than a month after 3.11 by Chubu Electric Power Company to complete construction of its Kaminoseki plant "to ensure energy security and prevent global warming," and the announcement by Kansai Electric Power Company that it would resume operations at three of its reactors that had been shut down for routine inspection. JAIF chair Imai Takashi articulated this view clearly at the organization's general assembly in June 2011 and invoked the community theme: "The accident at Fukushima Daiichi was caused by an earthquake and tsunami, the likes of which occur once in a thousand years. Yet it is regrettable that the accident has radically undermined the confidence in the safety of nuclear power generation. . . . Japanese society must be unified in support of the restoration of Fukushima."[97]

Politicians who held this view reminded the public that although the tsunami caused a meltdown in Fukushima Daiichi, "no one died" from the nuclear accident and the neighboring reactors at Fukushima Daini and

Onagawa safely shut down according to plans.[98] Yosano Kaoru, a former minister of state for economic and fiscal policy (and a former Japan Atomic Power Company employee) said that "there is no explaining God's work" and declared nuclear power to be safe. (Kanō went further, insisting that "radiation is good for your health.")[99] Yosano openly opposed any change to the sector and declared it would be "unjust" to make TEPCO bear full responsibility for an "abnormal" natural disaster beyond the capacity of the "highest intellect" to anticipate.[100] Nuclear power was, he insisted, "necessary to sustain current levels of Japanese wealth and economic power," and without it, Japan would be impoverished. In summarizing his views, Yosano captured the narrative with perfect pitch: "Because the incident [3.11] was well beyond any scientifically anticipated scale, there is no merit in reflecting on it."[101] He helped Kanō and Amari Akira—also identified with the utility industry—organize a caucus of Diet members to promote nuclear power.[102] One member of the caucus picked up where Yosano and Kanō left off and invoked the vulnerability trope: "Eliminating nuclear power is impossible. If we do that, Japan will revert to an agricultural economy."[103] Meanwhile, other politicians made a more indelicate case for nuclear power. The LDP's Ishiba Shigeru, a former defense minister, insisted that "it is important to maintain our commercial reactors because it will allow us to produce a nuclear warhead in a short amount of time. . . . It is a tacit nuclear deterrent."[104] Ishiba earlier had suggested that the nuclear accident originated in the fact that "Japan had introduced nuclear technology developed by American corporations without examining factors unique to Japan, such as geography, geology, weather conditions, and natural disasters."[105] In September 2012, the sitting defense minister, Morimoto Satoshi, publicly declared his support for nuclear power on the basis of its deterrent value and as a means to maintain Japan's nuclear weapons option.[106]

The notion of vulnerability was raised less provocatively by specialists in the think tanks and private sector who reminded the public that the stability of electric power supply in Japan—the best in the world—could not be taken for granted in the absence of nuclear power.[107] Toyoda Masakazu, a retired senior METI official who became chair of the authoritative Institute for Energy Economics (IEE), listed a number of "lessons from Fukushima," most of which point the way back to business as usual. In his view, the nuclear accident created rumors that were more harmful than reality— that Japanese exports were tainted or that visitors should avoid Japan. He warned that a decline in nuclear power supply would lead to electricity shortages that would hurt the macroeconomy, and that a shift to fossil fuels would increase costs and CO_2 emissions. He called for an "appropriate" safety and regulatory scheme and a "balance of responsibility" between government and industry.[108] Other IEE analyses forecast a 4 percent decline in the Japanese economy and a growth in jobless claims by two hundred thousand if reactors did not resume operation.[109] An unstable electric power supply would scare off investors, who would shift to offshore opportunities.[110]

Raising concerns about growth and jobs were potent, but defenders of nuclear power invoked another powerful variant of the vulnerability trope—the effect of a nuclear shutdown on Japan's technological future. Arguing that the survival of Tohoku Electric's Onagawa nuclear facility near Fukushima Daiichi was evidence that Japanese technology had long ago surpassed the original designs supplied by General Electric, Hokkaido University nuclear engineering professor Narabayashi Tadashi struck a technonational chord: "Japan should take credit for the high level of technology that saved Onagawa. . . . [I]f Japan should assume a non-nuclear stance it will not be able to preserve and protect such superb technology. . . . [I]t is vital to continue to pursue even higher technology, thereby protecting Japan's position as one of the world's frontrunners in this field, while also providing support to the Japanese economy in general with a broad based nuclear industry."[111]

Hamada Yasuo, president of the Japan Atomic Power Company, made a similar argument, saying that he is "quite sure Japan will continue to need nuclear power" because of its technological contributions.[112] One utility executive channeled Japan's 1990s technological confidence and told a shareholders' meeting after 3.11 that "our containment vessels are so strong and excellent that they could even withstand a Taepodong [North Korean missile] strike."[113] The IEE's Toichi also weighed in on the importance of nuclear expertise, expressing concern that Japan's hard-won technological leadership might be lost if construction of new reactors per the 2010 Basic Plan does not go forward.[114] On his account, alternative energy technologies are expensive, unreliable, and provide no near-term answers. From a technological perspective, nuclear power made more sense.[115]

TEPCO's own analysis of 3.11 defended its technological choices following a "black swan" event. According to one general manager, "We do not believe that the Fukushima Daiichi accident was caused by our choice of reactor design. We have to study the causes further. It was beyond our imagination and, thus, beyond our preparation with the government."[116] Indeed, in 2009, TEPCO had reported to the NSC that its Fukushima plant could withstand "even a large earthquake" and that it was designed to ensure "zero radiation impact in the vicinity."[117] In its interim report on the accident, TEPCO insisted that it had always complied with extant regulatory guidelines and that "necessary measures were taken" when those guidelines changed. Invoking the "sōteigai defense," TEPCO stated that no simulation studies and nothing in the recorded history of Tohoku could have prepared them for a seismic event of this magnitude: "The situation on the site was far beyond the originally estimated accident management conditions, and as a result, the expansion of the accident could not be prevented under the framework of the prepared safety measures."[118]

Keidanren defended this position vigorously. At a press conference less than a week after the disaster (and before the full extent of the damage to Fukushima Daiichi was known), Chairman Yonekura Hiromasa declared that "having a reactor that can withstand a once in a thousand year tsunami is fantastic. We should be confident about nuclear power." A month later, Nippon Steel's Mimura—also a Keidanren board member—spoke of Japan's strengths in dealing with such "unforeseen circumstances" (*sōteigai no jittai*).[119] Keidanren had the staff of a two hundred–member committee investigate the accident and compile data demonstrating that regulation of the reactor was not slack. They charted nine separate steps in the siting, design, and construction process at which the government required inspections and certifications as well as six separate inspections once the commercial reactor was online, adding that seven inspectors were on duty at Fukushima Daiichi at all times. Their data also support the view that the accident at Fukushima Daiichi was beyond imagination. They show that TEPCO had built Fukushima Daiichi to specifications that far exceeded NSC guidelines—including higher-than-required tsunami barriers, containment vessels that were double the specified strength, and more than double the specified number of external power lines. They documented how the actual height of the tsunami, the impact on the containment vessels, and the knockout of external power overwhelmed even these extra precautions.[120] A senior staff member explained that the committee's work would take time, and that it "should put off any quick decisions and wait a few years to make a rational (*gōriteki*) decision [on nuclear power]."[121] While warning against "hasty" (*busoku*) decisions, however, Keidanren argued in its first post-3.11 energy policy white paper for a rapid resolution of TEPCO's liability for the nuclear accident and for a quick decision on a midterm energy plan emphasizing supply stability and economies of scale—euphemisms for nuclear business as usual. Indeed, it repeatedly called for an end to the government's "stress tests" and for the quick restart of nuclear reactors that had been closed for maintenance but not restarted after the accident at Fukushima Daiichi.[122]

Realism. Different approaches to rational decision making is where the "business as usual" variant of the stay the course narrative yields to a realist alternative that more readily acknowledges mistakes made by the nuclear power industry. Sawa Akihiro, a former METI official and energy policy analyst, also has argued for a "cool headed and rational discussion" and against "emotional" responses to the disaster. After all, less-experienced nations are adapting nuclear power and need Japan's continued guidance, so "we must clearly understand that condemning or sealing nuclear power technologies could actually threaten safety" at home and abroad.[123] Sawa argues that the impact of a shutdown of nuclear power in Japan would be enormous—particularly in supply disruptions and in unsustainable cost and rate increases: the extra costs of imported fuel would add more than 3 trillion yen to the utilities import bill, which would translate into more than 1,000 yen per month more for residential users, 750,000 yen per month more for small factories, and more than 7 million yen per month extra for large plants.[124] He and other realists are committed to keeping Japan's nuclear reactors online, but are willing to countenance some structural change to the industry.

One of the leading voices for this position is Suzuki Tatsujirō, vice chair of the Atomic Energy Commission and a former professor of nuclear engineering at Tokyo University, who reflects on how "risk was not considered in a cool and calm manner" when nuclear power was being ramped up in the 1970s.[125] In Diet testimony and elsewhere, Suzuki has argued that everyone associated with the development of nuclear power in Japan—including himself—should feel responsibility for what happened at Fukushima Daiichi. While he understands there was a system malfunction, he usually avoided the term "nuclear village" to assign blame, calling it a "community" instead. At the same time, however, Suzuki also distanced himself from the "sōteigai defense."[126] He reports that the nuclear power industry had made many safety improvements (kaizen) over the years, but he did not call attention to them out of concern that it would invite questions about earlier safety lapses. He called for a break in this "vicious cycle," and directed the AEC to study risk openly. In the government's first public estimate—though not likely one that will satisfy critics—Suzuki's AEC placed the probability of a serious nuclear accident to be once in five hundred years at a cost of 3.9 trillion yen.[127]

At issue for this group of realists is not merely the extent to which risk had been de-emphasized in the rush to consolidate nuclear power, but the possibility that excessive risk aversion after 3.11 might cripple an important source of energy. They remind the public that risk exists in all large-scale engineering systems and requires systematic attention. Takeda Tōru, for example, warns that the nuclear "safety myth" could now easily be replaced by a "nuclear danger" myth or by a "practical renewable energy 'safety myth.'"[128] One economist tackles practicality from a different angle, arguing that "a narrow focus on renewables could seriously damage national interests" because foreign producers would overwhelm the Japanese market while Japanese consumers bear the enormous costs associated with a shift away from nuclear power. Japan should instead "advance nuclear technologies that would enable the operation of safer reactors."[129]

Many realists are not opposed to renewables in principle, but believe they cannot compete with nuclear power in the short or medium term. For example, Tanaka Nobuo, a former executive director of the International Energy Agency, has repeatedly argued that although renewables are theoretically possible, Japan needs nuclear power for the sake of environmental sustainability, energy independence, and security.[130] Tokyo Institute of Technology professor Kashiwagi Takao similarly advocates renewables and distributed energy systems, but insists that they be integrated into the existing system in order to ensure both stable supply and a low carbon outcome.[131] Arguing that "we need to be cautious before ruling out nuclear power," he believes that this combination of a stable base load supply and new energy technologies will boost Japan's export economy.[132] Sawa concurs, noting that realists place supply security and growth ahead of environmental protection. He believes that advocates of renewables make environmental concerns their top priority and were opportunistic in "picking their enemies." Critics of fossil fuels before 3.11, he says, switched quickly to nuclear power after the disaster. In his view, they have been "ideological" when Japanese energy planners should be, like him, "realistic."[133]

Simple life. Not many energy analysts would find much that is realistic in a third group of energy policy entrepreneurs. Nor would many judge them to be influential in the national discourse. Still, there are those who believe that 3.11 proved that Japan had come too far in the wrong direction, and must return to simpler times if it is to survive as a national community. Unlike critics of the nuclear village, who wish to see nuclear power displaced by solar and wind power, many of those who would return Japan to better times are antigrowth and do not seek a technological fix for what ails Japan. Supporters of both groups have signed the same petitions calling for creation of "a sustainable and peaceful society" and "coexistence with all living things on the earth," but they part ways in their preferences for growth and the nature of Japan's integration in the world economy.[134] "Simple life" advocates will be satisfied with conservation and slower growth.

Support for this approach can be found in government circles, as well as among intellectuals and religious leaders. The Environment Ministry, for example, seized on 3.11 as reason for renewed emphasis on "building a low carbon society in symbiosis with nature contributing through recycling and 'green innovation.'" In September 2011, six months after 3.11, it announced it would use its FY 2012 budget to respond to the catastrophe with a program of environmental conservation, built on "safety, sustainability, and peace of mind as urgent challenges."[135] Well before 3.11, a Tokyo University professor of sustainability studies, Takeuchi Kazuhiko, chaired a study for what was then the National Land Agency, calling for a "Grand Design for National Land" that concluded that rapid modernization had weakened the resolve to think strategically about disaster. After 3.11, he renewed calls for a "new disaster culture" that would start with a "bottom up review of energy use, resiliency, and life style change," central elements of this third narrative.[136]

In October 2011, Meiji University anthropology professor Nakazawa Shinichi, citing the weakness of the country's political response to 3.11, announced the formation of a Green Party on a platform of eliminating nuclear power, slowing growth, and achieving national self-sufficiency in agriculture.[137] But not all simple life interpretations of 3.11 come from the political Left.

Professor Umehara Takeshi, the conservative Kyoto University philosopher identified with cultural essentialism, squared off against Keidanren chairman Yonekura in a full-page debate on the future of nuclear power in the New Year's Day 2012 issue of the *Asahi Shimbun*. Yonekura's *sōteigai* argument that focused on stability and growth was met by Umehara's simple life argument from the Right. Umehara, who had been a member of the Reconstruction Design Council, saw the nuclear accident at Fukushima Daiichi as a "civilizational disaster" (*bunmeisai*) that can be repaired only by an immediate "return to co-existence with nature" (*kyōzon ni kaerō*). The quake and the tsunami may have been natural disasters, he argued, but the nuclear meltdown was man-made; it was a signal that the age of Enlightenment and its technological accoutrements had reached their limits. He told readers that Japanese culture had originated in a rice-planting society, and that until Western culture forced itself on the archipelago, the Japanese understood that human beings cannot control nature. Umehara insisted that 3.11 signaled it is time to recall lessons from that past. He called it "arrogant" (*omoi agari*) to imagine that humans can harness the power of the atom. It is more important to protect lives and the environment: "Compared to the western view that humans can conquer nature, in Japan we believe that all animals and plants and minerals are Buddhas (*kusaki kokudo shikkai jyōbutsu*)." This is the moment to depart from the path of "excessive consumption" and waste; it is time to build a new civilization based on "spirituality consistent with Japanese tradition and to give thanks for the blessings of nature."[138]

Umehara was joined by religionists, such as self-described "eco-priest" Naitō Kanpū, who founded a nongovernmental organization (NGO) called the Simple Life Diffusion Center, based on lessons from 3.11. Like Umehara, Naitō acknowledged the quake as an unprecedented natural disaster, but argued that "while it was said to be 'unimaginable' (*sōteigai*), the basic designs of nuclear plants, the relaxed approach to the possibility of natural events, the unskilled nature of even the most expert inspectors, and the awkward response to the crisis all add up to make this a man-made disaster." He rejects both nuclear power and other thermal power sources, preferring a shift to "sustainable energy."[139]

Though it does not have such deep pockets as either of the black swan narratives, and it is not as growth oriented or widely accepted as the nuclear village narrative, the simple life story also relied on appeals to all of the principal motifs in the post-3.11 Japanese discourse: *change* is imperative and requires replacement of inept *leaders*; *communitarianism* must be rediscovered and nurtured; and above all, programs must be implemented that address modern *vulnerabilities*. Even most critics of modernity acknowledge that modern Japan accomplished its industrial transformation thanks to cheap electricity. The most fundamental questions raised by the simple life narrative were thus no different from the competing energy change narratives after 3.11—they revolved around risk and the leadership entrusted with managing electric power. The battle lines in this national discourse were drawn over whether the economic model that worked in the past was worth the risks it manifestly poses in the present and future, and about whether there is a better alternative that may have been hidden by advocates of nuclear power.

The Battle Was Joined

The battle over post-3.11 energy policy started with a struggle for control of the institutions of decision making. The established METI-utility nexus—the old "give-and-take power triangle" (*mochitsu motaretsu no toraianguru*)—came under assault from new political and commercial actors as well as established players, and together they threatened to effect a new balance of power in both regulation and policy.[140] Speaking to this point, Iwate governor Tasso Takuya observed that "a power shift is under way" in energy policymaking.[141]

Some editorialists were more cautious than others, but most asked tough questions about the future of the industry and urged change. Two months after 3.11, the *Asahi Shimbun* asked if the system of private regional monopolies, including the ties between regulators and producers, should continue. It also questioned the future of nuclear power and asked whether private firms should be allowed to operate nuclear facilities and whether nuclear fuel should be reprocessed, stored, and used. The *Mainichi Shimbun* offered unambiguous answers to these questions. It compared the contemporary commitment to the electric power industry to that of the Imperial Navy to battleships—two cases with disastrous results in which senior officials stuck with obsolete technology as the world shifted around them.[142] Arguing that "the illusion of nuclear power safety has been torn out by the roots," the *Mainichi* editorial page opposed reactor restarts and called for an end to the nuclear fuel cycle program. Even the business-friendly *Nihon Keizai Shimbun*, which warned against an outright shift away from nuclear power and argued for "careful review" of data, also called for open debate on all structural features of the electric power industry. It even suggested that since Japan possesses the world's largest exclusive economic zone (EEZ), ample space might be available for the construction of offshore wind power generators.[143]

Public opinion shifted over time, as support for nuclear power dissipated. An early post-3.11 *Yomiuri Shimbun* poll found that more than half the public was in favor of either the status quo or an increase in nuclear power. But a *Mainichi Shimbun* poll two weeks later found the reverse—more than half expressed a preference for reducing or eliminating nuclear power.[144] By early June 2011, nearly three-quarters of the respondents to an *Asahi Shim-*

bun poll and two-thirds of those to an NHK (Japanese Broadcasting Corporation) poll agreed it would be best to phase out and abandon nuclear power.[145] A year after 3.11, more than half of those surveyed opposed the restart of the nation's nuclear plants and 80 percent reported that they did not trust government safeguards.[146] Keidanren understood the problem. Its energy white paper declared that the number one priority was to regain the "confidence of the Japanese people and international society."[147]

PROTEST

First, though, nuclear advocates would have to deal with open protest. In one of the most dramatic episodes, angry Fukushima parents visited Education Ministry officials who had raised the maximum allowable exposure to radiation for schoolchildren by 2,000 percent. Dumping bags of playground sand on the officials' desks, the parents asked the bureaucrats if they would let their own children play in it. In another instance, a NISA meeting was delayed for several hours when antinuclear activists demanded a presence in the deliberations.[148] Utility officials were protected by police from protesters in the streets, but they had to face angry shareholders. Shareholder meetings in Japan are famously uneventful affairs, where the rare protestor would ordinarily be ushered out of the hall (or, in the case of gangsters threatening blackmail, bought off ahead of time).[149] But during the first round of post-3.11 meetings, shareholders at six of the ten private utilities introduced antinuclear resolutions that stimulated serious discussion.[150] TEPCO's meeting attracted the most attention. Under the watchful eye of "busloads of riot police," nearly ten thousand shareholders were in attendance, the largest gathering in the history of the firm.[151] Angry hecklers could not be subdued by the repeated "profuse apologies" of TEPCO senior management, and their restiveness only increased as TEPCO management reappointed seventeen board members and the chairman. One particularly agitated shareholder was widely reported to have screamed: "Go jump in a reactor and die!"[152]

Despite predictions to the contrary, however, the meltdown of three reactors and displacement of hundreds of thousands of residents did not at first trigger mass protests against nuclear power.[153] The general public may have turned antinuclear, but in political terms it remained relatively unmobilized for more than a year after the accident. A rally in Kōenji near Tokyo attracted fifteen thousand in April 2011, but only about a thousand protesters marched in front of TEPCO headquarters in Tokyo on the three-month anniversary of 3.11.[154] An aggregately larger group marched and assembled nationwide in June without the benefit of a central organizing committee, but the most notable early protest was held on the grounds of the Meiji Shrine in Tokyo in September 2011, when an estimated sixty thousand people, led by Nobel laureate Ōe Kenzaburō, waved signs saying "Sayonara Nuclear Power!"[155] On the same day, protests of smaller scale were held in Nagoya and Fukushima, and organizers claimed to have collected one million signatures on a petition.[156] Connecting the people of Tohoku to the victims of the atomic bombings in Hiroshima and Nagasaki through the pacifist icon Ōe and through the petition's language did not have a measurable effect. Neither did an encampment of protesters on the grounds of METI, who exhorted the public to "Occupy Kasumigaseki" in response to the "Occupy Wall Street" protests in New York City. Whether these demonstrations were not adequately covered in the mainstream media, as some claim, or for some other reason, the encampments remained small and the numbers of antinuclear power protesters declined as the first anniversary of 3.11 approached.[157] Instead, social mobilization was personified in the volunteers who made their way in record numbers to Tohoku to help with reconstruction and in "citizen scientists" who collected data on radioactivity in their neighborhoods.[158] Accounts of the activities of both groups were infused with the themes of leadership, vulnerability, and, especially, community. Japanese citizens seemed more concerned than outraged during the first year after the disaster.

Even if opposition in the form of mass rallies was relatively muted (or at least not very visible to the public) during the first fifteen months after the accident, a group untethered to the issue of nuclear arms emerged that appealed directly to the electoral mechanisms of democratic politics. The Citizens' Vote to Decide Together on Nuclear Power (*Minna de Kimeyō 'Genpatsu' Kokumin Tōhyō*) launched a petition drive calling for referenda on nuclear power in urban Japan. Direct, policy-specific referenda have not been uncommon in postwar Japan, but more than 90 percent have been initiated by the central government to secure local approval for the merger of towns and villages into larger municipalities. Others, related to hot-button issues such as industrial pollution, U.S. military bases, and mayoral recalls, have had mixed success.[159] Under the Local Autonomy Law, petitions signed by one-fiftieth of the locality's eligible voters go to chief executives who are required to submit them to local assemblies with a formal recommendation for or against. The issue reaches the ballot on passage by the assembly. Since 1982, when the first referendum campaign was launched in Kubokawachō in Kochi Prefecture, twenty-nine campaigns against nuclear plant siting or nuclear fuel use acquired the requisite number of signatures. Only three ever reached the ballot.[160]

This one was different for several reasons. First, it was organized entirely through social network technology without financial support from business, trade unions, or other organizations. In June 2011, twenty persons responded to a "tweet" by the campaign's initiator, Imai Hajime. He knew none of them personally, and watched with satisfaction as the number of volunteers (each of whom donated at least 1,000 yen) expanded into the thousands.[161] Second, it was organized explicitly as a battle between urban and rural Japan. This was the first time referenda on nuclear power would be held in major urban centers where nuclear energy is consumed, rather than in the isolated rural districts where it is produced. This targeting had several strategic advantages to the antinuclear movement. First, since the Tokyo Metropolitan Government and the city of Osaka were major shareholders in TEPCO and Kansai Electric, respectively, the movement leaders anticipated that a rejection of nuclear power in these metropolises would have a severe impact on the firms themselves. Second, in targeting urban Japan, Imai was protesting inequalities in the distribution of subsidies and grants by the central government as well as the lack of representation for urban residents in nuclear power decisions. Aware of the fact that urban and rural residents have different political interests, Imai asked: "Why should 1 percent of the population get so much money? Tens of thousands of people get billions of yen—and that's just the reported figure. The only people making choices so far have been rural folk in areas where no one lives. But nuclear power affects cities and urban residents too. Nuclear power is a human problem involving pollution of air, water, and food supplies that is far reaching and that should be resolved by the majority of people."[162] Imai acknowledged that ending nuclear power would create economic hardships for rural people who have become dependent on subsidies to keep their communities intact. He was willing to support them with limited government assistance, but insisted that they first make better economic choices for themselves, choices that are safer for all Japanese.[163]

By January 2012, the organizers had enough signatures to present their petitions to Osaka mayor Hashimoto Tōru, and in February they claimed to have 260,000 signatures in Tokyo, well more than the 214,000 required by law to make their presentation to Governor Ishihara Shintarō.[164] Ishihara—although no friend of TEPCO—showed his hand first, characterizing the referendum movement as "hysterical and sentimental."[165] When the petition was formally presented to him with 323,000 signatures in May, he dismissed it summarily.[166] It was less clear at first if Osaka mayor Hashimoto Tōru, a nuclear power opponent and one of the brightest young stars on the Japanese political horizon, would support the campaign.[167] As it turned out, he did not, claiming that it interfered with his own plans for a démarche on Kansai Electric at the next shareholders meeting. He declared that a referendum would be "redundant and wasteful" and that his own election on an antinuclear platform had already settled the desire to "let the people decide."[168] The Osaka City Assembly followed Hashimoto's lead and rejected the petition in March.[169] The referendum movement had failed, and soon thereafter, Hashimoto reversed course and agreed to support the restart of Kansai Electric's nuclear reactors.[170]

At first there was no public push back. The residents served by Kansai Electric supported the Ōi restart by a slim margin, and an overwhelming majority (67%) "understood" Hashimoto's reversal.[171] But once the restart became an impending reality, networks of antinuclear groups that connected through social media under the loose umbrella of a "Metropolitan Area Nuclear Association" turned out large numbers of protestors in Tokyo, many of whom had never participated in a demonstration. On 22 June, some 11,000–45,000 people chanted their opposition to nuclear power (*"datsu genpatsu!"* or "Get Rid of Nukes!") and to the Ōi restart in particular (*"saikidō hantai!"* or "We Oppose the Restart!"). A week later, just one day before Kansai Electric pressed the Ōi restart switch, many tens of thousands more protestors congregated in front of the prime minister's office—and in an orderly line more than a kilometer long, stretching down to the government offices in Kasumigaseki—in what was described as the "Hydrangea Revolution," the largest public protest in Japan since the 1960s.[172] These protests continued and grew in the weeks that followed—on 16 July, at least seventy-five thousand persons gathered to protest nuclear power in Tokyo's capacious Yoyogi Park.[173] These public protests were joined by complaints that the discussion at the government's town hall energy policy meetings was being manipulated. At the first one in Sendai in mid-July, Tohoku Electric was accused of having inserted one of its own employees in the guise of a concerned citizen, and Environment Minister Hosono moderated the event sandwiched by bodyguards.[174]

ESTABLISHED PLAYERS

Hashimoto's reversal and delayed public outcry notwithstanding, the petition campaign and the growing public disaffection with nuclear power signaled anything but a return to "business as usual" for the utilities. Even old allies had taken new turns. Former prime minister Koizumi Junichirō asserted that many of the costs of nuclear power had been hidden, and appealed for a reduction in Japan's dependence on nuclear power and for an increase in alternative energy.[175] The LDP, which had mobilized a party caucus to support nuclear power immediately after 3.11, announced in July that it might modify its long-standing support; in February 2012, the party deferred a decision on the future of nuclear power.[176] Meanwhile, eight LDP Diet representatives, led by Kōno Tarō, had joined twenty-eight colleagues from across every aisle in an "Energy Shift" (*enshifu*) caucus chaired by Democratic Socialist Abe Tomoko. The DPJ contingent was led by Nagashima Akihisa, and Sonoda Hiroyuki of the "Rise Up, Japan!" party lent it additional conservative ballast. This suprapartisan caucus covered an unusually broad ideological spectrum and attracted think tank analysts and activists as well.[177]

For its part, the ruling DPJ also sent mixed signals, further deepening public concern about its leadership. Prime Minister Kan declared soon after 3.11 that his government would abandon Japan's 2010 Basic Energy Plan.

This meant taking some nuclear power plants off-line and suspending all plans for new construction. Kan's call for a "reset" of national energy policy, like his unvetted speech in Paris calling for a 20 percent target for renewables by 2020, was not cleared with the party's hierarchs.[178] Edano Yukio, his chief cabinet secretary, insisted immediately that Japan's "fundamental nuclear policy is not changing," and Deputy Chief Cabinet Secretary Sengoku Yoshito, a Kan confidant and longtime nuclear power enthusiast, also reiterated government support for nuclear energy.[179] Less than two weeks later, though, Edano and Genba Kōichirō, the national strategy minister, agreed on the goal of restructuring the utility industry, possibly separating generation from transmission.[180] A month passed, and Maeda Tadashi, one of Kan's senior economic advisers, called for the nationalization of all nuclear power facilities.[181] In July, Kan announced that no reactors would be put back online without "stress tests," a requirement that he did not discuss with his METI minister Kaieda Banri, who had been trying to convince officials in Saga Prefecture to approve the restart of reactors there. By July, the *Asahi Shimbun* was reporting that "Japan's nuclear policy appears to be in disarray."[182]

Part of the problem was incomplete policy coordination within the DPJ, a problem exacerbated by its earlier elimination of its Policy Affairs Council, the venue where disparate views had typically been consolidated into a party program and transmitted to the government. More important, the DPJ had run on an anti-LDP platform that *perforce* rendered it suspicious of nuclear power; it was divided on the issue. Both Kan and Sengoku came from a wing of the DPJ anchored by former trade unionists from the electric power industry's trade union federation, Denryoku Sōren, which supported nuclear power. But it was not until August 2010, just seven months before 3.11, that the trade union confederation Rengō declared its unambiguous support for nuclear power and lined up with the pronuclear DPJ hierarchs. Although DPJ politicians never received the level of financial support from the nuclear power trade unions that their LDP colleagues did from the utilities, many did come to depend on it. The Electric Power Political Action Committee (*Denryoku Sōren Seiji Katsudō Iinkai*) endorsed forty-eight DPJ candidates in the 2010 House of Councilors election, and made recorded contributions to several members of the Kan cabinet.[183] Then, seven months after the disaster of 3.11, Rengō reversed itself.[184] It did so again in May 2012, when Arai Yukio, the head of TEPCO's labor union, vowed revenge on the DPJ for abandoning nuclear power. Like the DPJ, for which it was the number one institutional base, Rengō was inconsistent and unsure about the best way (or indeed, any way) forward for national energy policy.

Kan's successor, DPJ party mate Noda Yoshihiko, did not clarify matters. Before his August 2011 selection as party chief (and thereby as prime minister), Noda laid out his energy policy preferences in the influential monthly *Bungei Shunjū*. Trying to split the difference between the nuclear village

135

and realist narratives, Noda declared that the "nuclear 'safety myth' has been shattered"; he supported the decommissioning of reactors that did not pass the "stress tests" then under way. But he also expressed serious concern about the power supply if reactors were to stay off-line too much longer. Noda also added his support for the export of nuclear power plants as part of Japan's "new growth strategy."[185] In his first policy speech to the Diet, Noda called for Japan's reactor fleet to be restarted but phased out in the long term.[186] The following month, he told leaders of the Communist and Democratic Socialist parties that the nuclear budget should be used for Tohoku recovery.[187] Few knew exactly what to make of government policy. One senior official in the cabinet secretariat suggested that the prime minister had "not yet made up his mind" on nuclear power. Keidanren and the utilities were said to be "bracing for the worst."[188]

Government policy remained inconsistent. On the same day in January 2012, Hosono Gōshi, the environment minister and "disaster czar," insisted it would be impossible to restart reactors more than forty years old, but the cabinet approved bills that would allow twenty-year extensions under "difficult" circumstances. The *Asahi Shimbun* editorialized that the government was issuing "confused" messages and demanded that all reactors in service for more than forty years be shut down as "the embodiment of Prime Minister Noda's pledge" to reduce national dependence on nuclear power.[189] Then, in May 2012, after two DPJ task forces produced different recommendations on restarts and the government was facing the shutdown of Japan's last operating reactor, it declared that two reactors at the Kansai Electric Company's Ōi complex in Fukui were safe to restart. At that point, however, the government had trouble securing the cooperation of either the residents or their local officials.[190] Officials seemed to be getting a bit desperate, as when the DPJ's Sengoku invoked the most disturbing variant of the vulnerability trope and declared that the failure to restart would result in "mass suicide."[191] But by then, public opinion had taken a strong turn away from nuclear power. In May 2012, Japan became entirely nuclear free for the first time since 1970, and nearly two-thirds of the public opposed restarts.[192] All of Japan's fifty-four nuclear reactors remained shut down for two months until the Noda administration and the business community could convince the governors and mayors in Kansai to reverse their opposition "temporarily."[193]

Was the DPJ actually determined to unseat the nuclear village, as it sometimes declared? Was it readying a return to business as usual? Or was it simply being realistic? The uncertainty was embodied in the formation of the Fundamental Issues Subcommittee of METI's newly reorganized Advisory Committee for Natural Resources and Energy in October 2011. The subcommittee was charged with outlining options for a fundamental rethink of Japan's 2010 Basic Energy Policy. Nippon Steel's Mimura Akio was appointed chair, but in a remarkable departure from past practice, half the members were nuclear village critics.[194] The subcommittee, a disparate set of experts charged by METI minister Edano Yukio to pursue "out of the box" thinking, would cover a broad swath of issues from the nation's fuel mix to its industrial structure. But it arrived at disparate, "inside the box," conclusions.[195] In the event, whether because the goal was to map out different paths or (as the media reported) because differences among members were too great, the subcommittee punted on specific policies in favor of a range of possible paths that were already known.[196] So whatever the DPJ's national energy policy was or would become, the government was losing points with an increasingly skeptical public for failing to lead and failing to reduce the perceived threat posed by nuclear power.

There were DPJ inconsistencies and false steps in the regulatory arena as well. When the DPJ was in the opposition, it had called for separating NISA from METI and for integrating it with the NSC. But after gaining power, the DPJ backed away to what it called a more "realistic" position.[197] The events of 3.11 changed that stance. In one of its first and firmest policy declarations, the government announced in April 2011 that it would separate the NISA from METI after all and move the NSC out of the Cabinet Office.[198] It declared that a new National Safety Agency—modeled on the U.S. Nuclear Regulatory Commission—would be established in April 2012 inside the Environment Ministry, with responsibility for regulating power plant operations and for directing responses to nuclear accidents. In a historic change, the environment minister would now be responsible for regulating nuclear power. But again, history would have to wait. In February 2012, birth of the new agency was stalled—yet another victim of bureaucratic turf battles and competing priorities within the rapidly weakening DPJ.[199] Finally, in late July 2012, the members of the new agency were formally nominated. Two, including a presumptive chair who had helped formulate the government's ambitious pre-3.11 nuclear energy policy, were denounced as "nuclear village" members by dissidents within the party.

Notwithstanding the nuclear village critique, which focused on the collusion between a unified METI and the nuclear power industry—or the argument by former Fukushima governor Satō Eisaku that it was METI, and not TEPCO, that served as the "castle keep" (honmaru) for nuclear power—the Japanese bureaucracy was long divided on the merits of nuclear power.[200] Different bureaus within METI have had different preferences for years, though one official suggested that opponents could not press too hard because the industry was lobbying the LDP heavily. In his view, units inside the ANRE had always supported the utilities, but the Manufacturing and Industrial Policy Bureaus had supported end users and were displeased that TEPCO had not cooperated more enthusiastically with auto-generators and IPPs.[201] But even within the ANRE, a Renewable Energy Division was established after the 2008 G-8 Hokkaido summit when it became clear that METI was being blamed for falling behind Germany in the introduction of alternative energy technologies. Moreover,

METI was always deeply divided over "back-end" disposal and repro-cessing policies.

After 3.11, a cadre of antinuclear METI officials, sidelined after the fuel cycle battle of the early 2000s, came to be working in the National Strategy Office (*Kokka Senryaku Shitsu*) of the Cabinet Office, from which they hoped to produce a "progressive energy and environment strategy" (*kakushinteki enerugii kankyō senryaku*).[202] This office staffs the government's top decision-making organ for energy policy, the Ministerial Council on Energy and the Environment (*Enerugii Kankyō Kaigi*), created in June 2011 and chaired by the minister for national policy. Ex officio members include METI and envi-ronment ministers (vice chairs) and the ministers of economy and finance; education and science; agriculture, forestry, and fisheries; and land, infra-structure, and transportation; as well as the deputy chief cabinet secretary. Much like the METI Advisory Committee, from which it would receive detailed reports, the council insisted that every aspect of post-3.11 energy policy—industry structure, fuel mix, risk assessment, regulatory control—be put in play and that energy strategies be developed "from scratch."[203] To that end—again, like the METI committee—the ministerial council included a wide range of interests. It was no surprise that the first report of the coun-cil contained both pro- and antinuclear recommendations.

After 3.11, in a pattern reminiscent of the early decades of nuclear power, new competitors emerged within government for jurisdiction, particularly the Environment Ministry. Its 8 billion yen request for renewable energy projects in Tohoku in the third supplemental budget in 2011 was the largest government spending ever in this policy area and a direct challenge to METI's "smart community" projects, nearly all of which had been devel-oped in collaboration with the utility industry.[204] Also, the Ministry of Agri-culture, Forestry, and Fisheries (MAFF) sought to build distributed energy supply systems in local communities.[205]

NEW PLAYERS

The truly new players came from outside the central bureaucracy alto-gether because even in the absence of coherent leadership or formal policy decisions, the electric power industry was already changing. In May 2012, for example, after the last nuclear power plant went off-line, electric power continued to flow through the national grid; the shortfall was made up by natural gas, coal, and oil-fired thermal plants combined with conservation. This undercut the utilities' (and Keidanren's) frequent insistence that the end of nuclear generation would threaten supply stability.[206] The real test came several months later, during the summer months of peak demand af-ter the first restart of a nuclear reactor at Ōi in Fukui Prefecture in July. But there were no supply disruptions or brownouts. This partial return to busi-ness as usual—or at least to a realist mix that was expected to include a reduced but still substantial share of nuclear power in the electric power fuel mix—was hotly contested from the beginning by newly empowered policy entrepreneurs armed with their own narratives about the lessons of 3.11.

Challengers began to emerge even within the electric power sector, where some smaller utilities that relied more on fossil fuels were starting to distance themselves from the nuclear giants, the Kansai Electric Power Company and TEPCO.[207] While the large utilities drove Keidanren's vigorous support for nuclear business as usual, even Keidanren began to hedge its bets. In a tacit acknowledgment that new energy producers were in the wings and new sectoral logics were in the offing, Keidanren argued in its first post-3.11 energy policy statement that "cooperation between centralized and distributed electric power sources" would enhance stability and efficiency of supply.[208] Indeed, the interests of auto-generators in the heavy industrial sector and of fossil fuel importers now were at odds with those of the more nuclear dependent utilities. Several auto-generators, such as Mitsubishi Chemical and Nippon Steel, announced plans to increase supplies to the grid and seemed poised to make new efforts at establishing IPPs.[209] So did entirely new entrants, such as the unlisted Nihon Techno Company, which announced plans for a medium-sized, gas-fired plant in Chiba.[210] Osaka Gas, which operated the largest generating plant not owned by an electric utility, similarly announced it would increase output by the equivalent of one nuclear power plant by 2020.[211] In addition, several major firms closely associated with nuclear power, like the vendor manufacturers Toshiba and Hitachi and nuclear fuel trader Marubeni, were already repositioning themselves.[212] Venture firms with an eye toward smaller-scale generation using renewables began to appear after the government committed to reducing dependence on nuclear power.[213]

Several localities, led by the Tokyo Metropolitan Government, also announced plans to challenge the regional monopoly system by building their own thermal power stations, increasing direct electricity supply from IPPs, and even contracting for supplies from electric utilities other than their local monopoly.[214] The governors of each of the prefectures in the Kanto region joined with the mayors of the region's largest cities to petition METI to allow competition in the electric power sector, and the mayor of a Tokyo ward invited IPPs to bid on a contract to supply power to more than one hundred public facilities under his jurisdiction.[215] Aichi Prefecture announced it would go all in on renewables and conservation, and eighty-eight mayors assembled in Sapporo to discuss renewable and "smart city" projects.[216] After learning that TEPCO planned a 30 percent hike in transmission fees for the use of its grid, the Tokyo Metropolitan Government pressed for the deregulation of power distribution. As Deputy Governor Inose Naoki declared, "we want to show we have various options over our electricity supply."[217] A Yokohama city official concurred, saying that "the current system is pretty one-sided. We want to have a multilateral relationship in terms of energy use."[218] And Iwate governor Tasso Takuya explained that energy will soon be supplied by a great many different firms, including local ones: "The role of the electric utilities is declining. . . . We cannot be so dependent upon Tohoku Electric."[219]

Governor Tasso was anticipating (and participating in) an enormous change, one to which the utilities and Keidanren would have to respond. After 3.11 there was a growing sense that the twentieth-century model of centralized, one-way flows of electric power could be displaced altogether. What some have called "prosumption"—a twenty-first-century system in which the majority of homes and firms both produce and consume electric power—would be enabled and perhaps driven by "smart" technologies that provide real-time load, demand, and storage information. In this energy future, centralized power generation and distribution on a controlled grid will be less prominent than networked, distributed power generated on an interactive and open grid.[220] In a high-profile fight in the Keidanren boardroom over the future of national energy policy, Mikitani Hiroshi, the president of one of Japan's largest Internet firms, Rakuten, withdrew from the business federation to protest its support for business as usual.[221] But Mikitani was not the most prominent "new technology" challenger to centralized energy production. That title belonged to Japan's foremost entrepreneur, Son Masayoshi, the founder of Softbank, another of Japan's telecommunication and Internet giants. Unlike Mikitani, Son elected to remain in Keidanren in order to "make change from within."[222]

Son was anointed a hero by those who wished to wean Japan from its dependence on nuclear power, and even by those who simply wished to cheer the assault on.[223] Son assumed leadership of a bloc of renewable energy supporters—firms, national politicians, local chief executives—in Japan's most ambitious nongovernmental energy initiative, what he called Japan's "New Strategic Energy Plan—Version 2.0." This self-described "paradigm shift in energy" was straightforward. If his new firm, SB Energy, could secure the regulatory assistance of local governments and the right price for his solar-generated power, he would invest 80 billion yen to build ten "mega-solar" power plants across Japan that would provide 100 gigawatts of clean, safe power and pay rent for the use of public land.[224]

It was relatively simple to gain support and attention after 3.11, when the national discourse emphasized community (everyone sought it), insecurity (everyone felt it), leadership (everyone missed it), and change (everyone anticipated it). After an initial private meeting with a select group of governors in April 2011, Son organized a "Natural Energy Council" (*Shizen Enerugii Kyōgikai*) in which thirty-five of Japan's forty-seven prefectures and seventeen of its nineteen designated cities agreed to participate.[225] The council's first public meeting in Tohoku in July attracted widespread national attention.[226] Son and the governors worked on a plan by which the local governments would provide access to unused government land in exchange for a share of the electric power and revenue from Son's megasolar farms. Son projected that by 2030 his project could generate the equivalent of the output of fifty nuclear reactors, 60 percent of Japan's electric power.[227] In a more grandiose codicil to the initiative, Son also proposed to help create a 36,000 km Asia-wide electric power "super grid" connecting China, Korea, Japan, Malaysia, Thailand, the Philippines, Singapore, and India on the model of the DESERTEC plan to connect Europe and North Africa.[228]

The domestic version of Son's scheme was embraced by Prime Minister Kan and other critics of the nuclear village, but met immediate opposition from the electric power establishment and its allies.[229] The latter focused on the limits to renewables, in particular on the differences in scale between a 1-gigawatt nuclear plant and a 4-kilowatt home solar array. Even when solar is scaled up to ten million homes, they argued, the cost would be the equivalent of five nuclear power plants, but the output would meet less than 4 percent of national demand. To produce the same volume of power as a single nuclear plant, photovoltaics would require a land area equivalent to all of central Tokyo (67 sq km), and 100 gigawatts of photovoltaic power was considered a pipe dream.[230] Japan should be less focused on the unreliable 20 percent of electric power that might come from renewables and pay more attention to the secure 80 percent that had to come from nuclear, gas, and other thermal fuels.[231] Suzuki Tatsujirō, the deputy chairman of the AEC, explained that while Son's planned capacity would help during peak load periods, "it would not be nearly sufficient to replace nuclear energy."[232] One METI official called the Son plan "primitive" because it was based on subsidies, rather than on market logics. [233] Meanwhile, Miyagi Prefecture, which takes pride in its forward-leaning renewable energy program, refused to participate in Son's Natural Energy Council because it "did not feel it would be appropriate to invest in a program led by a single private firm for which tax exemptions and other considerations would be made."[234] There were also widespread *ad hominem* attacks on Son that mocked his insistence on "change from within" and his call for "more diverse voices" in the energy policy debate. Defenders of the nuclear status quo painted Son as a non-Japanese outsider who is "only in it for the money"—a reminder that he is ethnically Korean and a suggestion that other firms are somehow more patriotic.[235] LDP representative Kōno Tarō deplored this reaction as "character assassination."[236]

Son acknowledged that renewables were not economically competitive, and so if his investments were to make economic sense, he and other investors would need policy assistance. Son's council called on the government to set an ambitious national target for renewable power, with a legal requirement that utilities purchase all renewable power generated by independent firms and guarantee their connection to the grid.[237] Son's policy intervention of choice was the Feed-In Tariff (FIT), a European policy that advocates say drives down the cost and accelerates the diffusion of alternative technologies.[238] Under a FIT, utilities are required to purchase all the electric power generated by specified alternative energy technologies at prices set according to the power source for fixed periods of time. The cost to the utilities of such purchases is passed along to ratepayers.

By 3.11, the FIT already had an uneven history in Japan. In 2003, the utilities and their allies opposed the first effort to introduce it, agreeing instead to a Renewable Portfolio Standard (RPS). Unlike the FIT, the RPS required only that utilities acquire a fixed volume—set by the government—of their power from renewable sources. Since much of that volume could be acquired in-house, the utilities were not forced to nurture competing firms. Realizing they needed to change the terms of that debate, activists struggled to reposition the FIT from the province of a "triple minority" in Japanese politics—left-wing, antigrowth, antinuclear activism—to one that would attract conservative support. They did so by associating renewables with terms such as "domestic made" (*kokusan*) so that those on the right—particularly "clean hawks" such as former LDP defense minister Aichi Kazuo—would feel it unpatriotic not to support alternative energy.[239] They also leveraged the government's commitment under the 1997 Kyoto Protocol to reduce greenhouse gas emissions.

A proto-FIT was finally adopted in 2009, but it applied only to solar power and had a loophole allowing utilities to deny independent solar producers access to the grid if, in their judgment, access would threaten supply stability.[240] As a consequence, solar power grew, but uncertainties persisted for investors and Japan still lagged behind most other developed economies in the use of renewable energy. In 2010, ten other OECD countries had each invested more than Japan in this sector—$3.3 billion.[241] Advocates continued their struggle, and ironically, they succeeded just in time for 3.11 to change the entire policy landscape. New FIT legislation—the Law of Special Measures concerning the Procurement of Renewable Electric Energy by Operators of Electric Utilities (*Denki Jigyōsha ni yoru Saisei Kanō Enerugii Denki no Chōtatsu ni kansuru Tokubetsu Setchi Hō*)—was submitted by the cabinet to the Diet on 11 March 2011, just hours before the disaster in Tohoku.

At first, the FIT was stalled in Japan's "twisted" Diet, where the opposition controlled the upper House of Councilors. But when Prime Minister Kan made FIT's passage a condition for his stepping down in August 2011, the LDP softened its opposition. Before they would sign on, however, antinuclear activists inside the party worked with the DPJ and others to remove power over FIT rate setting from METI and place it in the hands of an independent commission appointed by the Diet.[242] METI officials were not used to this sort of political leadership. According to one, "Before 3.11 bureaucrats and major firms used advisory councils to make energy policy. But this changed after 3.11. . . . This [rate setting commission] arrangement is extremely unusual, and my colleagues are confused and angry."[243] That there was little they could do about it did not stop them from trying to pack the five-member commission. In November 2011, pro–alternative energy Diet members from both the DPJ and the opposition—all members of the *ene-shifu* caucus—blocked the nomination of three METI-approved nominees to the FIT rate-setting commission, one of whom had already testified against the FIT.[244]

Setting FIT prices at a level high enough to stimulate investment in alternative energy without burdening consumers and slowing growth required getting costs right. But the actual costs of electric power by fuel source had long been obscured. Although Japanese electric power costs were among the highest in the world, nuclear power supporters had always trumpeted their cost advantages over fossil fuels and alternative energy sources such as solar and wind.[245] Opponents of nuclear power had insisted that the actual costs were shielded from public view. The official figure of 5–7 yen per kilowatt-hour vastly underestimated the true costs which, opponents said, ought to have included the full panoply of siting subsidies, safety measures, health and decontamination costs, decommissioning expenses, compensation claims, and the engorged expenses associated with spent fuel reprocessing and storage facilities.[246] Son insisted that the real pre-3.11 cost of nuclear power was 15–20 yen per kilowatt-hour; once costs associated with the accident were factored in, nuclear would prove to be by far the most expensive source of electric power.[247]

To sort through these competing claims, the Ministerial Council on Energy and the Environment created an independent cost verification commission in the National Policy Office. Like the FIT price committee, this commission quickly became the object of efforts by both sides to pack it with partisans.[248] In December 2011, it revised nuclear costs upward to 8.9 yen per

Table 2 Cost of Electricity Generation by Source, 2010

Electric Power Energy Source	2010 Cost (yen/kWh)
Nuclear	8.9
Coal	9.5
Liquefied Natural Gas (LNG)	10.7
Oil	22.1
Wind	9.4–23.1
Geothermal	9.2–11.6
Solar (PV)	33.4–38.3

Source: Cost Verification Committee of the Ministerial Energy and Environmental Council, reported by the Institute for Energy Economics at http://eneken.ieej.or.jp/en/jeb/1201.pdf

kilowatt-hour, far less than Son and his allies had hoped.[249] As a result, the cost of nuclear power still compared favorably with other sources.

In April 2012, in what appeared to some as rent seeking, many of the first FIT price proposals from industry groups and potential investors were twice what the government had estimated. Son personally claimed that any solar FIT price set lower than 40 yen per kilowatt-hour would force him to abandon his project as unprofitable.[250]

That would have been fine with his many opponents, who raised several substantive objections. The first concerned FIT costs and their consequences for investment. At a June 2011 meeting of Keidanren's New Growth Strategy Implementation Conference, Chairman Yonekura insisted that rapid introduction of high-priced FITs would require a sharp increase in electric power rates that would in turn create disincentives for investors. The FIT would drive down costs of alternative energy systems, but only at great cost to consumers and at just the moment when nuclear power costs were increasing. Domestic firms, he predicted, would move offshore and prospective foreign investors would go elsewhere.[251] A second objection was that by setting prices for each energy source, the FIT would hinder fuel mix competition. Fixed long-term prices would reduce incentives for innovation and hinder competition.[252] Opponents also suggested that the FIT subsidy would amount to a regressive consumption tax on an essential product. One retired TEPCO executive complained without any evident irony that "the FIT is a subsidy system and private companies should not receive subsidies. Governments are always seeking to take money from people and industry. The FIT is a camouflaged tax."[253] A senior Keidanren staff person argued that opposition to the FIT is also a matter of social equity: "Large landowners can set out solar panels and get paid by the utilities, while the renters in cities have to foot the bill."[254]

Undoubtedly, however, the often unspoken mother of all objections was, as an *Asahi Shimbun* editorial suggested, that the FIT would "demolish the assumption that electric power must be produced in large power plants."[255] For some, the choice between renewables and nuclear power was a replay of the 1980s battle between mainframes and personal computers or the 1990s battle between landlines and mobile telephony in which large-scale monopolies or oligopolies eventually had to give way to more nimble competitors. As one foreign critic of the "nuclear village" has expressed it, "the challenge is whether to protect a monopolized, centralized, expensive, and probable cul-de-sac power economy, or to opt to innovate a potentially world beating, decentralized smart power economy."[256] This is precisely the paradigm shift that animated Son—himself a big winner in the telephony wars—and helps explain why he would not be deterred.

Having monitored closely the transformation of the energy sectors in Western Europe and North America, METI was hardly unaware of this potential shift, of course. It knew that in 2010, feed-in from renewables outstripped off-peak electric power demand in Europe, and global investment in solar energy had grown from 2 to 22 trillion yen after 2002. As recently as 2003, Japan had more installed solar energy capacity than Germany, but once the German government introduced its own FIT, solar capacity soared to eight times the Japanese level. Japan, which had nearly half of the world's installed solar capacity in 2005, plummeted to just 12 percent in 2009.[257] METI had little to show for decades of efforts to nurture an alternative energy sector that might serve as an engine for export growth.[258] It had promoted nuclear plants and services, of course, but officials understood that the larger market would be in green and distributed technologies. One of its studies predicted the market for small- and medium-sized generators, storage systems, interactive grids, smart buildings, and other green technologies would triple by 2021 to 86 trillion yen—reaching roughly half the size of the automobile industry—and then would more than double again by 2031.[259] So even before 3.11, and even as it embraced the ambitious nuclear power goals of the 2010 Basic Energy Plan, METI had turned to renewables.

The challenge for the industrial policy bureaucracy was to position Japanese manufacturing firms on the frontier of these shifts without abandoning either nuclear power or conventional utilities. To do so, METI promoted a "smart community" program with the active support of Keidanren. After vetting proposals from twenty consortia, METI designated four demonstration projects in August 2010—in Yokohama, where the city teamed with Toshiba and other firms in a household energy management project; in Toyota City, where the municipality and Toyota Motors were to enable homes to supply more than 60 percent of their own energy requirements; in Kyoto, where the prefecture teamed with Mitsubishi Heavy Industries and other firms to connect homes and vehicles with data exchange on power use and demand; and in Kitakyushu, where IBM Japan was to help the city install waste heat exchangers in homes and factories. In each case except Kitakyushu, the regional electric power company was at the center of the plan, and trading companies, equipment vendors, and systems integrators all joined with energy users.[260] By integrating the transport, construction, telecommunication, and energy infrastructures with public administration across a range of firms, METI hoped to "facilitate the development of next generation technologies in related industries, establish international standards for these technologies, and eventually strengthen the competitiveness of Japan's environmental and energy industries."[261] The question was whether it could achieve these ends while defending so many of the core institutions of the existing power system.[262]

Local governments may not have been as keen on preserving the existing system, but they certainly were opportunistic. For example, Iwate governor Tasso joined the Son initiative, but also negotiated with Toshiba and Toyota about their alternative energy programs. As he explained, "The competition for alternative energy supply is good from the prefecture's perspective. It gives us a chance to choose what is best for us."[263] After 3.11, local chief executives were not only experimenting more aggressively than ever with nonconventional suppliers but, in backing away from nuclear power, they were also exercising political power in high-profile—and, in some cases, entirely new—ways. First, Tokyo Prefecture, which owned 2.7 percent of the shares of TEPCO, and Osaka City, which owned 8.9 percent of Kansai Electric Power, threatened to demand utility restructuring at shareholder meetings.[264] Some governors and mayors had more visible impact, temporarily blocking restarts of reactors that had gone off-line for regular maintenance. Local officials had no formal legal basis to do so, but host localities did have "safety agreements" with utility companies that stipulated "local consent" before "any significant actions," including postmaintenance restarts, could commence. Even if such "gentlemen's agreements" lacked the force of law, the post-3.11 environment of public mistrust armed mayors and governors with considerable de facto veto power.[265] In July 2011, Niigata governor Izumida Hirohiko announced that he would not approve the resumption of operations at the off-line reactors in Kashiwazaki, even after completion of their "stress tests."[266] Fukushima governor Satō Yūhei called for the decommissioning of all ten reactors in his stricken prefecture.[267]

The highest profile case of all was local opposition to Noda administration plans to restart Kansai Electric Power Company's Ōi reactors in April 2012. Kansai Electric depended on nuclear power for half its electricity supply, making its service region particularly vulnerable during the high-demand period in the summer. But Osaka mayor Hashimoto—who already had declared his opposition to nuclear power and was leading a new reformist party with national ambitions—used the occasion to declare "all-out war" on the DPJ. Although he lacked jurisdiction in the matter—Osaka is 100 km from Ōi and in a different prefecture—the mayor set eight "conditions" for allowing restarts there (including abolition of nuclear power, separating generation from transmission, and ending *amakudari*), and was taken seriously by media analysts and by the two-thirds of the electorate that opposed the restarts.[268] In late April 2012, he discussed his demands (and, presumably, his declaration of war) with Chief Cabinet Secretary Fujimura Osamu at the prime minister's office.[269] Meanwhile, the governors of Kyoto and Shiga, prefectures with territory within the 30 km Urgent Protective Action Planning Zone around the Ōi reactor, invoked community safety concerns and resisted the government as well. So did Nagoya mayor Kawamura Takashi, who argued that a nuclear accident at Ōi would contaminate his residents' water supply.[270] Hashimoto and the other local chief executives ultimately backed off under pressure from the business community, but not until after flexing their political muscle.

Governors and mayors had a history of invoking legal authority under related but not reactor-specific powers. In 2007, for example, the mayor of

Kashiwazaki City used a local fire protection law to stop operation of the Kashiwazaki reactors after the Chūetsu earthquake. In an earlier case in 1998, Aomori governor Kimura Morio had used his authority over ports and harbors to refuse docking rights to a ship carrying high-level nuclear waste from France and successfully demanded a guarantee that Aomori Prefecture would not become the final disposal site for the waste without local consent. In similar ways, local power—both de jure and de facto—was wielded aggressively after 3.11, particularly in Kansai. After the Kansai Regional Union—a coalition of prefectures we examine in chapter 6—appealed directly to the Diet for renewable energy legislation, it secured unprecedented agreement from Kansai Electric that *it*, and not the individual prefectures, would be the first to be informed in the event of a nuclear accident.[271] When negotiations for the Ōi restart began in the spring of 2012, it was the alliance, and not the individual local governments, that the central government consulted. In addition, governors began refusing to accept nuclear waste storage, raising the pressure on the central government to find a solution to a problem it long had left unsolved.[272] Although the Kansai cities and prefectures reversed their position in the face of prospective brownouts in the summer of 2012—two Ōi reactors were restarted on 2 July—there was every indication that the balance of power was shifting in Japan, and not just in the electric power sector.

Throughout that summer, as anti-nuclear power protests gathered force, the government held hearings in eleven cities on the future of nuclear power. It presented three scenarios for public discussion of the share of electricity that would be produced by nuclear power in 2030—25 percent, 15 percent, and zero options. The overwhelming majority (70%) of those who asked to speak at these sessions favored the zero option. In addition, the government received more than fifty thousand comments from citizens—fifty times more than normal when public views are solicited on a policy issue in this way.[273] The Noda government had indicated its preference for the fifteen percent option, which it would achieve by decommissioning ageing reactors. But under intense pressure from all sides, the government repeatedly delayed announcing the new policy. When it finally did so in the face of a looming Lower House election, the DPJ government opted for an inconsistent and ambiguous "zero" nuclear target for the medium and long term. This satisfied no constituency: pro-nuclear interests were upset that the government had tilted in favor of phasing out nuclear power which, the business community insisted, would raise energy costs and destroy the economy. Anti-nuclear activists were disappointed that existing plants would restart, that construction would resume for those with pre-3.11 permits, that the reprocessing and FBR programs would continue, that there were no assurances that the 40 year age limit on existing plants would be enforced, and that the target date for elimination of nuclear power was pushed forward from 2030 to the 2040s.[274] Then, as if to underline the government's own lack of resolve, it "backtracked" a week later when the cabinet failed to endorse its new policy.[275]

Conclusion

After 3.11, Japan's vigorous debate over energy policy was anchored to ideas about change, community, leadership, and vulnerability. Those who saw villainy in the nuclear village extolled the virtues of a shift to distributed, community-based electric power generation. They would unwind a collusive and dangerous industry and deliver decision-making power over energy to local governments and eager entrepreneurs. Others saw villainy in failed national leaders and false prophets who would unplug decades of critical investments in nuclear energy and leave Japanese industry and the entire nation more vulnerable than ever. In every corner of the nuclear power industry, change—profoundly consequential change, championed by well-entrenched interests and new entrants alike—hung in the balance. And narratives of change, rooted in fundamentally different political interests with different resources, competed to define Japan's energy future.

TEPCO—nobody's hero—was central to the discourse. Within moments of the disaster, a company whose top officers had been among the most powerful political actors in postwar Japan, which had been hiring one thousand new employees each year, and which had only months earlier raised 450 billion yen in an equity offering, became a "zombie firm."[276] Standard corporate defense mechanisms—apologies by, pay cuts for, and retirements of senior executives—proved wholly inadequate to regain public confidence. Middle- and upper-level managers were headhunted and snapped up by equipment manufacturers, trading companies, and IPPs. In addition, hundreds of younger employees—what one executive ruefully called "the future of TEPCO"—resigned and returned to their hometowns to work on local energy projects or in family businesses.[277] TEPCO, whose share price lost about 90 percent of its value within the first three months of the meltdown, posted a 600 billion yen loss between April and December 2011 before its share price stabilized at about one-twelfth of its pre-3.11 height.[278] By early 2012, it was in state receivership, kept on life support only to generate revenue to compensate its victims. In the first quarter of 2012 alone, the central government injected 800 billion yen into TEPCO, and the company asked for 2 trillion yen more.[279] In April, the Noda government agreed to provide 1 trillion yen from the Nuclear Damage Liability Facilitation Fund to keep the firm running. TEPCO, the world's largest private utility until 3.11, was the first institution in Japan's energy system for which the catastrophe delivered major change. When the deal was consummated in July 2012, however, the government owned just over half of TEPCO, which gave it control of the board of directors but fell short of the three-quarters ownership it would need (and for which it had an option) to carry out full reform of the firm.[280] Thus, even in the case of TEPCO, change in firm ownership did not necessarily portend thoroughgoing changes in operation or structure.

Change elsewhere moved slowly and more uncertainly, if it moved at all. Some of those who evoked the virtues of community would not be satisfied with the destruction of a single firm. For them, change meant structural transformation of the electric power industry itself. This involved the seizure of prerogatives by local public officials, a shift toward alternative energy sources, and the embrace of new forms of power generation and transmission—based primarily in an upgrade from "dumb" one-way to "smart" two-way interactive systems. The 3.11 catastrophe also opened the way to a breakup of the utilities into separate generation and transmission firms. In this sense, it enabled yet another avenue of assault on the core business model of the postwar system.[281] Keidanren would accept separation by function or by legal entity, but only if both operations remained under the control of the existing utilities. In its view, the demerits of more-ambitious structural change were more numerous (instability of supply, excess investment, efficiency losses) than the merits (price competition). Keidanren and the utilities squared off against a divided DPJ government, part of which held that the future of nuclear power and the restructuring of the sector were its top two energy priorities. Whether declaring the need for Japan to put it in gear or stay the course, each party to the debates on structural reform, avowed that it cared deeply about protecting social solidarity.[282]

Those most concerned with vulnerability focused on storage, reprocessing, and other elements of Japan's underdeveloped, overpriced, and accident-prone nuclear "back end."[283] Here too, despite the October 2011 AEC finding that reprocessed MOX fuel was twice as expensive as "once through" uranium fuel, the prospect for 3.11-induced change remained uncertain. When Prime Minister Kan declared in the Diet that he would shut down the FBR program, he was attacked for abandoning Japan's long-held dream of energy independence.[284] A week after Science Minister Nakagawa Masaharu insisted that the government would not abandon the fast breeder program because Japan had already invested too much in it, fellow cabinet minister Hosono Gōshi told the press that the government was actively considering decommissioning Monju. Both were responding to the first post-3.11 budget screening committee (Government Revitalization Unit) report that announced a modest 10 percent cut in the Monju budget.[285] As one observer has noted, "[A] non-nuclear Japanese future is anything but a sure bet . . . [and] even with a scale down of nuclear power, there is a possibility that the policy of reprocessing will continue as a matter of political inertia."[286]

The post-3.11 political entrepreneurs most concerned with the failures of government leadership focused on getting the fuel mix right and insisted on preserving Japan's global position as technological leader in the nuclear power business. As nuclear power plants went off-line one after another in the year after 3.11, Japan experienced a sudden and unavoidable shift in its fuel mix. Policy advocates clashed on whether to privilege renewable technologies and euthanize nuclear power or to constrain the enthusiasm for unproven alternatives, and power producers rushed back to fossil fuels. Natural gas, what one think tank called "Japan's trump card" (even though it was imported and carbon based), was the early big winner during this period of uncertain transition. Imports increased by 18 percent in FY 2011, at a reported cost of more than 1 percent of gross domestic product (GDP).[287]

Even nuclear power won a victory of sorts. Before 3.11, the nuclear power industry and METI had designated nuclear plant exports as central to Japan's "new growth strategy," a program fully endorsed by the DPJ government.[288] In an echo of industrial policies past, manufacturers would join forces and the government would provide development assistance to countries to acquire Japanese nuclear plant construction and services—an "export infrastructure package."[289] There were a great many prospective takers, including Turkey, Lithuania, Jordan, and Vietnam. Unable to finance new projects after 3.11, TEPCO backed out of leadership and abandoned its dream of following Électricité de France as a global producer of electric power. But 3.11 had virtually no effect on the larger national strategy. As Utsuda Shōei, chairman of the trading firm Mitsui Bussan, put it, "It is important that Japan continue to contribute globally through improved nuclear technology as a matter of national energy policy and diplomacy."[290] Utsuda was echoing Prime Minister Noda, who declared immediately upon taking office that "we will firmly respond to the interests of countries that are seeking to use nuclear power to generate electricity."[291] Six months after the meltdown at Fukushima Daiichi, the Japan Atomic Power Company signed an agreement with Vietnam to conduct a feasibility study for two reactors, and in December 2011, the DPJ-dominated House of Representatives voted to approve civilian nuclear power agreements with foreign countries.[292] Despite the widely reported decision by Germany to phase out nuclear power, and its rejection by Italian voters in a national referendum, the International Atomic Energy Agency reported that most national nuclear power programs were unaffected by 3.11.[293] Staying the course on nuclear exports was the natural policy choice of Japan's *sōteigai* narrators, and one of their few post-3.11 victories.

Just as in the security realm, the energy sector saw less change in the first year and a half after the catastrophe than one might expect, given the stridency of the various narratives, the vigor of the debate, and the expectations of analysts. Apart from the nominal demise of TEPCO, substantive policy change seemed more likely in local jurisdictions, where local executives were closer to their alienated constituents and further from the grand strategic battles being fought in Tokyo. We turn now to see how local governance may have changed.

Repurposing Local Government

> The centralized administrative system that Japan has had since Meiji which fuses national and local governance is corroded. It cannot be fixed, but must be reset from the beginning.
> —Osaka mayor Hashimoto Tōru, May 2012

Local public administration—the delivery of services to residents by subnational governments—is hardly as dramatic as war fighting or as awesome as the production and delivery of energy by massive industrial machines. But it is no less consequential. Education, welfare services, property registration, transportation, public safety, recreation, voting—indeed, nearly everything in the public sphere related to birth and life, death and taxes, is the work of neighbors. They are quotidian tasks—until they are not. As 3.11 demonstrated in riveting detail, the quality of local governments and the systems in which they are embedded can themselves be matters of life and death. Consequently, as for security and energy, "getting local government right" has become central to a renewed national debate cloaked in language of change, community, vulnerability, and leadership. And, as in these other cases, parties to the debate assumed positions consistent with existing preferences that were aligned with our three models of change.

To understand the arguments for change, we must first understand how Japanese local government is structured and how it has functioned.[1] Local government operates at two levels, each with an elected chief executive and legislative assembly. Together, the budgets of these "local public bodies" account for nearly 60 percent of all public spending in Japan.[2] There are forty-seven prefectures that govern at the level beneath the central government; the Ministry of Internal Affairs and Communications (MIAC) has nominal supervisory responsibility. Until 2000, as much as 70–80 percent of the work of the prefectures had been delegated by central government ministries and agencies (loosely coordinated by MIAC), an arrangement long seen as contributing to the fractured "vertical administration" described in chapter 2. Critics also judged these "agency-delegated functions" to be at odds with the guiding principle of local autonomy because they were conducted beyond the scrutiny of the prefectural assemblies.[3] There are more than 1,700 cities, towns, and villages at the level beneath (some say subordinated to) the prefectures. In an effort to rationalize the provision of municipal services, three waves of amalgamation—in 1888–1889, 1953–1961, and 1999–2010—expanded the size of these municipalities and shrank their number dramatically.[4] At the higher end are seventeen "designated," thirty-nine "core," and forty-three "special" cities that enjoy relative autonomy from the prefectural authorities.[5] Most public administration in Japan is local: in January 2010, 83 percent of Japan's 3.5 million public officials worked at the local level.[6] Despite reforms to the system of agency delegation, two-thirds of the central government's 330,000 employees still worked in "field offices" outside Tokyo as recently as 2006, and in 2007, ninety different central government bureaus still ran nearly five thousand field offices.[7]

Agency delegation is only one of five tutelary mechanisms by which the central government has exerted control over local government. The second, finance, has been similarly problematic. For most of the postwar era, only one-third of local government spending was funded from local taxes, inspiring the widely used catchphrase "30 percent autonomy" to describe the true state of local administrative affairs. As recently as 2009, despite a partial shift of income taxes from the national to the local tax base, local taxes still accounted for only 36 percent of the 100 trillion yen in local government spending. The rest came from hundreds of different transfers from the central government and a small but growing number of local bond issuances.[8] Local government finances have deteriorated dramatically since the early 1990s. The three prefectures hardest hit on 3.11 were already in precarious straits, with particularly high levels of dependence on central government financial transfers and little capacity to raise funds on their own.

The third tutelary mechanism, the power of the central government to grant or withhold approval and permission for some local policy initiatives, has likewise sustained central prerogatives. The fourth mechanism, "administrative guidance," is an omnibus term for the profusion of notifications, guidelines, memoranda, model legislation, and orders issued by central government agencies for implementation by localities. The final mechanism is the continuing practice by which the central government packs strategic positions in local governments with its own officials—local budget directors may have been seconded from the Finance Ministry, civil engineering bureau chiefs may be on loan from the Ministry of Land, Infrastructure, Transport and Tourism (MLIT), vice governors may have parachuted in from the MIAC. In short, delegated functions are often implemented by delegated officials with delegated funds according to delegated guidelines—all at the expense of local autonomy.

Naturally, the status of local autonomy has been disputed for decades. Localities seeking to expand their freedom responded to Tokyo's control in two ways. The first was overtly political. By the early 1970s, a time when national politics was still dominated by the conservative Liberal Democratic Party (LDP), opposition politicians on the left found that they could use bully pulpits at the local level. Cities with opposition-based mayors such as Yokohama, Osaka, and Kyoto, and prefectures with opposition-based governors, Tokyo being the most prominent, began to innovate in health care and education, as well as in environmental regulation, in ways that generated considerable public support. Within a few years, nearly half the population of Japan was living in municipalities or prefectures governed by a chief executive endorsed by the Socialist Party, the Communist Party, or both. The LDP responded creatively, co-opting many of these innovative programs.[9]

An important precedent had been set for Japanese democracy: voters had demonstrated that they would respond to substantive policy choices, and politicians learned that they needed more than business, family, or factional connections to be reelected. Competitive national elections of the sort now familiar in Japan originated (and persist) in local politics. Along the way, as we have seen with regard to military basing and the regulation of nuclear power, mayors and governors had learned how to exercise power despite their limited fiscal and administrative resources.[10] Some believe that 3.11 will further empower them, as mayors and other local politicians are being entrusted to decide where and how to rebuild their devastated communities.[11]

The second solution was both political and administrative. Local governments learned how to collaborate and, by doing more together, they learned how to get more from themselves and the center. Ironically, from the perspective of 3.11, the earliest forms of translocal policy coalitions were the Tokugawa-era "assistance agreements" (ōen kyōtei), promises of mutual aid in the event of a natural disaster. This practice was later enshrined in the 1961 Disaster Response Basic Law (Bōsai Taisaku Kihon Hō).[12] By the 1980s, horizontal linkages among localities were actively serving five different functions. The first was *communication*. Policy innovation diffused through a great many channels, but local governments learned through trial and error that they could rely at least as much on each other for new policy ideas as on higher levels of government. Second, as localities learned that they often could be more successful making collective demands on the center than by petitioning alone, they created nationwide and regional mechanisms designed to facilitate the *acquisition* of resources. Third, horizontal coalitions were also built as cheerleaders to *support* central government plans and programs. In some cases, petitioning by interest groups assembled by extralocal interests was required before new projects could be initiated. *Opposition* has long been a fourth function for coalitions of local governments. Some groupings have been partisan, others policy specific. The fifth function, *proposition*, came of age in the 1980s and has matured since, as localities became increasingly innovative, often generating new policy ideas well ahead of the central government.

While each of these forms of horizontal linkages continued to proliferate, the original function, assistance, was reinvented after the Hanshin/Awaji disaster in January 1995. In the first two months after that earthquake, other localities provided nearly two hundred thousand person-days of assistance from firefighters, social workers, civil engineers, medical specialists, and others. Ten thousand came from Osaka alone, and 175 workers dispatched from beyond the prefecture worked for six months or longer at Hyogo prefectural offices.[13] Soon afterward, the central government established a system for sharing fire departments, and in 2006, the National Association of Governors (NAG) developed a baroque mechanism for the transfer of officials to disaster-stricken areas; it proved too unwieldy to implement after 3.11.[14]

But the greatest impact bubbled up from the localities themselves. Mutual disaster assistance agreements (*bōsai sōgo kyōtei*) between localities— usually no longer than a single page—became the voluntary "risk hedge" of choice after Kobe.[15] Mayors pledge mutual assistance, including provision of shelter for displaced persons, and promise to provide relief supplies and seconded officials with expenses borne by the affected locality. Emergency response plans are exchanged and contacts are clearly stipulated. Localities are not required to register these agreements, and even MIAC does not know how many have been signed since 1995. One MIAC official seconded to Yamagata Prefecture reported that Yamagata had signed one of these agreements with each of its neighbors, and guessed they number in the thousands nationwide.[16] Tokyo crafted similar "wide area support" arrangements with each of its neighboring prefectures and special cities.[17] These agreements were far more than faint echoes of the Edo period. This newly robust but informal practice proved to be the most consequential of all in the aftermath of 3.11, when unaffected localities, acting entirely on their own, reached out to stricken localities to provide support.

This informal elaboration of horizontal ties proceeded in tandem with the limited (and repeatedly aborted) efforts at larger-scale decentralization by the central government. One example was the 1995 amendment of the Local Autonomy Law that would allow neighboring prefectures and municipalities to form regional councils to implement policies such as environmental regulation, tourism, and transportation systems that extend beyond the borders of the individual units. These "regional unions" (*kōiki rengō*) joined a variety of existing legal organs for horizontal cooperation, such as the outsourcing of services to neighboring localities, creation of partial affairs associations for service delivery, and use of joint facilities. Unlike most organs, which are limited to specific policy areas, however, the new regional unions could administer polices across functional areas. They require legislation at the local level and creation of a new administrative unit. While they cannot generate their own revenue and must depend on fees allocated from each member locality, they can assume the responsibilities of higher levels of government. They are therefore seen as an important prototype, or at least as a "more realistic alternative," for structural reform of the prefectures.[18] By July 2010, these various arrangements taken together accounted for more than 7,500 cases of translocal policy cooperation.[19]

Although it received only limited media attention, the formation of these regional unions was a major step forward for local autonomy. By July 2010, just fifteen years after the tool was created, nearly 2,300 localities were participating in 115 regional unions nationwide; there had been only 82 such arrangements in 2004.[20] More than half of these unions provide health services for aged and handicapped citizens, but in Kyushu, a regional union was used to harmonize tax ordinances, and a union of Tohoku prefectures invoked the model to harmonize ordinances in more than twenty areas as a first step toward what some hoped would become a "Tohoku State." The progressive development of horizontal solidarity was the course on which local governments found themselves when 3.11 struck—the only course on which decentralization was actually seeing progress. It was therefore the one from which local governments drew greatest strength as they sought to recover from the catastrophe.

Like local autonomy, decentralization has been elusive. Although there is widespread support for decentralization as an ideal, "everyone has a different idea about what form it should take."[21] In 1995, after decades of failed attempts to reform the prefectures by replacing them with "states," the LDP-backed Murayama government passed a Decentralization Promotion Law. This law created a committee with the declared goal of making local governments "equal" to the central government. In the 1990s, in the context of national-level administrative reform and a concern over local debt, support for prefectural mergers gathered new steam in the business community, and also among governors for the first time.[22] One of the first to take up the cause was Ōmae Kenichi, a management consultant, author, and prolific public intellectual who criticized the regional unions as "half-baked" and used the state system (dōshūsei) as a central platform.[23] In 1992, he established the Heisei Restoration Society (Heisei Ishin no Kai) as his political base. In 1995, he published a road map for switching to a state system, and his efforts would continue to reverberate across the next several decades and influence Hashimoto Tōru, the nationally ambitious Osaka governor (and later mayor) who shared his enthusiasm for the state system and for whom he continued to consult after 3.11.[24]

In April 2000, the number of local functions was increased and agency delegation was nominally abolished. The problem of local finances persisted, however. The next year, in what were called the Trinity Reforms to increase local revenues and local autonomy through decentralization, the Koizumi government set a goal to reduce tied grants and subsidies by 3 trillion yen per year, to reform the subsidy system that had kept localities on a short tether, and to reduce the local allocation tax. At least nominally, local governments would have fuller control of their revenues and greater freedom to implement policies of their choice. In announcing these reforms, Koizumi characteristically made the Cabinet Office responsible for decentralization, going over the heads of his Finance Ministry and MIAC.[25]

This was both cause and effect of opposition to reform by the ministries and agencies in the central bureaucracy. The bureaucracy pushed back vigorously, local finances remained unhealthy, and the chronic political competition between the LDP and the Democratic Party of Japan (DPJ) ensured that it would take nearly five more years for the political class to agree on how to proceed.[26] Ōmae, Keidanren, and others complained about the pace of change and pressed harder, arguing that the state system would "unleash the creativity" of the Japanese people, pull the nation back from the brink of fiscal insolvency, and eliminate the corruption and collusion that constrain national development (*oshoku ya dangō*).[27] In 2006, Ōmae declared that Koizumi was moving too cautiously, and pressed for the state system to be imposed once the remaining central field offices were integrated and prefectural unions constructed. Later that year, the LDP tried again to foster the large-scale transfer of central functions to local jurisdiction. And once again the plan involved strengthening horizontal intergovernmental coordination.

With progress on decentralization slowed from a perambulatory stroll to a crawl, Prime Minister Abe Shinzō appointed a special minister for decentralization reform, Masuda Hiroya, a former MIAC bureaucrat and governor of Iwate Prefecture, who committed himself to promoting "self-reliance and mutual cooperation" among localities. Prospects for reform got a further boost when Abe set up a ministerial post for the state system in 2006 and organized an initiative to create a "pilot" state system for Hokkaido and any other three or more neighboring prefectures.[28] Following Koizumi's lead, Abe did this through the Cabinet Office as a way to bypass opposition within the central bureaucracy, which stood to be slimmed down in the reform. Now, for the first time, the general idea enjoyed support from the NAG, the majority of whose members were finally convinced that a state system might actually reduce central oversight and deliver untied resources.[29] Proposals for a state system with nine, eleven, and thirteen states were floated, and a vigorous competition for regional leadership ensued. Different prefectures volunteered to become state capitals; Hiroshima and Okayama vied for leadership of a "Chūgoku state."[30] This final pre-3.11 effort to introduce the state system collapsed when the LDP surrendered power to the DPJ in 2009 and party boss Ozawa Ichirō reversed the DPJ's long-held support for the reform.[31]

Ozawa had famously argued in his 1994 *Blueprint for a New Japan* for a "new decentralization" that would "restrain the power of the central government . . . [which] suppresses people's potential and produces quiescent citizens overly dependent on authority."[32] He did not propose to abolish prefectures, but would devolve most of their functions to a single tier of three hundred municipalities—a number and scale reminiscent of the *han* (fiefs) before the Meiji modernization in the late nineteenth century. Delegated central functions would be abolished and, with the exception of a limited number of functions such as defense and public health, most administrative and fiscal responsibilities would become municipal. Local chief executives would no longer be treated as "approved representatives of the national government." So Ozawa never supported the state system, and when he had his chance to kill it after the historic electoral victory of the DPJ in 2009, he did so.

The new DPJ government under Hatoyama Yukio, armed with a series of now meaningless party manifestos promising to end centralized public administration, rejected an agreement hammered out by the previous government with the National Associations of Mayors and Governors, and pressed instead for what it called for "regional sovereignty reform."[33] Hatoyama, presumably under Ozawa's tutelage in this as in most matters, declared that he wished the positions of the central and local governments to be reversed, and proposed a new five-year plan that was a hodgepodge of measures, including an increase in local government control of revenues, revision of the Local Autonomy Law, abolition of the statutory limit on the size of local assemblies, disassembly of central government field offices, an end to all "tied" subsidies, establishment of a local judiciary, and (in yet another discursive echo) further enhancement of horizontal cooperation among local governments. Nothing was going to happen any time soon.[34] Even after Ozawa's star faded within the party, the DPJ never again returned to support of prefectural consolidation or the state system.[35]

By now, though, the localities were taking matters into their own hands—at least for those matters over which they had some control. Chief among them was horizontal cooperation, a mechanism that both parties and central government had flagged as essential to reform. In December 2010, just three months before 3.11, seven prefectures in the Kansai area, Japan's second most prosperous region, created the Kansai Regional Union (*Kansai Kōiki Rengō*). According to one of its architects, Hyogo governor Ido Toshizō, the governors allied to enhance industrial development and eliminate central government field offices, but also to deal collectively (and presciently) with crisis management.[36] Therefore, it should not be surprising that, as discussed in chapter 5, one of the most pointed challenges to plans by central government to restart nuclear reactors after 3.11 was made by local officials in the name of the Kansai Regional Union or that, in the first such agreement between a utility and a *federation* of local governments, Kansai Electric agreed to demands that the union be notified in the event of a nuclear accident.[37] Likewise, it should be no surprise that it was this particular coalition of local governments that was first off the mark with "counterpart support"—the most innovative form of assistance to Tohoku localities after 3.11, and possibly the most innovative policy initiative to emerge from the crisis overall.

Opened Windows

So challenges to the local government system were already under way when the central government seemed to fumble in its response to 3.11. Hyogo governor Ido connects the two: "3.11 revealed the weakness of excessive concentration of power in Tokyo. As a result, we will see even more effort to decentralize and the emergence of a local government system in Japan that is more balanced between Kanto and Kansai."[38] Citizens appreciated this. In an August 2011 survey, nearly 60 percent identified the central government as the least reliable source of information after a disaster—up more than 22 percent from a survey taken before 3.11—and more than one-fifth identified prefectures and municipalities as the most reliable sources of disaster information.[39] Post-3.11 dissatisfaction with the central government was palpable and widespread at the local level, and local officials were the immediate beneficiaries. As one former MIAC official acknowledged, "People always felt that the central government would help them, but now they are doubtful. Public trust in central officials is low, but it is growing for governors and mayors who have nowhere else to go and must work for the revitalization of their communities."[40] The nation's governors understood this and, as early as April, some 60 percent of them—including those who had nothing but praise for the SDF—expressed dissatisfaction with Tokyo's response.[41]

But sometimes the frustrations among local chief executives were less calculated and more heartfelt. The mayor of Rikuzentakata, an Iwate community devastated by the tsunami, lamented that central government officials and politicians treated him and his community as photo opportunities: "They come here and see the rubble and declare 'Wow, how awful! We can't let this be,' and then they go back to Tokyo, where they soon forget everything."[42] Mayor Toba's was not the only *cri de coeur*. Delays in central government assistance became especially prominent after his counterpart in Minami Sōma, Mayor Sakurai Katsunobu, pleaded for assistance on YouTube on 24 March and complained about the lack of information about the Fukushima Daiichi meltdown.[43] The day after his video went viral globally—at a time when more than 70 percent of his residents were displaced— the central government issued a voluntary evacuation order which, Mayor Sakurai says, merely threw the city's residents into further confusion. How could so many who were already "internally displaced" now face "voluntary relocation"? By April, Mayor Sakurai, who had endured the loss of thirty-six of his staff in the tsunami, had become so well known and powerful that he could confront the deputy chief cabinet secretary directly in Tokyo.[44] Given widespread perceptions of the failure of central government and given the deepening support enjoyed by local political leaders, 3.11 pushed the window wide open for local government reform.

Local officials were among the first to suggest that 3.11 would stimulate systemic change in Japan. Asano Shirō, a former governor of Miyagi Prefecture, said 3.11 was an opportunity for a complete overhaul of Japan's local government system.[45] Similarly, a former city mayor and leading local government reformer, Hosaka Kunio, wrote that 3.11 should be used as a "starting point for change of the entire system of public administration."[46] Iwate governor Tasso became convinced that "3.11 will make local governments stronger than ever," based on his frustration with the central government during the crisis, and suggested that a historic role reversal is under way. The central government depends more than ever on local governments for information and guidance, and local governments are coming to depend more than ever on each other.[47] Hyogo governor Ido took this further, pointing out disdainfully that central government officials seem clueless about their loss of legitimacy: "Most of those in the central government insist that 3.11 demonstrated the importance of their role, and oppose any shift in administrative authority to larger regional units or the elimination of field offices."[48] One MIAC central government official stationed in its Morioka field office agreed, confidentially: "There will be change in the system. The center has direct contact now with the municipalities. Our work is no longer mediated through the prefectures and there is real give and take in our discussions. Their basic stance is to not be dependent on us."[49]

Policy intellectuals were not far behind in connecting 3.11 with the prospects for system change. Meiji University professor Nakabayashi Itsuki saw an opportunity to use the Tohoku recovery as a test bed for innovative policy. In what he calls "recovery before the fact," 3.11 would provide a chance to incubate new ideas about public administration that could later be adopted nationally.[50] Hirayama Yōsuke, a professor of urban planning at Kobe University, declared the 3.11 "crisis as an opportunity," and laid out a program of community building that would have implications for local public administration across the country.[51] An *Asahi Shimbun* editorial in September 2011 argued that "the recovery effort ought to be used to review the relationship between central and local governments."[52] Even the vice chair of the Reconstruction Design Council predicted that local governments would now seize the lead in changing public administration.[53] Australian lawyer and policy analyst Joel Rheuben frames the issue and the expectations with particular clarity: "[A]s the potential frustration of dealing with a central government-focused reconstruction bureaucracy slows down regional initiatives and hollowed out local governments assess their long term viability, a very different type of regional governance could rise from the ashes of Northern Japan."[54]

Will the widespread enthusiasm for such change be sustained? Some, like a deputy mayor of Yokohama, think not. He ruefully suggested just six months after the catastrophe: "Yes, local government should change. And everyone was enthusiastic about the prospects for change, but I sense the enthusiasm has disappeared. Momentum has been lost and I am concerned."[55] As in security and energy, so expectations for post-3.11 change in local administration come in three narrative models: one that posits accelerated forward movement (put it in gear), one that argues for a deepening of extant trends (stay the course), and a third that suggests Japan should return to better times past (reverse course).

Narratives of Local Government Change

REDIMENSION JAPAN

Two arguments for putting it in gear sprouted from the ruins of 3.11. Both argued that it now was time to "redimension" local public administration. The first builds on decades of failed efforts to consolidate the prefectures and replace them with a limited number of "more efficient" states. The second rejects efforts to rationalize and consolidate public services, arguing instead for bringing local government closer to residents. I call the first "supersize me" and the second "localize me." Both leverage off the leadership and community tropes, and each is justified by proponents as the true lesson of 3.11.

"Supersize me." The 3.11 "supersize me" narrative is built on two components, each of which values scope and scale; the business community and its political and administrative allies spin both out of positive externalities from Tohoku reconstruction. The first is economic: The introduction of large-scale commercial operations as part of regional recovery would not only bring prosperity to the region but also open it to world trade, and consequently diffuse prosperity across Japan. On this account, Tohoku was a backwater because it had relied on small and medium enterprises. Fix problems of economic scale and the economy will deliver a bundle of public goods, including stable energy supplies, reduced taxes, deregulation, and labor market reform.[56] The second is administrative: Larger administrative districts—whether amalgamated municipalities or consolidated prefectures—would enhance efficiency and, presumably, reduce political noise in the delivery of public services. Fewer regions with wider jurisdiction will provide more effective leadership and ensure better public service.

"Supersizers" aimed to implement two different but closely connected mechanisms to attain scope and scale in public administration. Both had been in the wings for decades, their proponents waiting for an opportune time for wide-scale adoption.[57] The first is the "special zone" (*tokku*) model that the "localizers" wield even more effectively. Designed by the Hashimoto administration in the early 1990s and introduced by Prime Minister Koizumi a decade later, special zones are designated by the central government at the request of localities or private firms wishing to gain regulatory relief for specific products or programs.[58] When a special zone is established, a "central-local conference" is created to coordinate the views of the various central and local actors. The Cabinet Office nominally serves as a sort of traffic cop, directing line agencies and ministries to relax their regulatory grip in specific, approved cases.[59] The government has two goals for the special zone model: The first anticipates the community trope—to sustain the special features of local industry by connecting it to regional vitality. The second evokes the leadership trope—to diffuse successful examples to promote structural reform nationwide.[60] In 2010, there were fewer than five hundred proposals for such special zones, and most of the zones that had been approved had only limited impact.[61] They were largely ignored by localities—and derided by the business community—because, due to their narrowly targeted "one zone for one task" formula, they created more red tape than they eliminated.[62]

After 3.11, however, the Cabinet Office declared that "comprehensive special zones" would be a "break out" instrument for solving administrative problems and realizing "strategic growth."[63] When asked if he thought that special zones, even "comprehensive" ones, might help solve the problems of scope and scale in public administration, Nagoya mayor Kawamura Takashi (an outspoken "localizer," whose leadership during the crisis is examined later in this chapter) referred to central authorities as "idiots" (aho mitai).[64] Still, the status of special zones markedly improved after 3.11. The special zone became the modal format of the detailed reconstruction plans submitted by Tohoku prefectures, and the idea of a "comprehensive special zone" for the region was supported by the DPJ, the central bureaucracy, national groups, and Miyagi governor Murai.[65]

The second, more ambitious, reform to promote scope and scale after 3.11 was the phoenix-like "state system." The crisis provided the perfect opportunity to revisit the idea. In May, Keidanren, the most aggressive "supersizer," incorporated scale enhancement directly into its first post-3.11 policy program. It elevated disaster prevention and enhanced first-response capabilities on its long and varied list of public goods that the state system would engender.[66] In doing so, it reprised many of the recommendations it made after the Hanshin/Awaji earthquake in 1995, now substituting Tohoku for Hyogo as the ideal pilot region for administrative reform.[67] In this "Master Plan" and in subsequent reports, Keidanren called for rebuilding the affected areas "efficiently and effectively." The first step would be the creation of a Disaster Revival Special Zone (shinsai fukkō tokku), a comprehensive region-wide collection of appropriate regulations, tax breaks, financial support, and administrative measures to facilitate investment under the guidance of central authorities. Declaring that "views of the residents of the affected areas would be valued," Keidanren sought an "appropriate division of labor" between central and local governments and stressed the importance of considerable authority for a General Headquarters for Disaster Recovery. This headquarters, chaired by the prime minister, would draft legislation, coordinate budgets, and harmonize policy across ministries.[68] Keidanren imagined that the fruit of this special zone would include industrial clusters of higher-value-added, advanced technology firms and the development of "large scale and managerially sophisticated" primary producers who would rebuild the region. Construction of this special zone "control tower" (*shireitō*) would guide the nation to the state system.[69] According to a senior official there, "Keidanren prefers a Tohoku-wide special zone with a central government supervisory office (*fukkōchō*) that would pioneer the national consolidation of local government into a state system. The 'State of Tohoku' (*tohokushū*) would be a model for introduction of the state system nationwide."[70]

This is exactly what some governors and national legislators fear most about post-3.11 reform. Democratic Socialist Party Policy Affairs Committee chair Abe Tomoko called the state system "nothing other than a minicentralization," and compared it to prewar military organizations.[71] Former Fukushima governor Satō Eisaku did not go that far but, comparing the supersizers' strategy to the metaphorical diversionary fire that allows thieves to enter neighboring homes (*kajiba dorobō*), he warned that business and government leaders would use 3.11 to eliminate prefectures and to "capture localities."[72] Other governors, like Iwate's Tasso, reject the idea as distancing public administration from the citizens.[73] On his account, "the state system would be very hard for Tohoku. Our prefectures have well established functions and our size is already enormous. We'd need a helicopter to travel between Sendai and Morioka."[74] Hyogo governor Ido Toshizō is also very cool to the idea of the state system. He says that business leaders support it because "they don't want to have to bow to so many governors." The states, he says, would not be "local," but would remain dependent on the central government and its field offices: "It would be 'do as the central government says.'"[75] Ido insists on separating regional cooperation from regional consolidation. The former, which is critical, can be accomplished through regional unions, such as the Kansai Regional Union that he chairs.[76] One DPJ Diet member and former MIAC bureaucrat, Ogawa Junya, offered a more cynical explanation: he says that support and opposition to the state system is not a matter of policy orientation but "a calculation of gains and losses." Central government ministries and agencies would lose slots for retired officials, and most governors would not survive consolidation because each state needs only one governor and one capital city.[77]

But there was one influential supersizer among the region's leaders: Miyagi governor Murai Yoshihiro. He proposed to the Reconstruction Design Council a special zone within which commercial marine product and fishery firms could participate alongside (some say compete with) existing cooperatives to grow the industry in Miyagi Prefecture. His "Eastern Japan Recovery Zone" would involve a decade of tax breaks and central funding in eight areas including construction, agriculture, industrial consolidation, and seafood processing.[78] Embracing the "put it in gear" approach, Governor

"Of course it's good! The State System." Cartoon courtesy of Keizai Kōhō Center, Keidanren.

Murai invoked the errors of Hyogo Prefecture after the Hanshin/Awaji disaster. Hyogo erred by establishing a return to the status quo ante as its reconstruction goal. By planning to past benchmarks, Kobe lost out to other ports and manufacturing centers. Murai insisted: "people have a memory of pre-3.11 seared into their heads, but times change relentlessly. If we are going to make plans, it is essential that we focus on the shape of Japan and on the shape of Tohoku ten years from now."[79]

Dominating that future landscape in Miyagi, as in other localities dependent on primary industry, is the fact that half the fishery workforce is aged sixty or older and that many are not inclined (or likely) to return to the sea even after reconstruction. Murai knew that in a single day, Miyagi's fishing industry had added ten years to its demography. With a declining workforce and without new financial resources or technological innovation, only a fraction of the prefecture's 142 fishing ports would be rebuilt. The industry would die. He proposed, therefore, to supersize the industry by ending the licensing monopoly of the local fishing cooperatives and opening the ports to large commercial firms per the Keidanren agenda.[80] According to Gakushūin University professor Akasaka Norio, a Tohoku native and fellow member of the Reconstruction Design Council: "Governor Murai is not from Tohoku, but from Hokkaido. He was backed from the beginning by the business community and Tokyo think tanks that are trying to transform the region. That was the origin of his proposal."[81] Governor Murai and Keidanren were hardly alone. The idea of supersizing Japan after 3.11 stimulated a nationwide conversation. A Japanese-language Google search for disaster (*daishinsai*) and state system (*dōshūsei*) six months after the catastrophe surfaced nearly half a million hits. A citizens' group—the rump of Ōmae's 1990s initiative—asserted on its website that the national response to 3.11 would have been more effective had Japan already had a state system in place: prefectures would not have had an incentive to "siphon off assistance from neighboring prefectures" and would have had sufficient infrastructure to meet the challenge.[82] The group announced creation of "the first post-disaster state system café"—a website where citizens could discuss how things might have turned out differently if states, rather than prefectures, had been on the front lines of local public administration.[83] Another blogger representative of much of the Web chatter after 3.11, a member of the Japan Local Autonomy Research Association, headlined a "Connection between the State System and Regional Rebirth One Month after the Great Eastern Japan Disaster." Now, he insisted, was the chance to introduce the state system.[84] *Toyo Keizai*, the influential weekly, concurred, calling the state system a "cornerstone of nation building after the disaster," and its sister publication, *Shūkan Tōyō Keizai*, argued that it should be the "central axis" of national recovery.[85] In May 2011, 130 Diet members created a suprapartisan State System Discussion Group to discuss the creation of a "Tohoku State."[86] Your Party, a small but popular opposition party that champions decentralization, began calling for the state system to be applied in Tohoku. Evoking the community ideal, one of its leaders, Eguchi Katsuhiko, insisted that "we must use this opportunity to close the books on the centralized system and promote the state system as the basis for new nation building."[87]

Making things bigger was only one part of the argument that Japan needed to be redimensioned. A second argument held that making things smaller was the better way to proceed. The former had deeper pockets and longer legs, but the latter was more evocative and had tighter heartstrings. And it, too, won high-visibility support.

"Localize me." Considerable resistance to the state system and to other supersizing reforms survived 3.11; indeed, in some circles it stiffened. Much of the opposition was based on the view that the Heisei wave of municipal amalgamations—the first step toward a state system—had hindered 3.11 rescue and relief efforts.[88] Former Fukushima governor Satō insisted that several newly formed cities, such as Minami Sōma and Tamura, had become so large that emergency services were too far from residents to help them. Had the towns and villages not been merged, he argued, they could have saved more lives. The supersizers' counterproductive insistence on rationalizing services and efficiencies of scale led to "a chaotic situation" because it weakened the capacity of localities to respond precisely when responses were most needed.[89] One policy planner in the Iwate prefectural government agreed: "Amalgamation led to a reduction in the number of local officials, which surely had a negative effect on the emergency response: there were fewer first responders, fewer administrators to carry the load."[90] This was confirmed by the local media. The *Kahoku Shimpō* reported that due to amalgamation, the number of local government workers in Ishinomaki City, the second largest city in Miyagi and one of the hardest hit, had been reduced by 40 percent. Demands on the remaining officials—three hundred fewer than before amalgamation—overwhelmed them. There were also communication problems between city halls and branch offices that once had been town and village halls and now were understaffed.[91]

There was also the matter of inequality. Many of the amalgamated cities were in demographic and economic decline—indeed, this was part of the justification for their "rationalization." But neighboring localities that had agreed to accept nuclear power plants were, as discussed in chapter 5, enriched by subsidies and suddenly prosperous. Genkai in Saga, Onagawa in Miyagi, Higashi Dōrima in Aomori, and Kariwa in Niigata, as well as six towns along the Fukushima coast (Namie, Futaba, Ōkuma, Tomioka, Naraha, and Hirono), each judged that there would be no benefit from amalgamation—indeed, they would have to share the subsidies—and therefore opted out.[92] So, while some new cities ended up with skeletal services across a sprawling geography, the newly rich towns could bulk up services within their existing boundaries.[93]

Hyogo governor Ido Toshizō framed the problem in terms that point us toward the "localize me" narrative: "The Heisei amalgamation was a failure. All we did was reduce the number of mayors. Now some cities are larger than small prefectures. The flow of citizens to local officials was cut off, downtowns were strangled, and citizens have nowhere to go. We need smaller, not larger units of government."[94] While there were no obvious heroes or villains in the 3.11 "supersize me" narrative—except perhaps for Ozawa Ichirō, the former DPJ *éminence grise* who killed the final pre-3.11 state system proposal—there were many of both in the "localize me" alternative. For example, the head of the Policy Affairs Committee of the Democratic Socialist Party, Abe Tomoko, praised the mayors: "while the central government dawdled, the mayors took action. Excellent future mayors and governors will emerge from the crisis."[95] For Iwate governor Tasso, the 3.11 heroes were the small producers who will inherit a robust future in Tohoku. Others demonized the promoters of amalgamation and the state system. The *Asahi Shimbun*, for example, editorialized about the "dead hand of the central government" and wondered "why must local governments ask the central government for permission at every step while they are trying to decide on the future of their communities?"[96] Former Fukushima governor Satō attacks promoters of the state system and insists that putting efficiency ahead of public service is anathema.[97] Invoking an administrative variant of the leadership motif, others opposed the "supersize me" model by arguing that "efficiency-seeking structural reformers had destroyed farming and fishing villages."[98]

Crisis Management Center in Minami Sanriku. Only the steel frame survived the tsunami. September 2011. Photo by the author.

The most prominent Tohoku localizer, Iwate governor Tasso, stood resolutely across the aisle from the most prominent supersizer, his colleague and neighbor, Miyagi governor Murai. Tasso insisted that "intensifying the scope and increasing the scale, or introducing the techniques of large private commercial firms—what in the extreme would be the route of the Transpacific Partnership [a proposed regional free trade arrangement supported by Murai and Keidanren]—is absolutely unthinkable in Iwate's reconstruction."[99] Tasso believes "the answer is local" (*kotae wa genba ni aru*).[100] He accepts the use of special zones, but not the comprehensive version that the business community sees as leading to large-scale consolidation. He wants to apply them functionally, by promoting small local industry to enable "fair trade," and eschews Murai's preference for introducing large outsider firms in the name of "free trade." Tasso explained that "I have seen large scale commercial agriculture in the United States and Brazil. Iwate cannot compete with that. But we can export in niche markets. This is our advantage."[101] Tasso's vision for Iwate—and, he says, for Japan—is the French and Italian model in which high-quality, artisanal manufactures and agricultural products dominate world markets. He insists that for this to work, programs will have to be generated locally because there is "no substitute for local knowledge."[102] Soon after 3.11, he assembled an Iwate Prefecture Great Eastern Japan Disaster and Tsunami Revival Committee composed of planners (who had just returned from a site visit to Christchurch, New Zealand, where a major earthquake had recently struck) and social policy professionals, with representatives of local agriculture, fishery, forestry, and commerce. The result was a model plan for localized redevelopment.[103]

Tasso is not alone. Although the authors of the report of the Reconstruction Design Council do not say so directly, this approach won their support. Although they occasionally nodded at consolidated districts, they endorsed special zones that are narrowly functional and highly local in nature. Indeed, the report's first sentence links localities to the ideal of community, declaring that "we must focus on local communities and 'people who link with others' when going forward with reconstruction of the affected areas." It devotes an entire section to "Utilization of Special Zones and the Autonomy of Municipalities."[104] In the view of the council, "the fundamental principle for reconstruction is that the main actors should be the municipalities themselves, as it is the residents who are closest to their communities who understand local characteristics best. The national government should set overall policy . . . and make maximum use of the abilities of the municipalities . . . based on local wishes."[105] It is hard to find a more coherent statement of the "localize me" perspective. In laying out a strategy for putting Tohoku back in gear, the council report stressed local initiative, local knowledge, local resources, local training of medical professionals, and the value of localized and distributed energy systems "consistent with regional characteristics." It even called for optimizing on "business cycles that are internalized within the region."[106]

The sharpest confrontation between supersizers and localizers was to be found in the recovery plans submitted in May 2011 to the Reconstruction Design Council, a contrast that *Asahi Shimbun* editorialists aptly labeled "one nation, two systems."[107] Miyagi Prefecture presented a ten-year, eight-point plan for recovery that explicitly used 3.11 as an opportunity for structural change and new development. It was built around a comprehensive special zone, and each of eight functional items was organized around a different "special zone" (*tokku*). Relaxed regulatory conditions would permit reconstruction to proceed liberated from central government regulations.[108] The Miyagi plan would promote "community building" (*machizukuri*) by moving residents to high ground, separating residences from workplaces, and rebuilding public infrastructure. A second special zone would promote private investment, with a priority on manufacturing and low-carbon energy sources. A third was the controversial special zone concerning fisheries, aiming to vertically integrate the industry and make it "competitive." A fourth special zone would similarly use 3.11 to provoke the structural transformation of other primary production: Miyagi proposed to end small-scale agriculture in the name of economic efficiency. Additional proposals in transportation, health care, and energy were less controversial than those that would "introduce competition and new management techniques." It does not seem irrelevant that only two of the twelve members of the Miyagi Recovery Commission were local residents.

Iwate also focused on special zones, but took a more localizing approach. For starters, all nineteen members of its Recovery Commission were from Iwate.[109] Governor Tasso insisted that his first priority was to enhance the capacity of local communities to thrive and, deploying a horizontal strategy, built his program on two alliances of local governments, one in the coastal part of the prefecture and the other inland.[110] The Iwate plan emphasized many of the same substantive policy areas as others: community building, renewable energy, health-care services, debt restructuring, revitalization of primary industry, and education. But it proceeded on Tasso's belief that reconstruction should help reduce the presence of the central government and protect local producers against incursions from large commercial firms. One of Iwate's new special zones would enable the prefecture to purchase the flooded lands, make them effective for fish processing, and provide interest-free loans to small producers for land use and acquisition of equipment. Another would establish a Tohoku International Science and Technology Research Zone for marine industry and disaster research. Tasso claims that "independently generated local government information" was critical in directing relief efforts and guiding long-term plans.[111]

Governor Murai's plan immediately faced opposition from the Miyagi fishing families that managed to survive 3.11. Concerned that profits would be diverted from the local economy, the Miyagi chapter of the Japan Fisheries (JF) cooperative initially opposed the proposal outright.[112] Murai acknowledges that he ought to have consulted with the JF before submitting his proposal, but insists this was no reason to block a reform needed to preserve fishing in the prefecture.[113] He invoked the production of bell peppers in Miyagi, which became the nation's largest producer after trading firms modernized production there. It was a tough sell, however. The JF countered with the town of Onagawa, where a private firm had been allowed entry only to withdraw precipitously when salmon prices fell. It collected 14,000 signatures on a petition opposing the special zone and delivered it in June to Governor Murai. By late July, the JF's new chair, Kikuchi Shinetsu, allowed as how they could support corporate participation as long as the cooperative could retain its monopoly control of licensing.[114] Within a year after 3.11, however, the Miyagi fishing cooperatives were facing competition from new firms. The new entrants were not large corporations from Tokyo but corporations established by defectors from the cooperative, younger Miyagi fishermen who, like Governor Murai, believed the future of the Miyagi marine industry would not look like its past.[115]

Perhaps the most creative localizing policy to come from the 3.11 tragedy was the idea for Community Building Recovery Corporations (*fukkō machizukuri gaisha*, or CBRCs) proposed by Tokyo University professor Ōnishi Takashi, an urban planner and member of the Reconstruction Design Council.[116] Leveraging off three themes central to the post-3.11 discourse—change, community, and leadership—Ōnishi imagined that the CBRCs would jumpstart economic reconstruction at the street level by combining public and private resources in locally sourced, locally initiated, locally staffed, and locally managed ventures. To ensure that local economic prosperity would be a priority, he designed a program in which local citizens participate and lead the recovery. Mayors would continue to handle normal administrative matters, but would also assume the post of president of the CBRC, and local residents would be their employees. Capital would be provided by the prefectures and central government, but there would be no central direction or return to the status quo. Tohoku was rapidly aging, its industrial base thinning, and commercial districts hollowing out. So the CBRCs were to move quickly past reconstruction (*fukkyū*) and recovery (*fukkō*) to "creative recovery" (*sōzōteki fukkō*). It would require doing things differently at the local level. CBRCs that at first would clear rubble or rehabilitate fisheries, serving as employment generators for displaced citizens, would later start new ventures and become model entrepreneurs. When projects required new technologies, the CBRCs would train local residents to use them. Resources could be external, but leadership must be local.[117]

Professor Ōnishi's idea captured the imagination of a broad public after he proposed it in the influential "economic classroom" (*keizai kyōshitsu*) column of the *Nihon Keizai Shimbun* on 11 May. The article was widely circulated, and support for the program was included in a draft bill in the fall of 2011; reports of the formation of CBRCs soon appeared in the Tohoku press.[118] Professor Ōnishi believes the two key lessons of 3.11 were about community and leadership. Local citizens now *expect* local government to do more, and they have seen that local government *can* do more. In his view, local governments do not need a reshuffling of jurisdictions; they need an investment of real energy.[119]

SOLIDARITY

Nowhere were these lessons learned better and nowhere was local energy more authentic than in the vigorous efforts of local government to assist colleagues after 3.11. Unlike the enthusiasm generated by ideas about new administrative directions, cooperation across localities continued and deepened a horizontal integration and translocal cooperation that had long been under way. Localities were staying a course set decades earlier. Now, though, they would widen the path into a thoroughfare, and would do so by invoking community and leadership under the banner of "solidarity." Initially on their own accord and later with central government funding, they would house displaced persons, bundle and ship relief supplies, provide grants to local volunteer groups and nongovernmental organizations (NGOs), and dispatch battalions of their own employees to fill in for overwhelmed and, in some cases, missing officials in the affected areas.[120]

There was something special in this development. The more than 7,500 formal joint policy units (outsourced projects, regional alliances, partial affairs associations) discussed earlier—and even the mutual assistance agreements, which had increased dramatically in the past decades—were overwhelmed by the sudden cascade of prefectural and municipal support to affected localities. Within days, every prefecture in Japan had sent assistance to Tohoku, and within the first two weeks nearly five hundred prefectures and municipalities were providing goods and services. By the end of the first month, more than 2,500 municipal employees had been dispatched to the region.[121] By July, 57,000 had gone to work there.[122] More than seven months later, there were still more than 1,300 local officials on loan to Tohoku prefectures.[123] As of December 2011, workers dispatched from Kansai alone had logged more than 175,000 person-days of assistance on-site.[124] And in the first year, more than 77,000 local public officials had been seconded to support recovery efforts in Tohoku.[125]

These aggregate numbers mask the large commitments of particular cities and prefectures. As of 30 September 2011, for example, Yokohama alone had dispatched 3,385 city officials to Tohoku. More than one-third were teachers and school board officials, 15 percent were firefighters, 14 percent were environmental resource specialists, and the rest were distributed across the entire spectrum of functional specialities: medicine, civil engineering, social work, and so forth.[126] Nagoya spent 450 billion yen to support Rikuzen-takata, an Iwate city 600 km away where one out of four city officials per-ished in the tsunami and with which Nagoya had no prior relationship.[127] Mayor Kawamura conferred with Governor Tasso—a former DPJ colleague in the Diet—immediately after earthquake, and his first team fanned out across Iwate cities and towns within a week. A second team followed within days. Nagoya's assistance to Rikuzentakata was intended to be a "full spec-trum" (zenmen), long-term presence across functional areas: thirty-one of eighty-seven officials, most of whom rotated in and out in three-month de-ployments, were still there six months after 3.11.[128] By December 2011, Hyogo Prefecture had dispatched more than seven thousand employees, almost all to the Miyagi prefectural government. In addition, more than thirty thou-sand municipal employees from Hyogo cities—including 8,569 from Kobe and 3,072 from Awaji—served in Miyagi municipalities, and thirty-seven of them stayed there for up to ten months in "local support headquarters" cre-ated by Hyogo.[129] A small number of these horizontal pairings were based on formal "sister city" ties or on existing mutual assistance agreements, but most were initiated on the fly, much like the Nagoya-Rikuzentakata one.[130] The notion came to be called "paired" or "counterpart" support (pearingu or kauntaapaato shien, when based in English, or taikō shien, when based in Chi-nese), and was modeled on China's response after the 2008 Sichuan earth-quake, where localities were expected to provide much of the first response and continuing relief. The difference, of course, was that in China, pairings were assigned by the central government; in Japan, they were developed without central guidance.[131]

Indeed, local leaders and analysts claim—and some central officials concede—that localities seized the relief initiative after the central govern-ment failed to act decisively. Seguchi Kiyoyuki, a former central banker and China hand who was in Beijing during the Sichuan crisis, reports that he brought the Chinese model to the attention of the Ministry of Land, Labor, and Infrastructure just days after 3.11, but got no response.[132] Tokyo Uni-versity professor Ichikawa Mikiko, who had worked in Sichuan in 2008 and observed the benefits of "taikō shien" there, says that she presented the con-cept to MIAC in the hope that it would organize systematic pairing, but says that "it was an awful experience." She also appealed to Diet members who did "not accept the leadership challenge."[133] She then presented the idea to the Science Council of Japan, which, on 22 March, became the first national organization to issue a "pairing support" proposal. It called on unaffected localities to reach out to Tohoku localities on a one-to-one basis in a sort of domestic aid program. It also called for central government action and or-ganizational support from the NAG and the National Association of Mayors (NAM), little of which was forthcoming at first.[134] By late March, the NAG claims to have organized the secondment of more than six hun-dred officials to Tohoku.[135]

Peace Boat staff member Kobayashi Shingo and Self-Defense Forces troops unloading relief supplies at Ishinomaki. 2011. Photo by Yoshinori Ueno/Peace Boat, courtesy of Peace Boat.

At first, though, not everyone was sure that the dispatches would be a good idea, or that the central government was needed. Even as MIAC and the national associations of local governments were considering (or, as some insist, ignoring) these proposals, the newly formed Kansai Regional Union was positioning itself to be first out of the blocks. It met on 13 March, after Hyogo governor Ido, its chairman, and Kyoto governor Yamada Keiji—both former MIAC bureaucrats—agreed that a relief operation involving tens of thousands of local government employees and volunteers would be an excellent first project for the young organization.[136] Convinced that "the central government was all clogged up (*katamari*) and not responding," the Kansai Regional Union created a Disaster Area Contact Office and adopted a "pairing support" system that matched its members directly with Tohoku counterparts: Hyogo, Tokushima, and Tottori were paired with Miyagi; Kyoto and Saga with Fukushima; Osaka and Wakayama with Iwate.[137] Field offices were operating in each of these three prefectures within days. This first step was crucial to Governor Ido, who remembered that "we had a bad experience in Hyogo in 1995, when no one ever asked us what we needed. So we made sure to ask our counterparts in Tohoku what they needed."[138] The Kansai Regional Union also organized partnerships between Himeji and Ishinomaki, Amagasaki and Kesennuma, and Nishinomiya and Minami Sanriku. A grateful Minami Sanriku mayor Satō Jin extolled the Kansai effort, saying that it was faster than anything the central government could do.[139]

Some of the rhetoric surrounding the response of localities was breathless. Many saw it as something entirely new that could have come only from catastrophe. In its September cover story, for example, a leading journal of local public affairs invoked the widely held notion of 1995 as "Year One of Volunteerism" in Japan and declared 2011 to be "Year One of Local Solidarity" (*jichitai renkei no gannen*). The year 2011 would see "the beginning of the end of central government control" of local government.[140] The journal insisted that this was "epochal in the history of Japanese public administration" and pronounced that "a new age has dawned." Experience after 3.11 showed localities that they do not have to depend on the center alone.[141] Even Governor Tasso referred to "new relationships and forms of cooperation among localities" and predicted "some will be institutionalized, others will be ad hoc."[142]

The benefits to dispatching localities often went unmentioned in the exhilaration. The most prominent benefit was the irreproducible management training received by seconded officials. This was no simulation, after all, and their experience and new skills were highly desired by localities anticipating that their time may soon be coming.[143] According to Hyogo governor Ido, "The first officials we sent were those with the experience of handling the aftermath of the Hanshin/Awaji disaster. We followed them with waves of officials who needed to learn about crisis management. When they returned, we had weekly 'mini-conferences' so that they could report on what they learned to their groups."[144] In a circular to employees in late October 2011, the Hyogo Prefecture Disaster Prevention Office explained how it wished to capitalize on the knowledge accumulated by their dispatched personnel: "In order to create an effective policy to deal with the next major disaster," it would compile a record of their experiences in Tohoku. Likewise, the city of Nagoya organized a symposium attended by four hundred employees to review their experience in Rikuzentakata. One conclusion was the critical need to protect and maintain communications; another was less technical but no less important: "city officials must support government operations as their primary responsibility after a disaster no matter how badly they were affected personally."[145]

Some accounts fail to acknowledge that the central government reimbursed localities for the costs of these dispatches. The MIAC reports that in the five months from 8 April to 20 September 2011, 9.3 billion yen from the center's special transfer tax budget supported 80 percent of the costs of the dispatch of officials.[146] Three months later, the government decided to increase this to full support.[147] Although the process by which funds were requested and disbursed was unwieldy, reimbursement probably helped stimulate and sustain such a high level of counterpart support.[148] This suggests that rather than being idle or paralyzed, the central government may simply have been overwhelmed by the disaster. In the first year after 3.11, its ministries and agencies dispatched more than seventy thousand central government officials to Tohoku.[149] Confronted with demands by Diet members to expand and coordinate the partnering system, MIAC minister Katayama Yoshihiro (himself a former governor of Tottori Prefecture) begged off, applauding the localities for taking the initiative and praising them for their "greater flexibility."[150]

The sending localities did, of course, confront some problems. Some local governments, for example, found themselves shorthanded at home.[151] Citizens occasionally resisted the use of their tax money to help elsewhere, and some officials "got cold feet" (*bibiru*) when it came time for their extended dispatch to Tohoku.[152] But perhaps the most difficult problem was the disinclination of most prefectures and municipalities to process potentially radioactive debris from Tohoku in their disposal facilities. Miyagi and Iwate, neither of which had to evacuate any citizens due to the meltdown in neighboring Fukushima, had accumulated 10–20 times more debris from the tsunami than normal, and had nowhere to process it.[153] As helpful as prefectural governments were in other matters, only one—Tokyo—was willing to accept the debris as of November 2011.[154] Four months later, Aichi Prefecture, whose governor griped that the central government "is not doing anything," reluctantly agreed to build a disposal facility to handle 3.11 debris.[155] Seguchi Kiyoyuki had visited Sichuan two years after the quake and saw different residential areas being rebuilt competitively by partner cities Beijing and Shanghai, a development he contrasted with slower progress in

Japan more than a year after 3.11: "*Taikō shien* [counterpart support] for rescue and relief is easy. But we need it for the rebuilding phase as well, and we have no leadership at the center. If we had *taikō shien* ordered by the central government, all of the prefectures would be involved in helping with the disposal of 3.11 debris. Instead, only the really dedicated ones like Hyogo have gone that far."[156]

VERNACULAR PRESERVATION

Debate about the lessons of 3.11 for Japan's local public administration centered on two of our three change narratives. The first would *put it in gear*, either by expanding local jurisdictions in the name of efficiency (supersize me) or else by focusing on local strengths and building institutions that generate growth from the bottom up (localize me). The second would *stay the course* that local governments had been following for several decades, in which their mutual dependence and solidarity deepen and the center draws back in ways that enhance both local autonomy and policy innovation. The final narrative would *reverse course* in order to preserve a Tohoku vernacular that 3.11 threatened to destroy. This narrative of change builds on, and resonates with, themes of community and vulnerability more than with leadership.

Tessa Morris-Suzuki has explored the intellectual origins of this perspective, suggesting that at times of environmental degradation and crisis people are tempted to look back in time to find model communities that lived in greater harmony. In the Japanese case, this search has focused on the centuries-long Pax Tokugawa, the period before rapid industrialization when Japan was isolated and free of war. Some observers developed a longing for a return to an idealized Japanese society that "had attained a sustainable and balanced relationship with its natural environment."[157] This steady-state utopia is then explored for clues on how to improve contemporary life. An Environment Ministry Web page tells of a Japanese "waste not spirit [that] changed as Western culture was imported."[158]

Environmentalists adopting this perspective focus on the skillful use of irrigation and natural fertilizers, evoking a long-lost rural-urban balance. As Morris-Suzuki notes, government white papers on the environment adopt this story "to represent Edo society as embodying, in embryonic form, a distinctly 'Japanese' version of modernity which avoided the negative aspects of western modernization—great power rivalries, wars, and environmental destruction."[159] In 2003, a group calling itself "Japan for Sustainability" reported that Iwate Prefecture was a leader in Japan's "slow life" movement, which would make life "more humane, more natural, and more simple." Iwate was said to reject the values of "fast, cheap, convenient, and efficient" that had been embraced as essential for Japanese prosperity.[160] "Slow life summits" espousing slow pace (walking, not driving), slow wear (traditional clothing made of indigenous materials), slow food (prepared from local ingredients), slow housing (built of locally sourced materials), and slow industry (primary product–based and sustainable) have attracted the participation of localities from across Japan.[161]

In the context of 3.11, this perspective shares villains (globalization, big state) and heroes (small producers) with the "localize me" narrative, but it has most in common with the "simple life" narrative examined in chapter 5 in relation to nuclear power. Professor Umehara Takeshi has staked his claim to intellectual leadership here too. He considers 3.11 a "civilizational disaster" and argues for a return to traditional values that predate the distorting influence of the western world. In a meeting of the Reconstruction Design Council, he declared that "Tohoku culture is *jōmon* culture, a culture of forests and ocean. And it is a culture in which all living things live together symbiotically. This is the Tohoku culture we must protect."[162]

But "back to the future" has few intellectual champions, and it is further from the mainstream on local administration than the "reverse course" arguments in either security or energy policy. In fact, going backward is referred to by critics more often than it is championed by its own policy entrepreneurs. Without specifying who makes such claims, Reconstruction Design Council vice chair Mikuriya Takashi argues that many in Japan had begun to pursue the "simple life," which would lower consumption and growth and increase isolation—what he and others refer to as Japan's "Galapagos mentality."[163] Likewise, fellow council member Ōnishi Takashi says "many believe that Tohoku should keep what Tohoku has been like," but acknowledges that "even those who are most interested in preserving the vernacular in Tohoku are thinking how to fit huge seawalls with the traditional townscapes there."[164]

Indeed, some of those apparently most likely to argue for a return to traditional Tohoku values actually reject it. The most prominent example is Gakushuin University professor Akasaka Norio, a folklorist from Fukushima who has specialized in what he calls "Tohoku Studies" (*tōhokugaku*). Professor Akasaka is a frequent contributor to the award-winning magazine *Sendaigaku*, published "to enable residents of Tohoku to make decisions for themselves based on local knowledge, independent of information and opinions from Tokyo."[165] Professor Akasaka, also a member of the Reconstruction Design Council (as well as chair of its Fukushima-based local counterpart), is identified with the "simple life" movement and has written eloquently of Tohoku's long history of loss and discrimination. But he has a far less romantic view. Akasaka says Tohoku was an internal colony before the Pacific War, from which "boys became soldiers, girls became prostitutes, and peasants paid tribute [to Tokyo]."[166] He believes that 3.11 brought this colonial relationship into relief because little has changed: Tohoku workers are exploited by large firms from outside the region, and its residents shoulder the risk of hosting dangerous plants that provide electric power for people far away in Tokyo. Professor Akasaka has blogged about how he "wants to search for hope" for Tohoku—particularly if the region can experience the end of exploitative "cruel and Asia-like" factory conditions for its workers. He stresses that "there is a Tohoku that Tokyo does not see," in which "communities will survive in small villages and towns and will regenerate."[167]

But first, lessons must be learned. Akasaka disparages the temporary housing in which 3.11 disaster victims find themselves, arguing that until they demanded locally designed, locally sourced shelters, they ended up in whatever was in the inventories of large manufacturers.[168] He likewise disparages the "unthinkable reconstruction plans" (*tondemonai fukkō puran*) of designers who have ignored—or never even investigated—the region.[169] Still, Professor Akasaka insists that he does not stand for preservation for preservation's sake: "I do not oppose change—after all Tohoku's history of exploitation should end. But change must be on a human scale" consistent with local values.[170] He reports that efforts by residents to reproduce their original communities in the temporary housing units were frustrated by authorities who insisted on assigning residence by lottery—with the result that whole communities were lost.[171] Communities, he says, can be preserved even with entirely new built spaces and in new locations (for example, on higher ground) if their communal institutions—temples, shrines, cemeteries—come with them. But to remain alive, he insists, communities have to be surrounded by their memories, even memories of death.[172]

Clearly, there are differences about which vernacular to preserve. In any case, the post-3.11 discourse on local government is oriented toward putting it in gear and staying the course. So what lessons will be learned, and which narrative will prevail and guide change?

Conclusion: Lessons Learned and Opportunities Seized

The 3.11 catastrophe rekindled debate over several of the most contested preferences for local government reform—decentralization, local autonomy, and regionalization. A senior official of one of Japan's largest cities suggested a principal lesson of 3.11 was that "the inherited three layer model of center to prefecture to municipality did not operate. Localities had to organize to help localities."[173] Hyogo governor Ido agreed, and says that the "pairing support system will be institutionalized nationwide."[174] But it was clear that local governments were not going to wait for legal change, or even for guidance, to implement the lessons they learned. While the central government was probing 3.11 for lessons, virtually every prefecture and city started to enhance its programs for disaster prevention and response.[175] Tokushima governor Iizumi Kamon explained why at an NAG meeting: "The government should establish an overall vision, but since it cannot decide what its role should be, it is up to us governors to do so."[176]

But some governors, particularly in Tohoku, were unsure of the appropriate lessons for administrative reform.[177] All were positive about "counterpart cooperation," and Miyagi governor Murai and Fukushima governor Satō called for the system to be established immediately and nationwide. But judging region-wide administrative change to be "premature," they held different views about whether a regional union (kōiki rengō) like Kansai's or the state system (dōshūsei) made better sense for Tohoku. Some were concerned that a Tohoku Regional Union would become merely a "receptacle" (ukezara) for central government programs at a time when localizing reforms was more desirable. The same division was reflected in views about the state system. Governor Murai suggested that "it will be essential to introduce this in the future with public input," whereas Akita governor Satake Norihisa worried that the state system would introduce a new form of concentrated power. Local officials concede there is still a role for the central government, even if 3.11 showed that its relationship to the localities is shifting in real time. One Iwate planning officer described it vividly in structural terms: "Vertical administration (tatewari gyōsei) remains a problem for us, especially in areas of land use, finance, and ports and harbor management where we have to deal with overlapping jurisdictions of central ministries and agencies. But coming out of 3.11 our horizontal (yoko) and diagonal (naname) ties are stronger than ever."[178] One expert explained that Japan has been "creeping" toward efficiencies in policy delivery at the local level, but galloping toward new forms of collaboration that enabled a quick response to 3.11 despite confusion at the center.[179] The confusion seemed finally to clear a bit when the MLIT earmarked 1.5 billion yen for "counterpart support" in its FY2013 budget request.[180]

For its part, the Cabinet Office's Central Disaster Management Council issued an interim after-action report in March 2012.[181] The study took nearly a year to produce and focused primarily on evaluating the response of government agencies to the immediate crisis and identifying the (by then familiar) obstacles in communication, relief supply delivery, manpower shortages, fuel supply, shelter, and medical care. The report was filled with incremental recommendations for improving disaster response. It concluded that the central government, localities, private firms, and individuals each have unspecified roles and responsibilities in a disaster, and it promised to recommend unspecified legal changes in a final report. But it had little to say about the impact of larger changes in center-local relations on crisis management. More than a year after 3.11, Japan continued to await a comprehensive analysis.

The analysis lagged behind the politics, for the disaster struck at a particularly unsettled time for local government. In June 2011, a MIAC advisory council issued a report on how to devolve greater power to prefectures by having them assume central government functions. It proposed revisions of the Local Autonomy Law to further empower the prefectural alliances (*kōiki rengō*) that had played a leading role in postdisaster relief.[182] Indeed, after decades of false starts, populist leaders had already begun to seize the initiative, and 3.11 made it easier for them to deliver their anticenter message. In Nagoya, Mayor Kawamura, a former Diet representative who had moved to the local level with an anticenter message in 2009, cofounded an antitax party (*Genzei Nippon*) and was reelected in February 2011 with triple the votes of his DPJ rival. Kawamura was among the most active local chief executives supporting Tohoku after 3.11. But the most visible and vocal challenge to the local government system came from his ally, Hashimoto Tōru, the former governor of Osaka Prefecture who became mayor of Osaka City in November 2011 on a platform of local government reform. Unlike most governors, Hashimoto is an advocate of the state system: "There is no alternative but to invoke the state system, but nothing will happen if all we do is talk about it."[183]

Elsewhere, Hashimoto has said that reform has stalled because the central government is in Tokyo and its employees see the country only from Tokyo's perspective. His prescription, then, is to "leave local affairs to localities. This is, after all, where people were born and live and are best understood. . . . It is not pretty to hear, but localities are slaves (*reizoku*) to Kasumigaseki [the Tokyo district where the ministries of the central government are located]."[184] Wielding this issue to considerable effect—and, indeed, using it as a litmus test for political allies—he created a political party (*Osaka Ishin no Kai*) and a political training center, the Restoration Political Institute (*Ishin Seiji Juku*), in early 2012 to nurture candidates who would challenge both the DPJ and the LDP at the national level. Hashimoto's popularity was not a direct consequence of 3.11, but was empowered by it. His party's manifesto focused squarely on several issues that 3.11 brought into sharp focus: it advocated the state system, promised to replace the allocation grant system with a system of direct local taxation, sought to merge Osaka City and Prefecture, called for an end to nuclear power, and insisted on revising the constitution to enable direct election of the prime minister and to abolish the House of Councillors. Despite considerable criticism (including comparisons to Hitler and Mussolini and references to "Fascimoto" by establishment politicians), Hashimoto became Japan's most closely watched politician after 3.11.[185] His efforts spurred DPJ and LDP support for revisions of the Local Autonomy Law, which not only empowered regional alliances but also allowed all cities over a certain size to assume many prefectural prerogatives. None before him has ever threatened to transform local into national power across such a broad front. Then again, rarely has local government mattered so deeply to so many Japanese at the same time.

Conclusion

There are no villains in this story, only a dysfunctional system.
—Dr. Kurokawa Kiyoshi, 21 May 2012

Only 20,000 people died in Tohoku, but 30,000 Japanese commit suicide each year. Unlike World War II, 3.11 did not bring Japan to a tipping point.
—DPJ Diet representative Ogawa Junya, 18 November 2011

These epigraphs frame the mixed lessons that this book draws for Japanese politics and public policy after 3.11. In December 2011, Kurokawa Kiyoshi, a professor of medicine and former president of the Science Council of Japan, was appointed by both houses of the Diet to chair the newly created Committee to Investigate the Accident at the Tokyo Electric Power Company's Fukushima Daiichi Nuclear Power Plants.[1] In a nation where blue ribbon panels are common but often ineffectual—or else captured—this one was to be different. The Kurokawa Committee would be the first independent public investigatory commission in Japanese history. It was in, but not of, the Diet, and by design was insulated from the cabinet and the rest of the executive branch. It was also the first that could issue subpoenas to compel witnesses to testify.[2]

Although Dr. Kurokawa was by no means an outsider—he had been an adviser to former prime minister Abe and over the years had held dozens of official posts—he made no secret of his distrust of politicians and bureaucrats. In May 2011, he called for "a special committee that is 'independent' and 'outside' . . . the government," adding that "equally necessary is a quick and total information disclosure. . . . Transparency is the foundation of trust and credibility."[3] Months later, after the formation of the investigatory committee, Dr. Kurokawa expressed concern that "they will try to bury the report," and required that the hearings be webcast, that his press conferences be open to journalists beyond Japan's cartel-like press clubs, and that transcripts be made available in English as well as in Japanese to make sure the government knew the world was watching and, presumably, to encourage foreign pressure (*gaiatsu*).[4]

The Kurokawa Commission report, published in July 2012, was the first official broadside critique of how collusion between business and government contributed to the 3.11 catastrophe.[5] Emphasizing that 3.11 was a "man-made" disaster, it rejected the idea that 3.11 was unforeseeable, so rare an event as to excuse lack of preparedness (the "*sōteigai* defense" identified in chapter 2). It excoriated the Japanese regulatory system, arguing that "regulatory capture" (*kisei no toriko*) was borne of long-term, single-party rule. The commission insisted on transparency, and toward that end, called for reform of regulators, of operators, of Japan's crisis management system, and of the law. It also called for the Diet to assume responsibility for monitoring all of Japan's regulatory bodies. In his introduction to the report, Dr. Kurokawa went beyond Japan's institutional problems and assigned fundamental blame for the accident to the Japanese social system that generated a "mind set" in which "arrogant" elites defended their organizations ahead of the public interest.[6]

To the extent that the report identified institutional problems that could be changed and were independent of more resistant (and ineffable) cultural ones, Kurokawa suggested possibilities for structural change that extend far beyond the remit of his commission. It leveraged off a widespread appreciation in Japan that problems of national governance originate in opaque decision making. That view is no longer only the view of political activists. The vice chair of the Atomic Energy Commission testified in the Diet, for example, that Japan needs public forums on the Swiss model and should make sure that an independent Office for Technology Assessment conducts transparent investigations on the U.S. model.[7] Taken together—or at least taken at face value—such ideas suggest that amid the mythmaking, blame laying, and *gaiatsu* baiting after 3.11, some policy players and a mobilized citizenry were looking to address fundamental problems afflicting Japanese democracy. The concerns of these actors may line up with other observations in this book: that despite frustrating systemic issues and continued resistance to change, the 3.11 catastrophe may have stimulated a move toward more open debate and more transparent decision making. If that is so, the vigorous rhetoric of crisis suggests possibilities for a democracy more robust than ever before.

Representative Ogawa's observation, in contrast, aligns with a different and perhaps more insistent finding: that much of the crisis rhetoric will amount to little more than empty and self-serving chatter. Ogawa, a two-term Diet member and vice-chair of the Democratic Party of Japan's (DPJ's) Policy Affairs Committee, voiced an unpleasant (even indiscreet) truth about crises in general—that even citizens moved to help one another may not sustain their empathy or engage with larger discontents. Saying this, of course, directly contradicted the community motif that was so widely embraced after 3.11. This is one reason why so many of those who heard his claim that 3.11 was not big enough to stimulate change were dismayed, though some admitted they were discomfited only because a Diet member was expressing in public what they feared in private. Others—such as a fellow Diet member who asked, "Is he from western Japan?"—situated this comment as evidence of a weakness in the fabric of the national community.[8]

In a larger (or at least more indirect) sense, however, Representative Ogawa was commenting on the credulity of analysts and the manipulative efforts of policy entrepreneurs who plant false hopes for change. On this account, the rhetoric of crisis should be dialed back to a more realistic level that focuses on regaining what was lost rather than creating what cannot be. It suggests that resilience may be the best that 3.11 victims can expect from themselves and that indulgence may be the most they can realistically expect from others. Ogawa's remarks are a reminder that, much like the Edo Era aphorism introduced in the preface to this book, Japanese will "fall down seven times, [and] get up eight." Indeed, the iconic expression of communal determination after 3.11, "*Ganbarō Nippon*" (Let's hang in there together, Japan), expressed yearnings for restoration rather than for renovation. Ogawa directs us to a far less optimistic place than Dr. Kurokawa's comment, and insists that we privilege the less transformational elements in our analysis.

Ogawa reminds us that the Japanese thought about change and assumed it would come as a result of so enormous a catastrophe. Most commentators agreed that Japanese desperately needed change even before 3.11, and the calamity initially underscored that desperate need. There was immediate evidence of change—in the speed of the Self-Defense Forces (SDF) and local government response, in the enormous outpouring of volunteering, and in the public scorn for Tokyo Electric Power Company (TEPCO) executives and others who thought that "business as usual" was an appropriate and adequate response. But the evidence many months later suggests that the much-maligned system, seemingly maladapted to the challenges that contemporary Japan faces, was far more resilient than many had given it credit for. Greater public acceptance for the military, a larger sense of national community that flows from volunteer efforts, the mobilization of large-scale protest over nuclear power—in short, the hundred and one indicators that something new was being born—may not have been sufficient to stimulate long-term, large-scale change in Japan's core politics.

These two views mirror the persistent debate in post-3.11 Japan over whether region and nation should pursue a "restoration" (*fukkyū*) or something closer to a "renaissance" (*fukkō*). The shared initial character in these terms connotes "return" and "reversion," but the second characters provide a linguistic fork in Tohoku's (and Japan's) developmental road. *Kyū* evokes old times and reinforces the idea of rebuilding what once was. *Kō* is more forward leaning—it evokes a flourishing, a rise, a revitalization. This choice and its implications are everywhere in the discourse, from decisions about whether to rebuild homes along the Sanriku coast or to move everything to higher ground, to decisions about whether to transform the scope and scale of everything from fishing fleets to local public administration. In essence, the choice is a struggle about whether or not Tohoku should become the point of Japan's developmental spear. When the government finally created its *Fukkōchō* in 2012, it seemed to opt for active change. But when it officially named the new body the "Reconstruction Agency" in English, it revealed underlying ambiguities that persisted.

It is too early to know if Japan is on the cusp of a more open future, or if it is more likely to return to the status quo ante. But it is not too early to review the evidence why either could be in the offing—and why elements of both are likely to persist. Indeed, the two remarks point us to begin by interrogating the theories we bring to bear. Dr. Kurokawa's comment reminds us how determined, creative leaders and a mobilized public can nudge institutions, and Representative Ogawa's reminds us that we cannot know a priori the threshold beyond which crises stimulate change.

Leaders were everywhere in the rhetoric of the 3.11 crisis—and in the action that accompanied the talk—but they are less evident in our theories about change. When trying to explain change, social science discounts human agency and privileges great forces—utility in economics, power in political science, structure in sociology, culture in anthropology.[9] Then, as if to further insulate our analyses from choices made by individuals, much of our theory insists that change is most likely after a major perturbation to the system. We routinely posit that war, economic collapse, and natural disasters are likely catalysts for change because they "punctuate" the equilibrium, thereby stimulating the formation of new political cohorts and undermining the stability of long-standing institutions. They set loose the great forces that trump or animate the choices of great leaders.

Recent developments challenge the assumption that change requires large exogenous shocks. Kathleen Thelen and James Mahoney, for example, focus on how incremental changes that are part of normal politics can accumulate to transform institutions. Even without a major crisis, existing rules may be displaced by new ones, new rules may be layered atop existing ones, there may be drift in the application of existing rules, or leaders may apply new meanings to existing rules.[10] No such changes are necessarily the result of systemic shock, though shock can nudge them to the fore. In this way, many of the dynamics we observe in post-3.11 Japan suggest that the crisis may have unstuck incremental changes—in local government, national security, and energy policy—that had been accumulating but were jammed in the queue. Even in the high-stakes energy sector, where expectations for new directions were most inflated, systemic change seemed more likely to evolve from the piecemeal developments associated with normal politics—abetted, of course, by political entrepreneurs who used the crisis to argue for their preferred future. To be sure, 3.11 was a crisis, but it stimulated battles within existing pathways and generated solutions consistent with existing goals. There was very little that was novel in the 3.11 discourse, apart from the horrific experience of 3.11 itself.

What sort of changes were we looking for, and what sort of changes did we find? In looking for system change, we searched for shifts in the balance of power between business and government, between politicians and bureaucrats, between soldiers and statesmen, and between center and periphery. We found no shift that was not already under way, or at least not already in dispute, suggesting that Thelen and Mahoney are correct to remind us that "change and stability are inextricably linked."[11] If there was change, it was incremental, and much of it had already been in the plans of advocates. 3.11 was no big bang that shifted balances of power or suddenly delegitimated institutions. Indeed, it was striking how balances of power were *already* being jostled by political actors, working aggressively to sustain or seize prerogatives.[12] The measure to stimulate renewable energy and reduce dependence on nuclear power that the cabinet introduced just hours before the earthquake on 11 March itself—the Feed-In Tariff—is a powerful illustration. On 10 March 2011, political competitors had already engaged in that struggle for a decade or more, and 3.11 was merely another tool to enhance their claims.

Consider Representative Ogawa's words once more: why do we expect so much change when we do not know a priori the size of shock required to transform a political system? That threshold has rarely been theorized. Part of the reason we expect so much is no doubt because narrators in the media, academia, and the political class told us we should. A profusion of extravagant claims dominated the 3.11 discourse. Many were metaphorical: windows of opportunity were now open, a new chapter would begin, an antimilitary allergy would be shed, and greed would be washed away. Japan would experience national rebirth, a new start, a reset, a return, reform, regeneration, reconstruction, and recovery. The nation would undergo paradigmatic change and civilizational transformation. It was at an inflection point, a historic moment, a turning point that would lead to a new generation that would overhaul the nation and change everything.[13]

Once the idea of imminent change was embraced by pundits and the public—a clinch that seemed to happen instantaneously across the entire policy landscape—the crisis stimulated explanatory and hortatory narratives specific to each of the policy areas we have examined: security, energy, and local public administration. Political actors spun stories to help make sense of the disaster, always in ways consistent with what they already "knew" to be true. Hence, their stories were consistent with normal politics. Those who thought the utilities were villains before 3.11 insisted that 3.11 proved their point. Those who believed the DPJ was a collection of incompetent parvenus before 3.11 now had additional evidence to make their case. Supporters of the Japan-U.S. alliance and of the Japanese military renewed their claim that they were right all along—Japan and the world now had "proof of concept" after 3.11. We observed a continued, albeit intensified, competition among political actors armed with a new tool, the disaster itself. As Karl Von Clausewitz might have framed it, 3.11 was simply the continuation of normal politics by additional means.[14]

These new means, born on 11 March 2011, were populated by *existing* villains and heroes. And there were a great many of them. Fingers pointed everywhere—at TEPCO for its cupidity in the face of a disaster of its own making; at former prime minister Kan Naoto for meddling in the emergency—or for failing to do enough; at the Ministry of Economy, Trade and Industry (METI) and the Liberal Democratic Party (LDP) for creating moral hazard in the "nuclear village"; and at academics for being handmaidens to their conspiracy.[15] Cloth was cut to fit heroes' mantles as well: the entrepreneur Son Masayoshi would save Japan and lead it to a new technological frontier; the DPJ politician Hosono Gōshi had brought the alliance back from the precipice and established himself as a future prime minister; plant workers and local officials were lionized for their selflessness, like young Endō Miki, who was washed away as she stayed at her post at the Minami Sanriku emergency center, imploring residents to get to high ground; Fukushima Daiichi plant manager Yoshida Masao ignored orders from corporate headquarters and saved untold lives; the SDF was embraced as the most—and on some accounts, the only—effective arm of the central government; and even the much-maligned U.S. Marines were warmly applauded. The implication was that if Japan can eliminate the bad guys and/or reward the good guys, salutary change will follow.

Change was our first—and most contested—theme. We suggested three models of how it might be championed and applied them to security, energy, and local public administration. Model One involved an explanation of 3.11 requiring a vigorous, forward-leaning response. We anticipated that some narrators would insist that the catastrophe was a warning that Japan must abandon past practice and head in a new direction. In the security realm, they read 3.11 as a "wake-up call." The natural disaster was a test run of military preparedness, but the real threat would be much more challenging. In a war, troops and commanders would not use cell phones to coordinate responses and would not focus on rescuing civilians. They would be trying to attack and struggling to survive. Japan therefore needed to "put it in gear," and use this historic chance to prepare for its real enemies—on some accounts, even to move beyond the alliance with the United States. The SDF were heroes, of course, and even though they could not be blamed for the catastrophe, the real villains were China, Russia, and North Korea.

In the case of energy policy, this "forward-leaning" response would require transformation of the entire electric power sector. The lesson of the disaster was that nuclear power—until 3.11, the foundation of Japan's Basic Energy Plan and a key element of its New Growth Strategy—would have to be replaced by renewable energy. If a second economic renaissance were to occur, the regional monopolies, with centralized generation and one-way transmission that had powered the postwar miracle, would have to be replaced by distributed power sources and smart grids. The entire regulatory structure would have to be torn down and replaced with one that avoided capture by the firms and their allies in government. Since the villains in this narrative—TEPCO, METI, LDP, and Keidanren—were evil on the face of it, their collusive nuclear village would have to be dismantled root and branch.

In the case of local government, policy entrepreneurs identified two ways forward after 3.11, each portending a significant change in scope and scale of public administration. Japan could "supersize" or it could "localize." Advocates of the former, such as Keidanren, saw in 3.11 an opportunity to revive the endlessly debated but always deferred plan to eliminate prefectures and replace them with larger states. For them, the disaster proved that when districts are too small, authority is fractured and therefore hinders the effective delivery of public services. Creating special, comprehensive economic zones with relaxed central regulation would be the first step toward scaling up to a state system (*dōshūsei*) that would rationalize services and generate public goods, including free trade. Miyagi governor Murai Yoshihiro was eager to supersize primary industry in Miyagi and was a leading advocate of these special zones. The larger state system concept was embraced by Osaka mayor Hashimoto Tōru, undoubtedly the most celebrated young politician to burst on to the national scene after 3.11. The localizers, however, saw big firms and bigger states as the problem, if not as outright villains. The scale of local government was already too grand. They argued that had the government not forced the amalgamation of localities before 3.11, a great many more victims could have been rescued. In their view, moreover, small scale had economic benefits as well. It was small producers and their privileged position in global niche markets that would rescue the Tohoku economy. The face-off between Iwate governor Tasso Takuya, who embraced this view, and his neighbor, Miyagi governor Murai, cast the choice between supersizing and localizing in sharp relief.

If Model One demanded doing things differently and exaggerated 3.11 failures in order to justify change, Model Two required doing the same things better; it inflated the virtues of the status quo. This could mean doing more of the same or it could mean doing less of the same, but either way its proponents insisted that the catastrophe reinforced (or at least failed to fully negate) extant wisdom and practice. The lesson of 3.11 was that if change were to come, it should be in volume and quantity, not in kind, direction, or quality. Staying the course was the dominant perspective for national security, where alliance managers and defense analysts were delighted to see the Japanese military and the U.S. alliance accepted by an unprecedented majority of the general public. They weaved a "we told you so" narrative, maintaining that after years of their insisting on the value of the alliance and the quality of the SDF, both were now proven concepts. The lesson of 3.11 was that Japanese military power and the alliance could be enhanced at just the moment when the need for national security was becoming acute.

In the energy case, Model Two took two forms, each of which urged the government to stay the course on nuclear power. Each was justified by a "black swan" defense. Proponents insisted that since 3.11 was the consequence of an enormously unlikely—indeed, unimaginable (sōteigai)—confluence of events, no one could be held culpable for the damage that resulted. Both groups defending the status quo in energy had a more difficult task than in security, since they were forced to defend villainous businesses, not heroic militaries. The first cohort adopted a more defensive "business as usual" posture: any changes to the extant electric power sector—especially to the provision of nuclear power—would be unwise or, as one DPJ elder put it, "suicidal."[16] Changes could have perverse consequences: electric power supplies would decline, prices would rise, economic growth would stall, and both unemployment and pollution would increase; they could jeopardize operation of the most stable supply system in the industrial world and counter trends toward liberalization; or else they could waste resources and turn out to be futile.[17] Business as usual was therefore the best available option. The second group that urged staying the course on nuclear power contained self-declared realists who acknowledged that nuclear power was more risky than the industry and its regulators had acknowledged, and that this would and should change as Japan restarted its reactors. This group reminded the public that zero risk is impossible and urged planners to improve their designs and enhance transparency—the only ways to reduce risk to acceptable levels.

Model Two was most dynamic in the case of local governance, where local public officials, who had been inventing new forms of policy cooperation for decades, found their efforts rewarded many times over. Prefectures and major cities—sometimes in coalition, as in the Kansai Regional Union—were quick to identify "counterpart" localities in Tohoku, and charged ahead of the central government to determine and meet many of their needs. For their part, governors and mayors in the affected area could not wait for central government assistance and welcomed the demonstration by sibling localities that central guidance was unnecessary. Taking a page from the Chinese government's response after the Sichuan earthquake (taikō shien) and from a deepening of translocal ties already under way, prefectures and municipalities from across the nation stayed the course on collaboration. They fashioned ad hoc supply and administrative chains to two ends. First, by dispatching thousands of officials for extended tours of duty in the affected areas, they assisted Tohoku localities in desperate need. Distant neighbors collected, delivered, and distributed emergency supplies, helped plan new civil infrastructure, counseled pensioners, relocated refugees, taught children, and collected debris. Second, their extended dispatches provided invaluable training for their staff, experience that they reckon will be critical when disaster strikes at home. Governors and mayors, and the legions of public officials they dispatched, celebrated 2011 as "year one" of solidarity among local governments. In fact, however, they were deepening an important element of local autonomy that they had already done much to enhance. Their villains were insouciant or ineffectual central officials, and they were staying the course of an oft-overlooked policy innovation of long standing. That they got the central government to pay for much of this horizontal cooperation was one measure of their success.

Model Three was deployed by those who believed that 3.11 taught that Japan had already come too far. Rather than do something new and rather than do more or less of the same, Japan must reverse itself and undo what it has already done. Japan should turn back resolutely to an often-idealized status quo ante. This narrative did not compete effectively against those who argued for dramatic change or for staying the course. In security, this reverse course was taken up by supporters of disarmament. Its advocates acknowledged the performance of Japanese soldiers, but argued that SDF successes during the rescue and relief effort proved Japanese troops are at their best when wielding shovels, not when toting guns. Disarmament narrators squared off against their villains, militarists who, they argued, were drawing entirely the wrong lessons from 3.11. They rejected the disaster as an opportunity to make the SDF muscular or to enhance jointness in the alliance with the United States. Rather, proponents of the Model Three narrative insisted that 3.11 paved the way for Japan to abandon its ill-conceived postwar course toward rearmament. Japan should recapture the spirit of its peace constitution by creating a global disaster relief force.

In energy and local government, this Model Three narrative touched on many of the same themes, and some of its advocates, such as Umehara Takeshi, were the same. Theirs was a "back to the future" argument in which Japan should eschew growth and rediscover its origins as a society in which urban and rural societies were balanced and where the local vernacular was preserved. Evoking a romanticized pre-Meiji time when farmers provided food and city dwellers provided fertilizer in symbiotic balance, and both lived comfortably with less, advocates argued for recycling, conservation, and a "simple life." Some blamed 3.11 on science—particularly Western science—that smugly assumed human beings could control nature. Business elites that pursued profits by deploying dangerous technologies had steered the nation in the wrong direction, and the only effective solution was to dial notions of scientific progress back to manageable levels. Western ideas about enlightenment should surrender to Buddhist ideas about enlightenment, the latter being truer both to Japan and to nature.

The post-3.11 discourse was thus a duel among three very different prescriptions for change. The contest between putting it in gear (Model One) and staying the course (Model Two) was easily the most robust. Still, all three narratives captured valuable real estate in the national discourse and, importantly, none was congruent with normal "left-right" orientations, what in Japan are typically referred to as conservative (*hoshuteki*) and progressive (*shinpoteki*). Some Model One arguments, as in security, were dominated by conservative policy entrepreneurs, but the Model One argument for change in the energy sector was dominated by progressives. Of the two Model One arguments about local government, one was progressive, the other conservative. That most models were ideologically catholic undoubtedly made it easier for policy entrepreneurs to engage the public and acquire new allies. The question for analysts is the extent to which public opinion shifted as a consequence of all this chatter, and in what direction.

In security, the Model Two "proof of concept" seemed to prevail, but even some of its own advocates felt the need for Japan to put it in gear. Public opinion tilted further than ever before toward the legitimacy of the military and the alliance. Still, this new level of support did not embolden officials to seek new budgetary allocations or acquire major new weapon systems. Neither did 3.11 successes create major new levers of command and control or step up alliance cooperation. On the contrary, Japanese defense budgets continued to fall, and Japanese defense bureaucrats and alliance managers rebuffed U.S. exhortations to invoke the "bilateral coordination mechanism" during the first North Korean missile test after 3.11. Despite reports of U.S. bullying during the crisis, the Japanese public now trusted U.S. and Japanese soldiers more than ever, but decision makers remained hesitant to test this newfound support.

In energy, Model One villainization of the nuclear village dominated the national discourse, and every aspect of the extant power system was up for grabs. But when the dust settled, Japan's nuclear reactors did not remain off-line for long, the export of nuclear power was reaffirmed as a matter of national policy, and the institutions of the much-disputed "back end" of the nuclear fuel cycle—the Mutsu fast breeder reactor and the Rokkashomura reprocessing facility—remained intact despite dwindling public support. A new regulatory system was established, nuclear power was downsized, anti-nuclear activists became members of government advisory bodies, and a feed-in tariff was implemented to stimulate investment in renewable energy. Still, nuclear power remained a critical element of Japan's fuel mix. The DPJ's long-awaited, much-debated, and ultimately compromised post-3.11 national energy plan announced in September 2012 called for the long term elimination of nuclear power (the so-called "zero option"), but allowed for considerable growth from near zero levels that could keep Japan's nuclear reactors running well into the second half of the twenty-first century. So here, too, the Model Two narrative prevailed—at least in its realist variant.

Likewise, in local government the supersizers and localizers battled it out for control of a Model One narrative to "redimension" Japan, but neither would prevail, at least in the immediate term. The policy entrepreneurs with the greatest success in this area were those who locked arms in solidarity against the central government and stayed the course to enhance translocal solidarity and promote local autonomy. And while the reverse course narrative, Model Three, never became a major force in any of these post-3.11 policy discourses—and it certainly was not the policy choice of Japan's policymakers—advocates of a simpler life and slower growth actually had already had many of their dreams come true. Japan's per capita gross domestic product (GDP) has been flat since the early 1990s. Meanwhile, Singapore, Hong Kong, and Taiwan surpassed Japan in the mid-1990s and never looked back, and the Republic of Korea was poised to overtake Japan by 2017.[18]

Change was the most contested, but it was only one of four tropes used by post-3.11 Japanese policy entrepreneurs trying to tilt politics in their favored direction. The other three were deployed more uniformly. For every misleading, inflated, and contested claim that Japan was hovering on the cusp of major change, there were uncontested reminders of the nation's fundamental predicaments and strengths. It seemed obligatory for each analyst to remark on Japan's dearth of quality leadership, its unlimited potential for social solidarity, and the ever-present shroud of vulnerability. If these three additional motifs were mutually independent, we would be documenting squabbles across our cases studies about whether, for example, it is more appropriate to think about risk or change. Leadership might have squared off against community as alternative ways to eliminate structural problems in Japanese politics.

Rather than compete, however, all of the remaining themes were invoked in each case and were embedded in all three sets of change preferences. Like change, but without the confrontation, risk, leadership, and community were on everyone's lips—from Keidanren chair Yonekura Hiromasa, who insisted on staying the course of nuclear power, to Tohoku folklorist Akasaka Norio, who drew more limiting lessons from the catastrophe. Often, each trope was used to bolster the others. An important collection of the thoughts of eighty opinion leaders about post-3.11 Japan produced by the *Asahi Shimbun*, for example, opened by heralding change: "Delegating Society to the Next Generation." It thereupon struck the leadership chord, pleading not for strong leaders but for "proficient managers who can lead." Then, without missing a beat, it insisted that nothing less than "construction of the community and nation" must be entrusted to the next generation. Before the end of a short preface, the editors invoked *shimaguni Nippon*, the standard reference to Japan as a vulnerable "island nation." The *Asahi*'s collection is only one example where the most prominent themes of 3.11 were invoked not to compete with but to reinforce one another in order to highlight the legitimacy of some particular argument for change.[19]

These repeated incantations about Japan's leadership deficit, insistences on its natural bonds of community solidarity, and reminders of the risks to which the nation has long been subjected may have inflated hopes for change after 3.11. In the case of leadership, the incessant question seemed always to be whether new principals would replace failed incumbents and rise to the challenge. But this discourse, centered on former prime minister Kan and his DPJ successors, may have been more negative than was warranted. Kan, for his part, was perhaps less the fumbling amateur depicted by his political enemies than a leader with excellent "situational awareness."[20] It is worth noting, moreover, that Kan shifted from a pronuclear to an antinuclear power position. In doing so, he was the only principal in the entire 3.11 drama who actually changed his preferences in light of the catastrophe. His successor, Noda Yoshihiko, reversed Kan's energy policy and insisted on staying the course. This, too, undergirded effective leadership, for in the summer of 2012, Noda prevailed on long-standing opponents to the nuclear restart—powerful governors and mayors in the Kansai region—to reverse their position.

The remaining two tropes also may have inflated expectations for change and misdirected public opinion. Much of the discourse surrounding vulnerability and risk emphasized the resilience of the people of Tohoku. But resilience was not exactly an option: residents of the devastated areas were forced to innovate. Judging from the national fascination with post-3.11 disaster scenarios—including those predicting imminent devastation in Tokyo and other major urban areas—it seems that 3.11 may have convinced the Japanese that they live in an even smaller, even more vulnerable island nation.[21] Nor was the post-3.11 ideal of community straightforward. While many Japanese felt reassured by the appeals to social solidarity after the catastrophe, cheap talk of *kizuna* (bonds) and *tsunagu* (connection) were accompanied by a more consequential mistrust of the political class and the nation's core institutions of governance and the economy. Some Tohoku mayors were even sued by "victims' groups" for malfeasance during the crisis. Nearly a year after 3.11, 85 percent of the Japanese public was "dissatisfied" with the state of Japanese politics, and 65 percent felt Japanese politics was headed in the "wrong direction." Nearly two-thirds of the Japanese public disapproved of the government's recovery efforts, and only 16 percent were optimistic that the economy would improve. The leading causes of their dissatisfaction were politicians and parties.[22] Moreover, the majority of Japanese opposed the restart of nuclear power plants, even when faced with electricity shortages, and were more than willing to discard their prime minister in the midst of the crisis. Decline in support for the DPJ was not offset by increased support for the LDP or any other opposition party. Instead, the already large mass of unaffiliated voters expanded.

Our review of historical and comparative cases prepared us for these results more effectively than did social and political theory. Several of Japan's earlier natural disasters provided little grounds for optimism, and each presaged 3.11 in important ways. The Ansei (1854–1855) and Nōbi (1891) disasters were both plagued by civil unrest and high levels of distrust. The Meiji-Sanriku quake (1896) should have rendered the "sōteigai" defense itself unimaginable. The Kantō (1923) quake and fires stimulated expansive hopes for imaginative reconstruction that were dashed on the shoals of political reality and fiscal constraints. And while the Hanshin Awaji (1995) disaster was a watershed for civil society, Kobe was left behind as the rest of the nation struggled with postbubble economic challenges. Each of these cases—and even that of Hurricane Katrina (2005) in the United States—raised the same questions of leadership, community, vulnerability, and change. Each generated fleeting moments that flickered with lost opportunities and competing narratives about institutional transformation. They all reinforced appreciation of the indeterminacy of political change: past disasters, like the present one, were open-ended and susceptible to narrative construction. In every case, the evils of vertical administration—dysfunctions associated with competing administrative jurisdictions—dominated discourse as much as did heroes and villains. The wake of each disaster was filled with an unstable mixture of optimism and pessimism that informed (and frustrated) efforts to mobilize and recover. As a result, we observed then (as now) that more change was incremental than institutional. And some historical changes that were institutional, such as the empowerment of the military and enfeeblement of political parties after the Kantō quake, were not positive developments for Japanese democracy.

Likewise, the lessons we drew from disaster diplomacy by the United States in Bangladesh (1991), Indonesia (2004), Pakistan (2005), and Myanmar (2008); by Japan in Sichuan (2008); and by China as it manipulated Japanese assistance during the Sichuan disaster, each resonated with 3.11. Humanitarian assistance and disaster relief were always welcomed on the ground, but in no instance did they transform international relations. Rescue and aid have not trumped, and should never be expected to trump, normal international politics or the domestic dynamics that govern foreign and security policy. Operation Tomodachi was unlike the Japanese initiative in Sichuan or the U.S. one in Myanmar, and there was no evidence that it was orchestrated for the purpose, as one U.S. government official put it, to position the donor "to make a withdrawal from the Bank of Goodwill." A good thing, too, for if history is any guide, such an effort would surely have failed.

Some observers suggested that 3.11 would stimulate neighbors to reconsider their view of Japan as a menacing enemy, but there have been no disaster-related shifts in the regional balance of power. The mobilization of the SDF and Operation Tomodachi surely sent a clear message to China and North Korea about Japanese and alliance capabilities, but 3.11 did not become "the opportunity for building new relationships with the world."[23] To the contrary, despite initial goodwill, Chinese and Japanese mutual feelings of friendship dropped sharply in the months after 3.11.[24] And immediately after the catastrophe, just when neighbors and trading partners were most worried about the export of radiation and tainted goods, the Japanese government decided to reduce its official development assistance (ODA) budget by 20 percent.[25] By mid-2012, territorial disputes led to Tokyo's recall of its ambassador in Beijing and large scale violent demonstrations in China; and public distrust of Japan in South Korea forced a sudden cancellation of a military cooperation agreement.

As it turned out, then, 3.11 was just another episode in which the winning of hearts and minds consistently yielded to realist facts on the ground—the balance of power, extant rivalries, and ideological competition and domestic political struggle over foreign and security policy priorities. This was no less true of the alliance. Despite the warmth of the moment and despite the profound amity that Operation Tomodachi generated, immediate politics and longer-standing concerns combined to shape the subsequent U.S.-Japan relationship. Japan's struggles over basing issues, for example, and its timidity vis-à-vis implementation of emergency coordination mechanisms in the face of a North Korean missile launch revealed an ongoing lack of confidence in security policy and, perhaps, in the alliance that Operation Tomodachi did not seem to ameliorate. Complicating matters were larger battles between the political class and the bureaucracy, struggles among vertically fractured policymaking institutions, and an increasingly dire fiscal outlook. The result was uncertainty and policy gridlock, which hurt alliance policymaking more than Operation Tomodachi could help.

These theoretical, historical, and comparative baselines provided guidance for analysis of the specific cases of security, energy, and local governance. But while they point us to explanations for policy successes and failures in particular cases, they also direct us to where the policy areas overlap. None of these cases is best viewed in isolation. Where they meet combines with the central themes of post-3.11 discourse to reveal important dynamics in the Japanese policy process. Each pairing is associated with a different motif, and each highlights different possibilities for institutional change.

For example, after the nuclear reactor accident in Fukushima, debates about the future of nuclear power combined in newly transparent ways with concerns about national security. As the legitimacy of the Self-Defense Forces rose and that of utilities and energy regulators fell, new possibilities emerged for the management of Japan's comprehensive security. The military's concern about the protection of nuclear materials could no longer be subordinated to the utilities' preference for concealing risk. Immediately after the meltdown, the Ministry of Defense gained unrestricted access for the first time to Japan's nuclear power plants, and the Atomic Energy Commission created a working group on nuclear security, focusing on spent fuel, transportation, and other matters affecting vulnerability and risk.[26] At the same time, what once were *sotto voce* discussions about a possible nuclear deterrent came into the open, and pacifist groups found common cause with antinuclear power groups under the leadership of Nobel laureate Ōe

Kenzaburō.[27] Ōe addressed the antinuclear power rally in September 2011 as well as the annual meeting of the Article 9 Society, one of Japan's leading pacifist civic groups, as organizers claimed that "the issues surrounding nuclear power plants are those surrounding Article 9."[28] This argument seemed to gain new force in June 2012, when the Atomic Power Basic Law was revised without extensive debate to include the contribution of nuclear energy to "national security," arousing concern at home and abroad.[29] Viewed separately, energy and national security were each on similar policy vectors after 3.11—both poised to stay the course—but viewed together, they undergird new public conversations and suggest new possibilities for institutional change animated by concerns about vulnerability and risk.

The same can be said of the interaction between national security and local governance, where the leadership trope emerged to guide new forms of policy interaction. The legitimacy of both the military and local governments was enhanced by 3.11, their cooperation having evolved after the deadly disconnect in the wake of the Hanshin/Awaji disaster in 1995. By March 2011, they had been sharing disaster scenario plans and exercising together for several years, occasionally on a region-wide scale. But 3.11 was the first time that the National Association of Governors and the SDF collaborated in the

Antinuclear demonstration in Yoyogi Park, Tokyo; organizers estimated a crowd of 170,000 people. 16 July 2012. Photo by Masaya NODA/Japan Visual Journalists Association.

provision of relief supplies, and it was the first time that civilian authorities were able to use military bases as staging areas for transport.[30] Far more significant than the "parcel delivery services" (*takkyūbin*) provided by the military was the uncontested way in which the SDF was able to supplement or replace the functions of local governments during the crisis. Regimental commanders actually assumed leadership of some Tohoku localities, including the responsibilities of mayors and deputy mayors.[31]

After 3.11, moreover, some Japanese local governments began reaching out on their own to U.S. forces in ways that were previously unimaginable. Shizuoka Prefecture, for example, approached the U.S. military to strengthen disaster preparedness and cooperation. It was concerned that in the event of a future disaster the government might set up a U.S.-Japan bilateral coordination cell in Tokyo, instead of in Shizuoka. According to its director of emergency management, "we know from the March 2011 disaster that we must be willing to look to the United States for assistance."[32] Robert Eldridge, a U.S. Marine Corps public affairs officer in Okinawa, speaks of a "Shizuoka model" in which Japanese localities hedge against the failure of the central government to respond effectively in a crisis.[33] Whatever the reason, localities were prepared to lead if the center would not. And if the localities led, then the center would be further marginalized.

Japanese localities asserted themselves in creative ways vis-à-vis the energy sector as well. Indeed, in what may be the most revealing combination of our three cases, local government met energy policy at several critical junctures after 3.11. First came the issue of structural reform of the electric power sector. An animated discussion of separating transmission and distribution from power generation was connected to the development of community-based "smart grids" and alternative power sources. Governors and mayors flocked to the side of Son Masayoshi and other private champions of locally based renewable sources. Many local chief executives and local assemblies actively weighed unprecedented options. They could invest in and derive power from new producers by moving beyond exclusive reliance on large, regional monopolies. If they could establish local control of power generation and use—and if they could build an interactive rather than a one-way grid—they could also design a decentralized regulatory system. Distributed energy connected to decentralized administration opened room for regulatory innovation and, in particular, for community control.[34] Local governments could become the sources of electric and, possibly, political power for the nation.

This was particularly evident in a second area where localities and the energy sector met. The status quo featured special relationships among central government regulators, electric utilities, and rural communities that could be enticed to host nuclear power plants. After 3.11, however, other localities—particularly large urban centers—claimed a place at the policy table. Electricity-consuming communities that had never received the grants and subsidies lavished on producing communities claimed that their citizens were just as endangered by nuclear accidents as were residents who live in the shadow of the plants. They demanded a say in the future of nuclear power. In April 2012, seventy current or former mayors from thirty-five prefectures formed an antinuclear group that held its inaugural meeting in Tokyo.[35] Governors in the Kansai Regional Alliance and their allies in Osaka and Nagoya were even more assertive. Although they had no formal jurisdiction in the matter, they claimed that accidents in the Fukui-based Ōi reactors could contaminate their populations, and for months they resisted central government plans to restart the Kansai Electric Company's nuclear reactors in distant Fukui Prefecture. It was here, in the meeting of the energy and local government sectors, that the very nature of community—and of community power—in post-3.11 Japan was being negotiated.

In these several ways, the connections across our cases illuminate heretofore opaque policy dynamics. Those revealed by these combinations, when arrayed alongside those within each sector, offer us insight into key institutional relationships. We observe how 3.11 may have opened a new urban-rural cleavage in Japanese politics—a division that has attracted little attention in the literature on contemporary Japan. Not only did metropolitan governments promise to build their own power sources and establish a presence in the national energy policy community, but urban citizens' movements, such as the antinuclear referendum effort in Tokyo and Osaka, targeted rural-urban inequities and therefore touched a political chord for many voters.

Similarly, the nationwide outpouring of public spiritedness by volunteers was much more than a replay of the Hanshin-Awaji experience. It was not merely its unprecedented scale or effective use of new media technologies; civil society activism had fuller institutional consequences this time. Nongovernmental organization (NGO) activists who had cut their teeth on community organizing in Kobe brought more than a decade of disaster relief experience—at home and abroad—to Tohoku. They were embraced by the prime minister's office, where one of their leaders was appointed national coordinator of volunteer activities, and they worked closely with business organizations and the military, two nominal adversaries. Long-standing left-right cleavages may not have closed as a result, but new common ground surely was constructed.

Likewise, the enhancement of horizontal solidarity among local governments may have been the biggest untold story of all. And to the extent that it empowered local leaders with national ambitions, it could become one of the most important innovations to emerge from the 3.11 catastrophe. Most notably, Osaka mayor Hashimoto Tōru gained populist acclaim by declaring "war" against the central government, and attracted support from fellow local chief executives, including Tokyo governor Ishihara Shintarō, who signed on to his anticenter message despite major policy differences.[36]

Speaking on behalf of fellow mayors and governors—and with their active support—Hashimoto repeated endlessly that the system was broken and that, as in the nineteenth century, it could not be changed until individual leaders assumed responsibility. He argued that Japan's elite had grown accustomed to shirking responsibility, locking the system into inflexibility. In saying this, he sided with critics who saw parallels between the arrogance and false reassurances of contemporary Japanese leaders and those of wartime leaders, and he echoed Dr. Kurokawa's views of the nuclear village.[37] Hashimoto—himself criticized for Bonapartism—gained considerable traction by using the charge to characterize the entire national political establishment. In September 2012 he created a national political party, the Japan Restoration Party (Nippon Ishin no Kai) to prepare for the next lower house election.

In the policy realm, when it was necessary to reduce demand for electricity during periods of peak demand, it was a coalition of localities, not merely the business federation or the central government, with which Kansai Electric Power Company had to negotiate. This same coalition took the initiative to provide relief to the affected areas. Acting well in advance of the central government, coalitions of localities demonstrated new possibilities for local autonomy. Local governments clearly captured the imagination of the Japanese public. Indeed, the most lasting changes after 3.11 may not come from the most admired institutions in the crisis, the Japanese military and the Japan-U.S. alliance, nor from the most reviled (the electric power industry and government regulators). Rather, they may come from those that were ignored or at least taken for granted: Japan's localities. After all, *they* were the democratic institutions that stepped up when the center was gridlocked and unresponsive.

Of course, 3.11 also illuminated—and may have rearranged—some key institutional relationships that have always attracted attention. The most prominent is the balance of power between career bureaucrats and politicians. The DPJ took power in 2009 on a promise to assert political leadership over an entrenched and privileged bureaucracy. But it found out that it needed professional support after all. Its most successful arm, the military, possessed the competencies—organizational superiority, hierarchical command and control, self-sufficiency, discipline, an image of self-sacrifice—that matched perfectly the demands of the crisis. At the same time, the competencies of the political class (the ability to craft minimum winning coalitions and to transfer resources to win popular support) were less useful. Policy change, once the province of bureaucrats collaborating with interested actors in controlled settings, now was the object of open debate. With more actors involved and public opinion more engaged than ever, with the leading parties attracting historically low levels of popular support, and with the national Diet "twisted," the post-3.11 policy process seemed to stalemate sooner—and changed less—than many expected. Even the plan to create a National

Security Council to serve as a "command tower" for security policy and crisis management had not moved beyond the discussion phase a full year after 3.11, demonstrating the need for enhanced expertise in the Cabinet Office.[38] After the crisis—indeed, well after the crisis—Japan's political class looked more hidebound to more citizens than ever. It is no small irony that a catastrophe presented as testing the resilience of the Japanese people also turned out to demonstrate the resilience of a sclerotic political system.

The relationship between business and government was also affected. Collusion, long the accepted narrative of their relations, was replaced by confrontation, particularly over nuclear power. The federation of business organizations, Keidanren, rallied to the side of the electric utilities and argued that Japan should stay the course on nuclear power. But business and its allies in METI were no longer able to control the membership of advisory commissions that were to chart Japan's energy course. Nor was the business community fully united behind nuclear power. Some dissident Keidanren members disagreed about the desirability of nuclear power and the advisability of the feed-in tariff. Others rushed to explore and invest in new, non-nuclear, business opportunities in the energy sector. Mixed signals from within the DPJ likewise frustrated the business community, leading one senior Keidanren official to throw up his hands and declare "we just don't know who to lobby anymore!"[39]

Perhaps of greatest importance is what attracted no political attention after 3.11—the relationship between soldiers and statesmen. After the largest mobilization of Japanese forces since the Pacific War, and despite the persistence of what conservatives repeatedly referred to as Japan's "anti-military allergy," there was nary a whisper of concern about civilian control of the military. Japan's soldiers performed their rescue and relief work effectively, and no one could question their commitment to democratic values. When analysts compared the Great Eastern Japan Disaster (3.11) to the Great Kantō Disaster of 1923, they focused on Gotō Shinpei and his frustrated, grandiose dreams for reconstruction, not on the way the earlier disaster had empowered the Imperial military. No one was concerned that 3.11 might be 1923 redux and, while the party system seemed nearly as rickety as in 1923, public trust in the SDF as a legitimate institution in a democratic system soared to new heights. More than a year after 3.11, nearly nine in ten Japanese regarded the SDF highly, a sharp 20-point improvement from a decade earlier.[40] Even the governor of Okinawa reportedly stated after 3.11 that he welcomed the presence of the SDF there.[41]

Whither post-3.11 Japan? There was nothing peculiarly Japanese about the rush to form narratives and to join political battle after the catastrophe. Japanese political actors and policy entrepreneurs did what politicians and pundits do everywhere after a crisis—they hurried to explain what happened and in the process they assigned blame and pressed their cases on the public using familiar and reassuring appeals. They agreed broadly that a 3.11-like catastrophe must not be allowed to recur, but in the process they may have exaggerated the prospects for change. Let us return, then, to Representative Ogawa, the pessimist, and to Dr. Kurokawa, the optimist, for guidance on the larger lessons to be drawn from 3.11.

It should come as no surprise to find the disconnect that Representative Ogawa suggests between the rhetoric of crisis and political behavior. Politics is, after all, a perpetual game in which there is far more saying than doing. In a crisis, the hopes of citizens and the expectations of social scientists may soar, but politics is never suspended. Indeed, given the higher stakes, both words and action are likely to intensify. And this is what we observed in post-3.11 Japan. The catastrophe inspired motivational stories of leadership, community, and vulnerability that all pointed toward the desirability and, for some, the certainty of change. Civil society, building on its now considerable experience with disaster relief—and using new networking technologies—mobilized effectively with the business community and state actors.

Still, Japan's political leadership remained split and its bureaucracy unimaginative; its political parties were weak, its communities more fractured than most would admit. When public hearings on Japan's energy policy choices were finally held in the summer of 2012, many thought they seemed to be "mere staged formalities," and they were at first met with derision.[42] Yet despite unprecedented levels of civic activism and record low levels of trust in public institutions and leaders, citizens' intense sense of vulnerability did not provoke widespread protest of overall government dysfunction. When the balance finally shifted from volunteerism by concerned citizens to protests by outraged ones, the largest demonstrations—those held in Tokyo in June and July 2012—were focused on the restart of nuclear reactors, and never addressed the simultaneous breakup of the DPJ, the introduction of an unpopular consumption tax, or any of the other issues on the national policy agenda.

In the first two years after the disaster, politicians busied themselves with long-standing power rivalries. Votes of no confidence were threatened and sometimes held; cabinet ministers came and went as parties formed and split for reasons unrelated to 3.11. Normal politics never gave way to crisis politics. In short, we saw in 3.11 what we saw in previous crises in Japan and elsewhere: postdisaster periods do not exist in a separate domain. Normal constraints continued to operate, even during the crisis, even when social and political equilibrium was supposed to have been dislodged. In reminding us that we can overestimate the transformational potential of crises, that crises may have to be far bigger than 3.11 to stimulate sustained change, Representative Ogawa states a powerful case. We should not be surprised that "stay the course," Model Two, prevailed in most debates about policy change.

On the other hand, Dr. Kurokawa reminds us that a robust Japanese democracy filled with well-informed, active citizens eventually emerged from the crisis. For each leader who failed the test of agility and flexibility—and even if efforts to "put it in gear" were more often frustrated than not—there were policy entrepreneurs who directed innovative ideas for change at an engaged public. Despite the dysfunctions in Japan's political class, we have seen abundant evidence of creativity in its policy class. Political entrepreneurs from across the political spectrum in think tanks, private firms, and universities actively generated policy ideas. Antinuclear activists failed to block the restart of reactors, but they succeeded with the feed-in tariff, mobilized large protests, and came to be represented in councils of state. Government plans for staying a robust course on nuclear power were stymied after nationwide public hearings revealed a strong popular aversion to business as usual. Utilities and their business allies were by no means impotent, but they were put on warning that they would no longer enjoy unchallenged positions of regional or national leadership. Likewise, the SDF and the alliance with the United States emerged from the crisis set to deploy in a military contingency with public support, the Ground Self-Defense Force was poised to acquire amphibious landing ships, and the Ministry of Defense was better positioned to participate in the making of national security policy. Local governments, for their part, were freer of central control than ever before. They demonstrated that they could lead the center as often as the center leads them, and their stout, sustained calls for administrative reform were widely acknowledged by the media, the public, and the political class.

So we are left with a paradox. The 3.11 catastrophe was not the "game changer" many policy entrepreneurs desired. It did not cause structural change to the Japanese body politic. Normal politics prevailed, with all its imperfections, and "staying the course," rather than the more forward leaning "put it in gear," seemed to prevail across the three policy areas we have examined. Still, post-3.11 Japan belongs as much to Dr. Kurokawa as to Representative Ogawa. The rhetoric of crisis infused democratic politics, empowered new actors, stimulated long-awaited if piecemeal reforms, aroused considerable public protest, and may have pushed the policy process in the direction of transparency. At a minimum, the catastrophe opened all of these possibilities and, in a famously conservative system, the first months that followed the quake, the tsunami, and the meltdown provided encouraging (if limited) signs of change for those who hoped for a new style in Japanese politics. Would those early moves result in long-term alterations in the country's politics? Nearly two years later it was still too early to tell and too soon to conclude otherwise: a 3.11 master narrative was still under construction.

Notes

Any inconsistencies in identification of interviewees are owed to the requests of some for anonymity. Japanese names are in Japanese order, family name first.

Preface

1. This distinction was first made by my MIT colleague, Shun Kanda.
2. McCloskey 2011, 181–85.

1. The Status Quo Ante and 3.11

1. Vogel 1979 was just the first and most successful of many adulatory accounts of Japan in that period. See also Ouchi 1981 and Johnson 1982.
2. Ministry of Economy, Trade and Industry (METI) data in *Wedge*, November 2011, 13. The *Oriental Economist*, July 2011, reported that even before 3.11, one-third of all Japanese capital investment was done abroad, and that 3.11 would accelerate this, notwithstanding METI "guidance."
3. *Kyodo*, 6 September 2011. Organization for Economic Cooperation and Development (OECD) data reported in Shimabukuro, chap. 1, 2012. See also d'Ercole 2006.
4. *Japan Times*, 10 May 2011. National Police Agency data are online at http://www.npa.go .jp/safetylife/seianki/H23jisatsunojokyo.pdf.
5. See http://citigroup.com/citi/citiforcities/pdfs/hotspots.pdf (appendix 1). According to other data published in early 2012, the average income in Tokyo in 2009 was more than 21 percent higher than in the next richest prefecture, neighboring Kanagawa. Moreover, if the four capital area prefectures—all in the nation's top ten—are excluded, the average Japanese income was less than 36 percent the average level for Tokyo residents. *Yomiuri Shimbun*, 1 March 2012.
6. See Schaede 2008 and Fingleton 2012 for contrary views.
7. Keidanren, ed. 2011, 17. Lincoln 2011 also explains the underperformance of the Japanese economy by policy mistakes and argues that the government response was lethargic.
8. "On the New Growth Strategy," Cabinet Decision, 18 June 2010, http://www.kantei.go .jp/foreign/kan/topics/sinseichou01_e.pdf.

9. "Japanese Resilient, but See Economic Challenges Ahead," Pew Global Attitudes Project, 1 June 2011, http://www.pewglobal.org/files/2011/06/Pew-Global-Attitudes-Japan-Report-FINAL-June-1-2011.pdf.

10. *Seiron*, June 2011, 124.

11. The actual quote was "the politicians reign and the bureaucrats rule." See Johnson 1982, 154, 316.

12. The 2010 Party Manifesto is at http://www.dpj.or.jp/english/manifesto/manifesto2010.pdf. See Shinoda, forthcoming, for a review of the Democratic Party of Japan's (DPJ's) principles on governing Japan: (1) political leadership, (2) centralized decision making, and (3) cabinet policy coordination. The DPJ soon learned that it needed bureaucratic support and that coordination was hard to achieve.

13. See Government of Japan 2011 and 2012 for summaries of the costs and responses to the catastrophe.

14. Higashi Nihon Daishinsai Fukkō Kōsō Kaigi 2011.

15. *Mainichi Shimbun*, 28 May 2011.

16. *Kyodo*, 15 April 2011.

17. Ministry of Internal Affairs and Communications (MIAC) data provided on 17 October 2011.

18. Interview, Tokyo University professor Ichikawa Mikiko, 14 December 2011.

19. Fukushima 2011; Mikuriya 2011b, 91.

20. There are four nuclear power stations with fourteen reactors in the region where the quake and tsunami struck. All but the four at Fukushima Daiichi went safely into a state of cold shutdown.

21. Fukushima City pledged to decontaminate all private residences and public buildings in the city. *Asahi Shimbun*, 28 September 2011. Minami Sōma mayor Sakurai Katsunobu campaigned for the return of his citizens and the revitalization of his Fukushima community. See *Asahi Shimbun*, 7 May 2012.

22. *Tokyo Shimbun*, 25 August 2011.

23. *Asahi Shimbun*, 20 December 2012.

24. Interview, U.S. government scientist, 11 January 2012. A special investigative commission of the Diet reported that "there is no consensus among experts on the health effects of low dose radiation exposure." See Fukushima Nuclear Accident Independent Investigation Commission 2012, 39.

25. For a representative, single-day snapshot of news reports of radioactive contamination, see *Kyodo*, 21 April 2011, and *Asahi Shimbun*, *Mainichi Shimbun*, and *Tokyo Shimbun*, 30 August 2011. For a story about the "widespread panic" over the Tokyo water supply in late March 2011, see the special edition of *Shūkan Bunshun*, 27 March 2011, 46.

26. *Asahi Shimbun*, 26 November 2011.

27. *Asahi Shimbun*, 18 August 2011; *Kyodo*, 8 December 2011.

28. Gemba Kōichirō, then minister of national strategy, issued orders that these practices be stopped. *Mainichi Shimbun*, 19 April 2011.

29. Data from National Police Agency reported in *Asahi Shimbun*, 3 July 2011. See also Segawa 2011. Akasaka Norio tells of the ninety-year-old woman from Minami Sōma who, knowing she could never return to her home, left a note behind declaring: "The evacuation center will be my grave." See Washida 2012, 18.

30. *Asahi Shimbun*, 23 September 2011.

31. Toba 2011, 157.

32. Government of Japan 2011, 3; Higashi Nihon Daishinsai Fukkō Kōsō Kaigi 2011. For an early, detailed analysis of the costs of the disaster, see Nippon Seisaku Tōshi Ginkō 2011.

33. *Asahi Shimbun*, 29 April 2011.

34. The firms surveyed included Hitachi Automotive Systems, Toshiba Mobile Display, TDK, Mitsui Metals, Nippon Denpa Kōgyō, Epson, and others. *Nihon Keizai Shimbun*, 19 March 2011.

35. *Yomiuri Shimbun*, 4 May 2011.

36. Associated Press, 13 April 2011; *Oriental Economist*, May 2012.

37. *Yomiuri Shimbun*, 18 January 2012.
38. *Tokyo Shimbun*, 6 February 2012.
39. *Asahi Shimbun*, 10 September 2011, and data supplied by the Ministry of Internal Affairs and Communications (MIAC), 31 October 2011.
40. Kyoto-based Omron, for example. *Asahi Shimbun*, 17 June 2011.
41. *Kyodo*, 5 July 2011.
42. *New York Times*, 24 August 2011.
43. Nakasone 2011, 129.
44. *Yomiuri Shimbun*, 14 February 2012.
45. *Hokutō Kenkyū* 2011, 37.
46. *Yomiuri Shimbun*, 11 December 2011.
47. The food chain claimed this was due to concerns about cost, not origin. *Nikkei*, 13 February 2012.
48. Tasso 2011, 44.
49. *Kyodo*, 31 May 2011; Seguchi 2011, 3.
50. This is the sum of losses to the prefecture's primary industry, public facilities, and commercial industry. Fukushima 2011, 38.
51. *Yomiuri Shimbun*, 20 April 2011, and unpublished data supplied by the Tokyo Electric Power Company, 15 January 2012. See chapter 4 for more on the fiscal dependence of local governments on the nuclear power industry.
52. *Hokutō Kenkyū* 2011, 11.
53. *Kyodo*, 9 May 2012.
54. *Asahi Shimbun*, 12 October 2011, and 23 February 2012; *Japan Times*, 22 February 2012.
55. *Nihon Keizai Shimbun*, 5 March 2012.
56. *Asahi Shimbun*, 11 December 2012. Fukushima governor Satō Yūhei also wondered why this could not have happened sooner. See *Yomiuri Shimbun* and *Japan Times*, 10 February 2012.
57. *Asahi Shimbun*, 11 December 2012.
58. Interview, Professor Iokibe Makoto, The National Defense Academy of Japan, Yokosuka, 2 February 2012.
59. Interview, Professor Ichikawa Mikiko, Tokyo University, 14 December 2011.
60. See Howitt and Leonard 2009, 611–24; Bosner 2011. Asō 2003 is an excellent study of the history of Japanese emergency management.
61. Howitt and Leonard 2009, 617.
62. Asō 2003.
63. United Nations Centre for Regional Development 1995; Bosner 2011; David Rubens Associates 2011, 10–11. An editorial in the *Nihon Keizai Shimbun*, 18 March 2011, pointed out that the post-Kobe system never took into account the possibility of multiple simultaneous disasters, and criticized the lack of coordination between the government and private firms.
64. Otabe 2011 has a useful chronology of events. See also Yamada 2011. For a detailed chronology of the nuclear accident, see http://www.thebulletin.org/web-edition/columnists/tatsujiro-suzuki/daily-update-japan. Kingston 2012 is an excellent analysis of the crisis and the government's response.
65. International Atomic Energy Agency 2011.
66. Nagashima 2011, 136. Cleverly playing on the term "crisis management" (*kiki kanri*) and the prime minister's name, Nakasone Yasuhiro argues that 3.11 was "Prime Minister Kan's management crisis" (*kanri kiki*).
67. Interview, Ministry of Defense, 18 November 2011.
68. This is according to interviews with two principals on the prime minister's crisis management team, 7 July and 18 November 2011, in Tokyo and with members of the Reconstruction Design Council, 18 and 26 January 2012 in Tokyo.
69. Unpublished memo by Yamauchi Chisato, 22 July 2011, 1.
70. *Wall Street Journal*, 9 April 2011.
71. Interview, Iokibe Makoto, Yokosuka, 2 February 2012.
72. Interview, Akasaka Norio, Tokyo, 18 January 2012.
73. See Mikuriya 2011b, 65–66 and *Nihon Keizai Shimbun*, 18 March 2011.

74. *Asahi Shimbun*, 28 June 2011; Mikuriya 2011b, 69; *Yomiuri Shimbun*, 26 June 2011; interview, Iokibe Makoto, Yokosuka, 2 February 2012. Public support for a tax hike to pay for compensation to victims or for reconstruction had a remarkably short half-life. See *Asahi Shimbun*, 8 June 2011.

75. *Kyodo*, 17 March 2011.

76. Interview, Nagashima Akihisa, DPJ representative, Tokyo, 7 July 2011.

77. *Nihon Keizai Shimbun*, 18 March 2011.

78. Kan maintained authority to appoint the chair, the deputy chair, and "special advisors" to the Reconstruction Design Council, "as necessary." There was nothing in the enabling cabinet order that provided for professional staff. *Yomiuri Shimbun*, 12 April 2011. The council's vice chair provides an insider's view of the politician-bureaucrat divide in the council and reports that Prime Minister Kan asked him if he thought the bureaucrats could be trusted. Mikuriya 2011b, 67.

79. Fukushima Nuclear Accident Independent Investigation Commission 2012, 18, 33–34.

80. The report was by the independent Committee to Investigate the Accident at the Tokyo Electric Power Company's Fukushima Daiichi Nuclear Power Plants. See *Japan Times*, 17 March 2012, and the conclusion of this book. A leading political analyst suggested that by intervening in TEPCO's decision, Prime Minister Kan "arguably saved Japan from an even worse fate." See Okamura Jun's "Global Talk 21" blog entry at http://son-of-gadfly-on-the-wall.blogspot.com /2012/07/the-fukushima-reportsor-whom-do-i-trust.html.

81. As reported in *Asahi Shimbun*, 21 May 2011. At a hearing of the Diet's investigation commission in May 2012, Kan defended his 12 March site visit to the Fukushima Daiichi reactors, but acknowledged disarray in his government's communication and control functions during the crisis. See *Japan Times*, 29 May 2012.

82. For criticisms from across the political spectrum, see *Nihon Keizai Shimbun*, 18 March 2011; and *Asahi Shimbun*, 16 April 2011; *Yomiuri Shimbun*, 28 April 2011.

83. Matsumura 2011, 23.

84. Yokota 2011. For an alternative view, see Kingston 2012b.

85. Defense Minister Kitazawa repeatedly insisted that the Emergency Disaster Headquarters was sufficient for a prompt and authoritative handling of the crisis. For the criticisms, see Abe 2011, 37; *Asahi Shimbun*, 7 May 2011; Itagaki 2011, 123; Matsumura 2011, 23; *Seiron*, June 2011, 121; *Rippō to Chōsa* 320 (September 2011): 37.

86. *AERA*, 2 May 2011.

87. This account is from *Shūkan Bunshun*, 21 March 2011 (special edition), 36. It also reports on page 40 that Tokyo Electric Power Company (TEPCO) "ignored" Kan and appealed directly to the U.S. military for help. See also *Wall Street Journal*, 21 March and 9 April 2011.

88. *Yomiuri Shimbun*, 13 March 2011.

89. *Washington Post*, 23 February 2012.

90. Interview, Professor Morimoto Satoshi, Takushoku University, Tokyo, 13 July 2011.

91. See *Wall Street Journal*, 29 March 2011; *Asahi Shimbun*, 30 April 2011; and chapter 5 herein.

92. A special commission created by the Diet to investigate the accident was unequivocal. It concluded that 3.11 was "a profoundly man-made disaster—that could and should have been foreseen and prevented," adding that "our report catalogues a multitude of errors and willful negligence that left the Fukushima plant unprepared for the events of March 11." See Fukushima Nuclear Accident Independent Investigation Commission 2012, 9.

93. *Jiji Press*, 29 April 2011. See Ramseyer 2011 for an analysis of the law.

94. Agence France-Presse, 2 May 2011.

95. It is argued however that many of these guidelines were set by regulators and engineers who may not have been entirely independent. See chapter 4.

96. Interview, Suzuki Tatsujirō, vice chair of the Japan Atomic Energy Commission, Tokyo, 26 September 2011.

97. *Yomiuri Shimbun*, 4 May 2011; *Kyodo*, 14 May 2011; *Financial Times*, 17 May 2011; *Asahi Shimbun*, 15 June 2011; *Nihon Keizai Shimbun*, 15 November 2011. See Ōshika 2011 for a chronology of the compensation debate.

98. *Asahi Shimbun*, 7 November 2011.

99. *Bloomberg Businessweek*, 24 February 2012. See *Oriental Economist*, April 2012, for a detailed account of the compensation battle.

100. Slater, Nishimura, and Kindstrand 2012 is an excellent analysis. See also Koide 2011a, 104–6, and M. Takubo 2011, 23.

101. *Nikkei Shimbun*, 26 April 2011, is an early report of this phenomenon.

102. Slater, Nishimura, and Kindstrand 2012, 104.

103. Koide 2011b, 21.

104. Interim Report of Committee to Investigate the Accident at the Tokyo Electric Power Company's Fukushima Daiichi Nuclear Power Plants, 26 December 2011. The executive summary of the final report is available in English at http://icanps.go.jp/eng/SaishyuRecommendation.pdf. The report also vigorously criticized TEPCO. See 27 December 2011 press reports in *Asahi Shimbun*, *Financial Times*, *Japan Times*, and *New York Times*. See *New York Times* for more on SPEEDI. An internal memo from then Ministry of Education, Culture, Sports, Science and Technology (MEXT) minister Takaki Yoshiaki reportedly explained the decision to withhold the SPEEDI predictions because they were "too chilling" for public consumption. *Kyodo*, 4 March 2012.

105. *New York Times*, 18 May 2011.

106. *Oriental Economist*, May 2011, 2.

107. *New York Times*, 28 February 2012.

108. *Shūkan Bunshun*, 21 March 2011 (special edition), 37. On 3.11, the government ordered evacuations in a 3 km radius from the plant; on March 12, this was extended to 10 km, and after the explosion, to 20 km.

109. *Asahi Shimbun*, 12 April 2011.

110. Map prepared by U.S. Embassy, Tokyo, 31 August 2011.

111. *Kyodo*, 16 April 2011; *Yomiuri Shimbun*, 17 April 2011.

112. *Guardian*, 2 May 2011.

113. *Bungei Shunjū*, August 2011.

114. *Financial Times*, 7 July 2011.

115. *Kyodo*, 5 July 2011.

116. *Asahi Shimbun*, 10 September 2011.

117. *Yomiuri Shimbun*, 13 March 2011.

118. Associated Press, 1 June 2011; Komatsu 2011, 41.

119. *Asahi Shimbun*, 28 March and 3 April 2011; *Yomiuri Shimbun*, 14 April 2011. Ironically, according to his former wife, Ozawa stayed away from his home district for nearly a year because he was afraid of radiation. See http://japandailypress.com/11-page-letter-reveals-wife-divorcing-ozawa-after-he-fled-from-radiation-154369.

120. The Liberal Democratic Party (LDP) kept control of forty of the forty-one prefectural assemblies for which elections were held, and received fewer votes in all but one prefecture. *Asahi Shimbun*, 11 April 2011.

121. *Yomiuri Shimbun*, 16 April 2011; *Reuters*, 20 April 2011.

122. *Asahi Shimbun*, 14 April 2011.

123. Nishioka resigned from the DPJ to assume this post, but the president of the House of Councilors (HOC) is supposed to be politically neutral. See the editorial in *Asahi Shimbun*, 21 May 2011. See also *Nihon Keizai Shimbun*, 14 April 2011.

124. A survey in mid-April showed that 69 percent of respondents agreed with the idea of introducing a reconstruction tax to finance recovery in Tohoku. See *Nihon Keizai Shimbun*, 18 April 2011. This figure was significantly higher than earlier ones based on a March survey by the national broadcaster, NHK. By May, however, voter support for a reconstruction tax had declined to 26 percent. See *Bloomberg Businessweek*, 23 May 2011.

125. A poll in late April found 76.4 percent disapproval of the government's handling of the accident. See *Sankei Shimbun*, 25 April 2011. A week earlier, another poll by the *Asahi Shimbun*, 18 April, found that only 16 percent approved of the government's performance and nearly half said they "hope Kan quits soon." By July, Kan's support level was at a historic low of 12.5 percent. *Jiji Press*, 15 July 2011.

126. Izumi 2011.

127. In early April, nearly two-thirds of the Japanese people supported a DPJ/LDP "grand coalition." *Yomiuri Shimbun*, 4 April 2011; *Kyodo*, 16 April 2011. The *Oriental Economist* reports that LDP Policy Council head Ishiba Shigeru and LDP secretary general Ishihara Nobuteru both favored the idea of a grand coalition.

128. See the editorial in *Asahi Shimbun*, 21 May 2011. The chairs of both major business federations—Keidanren (Yonekura Hiromasa) and Keizai Dōyūkai (Hasegawa Yasuchika)— also protested the political posturing. *Kyodo*, 7 June 2011.

129. Mikuriya 2011b, 77.

130. Kingston 2012b, 189.

131. *Asahi Shimbun*, 26 December 2011.

132. Shinoda, forthcoming, is a useful account of Kan's dilemma. The renewables policy, known as a "feed-in-tariff," is discussed in detail in chapter 5.

133. Data supplied by the MIAC, 15 September 2011. See also Government of Japan 2011 and 2012.

134. Chinese offers to do more—including the dispatch of a People's Liberation Army Navy (PLAN) hospital ship—were rejected, as if it were payback for Beijing's refusal to accept Japanese military aircraft during the Sichuan relief effort (see chapter 3).

135. *Mainichi Shimbun*, 18 April 2011.

136. *Asahi Shimbun*, 19 June 2011; and Kawato, Pekkanen, and Tsujinaka 2012.

137. The aggregate number is reported in *Tokyo Shimbun*, 8 March 2012. Hyogo Prefecture provided 1.3 million yen grants to local groups with experience during the 1995 Hanshin/ Awaji disaster to send them to Tohoku to help build teahouses, medical facilities, beauty parlors, and other facilities. Data provided by the office of Hyogo governor Ido Toshizō, 22 December 2011. Kobe provided free buses for volunteers from its "Volunteer Plaza" to Tohoku. See Ido 2011, 132.

138. Interview, Hatakeyama Chiyoshi, NPO, Culture, and International Relations Division director, Iwate prefectural government, Morioka, 21 September 2011. (NPO is the Japanese acronym for nongovernmental organization, or NGO.)

139. Keizai Kōhō Sentā 2011b.

140. This is not a representative national sample, but it does reflect the civic activism of employees and affiliates of mainstream firms. The number was highest among those over sixty and under thirty. See Keizai Kōhō Sentā 2011a.

141. Data supplied by Keidanren, 28 February 2012.

142. *Jiji Press*, 26 April 2011.

143. *Tokyo Shimbun*, 8 March 2012.

144. See *Sōmushō Shōbōchō Saigai Boranteia Katsudō Jiretsu Deetabeesu* 2009; Avenell 2012b; Kawato, Pekkanen, and Tsujinaka 2012.

145. Interview, Nagasawa Emiko, NPO coordinator, Keidanren, Tokyo, 9 September 2011; Avenell 2012b; interview, Fuwa Masami, director, Office for Reconstruction Assistance, Japan International Cooperation Agency, Tokyo, 15 May 2012.

146. Avenell 2012b, 58.

147. Interview, Ogata Sadako, Tokyo, 15 May 2012.

148. See Peace Boat website at http://peaceboat.jp/relief/reports/shingo/ and photo on p. 172.

149. Avenell 2012b, 67.

150. Interview, Nagasawa Emiko, NPO coordinator, Keidanren, Tokyo, 9 September 2011.

151. Slater, Nishimura, and Kindstrand 2012, 96.

152. *USA Today*, 11 March 2011.

153. Interview, U.S. government official, Tokyo, 9 May 2012.

154. See "U.S. Giving in Response to Japan's March 11 Disaster Tops $630 Million," Japan Center for International Exchange, Special Report, http://www.jcie.org/311recovery/usgiving .html.

155. For excellent chronologies and summary data of these activities, see Feickert and Chanlett-Avery 2011 and Zielonka 2011.

156. For the decision on U.S. use of the Yamagata Airfield, see *Asahi Shimbun*, 16 March 2011.

157. Data supplied by U.S. Forces Japan, 20 July 2011.

158. Interview, Umemoto Kazuyoshi, North American Bureau director general, Ministry of Foreign Affairs, Tokyo, 15 July 2011.

159. Interview, senior U.S. Embassy official, 5 July 2011, and senior Ministry of Defense official, 21 July 2011. See also Nishihara 2011.

160. Interview, U.S. army officer, Tokyo, 9 September 2011. For more on U.S. recognition of the Japanese sensibilities, see *Yomiuri Shimbun*, 7 April 2011.

161. Interview, U.S. government officials, Tokyo, 5 and 7 July and 7 October 2011.

162. Interview, Masuda Kazuo, director of policy planning and evaluation, Ministry of Defense, Tokyo, 16 December 2011.

163. Kitazawa quoted in the *Wall Street Journal*, 22 April 2011. For an early analysis of the unprecedented intimacy between U.S. and Japanese forces, see *Asahi Shimbun*, 23 March 2011.

164. Interview, Ministry of Defense (MOD) official, Tokyo, 15 September 2011.

165. Interview, U.S. government official, Tokyo, 9 May 2012.

166. In one case, radiation data collected by the U.S. military was given to the Foreign Ministry and passed on to the Ministry of Science and Education, but not to the prime minister's office. See *Reuters*, 20 June 2012.

167. *Tokyo Shimbun*, 23 February 2012. According to a U.S. embassy official (interview, Tokyo, 12 July 2011), the Japanese government confessed to the U.S. government that it was having trouble getting information from TEPCO.

168. Interview, U.S. business executive, Tokyo, 10 January 2012.

169. Warden Message from U.S. Embassy via the American Club in Tokyo, 17 March 2011.

170. *Wall Street Journal*, 7 June 2011.

171. *Yomiuri Shimbun*, 4 May 2011, and interview with author, Tokyo, 16 December 2011.

172. Nagashima 2011, 136.

173. Nagashima Akihisa quoted in the *Wall Street Journal*, 7 June 2011. For Nagashima's full account—an effort to rebut critics who argue that Operation Tomodachi merely proved how dependent Tokyo is on Washington—see Nagashima 2011. See also the *Asahi Shimbun*, 30 April 2011, for an account of these glitches that concluded "the United States is not used to helping advanced countries while Japan is not used to receiving aid."

174. Interview, U.S. Embassy officials, Tokyo, 12 July and 7 October 2011.

175. Ibid.; see also Nagashima 2011, 136, and *New York Times*, 13 June 2011.

176. *Asahi Shimbun*, 21 May 2011.

177. Interview, U.S. Embassy official, Tokyo, 9 May 2012.

178. *Asahi Shimbun*, 21 April 2011. Six separate joint project teams were created with U.S. civilian experts from the Nuclear Regulatory Commission (NRC), the Department of Defense (DOD), and the Department of Health and Human Services. For a summary of U.S.-Japan cooperation on the radiological effects of the Fukushima meltdown, see *Asahi Shimbun*, 18 April 2011.

179. Interview, Hosono Group participant, Tokyo, 12 July 2012. This was corroborated by a retired senior government of Japan (GOJ) intelligence officer (interview, 29 June 2011). A U.S. participant explained that Kitazawa called for meetings with the U.S. side that included an unwilling TEPCO and an unwilling METI as well (interview, 7 October 2011).

180. Interview, Nagashima Akihisa, Tokyo, 7 July 2011.

2. Never Waste a Good Crisis

1. For useful theoretical treatments and literature reviews, see Katznelson 1997; Immergut 1998; Capoccia and Kelemen 2007; and Mahoney and Thelen 2010. Baumgartner and Jones 2009 offer a detailed empirical analysis of how policy change in the United States is "disjointed and episodic." Gourevitch 1986 is a particularly important comparative and historical study. See also Gershenkron 1966, which posits the Industrial Revolution as the shock that transformed the developmental strategies of late-developing states.

2. Samuels 2003.

3. The standard theoretical treatment is the notion of scientific revolution introduced in Kuhn 1996. For the example of Keynesianism, see Hall 1989. Mahoney 2000 and Pierson 2004 are canonical approaches to critical junctures that stress path dependence.

4. Freeman 1987.

5. Mannheim 1993. Mannheim's theory was further developed in Neumann 1939; Linton 1942; and Heberle 1951. For comparative applications, see Samuels, ed. 1977; Johnston 1992; and Nikolayenko 2007.

6. Mannheim 1993, 79, 365, 385.

7. Mikuriya 2011b. See Krauss 1974 for a study of the *ampo* generation. For a pre-3.11 analysis of political generations in Japan, see Boyd and Samuels 2008.

8. Kan is quoted in *CNN.com*, 22 April 2011.

9. Hay 1999, 318.

10. Baumgartner and Jones 2009, xxvii.

11. Kingdon 1995.

12. Here, Emanuel was channeling an Asian notion holding that there is opportunity in crisis. Borrowing from the Chinese, the Japanese word for "crisis" combines the Chinese characters for danger and opportunity. For a more academic formulation of the same idea, see Polsky 2000, 466.

13. P. Hart 1993, 46.

14. Hirschman 1991.

15. P. Hart 1993, 37–38, and Hay 1996, 254.

16. Stryker 1996 outlines the construction and use of "strategic narratives" by social scientists, rather than social scientists' interpretations of narratives constructed by policy actors. Still, the rules are the same: narratives are sequential and "not only tell us what happened but they also explain why it happened as it did and not otherwise" (305).

17. "Discourse coalitions" is from P. Hart 1993, 41. McCloskey 2011, 186, tells us that "[T]he rhetorical tetrad of fact, story, logic, and metaphor characterizes all human thought," adding that economies and polities are "continuously negotiated with words."

18. Clancey 2006b, 916.

19. McCloskey 2011, 182

20. P. Hart 1993, 39.

21. Sniderman and Theriault 2004; Chong and Druckman 2007; and Baumgartner and Jones 2009.

22. White 1981; Stone 1989; Linde 1993.

23. Gamson and Modigliani 1989, 5.

24. Van Oostendorp 2001.

25. Brysk 1995, 577.

26. For a recent review of the literature, see Borah 2011.

27. Gusfield 1981, 3.

28. Edelman 1988, 95.

29. Entman 1993.

30. Chong and Druckman 2007, 112.

31. Entman 2003, 7.

32. Samuels 2003. The original elaboration of *bricolage* in the sociological literature is Lévi-Strauss 1966.

33. Gusfield 1981, 8.

34. Nelson and Kinder 1996, 1055–78.

35. See Slater, Nishimura, and Kindstrand 2012.

36. McGraw and Hubbard 1966.

37. Sniderman and Theriault 2004, 158; Chong and Druckman 2007.

38. Snow and Benford 1988; Benford and Snow 2000.

39. Druckman 2001, 1045; 2004, 683.

40. Rochon 1998, 7–8.

41. Birkland 1997, 33.

42. Jennings 1999, 3.

43. Sasa Atsuyuki quoted in Otabe 2011.

44. Ishihara cited in Duus 2012, 176.

45. See "Fukushima Project," www.f-pj.org/e-index.html.

46. Interview, Abe Tomoko, Tokyo, 2 November 2011. See also the headline of the 4 November 2011 *Nihon Keizai Shimbun*: "Recovery Is Nation Building" (*fukkō wa kunizukuri*).

47. Former prime minister Hosokawa is cited in *Asahi Shimbunsha* 2011, 136–43. Professor Iio Jun is cited in *Oriental Economist*, May 2011, 7. See converging views by others in *Asahi Shimbunsha* 2011. See also Hirayama 2011.

48. See Hiroshi Izumi, "Post-Earthquake Politics: A New Paradigm?" Tokyo Foundation, 26 April 2011, http://www.tokyofoundation.org/en/articles/2011/post-quake-politics.

49. Wada cited in *Los Angeles Times*, 11 April 2011.

50. Mikuriya 2011b, 7. The chapter is reproduced from his OpEd column in the *Yomiuri Shimbun*, 14 March 2011.

51. Taggart Murphy, "3/11 and Japan: A Hinge of History?" *Japan Focus*, 21 April 2011.

52. This formulation was first deployed in *Yomiuri Shimbun*, 24 March 2011, and appears also in *Chūō Kōron* July 2011, 89–91 and in Mikuriya 2011b. "At last" is from Sakamoto 2011, 112, who makes the same argument for 3.11 as the punctuation mark at the end of the "postwar era."

53. *Yomiuri Shimbun*, 23 April 2011.

54. See also Kamiya 2011, 14–15, for predictions about a reenergized generation of Japanese youth. See *Asahi Shimbunsha* 2011, 116–22, for a debate about change between Imae Hajime, a civic activist, and an established Democratic Party of Japan (DPJ) politician, Maehara Seiji.

55. Mikuriya 2011b, 173.

56. Interview, Tokyo Electric Power Company (TEPCO) senior manager, 26 January 2012.

57. This echo of Hirschman's perversity thesis was argued by Imai Takashi, chairman of the Japan Atomic Industrial Forum, an industry group representing utilities and vendors, at its annual meeting in June 2011; see http://www.jaif.or.jp/english/news_images/pdf/ENGNEWS02_1336537903P.pdf. See also *Nihon Keizai Shimbun*, 12 July 2011, for the claims of Yosano Kaoru, who was minister for economic and fiscal policy on 3.11.

58. Sakurabayashi 2011a, 94.

59. Befu, 2001; Dale, 1986.

60. For Umehara's ideas about *jōmon* culture, see Umehara, 1983 and www.goipeace.or.jp/english/activities/award/award3-1.html. For a glimpse of how his views of 3.11 and a return to traditional culture resonated with the general public, see the blog of Komeito politician, Akamatsu Masao at www.akamatsu.net/index.php/wp/2011/07/02/3014.html. Chairman Iokibe said he found Umehara's repeated calls for a return to *jōmon* culture "distracting." Interview, Yokosuka, 26 January 2012.

61. http://homepage2.nifty.com/nicvhousan/eco_bozu002_1105031.html.

62. Uchiyama 2011.

63. Ibid., 94.

64. A surprising exception was the acknowledgment by Kyoto University professor Nakanishi Hiroshi who, in an otherwise very critical column, acknowledged that "it is unlikely anyone else would have handled it any faster or better." See *Sankei Shimbun*, 4 May 2011. Kingston 2012a argues that Kan was "scapegoated" by political opponents. See also the report by the independent Rebuild Japan Initiative Foundation, which characterizes Kan as having displayed presence of mind and urgency during the early hours of the crisis, http://bos.sagepub.com/content/early/2012/02/29/0096340212440359.full.pdf+html and the analysis of Okamura Jun at http://www.son-of-gadfly-on-the-wall.blogspot.com/2012/07/the-fukushima-reportsor-whom-do-i-trust.html.

65. *Asahi Shimbun*, 7 April 2011 (online English edition). Note that the next day's Japanese-language editorial in the *Asahi* actually praised the prime minister for his decision to mobilize the Self-Defense Forces (SDF). See chapter 3.

66. *Jiji Press*, 27 March 2011.

67. *Yomiuri Shimbun*, 24 March 2011, and *Nihon Keizai Shimbun*, 29 March 2011.

68. A symposium on the relevance of Gotō after 3.11 was held in Tokyo in mid-July 2011 across the street from the iconic Tokyo Institute for Municipal Research, which he built. It was attended by several hundred persons, http://goto-shimpei.org/. See also the *Los Angeles Times*, 11 April 2011.

69. See Kingston 2012 for a list of Kan's successes and for his supposition that much of the negativity in the narrative was owed to "malicious" initiatives by TEPCO to discredit the prime minister. For a lengthy report on Kan's mishandling of the crisis, see *Nihon Keizai Shimbun*, 14 April 2011.

70. Toba 2011.

71. *Kyodo*, 14 April 2011.

72. "Amateurs" is a term used by Professor Iwai Tomoaki of Nippon University, quoted in the *Wall Street Journal*, 9 April 2011.

73. *Wall Street Journal*, 9 April 2011; *New York Times*, 15 April 2011.

74. This critique is from Tokyo governor Ishihara Shintarō in *Seiron*, June 2011, 122.

75. Inoue Tadao, chair of the Institute for Nuclear, Biological, Chemical, and Radiological Defense, quoted in the *Japan Times*, 12 April 2011.

76. *Yomiuri Shimbun*, 19 April 2011.

77. A Japanese-language search for this term paired with "Great Eastern Japan Disaster" turned up more than one million hits in December 2011. See *Nihon Keizai Shimbun*, 16 March 2011, for a sober use of the term. Tokyo governor Ishihara preferred the terms "ignorant and wrong headed" (*muchi ya kanchigai*). See *Seiron*, June 2011, 122.

78. Nakasone is quoted in *Mainichi Shimbun*, 19 April 2011. Yonekura is cited in *Mainichi Shimbun*, 26 May 2011. See also *Wall Street Journal*, 9 April 2011. Even Iokibe Makoto, Kan's own appointee, spoke to the press of "the limits of a civic activist turned-politician having been revealed." See *Mainichi Shimbun*, 28 August 2011.

79. Abe 2011, 36.

80. *Yomiuri Shimbun*, 5 May 2011.

81. *Shūkan Bunshun*, 27 July 2011 (special edition), 16.

82. Interview, Ogata Sadako, Tokyo, 15 May 2012.

83. *Economist*, 24 May 2011.

84. *Nihon Keizai Shimbun*, 18 April 2011.

85. *Kyodo*, 1 May 2011. U.S. government officials, for their part, credit Kan with effective leadership. One asked rhetorically: "Who knows what would have happened if Kan hadn't screamed at TEPCO?" Interview, Tokyo, 7 October 2011.

86. *Higashi Nihon Daishinsai Fukkō Kōsō Kaigi* 2011, 2.

87. Dinmore 2006.

88. Interview, Takamizaka Nobushige, Ministry of Defense Policy Bureau chief, Tokyo, 7 July 2011.

89. See P. Hart 1993, 44, and Boin et al. 2008, 4. The notion of *sōteigai* as "evasion" and "concealment" has been remarked on by Japanese intellectuals as well. See, for example, Hatamura 2011, 86–88, 92.

90. *Asahi Shimbunsha* 2011, 182.

91. Kawano 2011, 5, 21.

92. *Asahi Shimbunsha* 2011, 173. Chapter 3 examines this claim.

93. *Yomiuri Shimbun*, 16 December 2011. The *Yomiuri* seems to have been conflicted on the *sōteigai* argument. An earlier editorial bore the headline: "We Must Never Again Allow the 'Unimaginable.'" See *Yomiuri Shimbun*, 18 April 2011. As we have noted earlier, a successful *sōteigai* defense is particularly critical for TEPCO, as the size of its ultimate liability depends on acceptance of the argument that 3.11 was a natural disaster, not a man-made one.

94. See, for example, Nakanishi 2011 and Nishio 2011.

95. Nakagawa 2000.

96. Professor Madarame Haruki, quoted in the *Japan Times*, 16 February 2012.

97. Hirose 2011, 1.

98. Handō, Hosaka, and Todaka 2011, 158, 163.

99. Hatamura 2011, 91.

100. See Professor Nakabayashi Itsuki's analysis in *Nippon Seisaku Tōshi Ginkō* 2011, 34.

101. The *Yomiuri Shimbun*, 22 April 2011, reported that the Japanese public regarded TEPCO and the government as equally culpable for the nuclear accident.

102. *Wall Street Journal*, 17 and 19 March 2011; *Financial Times*, 19 April 2011.

103. *Shūkan Bunshun*, 7 April 2011. These stories covered TEPCO's discharge of radiated water, cozy relations with its regulators, questions about its commitment to compensate victims, and so forth. In an earlier issue, it spoke of TEPCO as "the black monopoly firm." See *Shūkan Bunshun*, 27 March 2011.

104. *Financial Times*, 15 March 2011.

105. *Yomiuri Shimbun*, 11 April 2011; *Asahi Shimbun*, 18 April 2011; *New York Times*, 21 May 2011.

106. *Japan Times*, 15 February 2012.

107. Nishio 2011, 44–46. TEPCO reportedly refused to acquire remote sensor technologies and robots for fear that their deployment would shatter the "safety myth" that it had cultivated for the nuclear power industry. See *Asahi Shimbun*, 14 May 2011.

108. Katsunobu Sakurai 2011, 141. Mayor Sakurai's YouTube appeal is at http://www.you tube.com/watch?v=70ZHQ–cK40.

109. *Associated Press*, 13 April 2011.

110. *Asia-Pacific Journal*, 4 April 2011.

111. Column by William Pesek in *Bloomberg*, 24 May 2011. The *Economist*, 24 May 2011, added that TEPCO was "so big that it could co-opt or run rings around its regulators." TEPCO executives claimed that the public did not understand their struggles and resented being singled out as scapegoats for the disaster. One compared TEPCO's situation to that of Koreans in Tokyo after the Great Kanto Earthquake of 1923. Another insisted that the prime minister used TEPCO as a villain to maintain a grip on power. Remarkably, one retired TEPCO vice president even tried to shift blame by explaining that Prime Minister Kan was Korean. Interviews with current and retired TEPCO senior executives on 26 January 2011 and 3 February 2012. See also *Asahi Shimbun*, 14 July 2012.

112. Chief cabinet secretary Edano Yukio promised to do all he could to block officials from taking up post-retirement sinecures (*amakudari*) in the electric power industry. *Kyodo*, 13 April 2011, and *Financial Times*, 18 April 2011.

113. The weeklies report that officials demanded and received taxi rides, alcohol, and the services of hostesses from the utilities. See *Shūkan Bunshun*, 17 April 2011, 30.

114. Onuki 2011, 2; *Shūkan Bunshun*, 17 April 2011, 30; Kingston 2012b.

115. Satō Eisaku 2011, 100–101; *Yomiuri Shimbun*, 10 April 2011. As governor in the early 1990s, Satō had stopped operation of seventeen TEPCO plants in Fukushima. See Onuki 2011, 1. See also the editorial in the *Mainichi Shimbun*, 2 January 2012, which questions why Yasui Masaya, a Ministry of Economy, Trade and Industry (METI) official who had once ordered a cover-up of unflattering safety data, was put in charge of reform of the nuclear power safety regulations by the Noda government. See also the critical account by Hasuike Tōru, a former TEPCO employee who worked at Fukushima Daiichi and the brother of one of those kidnapped by North Korean agents in the 1970s: Hasuike and Onda 2011, 237.

116. *Asahi Shimbun*, 27 May 2011.

117. Otabe 2011, 1.

118. *Yomiuri Shimbun*, 15 January 2012. As discussed in chapter 3, the *sōteigai* defense does not apply to the SDF, which succeeded after 3.11 in part precisely because it imagined such a disaster and practiced effectively to deal with one.

119. See, for example, Smith 1985 on the importance of groups in Japanese society, and Katzenstein 1996 on Japan's purported "anti-majoritarian norm" of decision making.

120. See "Lessons Learned from the Great Hanshin-Awaji Earthquake Case," Kobe, 11 December 2008, www.jointokyo.org/files/cms/news/pdf/Kobe.pdf. This report also notes that in a 2003 survey of Kobe residents, people's ties within a community and family and the value of mutual assistance were referred to as the most important lesson of the disaster.

121. Seguchi 2011, 2, contrasts the looting of shops by Katrina victims with the sharing of rice balls by 3.11 victims. There were also occasional reports that, to the contrary, theft and assaults occurred in the affected areas, particularly in the temporary shelters.

122. *Nihon Keizai Shimbun*, 4 November 2011.

123. After all, the expression *"Ganbarō Tōhoku"* surfaced an additional eleven million hits, and neither of these captured nonelectronic forms of communication.

124. See Yokomichi 2010 for details on this *"Heisei gappei"* (Heisei era amalgamation of localities). The original plan was to reduce the number to just one thousand by 2010, but the government failed. Interview, Koyanagi Tarō, Sōmushō official, 13 October 2011.

125. Satō 2011, 124.

126. Interviews, local assemblyman and village head, Minami Sanriku, 12 January 2012. See also *Yomiuri Shimbun*, 18 March 2011, for an article on efforts to maintain existing communities in the temporary shelters.

127. *Higashi Nihon Daishinsai Fukkō Kōsō Kaigi* 2011.

128. Mikuriya 2011b, 42–43. His reference to an imminent shining light (*hikari ga sashite kuru*) is the title of a collection of poems by Kitamura Tarō, one of postwar Japan's most admired poets.

129. Ibid., 39.

130. The Miyagi plan is at http://www.cas.go.jp/jp/fukkou/pdf/kousou7/murai.pdf. For the Iwate plan, see Iwate Prefecture 2011. For the Fukushima plan, see Fukushima Prefecture 2011.

131. See the prime minister's statement, 11 April 2011, www.kantei.go.jp/foreign/kan /statement/201104/11kizuna_e.html. Note that he had used the term *kizuna* several months earlier in an address to the World Economic Forum in Davos, Switzerland.

132. *Mainichi Shimbun*, 13 December 2011.

133. The video is at www.kizuna-japan.com/kizuna_movie.html. Importantly, none of these messages take on a xenophobic cast. To the contrary, the song that overlays the images is partly in English, as are many of the graphic images themselves.

134. See www.Kadokawa-matsuri.com/program/?page_id=15.

135. *Asahi Shimbun*, 5 January 2012.

136. Rengō advertisement on Chiyoda subway line, January 2012.

137. See www.sakaya1.com/SHOP/njk007.html.

138. For a video of Ms. Endō's final moments and her broadcast, see http://www.youtube .com/watch?v=i6Kl08zHiJY. For Noda's eulogy, see http://www.kantei.go.jp/foreign/noda /statement/201109/13syosin_e.html. For Kobayashi's use of Endō to frame his account of 3.11, see Kobayashi 2011, 16. For a story on the first responders who are deceased, see *Sankei Shimbun*, 16 April 2011.

139. *Kyodo*, 26 August 2012.

140. *Asahi Shimbun*, 10 April 2011. Note that the word "Fukushima" is rendered in katakana (the Japanese writing system reserved mainly for imported words) to connote the invention of the term by the foreign media.

141. Penney 2011, 1. For a detailed investigative report on the alleged exploitation of subcontractors by TEPCO, see Takahashi 2011, 52–55. For details on these workers, see also the *Wall Street Journal*, 18 April 2012.

142. The TEPCO report is at www.tepco.co.jp/en/challenge/environ/pdf-1/10report-e .pdf. See p. 66. See also Jobin 2011.

143. Inose Naoki in *Chūō Kōron*, July 2011, 92.

144. *Asahi Shimbun*, 16 June 2011.

145. See a report on Yoshida's "unlikely" heroism in the *New York Times*, 13 June 2011. See also the account in *Asahi Shimbun*, 27 May 2011.

3. Historical and Comparative Guidance

1. Duus 2012, 175.
2. Busch 1962, 39.
3. Davison 1931, 56–57.
4. Busch 1962, 78–79.

5. Nōbi shook along an 80 km fault line. See Awata, Kariya, and Okumura 1998, at http://unit.aist.go.jp/actfault-eq/english/reports/h10seika/12seika.html. They conclude that this fault has a recurrence interval of 2,700 years.

6. Beard 1924, 11.

7. United Nations Centre for Regional Development 1995, xiii. Nearly 60 percent of prewar buildings in Kobe were destroyed, and fully one half of those erected during Japan's postwar high-growth period (1946–1965). Only 6 percent of the post-1986 buildings failed. See www .jointokyo.org/files/cms/news/pdf/kobe.pdf.

8. Hammer 2006; Smits 2006; Duus 2012. See http://pinktentacle.com/2011/04/namazu -e-earthquake-catfish-prints/ for an interesting collection of these images.

9. Smits 2006, 1052, 1066.

10. Clancey 2006a, 128.

11. Ibid., 130–31.

12. Ibid., 122.

13. See Fujitani 1996 and Samuels 2003 for accounts of the political use of the imperial institution.

14. Clancey 2006a, 132.

15. Ibid., 131.

16. The Imperial Earthquake Investigation Committee (*Shinsai Yobō Chōsakai*). Ibid., 151.

17. Beard 1924 is a particularly interesting contemporary account by a major American social scientist. See also Busch 1962; Seidensticker 1991; Hammer 2006; Duus 2012. Handō, Hosaka, and Mikuriya 2011a and Mikuriya 2011b draw parallels between 1923 and 2011.

18. Beard 1924, 17.

19. Kan 1975, chap. 1. For a glimpse of how reflective the Japanese military has become, and the extent to which it has come to embrace democratic norms, see the article by Satō Masahisa, a retired Ground Self-Defense Force (GSDF) general, who acknowledges that the imperial military used martial law to suppress freedoms after the 1923 quake: Satō 2011a, 103.

20. Kinney 1924, 3–4.

21. Davison 1931, 40.

22. Ibid., 18–22.

23. Beard 1924, 18, and Schencking 2006, 835; Dimmer 2011.

24. Beard 1924, 11.

25. Busch 1962, 173–74.

26. Beard 1924, 14–15.

27. Ibid., 18.

28. Mikuriya 2011b, 13–16.

29. Ibid., 14.

30. Schencking 2006, 870.

31. Beard 1924, 18, 21.

32. In one infamous incident, the *Kempeitai* (military police) abducted Ōsugi Sakae, an anarchist writer, his common-law wife, and their nephew (an American citizen) and murdered them in custody. See Humphreys 1995, 56–58. Kinney 1924, 14, refers to a similar incident.

33. Quoted in Allen 1996, 67–68.

34. Hammer 2006, 194.

35. Martial law continued until 15 October.

36. Davison 1931, 19.

37. Kinney 1924, 11; Busch 1962, 108–12; Hammer 2006, 159.

38. Hammer 2006, 167. Busch 1962, 111, reports that the government never conducted a serious investigation into the atrocities, nor did it ever punish appropriately those who committed them.

39. Hammer 2006, 168.

40. Quoted in Davison 1931, 50.

41. For an eyewitness account, see Kinney 1924, 12. See also Hammer 2006, 217.

42. Davison 1931, 21. An earlier account suggested that the Imperial military was idle, awaiting instructions from Tokyo, while the United States and other foreign navies bypassed them to provide early rescue and relief support. See Kinney 1924.

43. Admiral Edwin Alexander Anderson quoted in Hammer 2006, 219–20.

44. U.S. secretary of state Charles Evans Hughes quoted in Busch 1962, 34.

45. Hammer 2006, 246–48.

46. Humphreys 1995, 88.

47. Hammer 2006, 217, refers here only to the U.S. response, but notes also that the Soviets were turned away and the volunteers of other nations were also eyed with suspicion.

48. Schencking 2009.

49. Ibid.

50. Humphreys 1995, 52, 46–52.

51. Duus 2012, 178.

52. Schencking 2006, 2008, 2009.

53. Schencking 2008, 306.

54. Okutani Fumitomo, a Tenrikyō priest, quoted in Borland 2006, 889.

55. Busch 1962, 148.

56. Schencking 2006, 309–10.

57. Borland 2006, 891.

58. Ibid., 894.

59. Seidensticker 1991, 14–15. As home minister in charge of the police and protection of the emperor, Gotō had to assume special responsibility.

60. Estimates of total cost vary considerably. See Nagamatsu 2007, 373, and *Nihon Keizai Shimbun*, 21 March 2011. For reliable analyses of the Hanshin/Awaji disaster and its aftermath in English, see United Nations Centre for Regional Development 1995; Tierney and Goltz 1997; Edgington, Hutton, and Leaf 1999; Özerdem and Jacoby 2006; Kingston 2011. The best account in Japanese is Asō 2003.

61. Asō 2003, 114, details the "ossification of Japan's administrative structure" (*kōchaku shita nihon no gyōsei kikō*).

62. Midford, forthcoming, shows that the general public was ahead of elites in accepting the legitimacy of the Self-Defense Forces (SDF).

63. Nakagawa 2000.

64. See ibid. and Asō 2003, 72–76.

65. Asō 2003, 72–76.

66. Terry 1998, 233.

67. Tierney and Goltz 1997, 5.

68. Terry 1998, 232.

69. United Nations Centre for Regional Development 1995, 144; Tierney and Goltz 1997, 6–7.

70. United Nations Centre for Regional Development 1995, 144; Terry 1998, 237.

71. Tierney and Goltz 1997, 6.

72. United Nations Centre for Regional Development 1995, 151.

73. *Bōeishō* 2011a.

74. According to Özerdem and Jacoby 2006, 39, the mobilization was held up in Tokyo.

75. See Motoaki Kamiura, "Self Defense Forces Gain New Cachet as Emergency Responders," *Cultural News*, May 2011, www.culturalnews.com/?p=4689.

76. This is the view of Terry 1998, 236, and of Tierney and Goltz 1997, 7. See also Satō Masahisa 2011a, 62.

77. Interview, SDF flag officer, Tokyo, 16 December 2011.

78. Interview, senior U.S. military officer, Tokyo, 18 November 2011.

79. United Nations Centre for Regional Development 1995, 151.

80. Interview, former Hyogo governor Kaihara Toshitami, Kobe, 22 December 2011.

81. Özerdem and Jacoby 2006, 40.

82. Interview, former Hyogo governor Kaihara Toshitami, Kobe, 22 December 2011.

83. Terry 1998, 234. Governor Kaihara reports that he was happy to speak with U.S. ambassador Walter Mondale and to accept his offer of tarpaulins. Interview, Kobe, 22 December 2011.

84. This account is from United Nations Centre for Regional Development 1995, 171–72.

85. Leslie Helm, "Gangs Bridge Relief Gap after Quake," *Los Angeles Times,* 22 January 1995.

86. Avenell 2012a, 59.

87. United Nations Centre for Regional Development 1995, 175.

88. Interview, former Hyogo governor Kaihara Toshitami, Kobe, 22 December 2011.

89. Edgington, Hutton, and Leaf 1999, 15.

90. Despite Tokyo's provision of three supplementary budget outlays of 3.23 trillion yen, nearly half the reconstruction funds were derived from a municipal bond alone. See www.join tokyo.org/files/cms/news/pdf/kobe.pdf; www.city.kobe.lg.jp/safety/hanshinawaji/revival /promote/january.2011.pdf; www.mofa.go.jp/policy/economy/apec/1995/issue/info14.html; United Nations Centre for Regional Development 1995, 143; and Nagamatsu 2007, 372.

91. Edgington 2010.

92. And in key local industries, such as nonleather shoes and sake, it was far less. See www .city.kobe.lg.jp/safety/hanshinawaji/revival/promote/january.2011.pdf.

93. Mikuriya 2011a, 16–17.

94. Edgington, Hutton, and Leaf 1999, 15.

95. *Japan Times,* 26 January 1995; Tierney and Goltz 1997, 4; Nakagawa 2000; Özerdem and Jacoby 2006, 41.

96. For a local perspective, see http://tatsuki-lab.doshisha.ac.jp/~statsuki/papers/IAVE98 /IAVE98.html. See also Pekkanen 2006 for a detailed analysis of how Hanshin/Awaji volunteerism changed Japanese politics nationally. A short explanation is found at http://www.gdrc .org/ngo/jp-npo-law.html.

97. *Nippon Seisaku Tōshi Ginkō* 2011, 7.

98. Tierney and Goltz 1997, 4, 7; www.jishin.go.jp/main/w_030_f-e.htm.

99. Interview, Okamoto Atsushi, editor, *Sekai,* Tokyo, 13 September 2011.

100. Interview, SDF general, 16 December 2011.

101. One such exercise is reported in the *Wall Street Journal,* 25 October 2004. See chapter 4 for a detailed look at how these exercises evolved.

102. Louisiana Department of Health and Hospitals, "Reports of Missing and Deceased," 2 August 2006, http://www.dhh.louisiana.gov/offices/page.asp?ID=192&Detail=5248. I am grateful to Christopher Clary for his research assistance in support of this section.

103. *Washington Post,* 28 September 1998, paraphrases James Lee Witt, then head of the Federal Emergency Management Agency. He used similar language elsewhere. See, for example, *NBC News Transcripts,* 26 September 1998.

104. *Scientific American,* October 2001.

105. Access to the full series of articles is available at *Times Picayune,* http://www.nola.com /washingaway/. The article quoted appeared 24 June 2002.

106. Federal Emergency Management Agency, "Hurricane Pam Exercise Concludes," Press Release No. R6-04-093, 23 July 2004, http://www.fema.gov/news/newsrelease.fema?id=13051. See also U.S. House of Representatives 2006, 81–84.

107. U.S. House of Representatives 2006, chap. 16.

108. See, for example, U.S. Department of Justice, Office of Public Affairs, http://www.jus tice.gov/opa/pr/2010/December/10-crt-1420.html and http://www.justice.gov/opa/pr/2011 /April/11-crt-463.html.

109. See http://georgewbush-whitehouse.archives.gov/news/releases/2005/09/20050902 -2.html.

110. *Boston Herald,* 3 September 2005, and *New York Times,* 3 September 2005.

111. Joel Roberts, "Poll: Katrina Response Inadequate," *CBS News,* September 8, 2005, http://www.cbsnews.com/stories/2005/09/08/opinion/polls/main824591.shtml.

112. U.S. House of Representatives Select Bipartisan Committee 2006, 3.

113. The transcript of Mayor Nagin's interview is at http://www.jacksonfreepress.com /index.php/site/comments/transcript_new_orleans_mayor_c_ray_nagins_interview/.

114. Horne 2006, 3.

115. Sampling of *Associated Press, Associated Press Online,* and *New York Times* headlines from 9–10 September 2005.

116. Paglia in *Independent* (London), 3 September 2005.

117. Sullivan in *Sunday Times* (London), 4 September 2005.

118. Freedland in *Guardian*, 5 September 2005.

119. Frum in *National Post* (Toronto), 3 September 2005.

120. *New York Times*, September 8, 2005.

121. Dowd in *New York Times*, 12 September 2005.

122. Dionne in *Washington Post*, 13 September 2005. See also *New York Times*, 28 August 2006; *Washington Post*, 29 August 2006; and *New Republic*, 25 September 2006.

123. Lowry in *National Review*, 2 April 2007.

124. Also see Malhotra and Kuo 2008.

125. See Kelman and Koukis 2000; Kelman 2007, 2012. For a list of studies of disaster diplomacy, see http://www.disasterdiplomacy.org.

126. Among the 133 countries that offered assistance to the United States after Hurricane Katrina were rival states Cuba, Iran, and China.

127. Ker-Lindsay 2000; Akcinaroglu, DiCicco, and Radziszewsk 2011.

128. Gaillard, Clavé, and Kelman 2008. See also *Economist*, 20 July 2005, and *Guardian*, 14 August 2005.

129. Kelman and Koukis 2000; Kelman 2012.

130. *CBS News Transcripts*, 17 May 1991.

131. *Agence France Presse*, 15 May 1991.

132. McCarthy 1991, 31.

133. *New York Times*, 16 May 1991.

134. E-mail to Research Assistant Christopher Clary from U.S. defense official, Dhaka, 2 August 2011.

135. Smith 1995, 85–87.

136. Seiple 1991, 68.

137. Stackpole 1992, 116. See also Brig. Gen. Rowe, commander of 5th Marine Expeditionary Brigade (MEB), quoted in Seiple 1991, 88, 93; electronic correspondence with U.S. defense official, Dhaka, 2 August 2011.

138. Tripartite Core Group 2008, 1.

139. Ibid., 21.

140. *Guardian*, 23 May 2008.

141. See International Crisis Group, "Burma/Myanmar after Nargis: Time to Normalise Aid Relations" (Asia Report No. 161, Brussels, 20 October 2008), 6–7.

142. This was the largest and most effective overseas deployment of the SDF ever.

143. Beinert 2006, 194.

144. See http://www.terrorfreetomorrow.org/articlenav.php?id=56.

145. Admiral Mike Mullen, "What I Believe: Eight Tenets That Guide My Vision for the 21st Century" (U.S. Navy Proceedings, January 2006).

146. Wike 2012.

147. Bowers 2010, 132.

148. Bureau of Legislative and Public Affairs 2006, 3–4; Wilder 2008, 3; Bowers 2010, 132.

149. Crocker quoted by Bowers 2010, 133.

150. *Newsweek*, 4 September 2009; U.S. AID, *Pakistan Earthquake Relief*, 6, and "Fact Sheet—DOD Assistance to Pakistan."

151. U.S. AID, "Fact Sheet—DOD Assistance to Pakistan," 7.

152. See, for example, *Associated Press*, 10 October 2005; *Washington Post*, 13 October 2005; and *Wall Street Journal*, 22 December 2005.

153. Bowers 2010, 132.

154. Terror Free Tomorrow, *A Dramatic Change of Public Opinion in the Muslim World: Results from a New Poll in Pakistan* (Washington, DC: Terror Free Tomorrow, 2005).

155. Wilder 2008, 4.

156. Ibid., 26.

157. Pew Research Center, Global Attitudes Project, 2011.

158. Wike 2012.

159. The number of homeless is disputed, but no reported figure is less than five million. See http://www.factsanddetails.com/china.php?.itemid=407&catid=10&subcatid=65#8711. See also *BBC*, 1 September 2008; Restall 2008; Kokusai Kyōryoku Kikō 2009; Chen et al. 2010; Huang, Zhou, and Wei 2011; Zhang 2011.

160. *BBC*, 19 May 2008. For fuller comparisons, see Ayson and Taylor 2008 and Kapucu 2011.

161. As we see in chapter 6, this "partner support" system became a model in Japan after 3.11. For Japanese analysis of how it worked in China, see Hayashi and Masato 2011. For a positive but less effusive Chinese analysis of how the townships responded, see You, Chen, and Yao 2009, 384–85.

162. Shieh and Deng 2011, 185, 194.

163. Restall 2008, 80.

164. Ibid., 77–78, calls it the "renaissance" of Chinese civil society. Teets 2009 is less sure; she finds greater ambiguity in the robustness of Chinese civil society during and after the Sichuan event. See also Shieh and Deng 2011, 181.

165. Zhang 2011.

166. Restall 2008, 77.

167. See *BBC*, 12 June 2008.

168. See Restall 2008, 77–78; and Mine 2011, 3.

169. Ayson and Taylor 2008; Restall 2008, 79.

170. Wei, Zhao, and Liang 2009.

171. *Jiji*, 16 May 2008; *Kyodo*, 16 May 2008; *Xinhua*, 16 May 2008.

172. Interview, former Bank of Japan chief Beijing representative, Seguchi Kiyoyuki, Tokyo, 14 May 2012.

173. *Mainichi Shimbun*, 8 June 2008.

174. *Tokyo Shimbun*, 14 May 2008.

175. Ibid.; *Yomiuri Shimbun*, 14 May 2008.

176. *Mainichi Shimbun*, 8 June 2008. Vice Foreign Minister Onodera Itsunori also tied the mission to Japanese diplomacy. See Przystup 2008.

177. According to Japan International Cooperation Agency (JICA) officials, it is very unusual for a Foreign Ministry official to lead a Japan Disaster Relief (JDR) team, but this was an exceptional case. Interview, Ogata Sadako, former president, Japan International Cooperation Agency, and Fuwa Masami, director, Office for Reconstruction Assistance, Japan International Cooperation Agency, Tokyo, 15 May 2012.

178. For the full JICA report of the JDR mission, see Kokusai Kyōryoku Kikō 2009.

179. *Asahi Shimbun*, 31 May 2008.

180. Kokusai Kyōryoku Kikō 2009, 14.

181. *Yomiuri Shimbun*, 4 June 2008; *Kyodo*, 8 June 2008; Jyapan Purattofōmu 2009.

182. There was a basis for this: In 2007, China had signed the "Space and Major Disasters Agreement" and as a consequence, its National Space Administration received satellite images of the disaster area from Japan's Aerospace Exploration Agency. *Yomiuri Shimbun*, 24 May 2008; Kokusai Kyōryoku Kikō 2009.

183. *Kyodo*, 21 May 2008.

184. See http://www.zakzak.co.jp/top/2008_05/t2008052901_all.html.

185. *Mainichi Shimbun*, 15 May and 8 June 2008. The "avid interest" of the Chinese media in the Japanese relief effort was also reported by the Ministry of Foreign Affairs' (MOFA's) Koizumi, the leader of Japan's JDR team. See Kokusai Kyōryoku Kikō 2009.

186. *Mainichi Shimbun*, 20 May 2008.

187. For examples, see *BBC*, 12 June 2008 and 27 December 2008; *Los Angeles Times*, 29 July 2008; *New York Times*, 29 July 2008.

188. Qin quoted in *BBC*, 28 May 2008.

189. *Xinhua*, 17 and 18 May 2008. The JICA report lists all the Chinese and Japanese media that covered their JDR team.

190. For a video account of the photo, including an interview of the Xinhua reporter who captured the image, see http://www.youtube.com/watch?v=XoRDWylU1Jk.

191. Polls indicated that more than 70 percent of Shanghai residents reported their views of Japan had changed and 84 percent now held positive feelings toward Japan. See *Chōsa Nyuzu*, 22 May 2008, at http://news.searchina.ne.jp/dispcgi?y=2008&d=5022&f=research_0522_002.sthml.

192. For representative accounts, see *Chōsa Niyuzu*, 22 May 2008; Takarabe 2008; Mine 2011.

193. Kōmura's and Machimura's comments are reported in Przystup 2008.

194. See, for example, *Asahi Shimbun*, 29 May 2008; *Sankei Shimbun*, 29 May 2008. *Yomiuri Shimbun*, 29 May 2008, correctly reported the divisions within China on this issue.

195. This is the statement of People's Liberation Army (PLA) deputy chief of staff, Ma Xiaotian. *Asahi Shimbun*, 1 June 2008. One post was quoted in the *Financial Times* on 29 May 2008: "Yesterday their planes were dropping bombs. Today they are giving a little kindness to confuse the Chinese people." Another was quoted in the *Yomiuri Shimbun*, two days later: "[Allowing the SDF into China] is like letting the wolf into your room."

196. *Yomiuri* Shimbun, 29 May 2008; *Jiji Press*, 30 May 2008. Note that the Air Self-Defense Force (ASDF) chief of staff during this period was the nationalist Tamogami Toshio, who would soon lose his position.

197. *Yomiuri Shimbun*, 31 May 2008.

198. *Asahi Shimbun*, 28 June 2008.

199. *Nihon Keizai Shimbun*, 25 June 2008.

200. For documentation of this point, see Nakabayashi 2009.

4. Dueling Security Narratives

1. See "Outline of 'Public Opinion Survey on the Self-Defense Forces (SDF) and Defense Issues,'" Public Relations Office, Cabinet Office, March 2012, http://www.mod.go.jp/e/d_act/others/pdf/public_opinion.pdf.

2. Wike 2012 reminds us that Japanese views of the United States were already favorable before 3.11. Afterward, though, they soared to the highest level among the twenty-three nations surveyed by the Pew Global Attitudes Project.

3. The SDF even resorted to referring to tanks as "special vehicles" and to destroyers as "escort ships." See Frühstück 2007 and Samuels 2007 for more on this history of redefinition and self-restraint.

4. Midford 2011.

5. See "Outline of 'Public Opinion Survey,'" http://www.mod.go.jp/e/d_act/others/pdf/public_opinion.pdf.

6. Midford forthcoming, 1; See also jiji.com, 11 March 2012.

7. Interview, General Kimizuka Eiji, Tokyo, 16 December 2012.

8. Interview, Kimura Ayako, Tokyo, 22 November 2011.

9. *Der Westen* 2010.

10. Abe Shinzō quoted in the *Taipei Times*, 8 September 2011.

11. Nagashima 2011, 134.

12. Nakatani Gen quoted in *Asahi Shimbunsha* 2011, 43. Kamiya Matake, a professor at the National Defense Academy of Japan, uses the same "allergy" metaphor. See Kamiya Matake 2011, 15. As noted in chapter 2, most Japanese had long since been cured of this "allergy."

13. The former is Mizushima 2011b, 122, and the latter is Kamiya Matake 2011, 15.

14. Interview, North American Affairs Bureau director-general Umemoto Kazuyoshi, Tokyo, 15 July 2011.

15. *Yomiuri Shimbun*, 10 April 2011. See the 18 April 2011 editorials in the *Asahi Shimbun*, *Mainichi Shimbun*, *Nihon Keizai Shimbun*, and *Sankei Shimbun* for similarly effusive and optimistic evaluations of the alliance on the occasion of Secretary of State Hillary Clinton's post-3.11 visit to Japan.

16. Nishihara 2011, 1.

17. Interview, Ground Self-Defense Forces (GSDF) chief of staff Kimizuka Eiji, Tokyo, 16 December 2011.

18. Nishio 2011, 47.
19. Nakanishi 2011.
20. Tokyo vice governor Inose Naoki in *Chūō Kōron*, July 2011, 89.
21. Nishio 2011, 48.
22. Mamiya 2011, 111.
23. Kobayashi 2011, an account of 3.11, is an elaborate "wake-up call" entitled *A Theory of Defense*; see 56. He mocks those who suggest that Japan should be grateful for U.S. disaster assistance on 31–33.
24. Mamiya 2011, 106.
25. Takubo Tadae 2011, 191.
26. Satō Masahisa 2011a, 105.
27. Nakanishi 2011, 51.
28. Sasa Atsuyuki quoted in Otabe 2011, 45. For more on the Senkaku (Diaoyutai) Islands and Japan's other territorial disputes with its neighbors, see Samuels 2007.
29. See http://research.php.co.jp/research/foreign_policy/policy/post_3.php.
30. Nagashima 2011, 136–37.
31. Nakasone 2011.
32. *Yomiuri Shimbun*, 23 April 2011.
33. Sakamoto 2011, 113. See also Watanabe 2011.
34. Interview, GSDF Northeast Army policy adviser, Tokyo, 18 November 2011. The Ministry of Defense (MOD) official explained that there would have been more planning and exercises, but the electric utilities opposed crisis planning "for the effect it would have on citizens' sense of safety." As a result, he said, the SDF made its own plans for responding to natural disasters.
35. Interview, Takamizawa Nobushige, director general for policy, Ministry of Defense, Tokyo, 7 July 2011. Interview, Ono Hiroshi, director of Policy Planning Division, Bureau of Reconstruction, Iwate Prefecture, Morioka, 21 September 2011. Unpublished memo prepared by former MOD official Yamauchi Chisato, 22 July 2011. See also the interview with Lt. Gen. Kimizuka Eiji, commander of the Joint Task Force, in Otabe 2011, 48.
36. *Asahi Shimbun*, 8 April 2011.
37. See Asō 2011, chap. 2.
38. Sakurabayashi 2011a, 90.
39. For the English-language text of the emperor's message, see http://www.kunaicho.go .jp/e-okotoba/01/address/okotoba-h23e.html. Former prime minister Abe Shinzō claimed he carried the text of the emperor's statement with him every day, and criticized the *Asahi Shimbun* and the *Mainichi Shimbun* for not printing it in its entirety. See Abe 2011, 37. For other reactions to what has been called the emperor's "gracious approval" of the SDF, see Otabe 2011, 45 and Kubota 2011.
40. Interview, Nishi Masanori, director general of the MOD Bureau of Finance and Equipment, Tokyo, 21 July 2011.
41. Sakurabayashi 2011a, 94.
42. *Asahi Shimbunsha* 2011, 40.
43. See *Asahi Shimbun*, 30 April 2011; Kitamura 2011, 156; and Shikata 2011.
44. Interview, *Sekai* editor Okamoto Atsushi, Tokyo, 13 September 2011.
45. *Asahi Shimbun*, 30 April 2011. See Boyd 2012 for analysis of the full range of nationalist identities in play.
46. Mizushima op ed in *Asahi Shimbun*, 7 May 2011.
47. Kawasaki 2011, 79, 84.
48. *Akahata*, 19 April 2011.
49. See, for example, the blog of lawyer and peace activist Inoue Masanobu at http://www .news-pj.net/npj/9jo-anzen/20110406.html.
50. *Asahi Shimbun*, 7 May 2011.
51. Mizushima 1998.
52. Many Japanese derisively refer to Host Nation Support (HNS) as "the sympathy budget." The Socialists and Communists called for its reallocation to disaster relief. *Ryūkyū Shimpō*, 19 April 2011.

53. *Asahi Shimbun*, 7 May 2011; Mizushima 2011b, 122.

54. Kobayashi 2011, 102.

55. Satō 2011a, 100.

56. Interview, Ministry of Defense, Tokyo, 16 December 2011.

57. This section is based on the MOD's published evaluation (*Bōeishō* 2011a), on interviews with two MOD directors-general (Nishi Masanori on 21 July 2011 and Takamizawa Nobushige on 27 October 2011), and on an interview with defense analyst Morimoto Satoshi, Tokyo, 13 July 2011. (Morimoto became minister of defense in June 2012.) See also Shikata 2011, for an evaluation by a retired GSDF general.

58. According to MOD data supplied on 18 November 2011, 106,000 was the peak number in early May.

59. *Bōeishō* 2011a.

60. Ibid.

61. The MOD also acknowledges the "need to unify field communications more fully." See *Bōeishō* 2011a.

62. This, according to General Kimizuka in *Yomiuri Shimbun*, 4 May 2011. In May, more than two hundred SDF troops were reported to have lost family members on 3.11. By July, General Kimizuka revised that figure upward to 344. See *Jiji*, 4 July 2011.

63. *Asahi Shimbun*, 24 June 2011; and *Bōeishō* 2011a.

64. Interview, Takamizawa Nobushige, president, National Institute for Defense Studies, Tokyo, 27 October 2011.

65. *Bōeishō* 2011a; interview, senior military officer, MOD, Tokyo, 18 November 2011; and *Nihon Keizai Shimbun*, 13 March 2012.

66. *Asahi Shimbun*, 7 May 2011 and see photo on p. 172. Peace Boat publicly thanks the SDF on its website, http://pbv.or.jp/blog/?p=316. An MOD official reported that although Socialist Party prefectural and municipal assembly members privately conveyed their gratitude to SDF and MOD officials, no similar expression of gratitude was posted on the party's website. Interview, GSDF Northeast Army policy advisor, Tokyo, 18 November 2011.

67. The MOD identified "improved integration with private firms in crisis situations" among its lessons learned in its after-action report. See *Bōeishō* 2011a. In one of the first major military exercises after 3.11, GSDF units were moved from Hokkaido to Kyushu by private ferry firms. See http://newpacificinstitute.org/jsw/?p=8758.

68. Interview, senior military officer, MOD, Tokyo, 16 December 2011; and former minister of defense Nakatani Gen, quoted in *Asahi Shimbunsha* 2011, 43. See also Tanida 2011. It surely helped that Miyagi governor Murai and General Kimizuka were classmates at the National Defense Academy.

69. Interview, Governor Tasso, Morioka, 22 September 2011.

70. *Asahi Shimbun*, 7 May 2011.

71. Interview, MOD advisor to the Northeast Army, Tokyo, 18 November 2011.

72. Interview, GSDF chief of staff Kimizuka, 16 December 2011. Concern about the MOD and SDF role in local administration during a crisis when local functions have deteriorated was also expressed in the official MOD evaluation. See *Bōeishō* 2011a.

73. Interview, Ono Hiroshi, director, Policy Planning Division, Iwate Prefecture Bureau of Reconstruction, Morioka, 21 September 2011.

74. This was reported on the 13 July 2011 NHK (Japan Broadcasting Corporation) documentary show "Close Up Gendai," which reviewed approvingly the handling of local administration by the SDF.

75. The full list is at *Bōeishō* 2011b, 363, 373.

76. Data supplied by the MOD, 1 February 2012.

77. Government of Japan 2011, 4; and interview, senior MOD planning official, Tokyo, 7 July 2011.

78. Interview, Mayor Kawamura, Nagoya, 12 January 2012.

79. *Mainichi Shimbun*, 22 April 2011.

80. This is the conclusion drawn by the MOD. See *Bōeishō* 2011a.

81. Interview, MOD official, Tokyo, 18 November 2011.

82. Interview, senior MOD official, Tokyo, 27 October 2011.

83. Interview, TEPCO general manager, Tokyo, 26 January 2012. "Utterly insufficient cooperation from the utilities" was confirmed by an MOD director general, interview, Tokyo, 27 October 2011, and by former GSDF officer Nakamura Shingo in *Asahi Shimbunsha* 2011, 40.

84. Interview, Kimura Ayako, counselor, minister's secretariat, MOD, Tokyo, 22 November 2011.

85. Midford 2011, 106–7, reports on results from a 2000 cabinet poll. These results were reconfirmed in January 2012. See http://www.mod.go.jp/e/d_act/others/pdf/public_opinion.pdf.

86. *Yomiuri Shimbun*, 15 January 2012.

87. *Mainichi Shimbun*, 18 April 2011.

88. *Yomiuri Shimbun*, 18 December 2011.

89. The survey is at http://www.mod.go.jp/e/d_act/others/pdf/public_opinion.pdf. See also *Asahi Shimbun,* 11 March 2012. For some of the more striking portrayals of the SDF in the media, see the front-page photograph of SDF troops taking time to vote with absentee ballots in the nationwide local election in the 4 April 2011 edition of the *Yomiuri Shimbun*. See also Asō 2011; Nishihara 2011; Otabe 2011; Sakurabayashi 2011b; Kobayashi 2011; Satō Masahisa 2011a; *Shūkan Taishū* 2011. More realistic accounts with details of injuries, including stress and fatigue associated with the collection of corpses, can be found at *Shūkan Bunshun* 2011 and *Tokyo Shimbun*, 14 April 2011.

90. *Bōeishō* 2011a.

91. One Iwate Prefecture official described this as "clearly a decision from the top." Interview, Morioka, 21 September 2011. In June 2012, soldiers marched in full battle dress through Tokyo neighborhoods for the first time in forty-two years. *Kyodo*, 12 June 2012.

92. These data were provided by the MOD, 2 November 2011, and in interviews with MOD officials, Tokyo, 29 September and 27 October 2011.

93. Simpson 2011.

94. *Bōeishō* 2011a.

95. *Asagumo*, 6 October 2011.

96. See *Nihon Keizai Shimbun*, 22 April 2011; and *Kyodo*, 29 June 2011.

97. Interview, MOD official, Tokyo, 29 September 2011; and reports on 30 September 2011 in *Jiji*, *Kyodo*, and *Nihon Keizai Shimbun*, inter alia. See also *Yomiuri Shimbun*, 14 September 2011.

98. See, for example, Shikata 2011, who praised the SDF for being well equipped and argued that 3.11 highlighted the indispensability of some equipment that budget cutters usually find easy targets.

99. *Yomiuri Shimbun*, 14 September 2011.

100. On 3.11, the Maritime Self-Defense Forces (MSDF) had only three Ōsumi-class transports. One was in dock for maintenance and another, ironically, was in transit to Indonesia to participate in a disaster relief exercise. See *Yomiuri Shimbun*, 27 April 2011. Also Tanida 2011 and Mizokami 2011. On robots, see *Nihon Keizai Shimbun*, 4 April 2011.

101. See Katsumata Hidemichi in *Yomiuri Shimbun*, 27 April 2011.

102. *Sankei Shimbun*, 24 July 2011.

103. *Kyodo*, 17 July 2011.

104. Interview, Takamizawa Nobushige, Tokyo, 7 July 2011.

105. *Bōeishō* 2011a.

106. Interview, participating U.S. military officer, Tokyo, 11 January 2012. The officer explained that the MSDF and the U.S. Navy found cooperation easier to achieve than did the countries' ground forces, and noted regretfully that it took perhaps ten days to two weeks, rather than a few days, for these units to really hit their stride. E-mail correspondence, 18 March 2012. See also *Yomiuri Shimbun*, 7 April 2011.

107. Interview, Nishi Masanori, Tokyo, 21 July 2011.

108. Interview, Tokyo, 9 May 2012.

109. Interview, Col. Gregg Bottemiller, U.S. Forces Japan (USFJ), Tokyo, 22 July 2011. See also *Yomiuri Shimbun*, 23 August 2011.

110. Personal correspondence, 27 September 2011.

111. Interview, GSDF chief of staff Kimizuka Eiji, Tokyo, 16 December 2011.

112. See http://www.cfr.org/japan/us-japan-alliance-transformation-realignment-future-october-2005/p20745.

113. Interview, director of policy planning and evaluation, Masuda Kazuo, Tokyo, 16 December 2011; and interview, Colonel Mark Hague, U.S. Forces Japan, Tokyo, 20 December 2011.

114. Claims that the Bilateral Coordination Mechanism and the Bilateral Coordination Cells developed under the 1997 guidelines were implemented within hours are mistaken. See Center for International and Strategic Studies 2011, 32–33.

115. Private correspondence, U.S. military participant, 19 December 2011. Some suspect that this was because no exercise scenario anticipated a disaster on the scale of 3.11. See, for example, *Yomiuri Shimbun*, 7 April 2011.

116. Interview, U.S. military officer, Tokyo, 10 December 2011.

117. Interview, U.S. government official, Tokyo, 12 July 2011.

118. Interview, U.S. government official, Tokyo, 7 October 2011. One retired Defense Ministry official explained that this was due to the fact that the commander of USFJ has no operational responsibility for U.S. forces based in Japan, leading him to conclude that the alliance itself is therefore much like a "papier-mâché tiger" (*hariko no tora*). Interview, Tokyo, 22 July 2011.

119. Interview, participating U.S. military officer, Tokyo, 11 January 2012.

120. Feickert and Chanlett-Avery 2011 is an excellent summary of Operation Tomodachi. See also *Asahi Shimbun*, 18 and 30 April 2011.

121. Interview, James Zumwalt, deputy chief of mission, U.S. Embassy, Tokyo, 5 July 2011.

122. Center for International and Strategic Studies 2011, 33.

123. Prime Minister Kan quoted in *Asahi Shimbun*, 21 May 2011 and in *Shūkan Bunshun* 2011, 37. For his expressions of gratitude, see *Kyodo*, 4 April 2011; *Stars and Stripes*, 11 April 2011.

124. Interview, General Kimizuka, Tokyo, 16 December 2012. For background on Goldwater-Nichols DOD Reorganization Act of 1986, see Locher 2002.

125. *Bōeishō* 2011a.

126. Interview, Nishi Masanori, director-general of the MOD Bureau of Finance and Equipment, Tokyo, 21 July 2011; interview, former MOD official Yamauchi Chisato, Tokyo, 22 July 2011; interview, Takamizawa Nobushige, president of the National Institute for Defense Studies, Tokyo, 27 October 2011.

127. Interview, U.S. official, Tokyo, 12 July 2011; interview, defense analyst Morimoto Satoshi, Tokyo, 13 July 2011; and interviews, Japanese MOD officials, Tokyo, 2 and 27 October 2011.

128. *Bungei Shunjū*, July 2011, 236; *Asagumo*, 6 October 2011; *Nihon Keizai Shimbun*, 13 March 2012.

129. Ministry of Defense 2011. For a secondary account, see *Yomiuri Shimbun*, 23 August 2011.

130. Interview, former MOD official, Tokyo, 22 July 2011.

131. Interview, Takamizawa Nobushige, Tokyo, 7 July 2011.

132. Interview, Nishi Masanori, Tokyo, 21 July 2011.

133. *Bōeishō* 2011a.

134. Kitamura 2011, 158–59; and Mizokami 2011.

135. Interview, Nagashima Akihisa, Tokyo, 7 July 2011.

136. Interview, U.S. military officer, Tokyo, 11 January 2012.

137. Interview, Takamizawa Nobushige, Tokyo, 7 July 2011.

138. *Kyodo*, 28 August 2012.

139. Tanida 2011; *Yomiuri Shimbun*, 25 December 2011; *Nihon Keizai Shimbun*, 24 February 2012.

140. Interview, MOD official, Tokyo, 18 November 2011; and data supplied by MOD, 27 November 2011. The MOD sought to acquire three next-generation UHX rescue helicopters to replace the four UH-60J helicopters that were submerged on 3.11 in Miyagi. It also had to find a way to replace eighteen F-2 fighters that were damaged by seawater. See *Nihon Keizai Shimbun*, 21 April 2011; *Aviation Week*, 19 July 2011; *Asahi Shimbun*, 16 September 2011.

141. Kan is quoted in *Asahi Shimbun*, 18 August 2011.

142. Interview, Yokosuka, 2 February 2012.

143. *Defense News*, 10 September 2012.

144. Interview, senior Japanese military officer, Tokyo, 18 November 2011.

145. Interview, Takamizawa Nobushige, president, National Institute for Defense Studies, Tokyo, 27 October 2011; and interview, TEPCO general manager, Tokyo, 26 January 2012.

146. Quoted in *Kyodo*, 6 April 2011.

147. *Shūkan Posuto*, 29 April 2011; *Akahata*, 29 March 2012.

148. See Mizushima 2011b, 119–21; *Yomiuri Shimbun*, 10 April 2011; *Asahi Shimbun*, 11 May 2011; *Tokyo Shimbun*, 2 May 2011; *Kyodo*, 22 June 2011. Democratic Party of Japan (DPJ) Diet member Nagashima Akihisa says that for some, Operation Tomodachi was further evidence that U.S. forces in Japan are an "occupying army." See Nagashima 2011, 136.

149. *Tokyo Shimbun* editorial, 2 May 2011.

150. Kobayashi 2011, 65. In a lengthy critique of U.S. motives, the weekly magazine *Shūkan Posuto*, 29 April 2011, concurred, referring to the withdrawal of the carrier as "Reagan's getaway." The HNS argument was also made by Mizushima 2011b, 121, who suggests that Operation Tomodachi was "merely a payment to substantiate the arrangement" (*teigaku kyūfukin*).

151. *Japan Times*, 18 January 2012.

152. *Ryūkyū Shimpō*, 18 March 2011; and *Okinawa Times*, 9 April 2011.

153. Professor Gabe Masaaki quoted in *Ryūkyū Shimpō*, 26 April 2011.

154. *Komentoraina*, 21 April 2011.

155. See http://www.pewglobal.org/2011/07/13/chapter-2-views-of-the-u-s-and-ameri can-foreign-policy/.

156. *Associated Press*, 5 September 2011.

157. *Kyodo*, 3 December 2011.

158. *Jiji Press*, 13 April 2011.

159. See *Asahi Shimbun*, 7 April 2011; and *Nihon Keizai Shimbun*, 17 April 2011 for early analyses predicting this outcome.

160. This account is based on an interview with a meeting participant, Tokyo, 9 May 2012.

161. *Bōeishō* 2011b, 80–82. One USFJ official explained that U.S. forces have had "access" to Japanese facilities for landing and refueling for some time. But "use" of these facilities requires coordination with a number of central government ministries and agencies. Interview, Colonel Mark Hague, U.S. Forces Japan, Tokyo, 20 December 2011.

162. Interview, Morimoto Satoshi, 13 July 2011; and interview, Masuda Kazuo, director of policy, planning, and evaluation, MOD, 16 December 2011.

163. Interview, Northeast Army policy advisor, MOD, Tokyo, 18 November 2011. *Nihon Keizai Shimbun*, 17 April 2011, reported that Japan "caught a glimpse" of how this might work in the future. There also have been calls for a formal agreement between the U.S. military and local governments allowing regular drills in anticipation of natural disasters. See Satō Masahisa 2011b, 69.

164. Interview, Kimura Ayako, counselor, minister's secretariat, MOD, Tokyo, 22 November 2011.

165. For background on the treaty and the alliance, see Samuels 2007. The best work on basing issues is Smith 2006.

166. *Kyodo*, 22 July 2011.

167. See *Asahi Shimbun*, 10 and 13 April 2011.

168. *Asahi Shimbun*, 13 April 2011.

169. *Kyodo*, 14 June 2011; *Nihon Keizai Shimbun*, 27 June 2011.

170. Kitazawa is quoted in *Asahi Shimbun*, 30 April 2011.

171. McCain is quoted in *Jiji*, 13 April 2011.

172. *Asahi Shimbun*, 14 June 2011.

173. *Yomiuri Shimbun*, 10 March 2012.

174. *Japan Times*, 14 February 2012 (emphasis added). See also *Yomiuri Shimbun*, 10 March 2012. Analysts suggest that Iwakuni had already reached the political limits of cooperation with the U.S. military.

175. *Nihon Keizai Shimbun*, 21 April 2012.

176. Personal correspondence from U.S. government official, 20 March 2012.

177. Logan 2012.

178. *Asahi Shimbun,* 21 April 2012.

179. See *Nihon Keizai Shimbun,* 20 May 2011; *Economist,* 24 May 2011; and *Kyodo,* 4 September 2011.

5. Debating Energy Policy

1. This short history of nuclear power in Japan is from Samuels 1987, chap. 6.

2. Oshima 2010, 36–44; Nakamura and Kikuchi 2011, 898. These figures are disputed. The International Atomic Energy Agency reports that the share of nuclear in Japanese government energy research and development (R&D) in 2010 was 55 percent, far lower than the figure reported here, but still by far the highest in the world. The next highest was France, which spent 38 percent of its national energy research budget on nuclear power. See International Energy Agency 2012, 22. Other analysis suggests that these numbers are understated. One former local government official reports that 2 trillion yen were spent on construction of the Fukushima Daiichi and Daini reactors alone. Include other transfers, grants, and subsidies, and the total cost was more than 4 trillion yen. See Ōhira 2011, 128.

3. *Daiyamondo,* 21 May 2011, cites Ministry of Economy, Trade and Industry (METI) data and provides analysis of the structure of the contemporary nuclear power industry.

4. The 1956 Long-Term Plan stipulated the need for reprocessing and for a fast breeder reactor (FBR) project. The FBR (Monju) was designated a national project in 1967, even before construction of the first commercial light water reactor (LWR). See Suzuki 2000, 4

5. Critics of this policy—a study group including former METI officials who lost their battle with the nuclear power industry—produced and circulated an unsigned, no-holds-barred critique. See http://www.kakujoho.net/rokkasho/19chou040317.pdf. In their view, the Japanese government "cannot quit and will not stop" reprocessing because it cannot admit its mistake; because it does not have a way to reimburse the utilities for more than 2 trillion yen in sunk costs; and because of a system of "extortion by subsidy," in which too many localities and too many politicians derive benefits from the enormous funding that sloshes around the projects. Interview, study group member, Tokyo, 30 September 2011.

6. See, for example, Koide 2011b, 33. For additional criticism of the reprocessing program from within academic circles, see Genshiryoku Mirai Kenkyūkai 2003b.

7. Japan has the only commercial-scale reprocessing facility in a non-nuclear weapons state. Its Rokkasho facility is capable of separating 8 metric tons of plutonium from spent fuel each year. Takubo Masa 2011.

8. This stockpile was more than 43 tons in 2007. See http://www.wise-uranium.org/epasi .html#JP.

9. Suzuki 2000, 10; and Takubo Masa 2011, 21.

10. Scalise 2009, 111; Keidanren Kankyō Honbu 2011, 35.

11. *Daiyamondo,* 21 May 2011, 32.

12. *Shūkan Bunshun,* 27 March 2011 (special edition), 99; *Wall Street Journal,* 30 March 2011; *Financial Times,* 24 October 2011. In April 2012, Prime Minister Noda proved the point by approving a 1 trillion yen bailout of Tokyo Electric Power Company (TEPCO) and by appointing Shimokobe Kazuhiko, one of the seven experts responsible for setting the terms of that bailout, as chairman. See *Japan Times,* 20 April 2012.

13. This exemption is from Part II, Chapter 1, Section 3 of the law. The law, as amended in 2009, is available at http://www.oecd-nea.org/law/legislation/japan-docs/Japan-Nuclear -Damage-Compensation-Act.pdf.

14. *Kyodo,* 22 March 2007; and *Yomiuri Shimbun,* 31 March 2007.

15. The chief investigator of the Monju accident knew of efforts by his superiors to suppress evidence of a cover-up, and committed suicide. See Kingston 2004, 19. In October 2000, six Tōkai-mura executives were convicted of negligence but received suspended sentences. See http://www.wise-uranium.org/eftokc.html. The July 2011 special issue of *Shūkan Ekonomisuto,* 79, gives a list of nuclear accidents worldwide, beginning with the Canadian Chalk River heavy water reactor in December 1952.

16. Suzuki 2000, 24, 29.

17. Aldrich 2008 is an excellent account of this process.

18. See Aldrich 2008, 136–38, for time series data on public acceptance, which dropped over time as accidents occurred at home and abroad.

19. It also may have led the utilities to build their nuclear facilities far from Japan's densely packed urban centers despite higher costs and the inefficiencies of long-distance transmission. See Scalise 2009, 122; and Koide 2011a. For a map of Japan's fifty-four nuclear reactors—all on the coast—see *Nihon Keizai Shimbun*, 7 May 2011. How open discussion of risk was avoided in the development of the nuclear power industry is explored in Suzuki, Takeda, and Mizuno 2011.

20. *Washington Post*, 7 March 1994. See Pluto Boy on the web at http://woody.com/2011 /08/03/plutonium-kun/ and at http://fs200.www.ex.ua/get/157199220113/98cbe540e32ff 5fa617dbcb162372d27/24097038/pluto-kun-subbed.mp4. For a story of how Pluto Boy became the object of ironic tweets after 3.11, see http://news.linktv.org/videos/anime-characters-tweet -on-fukushima-disaster.

21. Ramseyer 2011. Kawato, Pekkanen, and Tsujinaka 2012 report that fourteen lawsuits had been filed since the late 1970s against power companies or the government seeking to block or close nuclear power plants, and none had succeeded. Iida 2011b and Avenell 2012a describe the efforts of Takagi Jinzaburō, a nuclear scientist who led Japan's antinuclear movement.

22. Suzuki 2000, 6; Iida 2011b, 19; and http://www.pref.fukui.jp/doc/dengen/kufukin_d /fil/001.pdf. "Cooperation funds" doubled between 1976 and 1983.

23. These totaled more than 120 billion yen in 2009. *Daiyamondo*, 21 May 2011.

24. Nakamura and Kikuchi 2011, 896.

25. In addition to its nukes, rural Fukui Prefecture hosts twenty-nine hydropower generators, three conventional thermal plants, and two wind farms. In 2010, its generators produced nearly one-quarter of the nation's electric power. See http://www.pref.fukui.jp/doc/dengen/.

26. Kingston 2012b, 205.

27. Aldrich 2008.

28. Most of these costs were borne by taxpayers. *Kyodo*, 2 May 2012.

29. Aldrich 2011 calls this a "culture of dependency." See also Aldrich 2008; Nakamura and Kikuchi 2011; and Ōhira 2011. For "addiction to subsidies," see the cover story in *Daiyamondo*, 21 May 2011; and Onitsuka 2012.

30. *Reuters*, 3 August 2011.

31. *Asahi Shimbun*, 8 July 2011.

32. See *Kyodo*, 5 October 2011; and *Jiji*, 7 December 2011. A government commission found abuses in the public hearing process starting in 2006. *Yomiuri Shimbun*, 1 October 2011.

33. See Suzuki 2000, 12; and *Wall Street Journal*, 3 January 2012. Aldrich 2008, 137, provides other examples.

34. Stigler 1971 is the classic analysis of this phenomenon. Kageyama and Pritchard 2011 call it a "culture of complacency." Scalise 2009, 107, argues that "no single actor . . . holds a clear consistent advantage over other interest groups" in the electric power policy process.

35. The Nuclear Safety Commission (NSC) has been populated almost entirely by pronuclear experts, many of whom have received grants from the power companies. See Kageyama and Pritchard 2011. These firms have repeatedly hired retired government officials and are accused of using their relationships with regulators to avoid costly safety improvements. *Asahi Shimbun*, 19 April 2011.

36. Nakamura and Kikuchi 2011, 894; *Yomiuri Shimbun*, 16 June 2011.

37. The Nuclear and Industrial Safety Agency (NISA) report is from *Tokyo Shimbun*, 15 November 2011. For more on conflicts between promotion and regulation of the industry, see Scalise 2009, 50; Kageyama and Pritchard 2011; and *Wall Street Journal*, 28 March 2011.

38. See the July 2011 report of the Energy and Environmental Council, http://www.npu.go .jp/policy/policy09/pdf/20110908/20110908_02_en.pdf.

39. Interview, TEPCO general manager, Tokyo, 26 January 2012. A METI energy official explained that independent power producers (IPPs) may also have been unsuccessful because the utilities limited their access to the grid "claiming they would hurt stability of supply." Interview, Matsuda Yōhei, deputy director, Commerce and Information Policy Bureau, METI, 9

December 2011. For data on the initial failure of IPPs, see http://jref.or.jp/images/pdf /20110912_presentation_e.pdf.

40. See the outline compiled by the Institute of Energy Economics at http://eneken.ieej.or .jp/en/jeb/1005.pdf; METI, 2010; and Scalise 2012a.

41. See also http://www.enecho.meti.go.jp/info/committee/kihonmondai/1st/sanko1_1 .pdf.

42. Interview, Sawa Akihiro, Tokyo, 28 October 2011.

43. METI data supplied by Sawa Akihiro, 28 October 2011.

44. For claims that nuclear power is "too big to fail," see Suzuki 2000, 2; and *Daiyamondo*, 21 May 2011, 28.

45. Kikkawa 2011, 36–38; Mikuriya 2011b, 15; Watanabe 2011; Kashiwagi 2012. Even Sawa Akihiko, a prominent defender of nuclear power, acknowledged that "3.11 created fluidity and made new solutions possible. Energy policy options have suddenly increased and there are new opportunities for change." Interview, Sawa Akihiko, Tokyo, 28 November 2011.

46. *Asahi Shimbun*, 11 May 2011.

47. Koide 2011b, 10.

48. On 11 September 2011, six months after the disaster, a Japanese-language Google search for "nuclear village" surfaced twenty-six million hits.

49. See Iida 1997. Iida had worked at the Fukushima Daiichi facility for a Toshiba subcontractor. See *Yomiuri Shimbun*, 16 June 2011. In addition to working for the vendor, Iida worked at the Central Research Institute for the Electric Power Industry (CRIEPI) and for the Federation of Electric Utilities. After leaving the industry, he became the executive director of the Institute for Sustainable Energy Policies. Interview, Iida Tetsunari, Tokyo, 28 September 2011. In July 2012 Iida was defeated in a gubernatorial election in Yamaguchi prefecture that was widely seen as a national referendum on nuclear power.

50. DeWit 2011a, 6. DeWit has also referred to the "tightly focused rent seeking" of the electric utilities in collusion with "a wide swath of the political class." See DeWit, Iida, and Kaneko 2012, 156.

51. See, for example, Kōno 2011 and Satō Eisaku 2011. Satō, who claims to have been the victim of a vendetta by the nuclear power industry after he pulled the plug on a project in Fukushima, offers a companion metaphor to describe the collusion within the nuclear village: "badgers in the same hole" (*onaji ana no mujina*). See *Shūkan Bunshun*, 27 March 2011 (special edition), 89.

52. *Asahi Shimbun*, 19 June 2012. This is from the English summary of the report: Fukushima Nuclear Accident Independent Investigation Commission 2012, 20. The full report in Japanese is at http://naiic.go.jp/report/. It does not use the term "nuclear village," but refers repeatedly to "regulatory capture." See section 5.2, headed "The Regulatory Authorities That Were Captured by TEPCO and the Federation of Electric Power Companies" (*Tōden · Denjiren no Toriko to natta Kisei Tōkyoku*) at 505–24.

53. *Yomiuri Shimbun*, 16 June 2012.

54. This story offers lurid details on the money, interests, and personal connections at play inside the nuclear village. See *Daiyamondo*, 21 May 2011.

55. Suzuki, Takeda, and Mizuno 2011, 26. Suzuki came under criticism in the press for attending a closed-door meeting in April 2012 that the media labeled a "preposterous . . . gathering of nuclear villagers." *Mainichi Shimbun*, 24 May 2012.

56. The Diet's Fukushima Nuclear Accident Independent Investigation Commission addresses the lack of regulatory transparency in sections 1.2.4 (91) and 5.4.4 (556) of its report.

57. Kōno 2011, 76.

58. *Japan Today*, 3 April 2011.

59. Interview, Iida Tetsunari, Tokyo, 28 September 2011. For "ethically suspicious rapport," see Nakamura and Kikuchi 2011, 896.

60. Hasegawa 2011, 110. One blogger, a tax accountant named Morita Yoshio, concurs, comparing the nuclear village to the Kwangtung Army in Manchuria. These sorts of organizations, he argues, cut off debate and criticism and "descend into depravity." See http://www.moritax .jp/column/003/post-92.html. Another blogger speaks of the business-government-academia

iron triangle as a "guild-like swarm that operates in the deep darkness." See http://www.rui
.jp/ruinet.html?i=200&c=400&m=248670.

61. *Shūkan Bunshun*, 27 March 2011 (special edition), 90.
62. DeWit 2011a, 1.
63. Iida 2011b, 40.
64. Segawa 2011; and *Shūkan Bunshun*, 27 March 2011 (special edition), 92–93.
65. Hasegawa 2011, 110–11, for example. Soon after 3.11, TEPCO removed its safety claims from the web and from its publicity materials according to Nakamura and Kikuchi 2011, 895.
66. See the lists of grants compiled by antinuclear activists at http://www47.atwiki.jp/goyo-gakusha/pages/1225.html.
67. Interview, Suzuki Tatsujirō, Atomic Energy Commission vice chair, Tokyo, 26 September 2011. For a related story, see *Mainichi Shimbun*, 27 September 2011.
68. *Kyodo* and *Asahi Shimbun*, 1 January 2012.
69. *Asahi Shimbun*, 6 February 2012.
70. Koide remained an assistant professor for forty years. After a commercial network broadcast a documentary on Koide and colleagues—the so-called Kumatori Six, who were relentless critics of the nuclear power industry—the Kansai Electric Power Company reportedly withdrew all advertising. For his own account, see Koide 2011a and 2011b. A secondary account by Yoko Hasegawa is at http://hasegawa.berkeley.edu/Papers/Koide.html.
71. See Anzai 2011; and *Asahi Shimbunsha* 2011, 177–78. Such "village ostracism" was a form of punishment in feudal Japan. Iida has suggested that Japanese academics fear ostracism even more than they appreciate the funding. Interview, Iida Tetsunari, 28 September 2011.
72. Ishibashi 2011, 131.
73. Interview, Kōno Tarō, Liberal Democratic Party (LDP) Diet representative, Tokyo, 16 September 2011; *Asahi Shimbun*, 23 September 2011.
74. *Asahi Shimbun*, 19 April 2011; *Financial Times*, 19 April 2011.
75. *Mainichi Shimbun*, 27 September 2011.
76. Kageyama and Pritchard 2011; *Wall Street Journal*, 28 March 2011; *Asahi Shimbun*, 19 April 2011. See *Daiyamondo*, 21 May 2011, 33, for the list of METI *amakudari* (literally, descent from heaven) placements in each utility.
77. *Shūkan Bunshun*, 27 March 2011 (special edition), 90; *Asahi Shimbun*, 19 April 2011. Scalise 2009, 50, 53, inter alia, discounts the importance of *amakudari* in the nuclear power sector.
78. Hasegawa 2011, 110; *Kyodo*, 23 July 2011; *Asahi Shimbun*, 9 October 2011. See *Tokyo Shimbun*, 3 June 2011, for a fuller historical account of TEPCO's political giving. Scalise 2012a, 148, dismisses these political links as "circumstantial at best." Elsewhere, he has compiled data to demonstrate that the 70 percent figure is inflated and misleading. See Scalise 2009, 57–64.
79. Representative Kōno tells how one fellow LDP representative approached TEPCO and promised to "keep Kōno quiet" for twice the normal donation. He also tells of asking tough questions about nuclear safety and being attacked for being a "communist" by TEPCO-affiliated LDP politicians. "My questions never were answered," he says. Interviews, Kōno Tarō, LDP Diet representative, 16 September and 21 November 2011.
80. *Asahi Shimbun*, 5 and 6 October 2011.
81. *Asahi Shimbunsha* 2011, 171–73. The other two utility executives were Hasegawa Kiyoshi, Japan Socialist Party (JSP) and Fujiwara Masashi, Democratic Party of Japan (DPJ). See Scalise 2009, 64–65.
82. Ōhira 2011, 128–29.
83. *Mainichi Shimbun*, 11 July 2011; *Asahi Shimbun*, 15 July 2011.
84. *Shūkan Bunshun*, 27 March 2011 (special edition), 88–93. This confirms Iida's personal account in the *Yomiuri Shimbun*, 16 June 2011.
85. *Yomiuri Shimbun*, 16 June 2011.
86. For the list of committee members and their affiliations, see Kōno 2011, 72–77. TEPCO insists that it had always complied with existing tsunami guidelines and that it had asked the committee to consider higher estimates that had come to its attention, which the committee declared were unreliable. See TEPCO's report at http://www.tepco.co.jp/en/press/corp-com/release/betu11_e/images/111202e13.pdf. In an interview, a TEPCO executive acknowledged

that "professors" had warned of a larger than anticipated tsunami, but said that "we did not believe them because they were too academic and the Civil Engineering Association did not accept them." He also acknowledged that utility officials were members of the commission that rejected the warnings. Interview, TEPCO executive, Tokyo, 26 January 2012. See also Fukushima Nuclear Accident Independent Investigation Commission 2012, 16 (English) and the commission's more detailed criticism of TEPCO and its regulators to take the report seriously in Japanese at Kokkai Tōkyō Denryoku Fukushima Genshiryoku Hatsuden Jiko Chōsa Iinkai 2012, sec. 1.2, esp. 91–93. See also *Asahi Shimbun*, 26 August, 2011; Kageyama and Pritchard 2011; and *Yomiuri Shimbun*, 26 August 2011.

87. Iida 2011b, 27; and *Yomiuri Shimbun*, 16 June 2011.

88. This former NISA head is unnamed. *Mainichi Shimbun*, 27 September 2011.

89. For a blog representative of this view, see http://blog.livedoor.jp/yamagata1111/archives/51767766html.

90. See Kokkai Tōkyō Denryoku Fukushima Genshiryoku Hatsuden Jiko Chōsa Iinkai 2012, sec. 5.4, 548–76.

91. *Kyodo*, 28 April 2011.

92. *Asahi Shimbun*, 11 May 2011; Associated Press, 18 May 2011; and *Nihon Keizai Shimbun*, 19 May 2011.

93. Interview, senior official, National Policy Unit, Cabinet Office, Tokyo, 12 October 2011.

94. *Japan Today*, 3 April 2012.

95. Kanō is in *Asahi Shimbunsha* 2011, 172. Interview, Masumoto Teruaki, Tokyo, 3 February 2012.

96. See Hatamura 2011, 88–89.

97. See http://www.jaif.or.jp/english/news_images/pdf/ENGNEWS02_1336537903P.pdf.

98. "No one died" is attributed to Yosano Kaoru, in Osnos 2011. Nishiyama Hidehiko, a senior NISA official, is quoted widely on Japanese blogs as having declared on 13 April 2011 that "only 29 people died in the Chernobyl accident" and that because that was an explosion, it is entirely different from Fukushima Daiichi. See, for example, http://www.sponichi.co.jp/society/news/2011/04/13/kiji/k20110413000616640.html and http://www.geocities.jp/angelo_de_rosa/TOKYOniGENPATSUwoFRASIinglese.html.

99. *Asahi Shimbun*, 5 May 2011.

100. *Jiji*, 20 May 2011.

101. Yosano's view, which attracted enormous criticism in the blogosphere, can be found at http://niconicositaine.blog49.fc2.com/blog-entry-1872.html. This criticism became so intense that Yosano's aide, Diet representative Tsumura Keisuke, offered a clarification: "The Minister was expressing how human beings must have the highest respect for nature." See http://mojimojisk.coco-log-nifty.com/lilyyarn/2011/05/post-8515.html.

102. *Asahi Shimbun*, 5 May 2011.

103. Unnamed caucus member cited in Hasegawa 2011, 109.

104. Ishiba is quoted in the *Wall Street Journal*, 28 October 2011. An editorial in the *Yomiuri Shimbun* concurred. Some have suggested that the post-3.11 change in the Atomic Energy Basic Law to include reference to "national security" raises these same questions. See http://www.idsa.in/idsacomments/Japansclearnuclearambition_sakhan_110712.

105. Ishiba quoted in *Yomiuri Shimbun*, 7 July 2011.

106. Kyodo, 6 September 2012.

107. This is argued by Toichi in the LDP newspaper *Jiyū Minshu*, 2 August 2011.

108. Toyoda 2011, 2.

109. Institute for Energy Economics (IEE) estimates cited in Center for International and Strategic Studies 2011, 16.

110. This was an explicit concern of Japan Atomic Industrial Forum (JAIF) chair Imai. See http://www.jaif.or.jp/english/news-images/pdf/ENGNEWS02_1309841709pdf.

111. See http://www.yoshiko-sakurai.jp/index.php/2011/09/27/can-japan-survive-without-nuclear-power-plants. Others suggest that what saved Onagawa was the seawall built by Tohoku Electric Power Co. at a height recommended for the TEPCO facility in Fukushima, but

passed over for financial reasons. A decade before 3.11, American researchers wrote that the General Electric LWR design installed at Fukushima Daiichi had "stifled the development and introduction of safer, cheaper nuclear power plants" around the world. See Lidsky and Miller 2002, 133. For more on Japan's technonational ideology, see Samuels 1994.

112. *Enerugii Fōramu*, 1 October 2011, 92.

113. Toyomatsu Hideki of the Kansai Electric Power Company is cited at http://hiroakikoide .wordpress.com/2011/06/30/hoch-jun30/.

114. *Jiyū Minshu*, 9 August 2011.

115. *Asahi Shimbun*, 14 July 2011.

116. Interview, TEPCO senior executive, Tokyo, 26 January 2012.

117. *Wall Street Journal*, 16 March 2011.

118. See TEPCO's interim report at http://www.tepco.co.jp/en/press/corp-com/release /betu11_e/images/111202e13.pdf.

119. Yonekura's comment was widely reported on the web, and confirmed by a Keidanren staff person on 20 October 2011. Mimura is quoted in *Nihon Keizai Shimbun*, 21 April 2011.

120. Internal data supplied by Keidanren, 17 and 20 October 2011.

121. Interview, Keidanren senior staff member, Tokyo, 12 October 2011.

122. Nippon Keizai Dantai Rengōkai 2011a.

123. Sawa cited on *Business Wire*, 17 October 2011.

124. Data provided from slides during interview, Sawa, 28 October 2011.

125. Suzuki, Takeda, and Mizuno 2011.

126. Suzuki 2011 (26 April testimony) and interview, Tokyo, 26 September 2011.

127. Suzuki, Takeda, and Mizuno 2011, 25; and *Yomiuri Shimbun*, 25 October 2011. Professor Murakami Yōichirō (2011) insists that he too attacked the "safety myth" and tried to end the "taboo" when he chaired a METI advisory panel on nuclear safety in the 1990s.

128. Suzuki, Takeda, and Mizuno 2011, 27.

129. Ohashi 2011.

130. See http://www.siew.sg/energy-perspectives/global-energy-trends/nobuo-tanaka -shares-21st-century-energy-security-vision and http://www.siew.sg/energy-perspectives /global-energy-trends/5-questions-former-executive-director-international-energy.

131. Kashiwagi comments at Keidanren seminar, 9 November 2011. See also http://www .iri.titech.ac.jp/old-iri/html/english/research/project/pj001.html.

132. Kashiwagi 2012.

133. *Business Wire*, 7 August 2011; and interview, Sawa, Tokyo, 28 October 2011.

134. A representative petition is at http://english.roukyou.gr.jp/Petition_form.pdf. Note its concern about the vulnerability of the population, and its call for community, leadership, and change—all four narrative tropes.

135. See http://www.env.go.jp/press/.php?serial=14223.

136. Takeuchi Kazuhiko 2011, 6–7. It is worth noting, though, that as recently as October 2010, Professor Takeuchi shared a platform with the Atomic Energy Commission (AEC) chairman, Kondo Shunsuke, who argued for "the harmony of nuclear power and society." See http://www .n.t.u-tokyo.ac.jp/modules/news/article.php?storyid=29.

137. *Tokyo Shimbun*, 3 October 2011. See also http://ajw.asahi.com/article/behind_news /politics/AJ201203200067. The party was formally launched in July 2012. See *Asahi Shimbun*, 29 June 2012.

138. *Asahi Shimbun*, 1 January 2012.

139. See http://homepage2.nifty.com/nichousan/eco_bozu002_1104051.html.

140. See *Daiyamondo*, 21 May 2011, 36, for an interesting characterization of this power triangle, which places the utilities at the middle of exchanges with general contractors, politicians, and others.

141. Interview, Governor Tasso, Morioka, 22 September 2011.

142. *Mainichi Shimbun*, 18 July 2011. *Denki Shimbun*, 19 October 2011, and Handō, Hosaka, and Todaka 2011, 158, also compare "absolutely unsinkable" battleships and "absolutely safe" nuclear power. Parshall and Tully 2005, 413, argue that a similar inflexibility plagued the Japanese military during World War II.

143. *Asahi Shimbun*, 11 May 2011; *Mainichi Shimbun*, 18 July 2011 and 7 March 2012; *Nihon Keizai Shimbun*, 5 October and 13 December 2011, and 10 January 2012. In a 16 February 2012 editorial, the *Asahi Shimbun* called for the dissolution of TEPCO and a thorough restructuring of the entire electric power sector. By October 2011, even Keidanren's Yonekura announced he was open to full debate on splitting transmission and generation, as long as it was done "from the perspective of users." See Keidanren Kankyō Honbu 2011.

144. *Yomiuri Shimbun*, 4 April 2011; *Mainichi Shimbun*, 18 April 2011.

145. The two polls were both reported on 14 June 2011. The *Asahi Shimbun* tracked a steady decline of support for nuclear power and confirmed this movement in public opinion. A Pew Research Center study found Japanese public opinion more evenly split. *Agence France Presse*, 2 June 2011.

146. *Asahi Shimbun*, 13 March 2012. The poll also found that women opposed these restarts at a much higher rate (two-thirds) than men (less than half). These results were duplicated two months later. See *Asahi Shimbun*, 21 May 2012.

147. Nippon Keizai Dantai Rengōkai 2011a, 3.

148. *Guardian*, 2 May 2011; Associated Press, 18 January 2012.

149. Szymkowiak 2002.

150. *Asahi Shimbun*, 18 June 2011.

151. *Financial Times*, 28 June 2011.

152. *Asahi Shimbun*, *International Herald Tribune*, *Nihon Keizai Shimbun*, 29 June 2011.

153. For the prediction of democratic participation "at a new level," see Suzuki, Takeda, and Mizuno 2011, 28. See also Kawato, Pekkanen, and Tsujinaka 2012.

154. Aldrich 2012, reports on the Kōenji demonstration. The TEPCO marchers were met by rightists who tried to shout them down. *Agence France-Presse*, 11 June 2011.

155. Kawato, Pekkanen, and Tsujinaka 2012, 107. Slater, Nishimura, and Kindstrand 2012 argue that social media activated networks of once-disaffected youth after 3.11.

156. *Asahi Shimbun* and *Jiji.com*, 19 September 2011. For a copy of the petition in English, see http://cnic.jp/english/topics/policy/10million.html.

157. *Asahi Shimbun*, 12 February 2012. The dearth of coverage was decried by one encamped demonstrator in an informal conversation on 31 October 2011 outside METI, and by Slater, Nishimura, and Kindstrand 2012.

158. "Citizen scientists" is the apt characterization of Daniel Aldrich during a lecture at Temple University Japan, 25 November 2011. Kawato, Pekkanen, and Tsujinaka 2012, 81, refer to "shadow monitoring" of official data sources.

159. See *Asahi Shimbun*, 22 January 2012.

160. The three referenda were: in Makimachi (Niigata) in 1996, in Kariwa (Niigata) in 2001, and in Umiyama (Mie) in 2011. In some of these cases, nuclear plans were aborted before the local assembly had to act. For a full list, see http://kokumintohyo.com/osaka/wp-content/uploads/2012/01/attached.pdf.

161. Interview, Imai Hajime, Tokyo, 3 February 2012.

162. Ibid. For elaboration of this point, see http://www.magazine9.jp/other/imai/index3.php.

163. See http://www.magazine9.jp/other/imai/index3.php.

164. *Asahi Shimbun*, 22 January and 9 February 2012.

165. *Asahi Shimbun*, 22 January 2012.

166. *Japan Times*, 12 May 2012.

167. Hashimoto's initial response is at http://kokumintohyo.com/osaka/. Imai called it "cloudy" (*kumorizora*). Interview, Imai Hajime, Tokyo, 3 February 2012.

168. Others suspected that the business community persuaded him to relent. See *Japan Times*, 24 February and 7 June 2012.

169. *Asahi Shimbun*, 28 March 2012.

170. *Asahi Shimbun*, 1 June 2012.

171. *Japan Times*, 7 June 2012; *Yomiuri Shimbun*, 18 June 2012.

172. Police estimated seventeen thousand protesters, and organizers insisted there were two hundred thousand at the second demonstration on 29 June. See *Asahi Shimbun*, 30 June 2012

and Williamson 2012. For a video account, see http://www.youtube.com/watch?v=hiIwLgvYyq8. For videos of the first rally, see http://www.ustream.tv/recorded/23481490, and for a blogged account, see http://www.asyura2.com/12/genpatsu24/msg/916.html. The first demonstration was not broadcast on NHK (Japan Broadcasting Corporation) and estimates of the number of participants ranged from eleven thousand in the conservative *Sankei Shimbun* to forty-five thousand in the antinuclear *Tokyo Shimbun*.

173. Seventy-five thousand is the police estimate. Organizers claimed 170,000 protestors assembled. See Bloomberg, 16 July 2012; *Kyodo*, 16 July 2012; and http://news.tbs.co.jp/news eye/tbs_newseye5082487.html. See photo on p. 194.

174. The photo of Hosono and his bodyguards in Sendai appeared in the *Japan Times* on the same day as the Yoyogi demonstration, 16 July 2012. For protest of manipulation of the town hall meetings, see also *Kyodo*, 14 July 2012.

175. *Kyodo*, 18 September 2011; and *Yomiuri Shimbun*, 19 September 2011.

176. *Mainichi Shimbun*, 14 July 2011; *Asahi Shimbun*, 16 February 2012.

177. Membership list provided by Representative Abe Tomoko, 2 November 2011.

178. *Asahi Shimbun*, 11 May 2011; *Tokyo Shimbun*, 3 June 2011.

179. *Daiyamondo*, 21 May 2011. Kan, too, had been an active supporter of nuclear plant exports before 3.11. Hasegawa 2011, 108, says that Kan had "stepped on the tiger's tail" and the *Tokyo Shimbun*, 3 June 2011, suspected that the vote of no confidence supported by Ozawa and others in the DPJ was manipulated by the nuclear power industry.

180. *Asahi Shimbun*, 19 May 2011.

181. *Asahi Shimbun*, 23 June 2011.

182. *Asahi Shimbun*, 8 July 2011.

183. For a list of these politicians, see *Daiyamondo*, 21 May 2011, 33, and Hasegawa 2011, 110. See also *Asahi Shimbun*, 16 June 2011; and *Kyodo*, 13 July 2011.

184. *Kyodo*, 5 October 2011; *Asahi Shimbun*, 30 May 2012

185. *Asahi Shimbun*, 26 September 2011; Noda 2011. For more on Japan's nuclear export strategy, see http://www.enecho.meti.go.jp/policy/nuclear/pptfiles/0602-6.pdf.

186. *Asahi Shimbun*, 13 September 2011; *Yomiuri Shimbun*, 8 October 2011.

187. *Yomiuri Shimbun*, 8 October 2011.

188. *Asahi Shimbun*, 12 September 2011; interview, Tokyo, 12 October 2011.

189. Associated Press, 18 January 2012; *Asahi Shimbun*, 19 January 2012; *Kyodo*, 2 February 2012.

190. *New York Times*, 14 April 2012; and *Oriental Economist*, April 2012, 4.

191. *Kyodo*, 17 April 2012.

192. *Mainichi Shimbun*, 8 May 2012.

193. *Yomiuri Shimbun*, 13 June 2012.

194. *Nihon Keizai Shimbun*, 27 September and 3 October 2011; *Kyodo*, 4 October 2011.

195. See the Fundamental Issues Subcommittee reports in English at http://www.meti.go .jp/english/press/2011/pdf/1220_05a.pdf.

196. The lack of consensus was reported by *Asahi Shimbun*, 28 March 2012. The final report in June 2012 narrowed the choices down to three. *Reuters*, 29 June 2012.

197. *Yomiuri Shimbun*, 16 June 2011.

198. *Yomiuri Shimbun*, 20 April 2011; *Reuters*, 3 August 2011; *Wall Street Journal*, 15 August 2011.

199. *Japan Times*, 14 May 2012.

200. Samuels 1987; Scalise 2009; Satō Eisaku 2011.

201. Interview, Matsuda Yōhei, deputy director, Commerce and Information Policy Bureau, METI, 9 December 2011.

202. Interview, Kōno Tarō, Tokyo, 16 September 2011; planning documents provided by— and interview with—former METI official now in the National Strategy Office, Tokyo, 12 October 2011; comments of Tokyo Institute of Technology professor Kashiwagi Takao at Keidanren seminar, 9 November 2011.

203. Energy and Environmental Council 2011.

204. See Energy Conservation and Renewable Energy Department, Agency for Natural Resources and Energy 2010. Keidanren reports that the Energy Ministry insists that the potential

for renewables is much higher than METI suggests. A memo entitled *Enerugii Seisaku wo meg-uru Saikin no Dōkō to Keidanren no Torikumi* [Recent Trends in Energy Policy and Keidanren's Efforts] was supplied by Keidanren staff on 12 October 2012. See also Iida 2011d, 110–11.

205. DeWit 2011a, 8; *Yomiuri Shimbun*, 14 September 2011.

206. See Keidanren Kankyō Honbu 2011. This report also warned that investor confidence would be undercut by a shift away from nuclear power.

207. Tohoku Electric even threatened to demand tens of billions of yen in compensation from TEPCO for failing to meet the terms of its supply contract after 3.11. *Kyodo*, 31 May 2011.

208. Nippon Keizai Dantai Rengōkai 2011a. See Hasegawa 2011 for more on divisions within the business community.

209. *Nihon Keizai Shimbun*, 16 April 2011. Toyota Motors announced plans for an IPP-like collaboration with Tohoku Electric in August 2011. See *Mainichi Shimbun*, 26 August 2011. See *Asahi Shimbun*, 31 July 2012 for more on how business was divided on the question of nuclear power.

210. *Reuters*, 27 September 2011.

211. *Yomiuri Shimbun*, 12 December 2011. According to one TEPCO executive, the entry of gas utilities into the electric power business was supported by METI after 3.11; interview, Tokyo, 26 January 2012.

212. Using funds borrowed from a Japanese sovereign wealth-like fund, the Innovation Network Corporation of Japan, Toshiba bought the Swiss firm Landis Gyr, a smart metering innovator, for $2.3 billion. *Bloomberg*, 19 May 2011; Hitachi president Nakanishi Hiroaki announced plans to target the "smart cities" sector in the same Tohoku press conference where he reaffirmed Hitachi's commitment to nuclear power at home and abroad. See *Denki Shimbun*, 19 October 2011; Marubeni partnered with China's JA Solar to import photovoltaic (PV) panels. *Nihon Keizai Shimbun*, 23 November 2011.

213. For a description of some of these new entrants, see *Nihon Keizai Shimbun*, 31 August 2011. See also http://www.jwd.co.jp/pdf/news/091030_release.pdf for news deals struck by the Japan Wind Development Company, founded by a former oil trader at Mitsui Bussan.

214. *Nihon Keizai Shimbun*, 21 November 2011; *Yomiuri Shimbun*, 22 November 2011.

215. *Wall Street Journal*, 6 February 2012; *Kyodo*, 10 February 2010.

216. *Enerugii Fōramu*, 1 July 2011; *Kyodo*, 17 October 2011; *Yomiuri Shimbun*, 18 October 2011.

217. *Kyodo*, 26 February 2012.

218. Nagura Naoshi, quoted in the *Washington Post*, 28 October 2011. See *Shizen Hogo*, September/October 2011, 15, for another local initiative involving Nagano Prefecture and several of its universities, civic groups, and municipalities.

219. Interview, Governor Tasso, Morioka, 22 September 2011.

220. Klose et al. 2010 is a useful outline of this transformation.

221. *Diplomat*, 30 May 2011. After Mikitani left, Keidanren officials suggested it was because he was denied a senior post in the organization. Interview, senior staff, Tokyo, 12 October 2011.

222. *Nihon Keizai Shimbun*, 16 November 2011.

223. Son embraced the role of hero. See, for example, the introduction to Son and DeWit 2011, 1. *AERA*, 30 May 2011, called Son the leader of Japan's antinuclear movement. See also *Asahi Shimbun*, 16 June 2011.

224. *Jiji*, 13 July 2011; see http://www.newsweekjapan.jp/headlines/business/2011/11/60839.ph.

225. See http://www.kaden.watch.impress.co.jp/docs/news/20111122_492782.html.

226. *Nihon Keizai Shimbun*, 13 July 2011.

227. *Kyodo*, 13 July 2011.

228. *Kyodo*, 12 September 2011; see http://jref.or.jp/images/pdf/20110912_presentation_e.pdf.

229. *Asahi Shimbun*, 16 June 2011.

230. Wind would require 3.5 times more (246 sq km). Keidanren Kankyō Honbu 2011, 11; *Asahi Shimbun*, 12 April 2012.

231. Sawa 2011b, 1.

232. Interview, Suzuki Tatsujirō, Tokyo, 26 September 2011. See the article by Iida 2011d for a rebuttal.

233. Interview, Matsuda Yōhei, deputy director, Commerce and Information Policy Bureau, METI, 9 December 2011.

234. Interview, Takahashi Heisho, Miyagi Prefecture Planning Bureau environment section chief, Sendai, 20 September 2011.

235. One retired TEPCO senior executive invoked what he called a "Korean adage" about "throwing stones at a horse in the river" (*kawa ni otoshite uma wa ijimero*) to describe how Son was taking advantage of "TEPCO's current weakness." He then paired Son with TEPCO's leading 3.11 villain, former prime minister Kan Naoto, suggesting that "Kan and Son were very close. They shared the same foundations. Both are Korean." (There is no evidence that the former prime minister is ethnically Korean.) Interview, Masumoto Teruaki, 3 February 2012. Son responds to criticisms that he is rent seeking and opportunistic at http://kaden.watch.impress.co.jp/docs/news/20110912_476956.html.

236. Interview, Kōno Tarō, Tokyo, 16 September 2011.

237. See http://www.kaden.watch.impress.co.jp/docs/news/20111122_492782.html.

238. See DeWit, Iida, and Kaneko 2012 and the supportive editorial in *Asahi Shimbun*, 5 September 2011.

239. Interview, Iida Tetsunari, executive director of Institute for Sustainable Energy Policies, Tokyo, 28 September 2011.

240. DeWit, Iida, and Kaneko 2012, 165, say this was a "deliberately hobbled version that the nuclear village hastily drafted and got passed . . . in order to preempt the DPJ election manifesto promise of a German-style comprehensive FIT." Son has objected to its "opaque loophole." See http://www.kaden.watch.impress.co.jp/docs/news/20111122_492782.html.

241. Fairley 2011.

242. Interview, Kōno Tarō, LDP Diet representative, 21 November 2011. See also the account by Shinoda forthcoming.

243. Interview, Matsuda Yōhei, deputy director, Commerce and Information Policy Bureau, METI, Tokyo, 9 December 2011.

244. Interview, Kōno Tarō, LDP Diet representative, Tokyo, 21 November 2011; *Asahi Shimbun*, 30 November 2011; DeWit 2011b.

245. Only Italian industry pays more for electric power than Japanese industry, and only German and Italian home owners pay more than Japanese home owners. See Keidanren Kankyō Honbu 2011, 35.

246. For an estimate of the latter, see http://kakjoho.net/rokkasho/19chou040317.pdf and *Reuters*, 24 February 2012.

247. Son and DeWit 2011. Koide 2011a, 111, reports Oshima Keiichi estimated that nuclear power cost 10.7 yen per kilowatt-hour from 1970 to 2007. See also Iida 2011c, 20, who argues that the costs of postaccident compensation alone would come to 16 yen per kilowatt-hour, even when amortized over decades.

248. Interview, Suzuki Tatsujirō, AEC vice-chairman, 26 September 2011; *NHK On-Line*, 11 October 2011.

249. One editorial also argued that the figure was still too low. See *Mainichi Shimbun*, 29 December 2011.

250. *Yomiuri Shimbun*, 12 April 2012. In April 2012, the pricing panel recommended a solar price of 42 yen per kilowatt-hour. Investors lined up to take advantage of this nearly risk-free program. More than one hundred 1-megawatt or above megasolar projects were under way when the FIT went into effect on 1 July 2012. New deployments of solar and wind generators constructed at costs in excess of 600 billion yen would provide power equivalent to that of two nuclear reactors by 2014. See the report in the *Nihon Keizai Shimbun*, 28 June 2012.

251. Keidanren Kankyō Honbu 2011. A senior Keidanren staff person explained that the business community would accept the FIT if the price were the same for renewables as for conventional power sources—which would undermine the purpose of the FIT. He also suggested that they could support the FIT if the subsidy were paid out of central government revenue rather than as a tax on electricity rate payers; interview, Tokyo, 20 November 2011.

252. Sawa 2011b, 2.

253. Interview, Masumoto Teruaki, former TEPCO vice president, Tokyo, 3 February 2012. For a list of objections to the FIT from an opponent, see Sawa 2011b, 2; and from a proponent, see Iida 2011c, 31.

254. Interview, Saitō Tadashi, Keidanren director of political and social affairs, Tokyo, 14 September 2011.

255. *Asahi Shimbun*, 21 June 2011.

256. DeWit 2011a, 1.

257. See Klose et al. 2010, 8; and Iida 2011c, 28–30.

258. See Samuels 1987 for a review of some of the earliest efforts.

259. *Nihon Keizai Shimbun*, 17 September 2011.

260. According to one METI official, the ministry was particularly excited about the Kitakyushu project in which IPPs are prominent. He explained that the electric power companies kept IPPs out of the others. Interview, Matsuda Yōhei, deputy director, Commerce and Information Policy Bureau, METI, 9 December 2011. For fuller information on each of the projects, see Energy Conservation and Renewable Energy Department, Agency for Natural Resources and Energy 2010.

261. See http://www.meti.go.jp/english/policy/energy_enviornment/smart_community /index.html. The "smart communities" concept has already been exported to India and is being actively promoted across Southeast Asia by the METI-related New Energy Development Organization and 647 private firms. See Information Economy Division 2011, 4. For its part, Toshiba imagines a 900 billion yen market for integrated infrastructure by 2015 and has invested in "smart city" projects in Lyons and Jianxi, as well as in localities across Japan. See http://www.toshiba.co.jp/about/press/2011_09/pr_j3002.htm and http://www.toshiba.co .jp/about/press/2011_10/pr_j2701.htm. Note, too, that several of the sixteen projects that were not designated for METI funding were pursued privately.

262. For their part, the utilities were also experimenting with smart grids. See, for example, http://www.kyuden.co.jp/press_110225-1.html, http://www.energi.co.jp/press/10/p100706 -1.html, and http://www.solarfrontier.com/Projects/Niigata+Megasolar/69. Note, too, that the post-3.11 Keidanren Master Plan pushed for the relaxation of regulations that inhibited siting of renewable energy systems. See Nippon Keizai Dantai Rengōkai 2011b, 49.

263. Interview, Governor Tasso, Morioka, 22 September 2011.

264. Interview, TEPCO senior manager, 26 January 2012. Tokyo and Osaka asked tough questions at the June 2012 utility shareholder meetings that effected no changes. *Asahi Shimbun*, 28 June 2012.

265. Many of these "safety agreements" are now disclosed by local governments on the Web. See, for example, http://www.atom.pref.fukui.jp/anzen/index.html.

266. *Nihon Keizai Shimbun*, 27 November 2011.

267. *Asahi Shimbun*, 1 December 2011. Two months earlier, a suprapartisan group of local assembly representatives from localities across Japan that host nuclear plants had organized themselves into an association to decommission existing nuclear reactors. See *Asahi Shimbun*, 27 October 2011.

268. *Asahi Shimbun*, 11 and 15 April 2012; *Jiji*, 21 April 2012; *Mainichi Shimbun*, 8 May 2012.

269. *Mainichi Shimbun*, 25 April 2012.

270. *Kyodo*, 8 May 2012.

271. *Kyodo*, 3 March 2012; *Asahi Shimbun*, 22 March 2012.

272. *Asahi Shimbun*, 16 June 2011.

273. *Kyodo*, 12 August 2012.

274. *Asahi Shimbun*, 12 September 2012; *Japan Times*, 12 September 2012. It was noted by one reporter that if new plants are completed and if they are allowed to continue operation beyond their fortieth year, Japan could still have nuclear plants operating in 2070. See *New York Times*, 12 August 2012.

275. *Wall Street Journal*, 18 September 2012.

276. For detailed analyses of TEPCO's transformation in the business press, see *Shūkan Bunshun 2011*, 27 March 2011 (special edition), 95–101; *Shūkan Tōyō Keizai*, 23 April 2011, 32–48; *Financial Times*, 13 February 2012; and http://www.diamond.jp/articles/-/15582.

277. Interview, senior executive, TEPCO, Tokyo, 26 January 2012.
278. See Scalise 2011a, 204, and http://stocks.finance.yahoo.co.jp/stocks/detail/?code=9501 .T&d=1y.
279. *Oriental Economist*, April 2012, 5.
280. *Bloomberg*, 21 May 2012; and *Kyodo*, 22 May 2012.
281. Like most recommendations for post-3.11 reform, this idea was not new. MITI minister Satō Shinji had announced his preference for the separation of transmission from generation in 1997. See Scalise 2009, 242. See also Kikkawa 2004 and 2011, 36–38. Sawa 2011c argues that foreign experiences with liberalization and structural reform have been uniformly negative. Scalise 2012b is a post-3.11 analysis of prospects for the restructuring of the transmission and distribution businesses.
282. Interview, senior energy policy staff member, Keidanren, Tokyo, 10 October 2011; interview, senior official, National Policy Unit, Cabinet Office, Tokyo, 12 October 2012; and Keidanren Kankyō Honbu 2011.
283. See the strongly argued editorial calling for an end to the nuclear fuel cycle policy in *Mainichi Shimbun*, 22 November 2011.
284. See the editorial in *Nihon Keizai Shimbun*, 9 August 2011; *Yomiuri Shimbun*, 25 October 2011.
285. *Kyodo*, 31 October and 28 November 2011; *Mainichi Shimbun* 22 November 2011; *Yomiuri*, 22 November 2011.
286. Takubo Masa 2011, 19–20.
287. See http://www.siew.sg/energy-perspectives/global-energy-trends/asian-premium -gas-strikes-lng-importing-countries; and *Enerugii Fōramu*, 1 July 2011. Imports of oil for power generation, a last resort, more than doubled in the same period. See http://eneken.ieej.or.jp /data/4325.pdf.
288. Toichi 2003; Sano 2011.
289. In 1998, Toshiba and Hitachi created the Asia Promotional Organization to promote foreign sales of boiling water reactors; see Kido 1998. One of the partners in the nuclear export public-private venture was the Innovation Network Corporation of Japan, itself a public-private organization (*Sangyō Kakushin Kikō*) with 89 percent public funding and nineteen corporate participants. See www.incj.co.jp/english/index.html. For information on the METI-led International Nuclear Energy Development of Japan Co. Ltd., in which TEPCO was the largest shareholder, see http://www.jined.co.jp/pdf/101022-e.pdf; and for METI's analysis of the global nuclear energy market, see http://www.enecho.meti.go.jp/policy/nuclear/pptfiles/0602 -6.pdf.
290. *Nihon Keizai Shimbun*, 3 October 2011.
291. *Asahi Shimbun*, 26 September 2011.
292. *Wall Street Journal*, 28 September 2011; *Tokyo Shimbun*, 2 December 2011; *Yomiuri Shimbun*, 2 December 2011; *Nihon Keizai Shimbun*, 7 December 2011.
293. International Energy Agency 2012, 22–24.

6. Repurposing Local Government

1. The classic account is Steiner 1965. This section is derived in part from Samuels 1983, chap. 2. See also Steiner, Flanagan, and Krauss 1980; and Reed 1986. For analysis of recent developments in Japanese public administration in English, see Jain 2011 and the papers by Yokomichi Kiyotaka listed at http://www.grips.ac.jp/faculty/yokomichi_kiyotaka.html.
2. Data provided by National Association of Governors, 1 November 2011.
3. This principle and all fundamental matters related to the local government system in Japan are enshrined in the Local Autonomy Law that was promulgated alongside the constitution in May 1947. See Steiner 1965 for the origin, and Rheuben 2007 and Jain 2011 for details on the nominal curtailment (except for cases of "national uniformity") of "agency delegated functions."
4. There were more than seventy thousand localities before the "Meiji amalgamation," and there were still nearly thirty-five hundred until the most recent "Heisei amalgamation." There

are still some five hundred municipalities with fewer than ten thousand residents—and in several rural prefectures, these small communities comprise the majority of localities. Data provided by MIAC, 31 October 2011.

5. Like an airline mileage program, each one of these designations comes with a different level of privileges. Examples of "designated" cities—those with populations of more than five hundred thousand—are Kobe, Kyoto, Fukuoka, Nagoya, Yokohama, and Osaka. "Core" cities qualify with three hundred thousand residents and "special" cities, a category added in 1998, are municipalities with more than two hundred thousand residents. See Hayashi 2009; Yokomichi 2010; and Yamazaki 2012.

6. Bōeishō 2011a, 35.

7. Masuda 2007.

8. Data provided by the National Association of Governors, 1 November 2011. Interview, Professor Hatakeyama Eisuke, National Graduate Research Institute for Policy Studies, Tokyo, 21 July 2011.

9. See Pempel 1982 for an account of "creative conservatism."

10. Jain 2011, 164, for example, argues that localities "have created opportunities for leadership, particularly through new policy initiatives and innovative ideas."

11. Interview, Ichikawa Mikiko, Tokyo University professor, Tokyo, 14 December 2011; Interview, Ōnishi Takashi, Tokyo University professor, Tokyo, 14 December 2011; interview, Mayor Kawamura Takashi, Nagoya, 12 January 2012.

12. Article 12, paragraph 2 of the law stipulates that local governments can sign mutual assistance agreements in order to deal with disaster relief.

13. June 1996 Hyogo Prefecture data supplied by MIAC on 4 November 2011.

14. Interview, Susume Kenichi, MIAC official, Tokyo, 2 November 2011. The overengineered National Association of Governors (NAG) scheme was a ten-page contractual document: "Agreement Document Related to Regional Assistance in Time of a Disaster among the Nation's Prefectures" (Zenkoku Todōfuken ni okeru Saigai no Kōiki Ōen ni kansuru Kyōteisho). See also United Nations Centre for Regional Development 1995, 146; Kamiya Hideyuki 2011, 2.

15. Tierney and Goltz 1997 observed the post–Hanshin/Awaji proliferation of these agreements. "Risk hedge" was the term used by MIAC official Koyanagi Tarō, interview, Tokyo, 31 October 2011.

16. Interview, Koyanagi Tarō, Tokyo, 31 October 2011. This order of magnitude was confirmed by Meiji University professor Kitaōji Nobusato, a consultant to Shizuoka Prefecture for emergency planning. Interview, Tokyo, 3 October 2011. See Sankei Shimbun, 2 April 2011, for a report on how Tottori Prefecture came to the aid of Niigata Prefecture after the 2006 Chūetsu earthquake, and how it used this same "Employees' Disaster Support Corp" to aid Hyogo Prefecture after a 2009 typhoon.

17. Nakabayashi 2009.

18. Interview, Ogawa Junya, Democratic Party of Japan (DPJ) Diet member and former MIAC official, Tokyo, 18 November 2011. See also Jain 2011, 171.

19. Data provided by MIAC, 31 October 2011. See also Rheuben 2007, 5, and Yokomichi 2010, 7–9.

20. Data provided by MIAC, 31 October 2011.

21. Interview, Fujiwara Michitaka, National Association of Governors, Tokyo, 1 November 2011.

22. See Rheuben 2007.

23. Ōmae calls the idea of regional unions a "half baked state system" (chūto hanpa na dōshū-sei) at http://www.nikkeibp.co.jp/sj/2/column/a/55/index.html.

24. Ōmae 1995. See also Yoshitomi 2011.

25. Jain 2011, 174. Note that this was part of a larger initiative by Prime Minister Koizumi to centralize policy in the Cabinet Office. See Uchiyama 2010.

26. According to one scholar, the Decentralization Promotion Bureau in the MIAC is dedicated to eliminating the central field agencies, but every ministry and agency has argued for the criticality of the mission of their own field office. Interview, Professor Hatakeyama Eisuke, Graduate Research Institute for Policy Studies, Tokyo, 21 July 2011.

27. See http://www.doshusei.org/.

28. This followed a report from Liberal Democratic Party (LDP) study group concluding that prefectural consolidation would save the government 11 trillion yen per year and reduce public employment by more than one hundred thousand workers. See Rheuben 2007, 4–6. Masuda 2007 is a firsthand account from the minister in charge.

29. Masuda 2007, 416.

30. Ibid.

31. Interview, Ogawa Junya, DPJ Diet member, Tokyo, 18 November 2011. A MIAC official confirmed that the government has been led in different directions by the political class (*"'yes' de ari, 'no' de aru"*). Interview, 31 October 2011. A Keidanren official suggested that Ozawa reversed course because the state system would eliminate entire election districts controlled by the DPJ. Interview, Tokyo, 14 September 2011.

32. Ozawa 1994, 76.

33. The 2003 DPJ manifesto spoke of "building a society in which regions can decide local issues for themselves." In 2005, the party promised to convert 90 percent of tied grants to block grants allocated to broad policy areas, such as social welfare and education. Both these platforms were echoed as one of the "Five Principles" in the 2009 DPJ manifesto.

34. Writing just before 3.11, one leading local government scholar said that due to political instability at the center, "it is fair to say that the road [to these reforms] will not be easy." See Yokomichi 2011, 24.

35. Ozawa finally left the DPJ in July 2012.

36. Interview, Governor Ido, Kobe, 22 December 2011.

37. *Kyodo*, 3 March 2012. In the event, however, the regional union could not resist the pronuclear pressure and announced it would accept the government's decision to restart the Ōi reactors. See *Kyodo*, 31 May 2012.

38. Interview, Governor Ido, Kobe, 22 December 2011.

39. *Kyodo*, 26 August 2011.

40. Interview, Professor Yokomichi Kiyotaka, Tokyo, 15 July 2011.

41. *Nihon Keizai Shimbun*, 29 April 2011.

42. Toba 2011, 149.

43. Mayor Sakurai compares the distant, unsympathetic, and insufficient response of the Tokyo Electric Power Company (TEPCO) to that of Tohoku Electric Power Company, whose thermal plant in his city was badly damaged by the tsunami. See Sakurai 2011, 142–43.

44. *Mainichi Shimbun*, 24 May 2011; Sakurai 2011, 134–36.

45. *Asahi Shimbunsha* 2011, 26–29.

46. See http://www.blog.goo.ne.jp/hosakakunio.

47. Interview, Governor Tasso, Morioka, 22 September 2011.

48. Interview, Governor Ido, Kobe, 22 December 2011.

49. Interview, MIAC central government official, Morioka, 20 September 2011.

50. *Nippon Seisaku Tōshi Ginkō* 2011, 4.

51. Hirayama 2011.

52. *Asahi Shimbun*, 13 September 2011.

53. Mikuriya Takashi in *Yomiuri Shimbun*, 29 April 2011.

54. Rheuben 2012, 11.

55. Interview, deputy mayor of Yokohama, 30 September 2011.

56. Center for International and Strategic Studies 2011, xxi, 12; Keidanren 2011.

57. See Keidanren 1995 and Nippon Keidanren 2006 for pre-3.11 arguments for how state system reform would enhance Japan's national competitiveness.

58. For background on the "special zone" model, see Naikaku Kanbō Chiiki Kasseika Tōgō Jimukyoku and Naikakufu Chiiki Kasseika Sokushinshitsu 2011.

59. One expert points out that even though the Cabinet Office is designated to run interference for the localities, it is populated by secondees from the very agencies and ministries it is trying to constrain. Interview, Professor Hatakeyama Eisuke, Graduate Research Institute for Policy Studies, Tokyo, 21 July 2011.

60. See Naikakufu Kōzō Kaikaku Tokku Tantōshitsu 2008.

61. See ibid. for a game attempt to list the (markedly limited) benefits of these special zones, for example, efficiencies gained through ride-share programs, cost savings achieved through privatization of jail management, and the joint purchase of recycling equipment. Perhaps the most famous (and common) special zones (seventy-one of them) have been for the production and sale of unrefined sake to tourists.

62. *Asahi Shimbun*, 16 June 2011; interview, Koiki Genichi, deputy section chief, Regional Recovery Support Section, Planning Bureau, Miyagi Prefecture, Sendai, 20 September 2011. One particularly illustrative case of the pettiness of some of these special zones was that of the special zone application by Kusaka City in Saitama Prefecture, which sought regulatory relief so that it could build elementary and middle schools with ceilings that were 0.3 meters lower than the height required by the Ministry of Education. See the account in Naikakufu Kōzō Kaikaku Tokku Tantōshitsu 2008, 9.

63. Naikaku Kanbō Chiiki Kasseika Tōgō Jimukyoku and Naikakufu Chiiki Kasseika Sokushinshitsu 2011, 1.

64. Interview, Mayor Kawamura Takashi, Nagoya, 12 January 2012.

65. Higashi Nihon Daishinsai Fukkō Taisaku Honbu Jimukyoku 2011; interview, Ono Hiroshi, director of Policy Planning Division, Bureau of Reconstruction, Iwate prefectural government, Morioka, 21 September 2011; Naikaku Kanbō Chiiki Kasseika Tōgō Jimukyoku and Naikakufu Chiiki Kasseika Sokushinshitsu 2011, 7.

66. See Nippon Keidanren 2008; Keidanren, 2011; and http://www.kkc.or.jp/doushusei/about/social.html for Keidanren promotion of the state system. The Keidanren home page has a tab devoted to educating the public about the virtues of the state system. See http://www.kkc.or.jp/doushusei/ for an accompanying *manga*, entitled: "Of Course It's Good! The State System." See also http://www.kkc.or.jp/doushusei/about/opinion/html and, for a particularly sophisticated analysis by a Keidanren task force, see Hayashi 2009. Professor Hayashi of Kwansei Gakuin University, was subsequently appointed a member of the government's Local Government System Research Council in 2011. This view of the state system is consistent with that of former Iwate governor and Minister of Internal Affairs and Communications Masuda Hiroya. See Masuda 2007.

67. Compare Keidanren 1995 to Keidanren 2011.

68. Nippon Keizai Dantai Rengōkai 2011b, 44–47.

69. This was made explicit in 2006, when Prime Minister Abe Shinzō introduced a "State System Special Zones Promotion Law."

70. Interview, Saitō Tadashi, director political and social affairs, Keidanren, Tokyo, 14 September 2011.

71. Interview, Abe Tomoko, Tokyo, 2 November 2011.

72. Satō 2011, 121. He repeats this metaphor in Satō and Tamogami 2011, 130.

73. Interview, Ono Hiroshi, director of Policy Planning Division, Bureau of Reconstruction, Iwate prefectural government, Morioka, 21 September 2011. Masuda Hiroya, a previous Iwate governor, was a strong supporter of the creation of a Tohoku state. See Masuda 2007.

74. Interview, Governor Tasso, Morioka, 22 September 2011.

75. Interview, Governor Ido, Kobe, 12 January 2012.

76. Ibid.

77. Interview, Ogawa Junya, Tokyo, 18 November 2011. This was reiterated in interviews with officials at the National Association of Governors and the MIAC, 31 October 2011, and 1 November 2011. Ōmae Kenichi's view is at http://www.nikkeibp.co.jp/sj/2/column/a/55/index1.html.

78. *Kahoku Online Network*, 30 May 2011.

79. *Hokutō Kenkyū* 2011, 10; and *Yomiuri Shimbun*, 7 June 2011.

80. *Asahi Shimbunsha* 2011, 162; and *Hokutō Kenkyū* 2011, 10–11.

81. Interview, Akasaka Norio, Tokyo, 18 January 2012.

82. See http://doshusei.dtiblog.com/blog.entry-171.html.

83. See http://doshusei.dtiblog.com/blog.entry-172.html.

84. See http://www.yamashika.cocolog-nifty.com/chiki/2011/04/post-9491html.

85. *Tōyō Keizai*, 8 September 2011 (online edition); and *Shūkan Tōyō Keizai*, 27 August 2011.

86. *Mainichi Shimbun*, 18 May 2011.

87. See http://www35.atwiki.jp/kolia/pages/763.html. Eguchi quoted in *Shūkan Tōyō Keizai*, 27 August 2011.

88. For the view that amalgamation was a first strategic step toward a state system, see http://www.keidanren.or/english/journal/200007.html.

89. Satō 2011, 124.

90. Interview, Ono Hiroshi, director of Policy Planning Division, Bureau of Reconstruction, Iwate prefectural government, Morioka, 21 September 2011.

91. *Kahoku Shimpō*, 16 October 2011.

92. Data supplied by MIAC, 31 October 2011. Interview, MIAC official, Sendai, 20 September 2011.

93. Information about untrusting neighbors is drawn from author interviews with citizens of Minami Sanriku as part of the Massachusetts Institute of Technology (MIT) Japan 3.11 Initiative: http://japan311.scripts.mit.edu/wp/, 23 January 2012.

94. Interview, Ido Toshizō, Kobe, 22 December 2011.

95. Interview, Abe Tomoko, Tokyo, 2 November 2011.

96. *Asahi Shimbun*, 13 September 2011.

97. Satō and Tamogami 2011, 130.

98. This perspective is made pointedly by the Tohoku newspaper *Kahoku Shimpō*, 12 May 2011.

99. Tasso 2011, 46.

100. Ibid., 43.

101. Interview, Tasso, Morioka, 22 September 2011.

102. Tasso 2011, 45.

103. Ibid., 42.

104. *Higashi Nihon Daishinsai Fukkō Kōsō Kaigi* 2011, 4, 36.

105. Ibid., 16.

106. Ibid., 7, 19, 33.

107. *Asahi Shimbun*, 16 June 2011. Fukushima's "Recovery Vision" was shallower and argued more weakly than those of its neighbors. Acknowledging that its leaders and residents had not clearly appreciated the dangers of nuclear power—effectively an admission that they allowed themselves to be bribed by TEPCO and METI—the report proclaimed its commitment to environmentally friendly energy sources and to the reclaiming of one of the world's most widely polluted plots of land. It was filled with bromides about building a "disaster resilient society" and the "rebirth of regional solidarity." Sadly, however, it seemed the product of a beleaguered, exhausted, remorseful, and nearly paralyzed local government. See Fukushima Prefecture 2011.

108. Miyagi's plan is at http://www.cas.go.jp/jp/fukkou/pdf/kousou7/murai.pdf. See also Miyagi Prefecture 2011.

109. See http://greattohokurevival.blogspot.com/2011/05/miyagi-and-iwate-recovery-commissions.html#more.

110. This is based on Iwate Prefecture 2011; interview, Governor Tasso, Morioka, 22 September 2011; and Tasso 2011.

111. Tasso noted proudly that his office's surveys of residents in temporary shelters had a 92 percent return rate. Interview, Morioka, 22 September 2011.

112. See *Kahoku Shimpō*, 12 May 2011 and http://www.japan-press.co.jp/modules/news/index.php?action=List&categoryid=49.

113. *Asahi Shimbunsha* 2011, 164.

114. *Kahoku Online*, 28 July 2011. See the supporting view of Nagaya Nobuhiro, a director of the National Association of Fishery Cooperatives, in *Asahi Shimbunsha* 2011, 165–67.

115. *Yomiuri Shimbun*, 5 March 2012.

116. For details of the proposal, see *Nippon Seisaku Tōshi Ginkō* 2011; Ōnishi 2011; and http://www.jamgr.jp/news/. As with so many other proposals reviewed in this book, this one existed before 3.11, and was reinvented with new urgency and legitimacy.

117. Ōnishi 2011.

118. The government's draft bill for a Special Regional Recovery Zone for the Great Eastern Japan Disaster (*Higashi Nippon Daishinsai Fukkō Tokubetsuku Iki Hōan*) offered financial support and regulatory relaxation, per the comprehensive special zones reviewed in this chapter. But it also included measures to support Community Building Recovery Corporations (CBRCs) by name. For an early report of a CBRC in Rikuzentakata, see *Iwate Nippō*, 20 October 2011. Professor Ōnishi also reported that in Kesennuma, local assemblymen set up a workers' association and provided jobs to unemployed citizens, something he called a "primitive" version of the CBRC. After the council ended, he established study groups to promote and conduct surveys of CBRCs in Tohoku. Interview, Tokyo, 14 December 2011.

119. Interview, Professor Ōnishi, Tokyo, 14 December 2011.

120. The National Police Agency reported that seventeen prefectures provided shelter to more than 160,000 persons within the first three weeks after 3.11. See *Sankei Shimbun*, 2 April 2011. In one prominent example, Saitama Prefecture opened its public sports arena and made shuttered schools available for temporary housing. Niigata offered to host all of the residents of Minami Sōma. See Kamiya Hideyuki 2011; Sakurai Katsunobu 2011, 134.

121. Komatsu 2011, 38; *Sankei Shimbun*, 28 March 2011.

122. MIAC data are at http://www.soumu.go.jp/main_content/000125227.pdf.

123. MIAC data provided 25 October 2011.

124. Compiled from data supplied by the office of Governor Ido Toshizō, 22 December 2011.

125. *Tokyo Shimbun*, 3 March 2012.

126. Data supplied by Yokohama City Hall, 7 October 2011. For additional cases, see Komatsu 2011; and *Sankei Shimbun*, 2 April 2011.

127. Interview, Nagoya, 12 January 2012. See also *Mainichi Shimbun*, 2 July and 24 July 2011, for more on Nagoya's "all out support" for Rikuzentakata.

128. Data supplied by interviews with Nagoya City officials at the "Disaster Victims Assistance Hall," Rikuzentakata Temporary City Hall, 22 September 2011; and *Nagoyashi Hisai Chiiki Shien Honbu*, 12 January 2012.

129. Compiled from data supplied by the office of Governor Ido Toshizō, 22 December 2011. In addition, Hyogo agreed to employ one thousand disaster victims for up to two years and staffed "one stop" consultation desks (*sōgō sōdan madoguchi*) for Tohoku residents who had questions on any aspect of postdisaster concern. *Yomiuri Shimbun*, 4 July 2011.

130. Nihon Gakujitsu Kaigi 2011.

131. See chapter 3 for the way the Chinese government organized the pairing of local governments in 2008. The Japanese pronunciation of the Chinese model is *taikō shien*. According to Hayashi and Akihara 2011, the Japanese adopted the English and Chinese terms because there is no equivalent word in Japanese for the one-on-one idea embedded in the notion of "pairing" and because the combination of Chinese characters in "*taikō*" does not exist in Japanese.

132. Interview, Seguchi Kiyoyuki, Tokyo, 27 December 2011. See his article in *Yomiuri Shimbun*, 18 March 2011.

133. Interview, Ichikawa Mikiko, 14 December 2011. See also Ishikawa 2011.

134. See Kamiya Hideyuki 2011; *Shūkan Tōyō Keizai*, 4 June 2011; http://financegreenwatch.org/jp/?p=723; and http://scienceportal.jp/news/daily/1103/1103221.html. See also Komatsu 2011, 39. Professor Ichikawa says that she went to the Science Council because these other organizations were not working well together. Interview, Tokyo, 14 December 2011. Mayor Kawamura, when asked about the role of these national associations, responded with a derisive "Hmmmmm." Interview, Nagoya, 12 January 2012. Former Hyogo governor Kaihara said simply "they didn't move" (*ugokenakatta*). Interview, Kobe, 22 December 2011.

135. NAG data supplied 1 November 2011.

136. Ido 2011, 127–31; Kamiya Hideyuki 2011, 4; *Sankei Shimbun*, 28 March and 2 April 2011; *Asahi Shimbun*, 15 April 2011; *Mainichi Shimbun*, 24 May 2011; *Nihon Keizai Shimbun*, 30 May 2011.

137. Interview, Hyogo governor Ido Toshizō, Kobe, 22 December 2011. One of his predecessors as governor, Kaihara Toshitami, concurred, saying that "the central government was not able to cope." Interview, Kobe, 22 December 2011.

138. Interview, Hyogo governor Ido Toshizō, Kobe, 22 December 2011.

139. *Mainichi Shimbun*, 24 May 2011.

140. Kamiya Hideyuki 2011, 2. This description appeared in the broadsheets even earlier. See, for example, *Sankei Shimbun*, 2 April 2011.

141. Kamiya Hideyuki 2011, 6.

142. Interview, Governor Tasso, Morioka, 22 September 2011.

143. See *Shūkan Tōyō Keizai*, 4 June 2011. *Sankei Shimbun*, 2 April 2011, reports that this was the motivation of Shizuoka Prefecture. Interview, Susume Kenichi, MIAC official, 2 November 2011.

144. Interview, Governor Ido Toshizō, Kobe, 22 December 2011. By January 2012, Hyogo had organized forty-six such conferences.

145. Data supplied by *Nagoyashi Hisai Chiiki Shien Honbu*, 12 January 2012.

146. Data supplied by MIAC, 4 November 2011. The first emergency allocation for this purpose was 5.8 billion yen in April 2011. See Komatsu 2011, 42.

147. *Nihon Keizai Shimbun*, 11 December 2011. I am grateful to Professor Nishikawa Masashi of Aoyama Gakuin University for calling my attention to this aspect of the dispatch.

148. Data and flow chart of application process provided by Yokohama City Hall, 20 October 2011.

149. *Tokyo Shimbun*, 8 March 2012.

150. See *Shūgiin Sōmuiinkai Gijiroku*, 19 April and 17 May 2011.

151. *Shūkan Tōyō Keizai*, 4 June 2011; interview, Nagoya mayor Kawamura, Nagoya, 12 January 2012.

152. This according to Nagoya mayor Kawamura, interview, Nagoya, 12 January 2012.

153. *Yomiuri Shimbun*, 12 November 2011.

154. *Tokyo Shimbun*, 1 February 2011; *Asahi Shimbun*, 29 September 2011; *Kyodo*, 19 November 2011; *Sankei Shimbun*, 30 December 2011. In May 2012, protestors in Kyushu blocked trucks attempting to deliver debris from Miyagi despite certification that it was safe. *Kyodo*, 23 May 2012.

155. *Yomiuri Evening News*, 25 March 2012.

156. Interview, Seguchi Kiyoyuki, former Bank of Japan Beijing representative, Tokyo, 14 May 2012.

157. Morris-Suzuki 1995, 36.

158. See http://www.env.go.jp/recycle/3r/approach/hokusai_en.pdf, 8.

159. Morris-Suzuki 1995, 48.

160. See http://www.japanfs.org/en_/newsletter/200310-1.html.

161. See http://www.japanfs.org/en_/newsletter/200310-1.html#to.

162. See http://www.cas.go.jp/fukkou/pdf/kousou2/gijiyousi.pdf, 22. The published record of the council's discussions does not attribute statements to individual members. But this was confirmed as Umehara's by two members of the council. Interviews, 18 January 2012, and 2 February 2012.

163. Mikuriya 2011b, 22–23. Japan's "Galapagos syndrome"—its inward orientation—was used to explain the failure of some Japanese manufacturing design to catch on globally. Concern was widespread well before 3.11. See, for example, Yoshikawa 2010; http://news.searchina.ne.jp/disp.cgi?y=2012&d=0426&f=business_0426_080.shtml; and http://www.nri.co.jp/navi/2008/080213_1.html.

164. Personal correspondence, 9 January 2012.

165. *Mainichi Shimbun*, 8 January 2012.

166. *Asahi Shimbun*, 10 September 2011.

167. See http://sankei.jp.msn.com/lif/news/110620/art11062007240001-n1.htm.

168. *Asahi Shimbun*, 10 September 2011.

169. Washida 2012, 73.

170. Interview, Professor Akasaka, Tokyo, 18 January 2012.

171. Akasaka reflects on this in Washida 2012, 64–65.

172. Washida 2012, 67–68.

173. Interview, Yokohama, 30 September 2011.

174. Interview, Hyogo governor Ido, Kobe, 22 December 2011.

175. *Yomiuri Shimbun*, 15 July 2011; Yamazaki 2012.

176. *Yomiuri Shimbun*, 13 July 2011.

177. This is based on a report in *Kahoku Shimpō*, 6 February 2012.

178. Interview, Ono Hiroshi, director of Policy Planning Division, Bureau of Reconstruction, Iwate prefectural government, Morioka, 21 September 2011.

179. Yokomichi 2010 speaks of "creeping."

180. Personal correspondence, Seguchi Kiyoyuki, former Bank of Japan official, 10 September 2012.

181. Individual agencies and ministries had conducted their own reviews, but this was the first to emerge from the Cabinet Office. See Chūō Bōsai Kaigi Bōsai Taisaku Sokushin Kentō Kaigi 2012 at http://www.bousai.go.jp/chubou/suishinkaigi/chukan_hontai.pdf.

182. *Kyodo*, 25 June 2011.

183. This blog post of a 21 January 2012 Hashimoto tweet can be found at http://wondrousjapanforever.cocolog-nifty.com/blog/2012/01/post-405b.html.

184. See http://www.hashimoto-toru.com/policy/.

185. LDP president Tanigaki Sadakazu's comparison is quoted in *Japan Times*, 27 March 2012. Yoshitomi 2011 is a pre-3.11 biography of Hashimoto.

Conclusion

1. The report of the Kurokawa Committee is referenced in chapter 5 of this study. The full report in Japanese, Kokkai Tōkyō Denryoku Fukushima Genshiryoku Hatsuden Jiko Chōsa Iinkai 2012, is at http://naiic.go.jp/report/. The English summary is at http://naiic.go.jp/en/report/. The international media expressed concern that this summary was not a direct translation of the Japanese version. See the press conference held on 5 July 2012 at the Foreign Correspondents' Press Club in Tokyo: http://inagist.com/all/221482359596388352/.

2. According to page 16 of the English summary of the Kurokawa Committee's final report, "the Commission was forced to exercise our legislative right to demand such information from NISA [Nuclear and Industrial Safety Agency], after NISA failed to respond to several requests."

3. See http://www.kiyoshikurokawa.com/en/2011/05/first-step-towards-structuring-new-japan.html.

4. Interview, Kurokawa Kiyoshi, Tokyo, 21 May 2012. The library of committee broadcasts is at http://www.shugiintv.go.jp/en/index.php?ex=VL. For more on these press clubs, see Freeman 2000.

5. See Kokkai Tōkyō Denryoku Fukushima Genshiryoku Hatsuden Jiko Chōsa Iinkai 2012, chap. 5.

6. In his English-language preface, Dr. Kurokawa went even further, suggesting that 3.11 was somehow idiosyncratic and "Made in Japan," an argument that undermined some of his larger analysis. See Curtis 2012, Dickie 2012, and Shimazu 2012 for critiques of the effort to essentialize the causes of 3.11 for the foreign audience.

7. Diet testimony of Suzuki Tatsujirō, 26 April 2011. Suzuki was later criticized in the press for participating in closed sessions limited to the "pro-nuclear faction." See *Mainichi Shimbun*, 24 May 2012. Suzuki denied any wrongdoing and "hopes this incident can be a trigger to reform the institutional arrangement of JAEC [Japan Atomic Energy Commision] (and other advisory councils) in Japan." Private correspondence, 29 May 2012. See *Kyodo*, 9 July 2012, for a report on the JAEC's practice of holding closed-door meetings ahead of its public ones.

8. Representative Ogawa offered this observation in an interview on 18 November 2011. The question about his origin was from Representative Kōno Tarō, 21 December 2011. Representative Ogawa is from Shikoku in western Japan.

9. I have developed this argument in Samuels 2003.

10. Mahoney and Thelen 2010.

11. Ibid., 9.

12. This is consistent with the expectations of Kingdon 1995.

13. Each of these claims is documented earlier in this study.

14. For his famous definition of war as "nothing more than the continuation of politics by other means," see Von Clausewitz's, *On War*.

15. Recall that this narrative had first appeared more than a decade earlier. See Iida 1997.

16. The speaker was Sengoku Yoshito. See *Kyodo*, 17 April 2012.

17. Perversity, jeopardy, and futility are the three elements in the "rhetoric of reaction." See Hirschman 1991.

18. See http://www.economist.com/blogs/graphicdetail/2012/04/daily-chart-16.

19. *Asahi Shimbunsha* 2011.

20. Michael Cucek, a leading foreign analyst of Japanese politics, concluded in *Shisaku*, his 8 March 2012 blog, that "Prime Minister Kan Naoto performed his job to what were the limits of what was humanly possible." See also Funabashi and Kitazawa 2012.

21. See, for example, *Yomiuri Shimbun*, 24 January 2012; *Sankei Shimbun*, 2 April 2012; *Asahi Shimbun*, 14 April 2012; http://www.bousai.metro.tokyo.jp/japanese/tmg/assumption_h24 .html; http://www.bousai.metro.tokyo.jp/japanese/tmg/pdf/20120418gaiyou.pdf; and http:// www.mxtv.co.jp/mxnews/news/201204186.html.

22. *Tokyo Shimbun*, 3 January 2012; and http://www.pewglobal.org/2012/06/05/japanese -wary-of-nuclear-energy/.

23. Mikuriya 2011b, 24.

24. *China Daily*, 12 August 2011.

25. *Asahi Shimbun*, 8 April 2011. After Democratic Party of Japan (DPJ) backbenchers protested, the official development assistance (ODA) budget was cut by 10 percent. See *Yomiuri Shimbun*, 17 April 2011.

26. Interviews, Takamizawa Nobushige, director general for policy, Ministry of Defense, Tokyo, 7 July 2011, and Suzuki Tatsujirō, AEC vice-chair, 26 September 2011.

27. Avenell 2012a explains why these two groups had difficulty coming together before 3.11.

28. *Kyodo*, 20 November 2012.

29. See the editorial in *Mainichi Shimbun*, 23 June 2012.

30. Interview, Fujiwara Michitaka, director of decentralization reform promotion, National Association of Governors, 1 November 2011.

31. The term "parcel delivery service" and the description of the roles of regimental commanders are from interview, senior Self-Defense Forces (SDF) officer, Tokyo, 18 November 2011.

32. Kobayashi Satoshi is quoted in the *Marine Gazette* at http://www.marines.mil/unit /mebjapan/Pages/2011/111123-disa. Aichi, Mie, and Kochi Prefectures also approached the U.S. military on their own. See *Japan Times*, 3 March 2012.

33. Telephone interview, Robert Eldridge, deputy assistant chief of staff, Government and External Affairs, Marine Corps Installations Pacific, 10 June 2012.

34. Interview, Abe Tomoko, Democratic Socialist Party (DSP) Diet representative, 2 November 2011.

35. *Kyodo*, 29 April 2012.

36. See *Japan Times*, 20 May 2012, for Hashimoto's plan to solicit support from chief executives in Tokyo, Kitakyushu, Okinawa, and other localities.

37. See Handō, Hosaka, and Todaka 2011 for the wartime comparison, and Parshall and Tully 2005, 413, for British field marshal William Slim's reminiscences of inflexible Japanese commanders.

38. *Asahi Shimbun*, 2 March 2012.

39. Interview, senior Keidanren official, Tokyo, 31 May 2012.

40. See http://www.pewglobal.org/2012/06/05/japanese-wary-of-nuclear-energy/.

41. This was described as providing the Ministry of Defense (MOD) "a big boost" and as "very encouraging." Interview, Kimura Ayako, counselor, Minister's Secretariat, Ministry of Defense, 22 November 2011.

42. Not only were questions from the floor disallowed, but in one case, an electric power company official was tapped to speak in the guise of an ordinary citizen. See *Kyodo*, 14 and 16 July 2012.

References

Abe, Shinzō. 2011. "Watakushi Nara Kō Yaru" [If it were me, this is what I would do]. *WiLL*, July, 28–37.

Akagi, Akio. 2011. "Sōteigai no Anzen to Baishō" [Security and compensation for the unimaginable]. *Sekai*, August, 194–211.

Akcinaroglu, Seden, Jonathan M. DiCicco, and Elizabeth Radziszewsk. 2011. "Avalanches and Olive Branches: A Multimethod Analysis of Disasters and Peacemaking in Interstate Rivalries." *Political Research Quarterly* 64: 260–75.

Aldrich, Daniel P. 2008. *Site Fights: Divisive Facilities and Civil Society in Japan and the West*. Ithaca, NY: Cornell University Press.

———. 2011. "Nuclear Power's Future in Japan and Abroad: The Fukushima Accident in Social and Political Perspective." *ParisTech Review*, 25 August, http://www.paristechreview.com/2011/08/25/nuclear-fukushima-accident-social-political-perspective/.

———. 2012. "Networks of Power: Institutions and Local Residents in Post-Tohoku Japan." Chap. 7 in *Natural Disaster and Nuclear Crisis in Japan: Response and Recovery after Japan's 3-11*, edited by Jeff Kingston. London: Nissan Monograph Series, Routledge.

Allen, J. Michael. 1996. "The Price of Identity: The 1923 Kanto Earthquake and Its Aftermath." *Korean Studies* 20: 64–93.

Ames, Chris, and Yuiko Koguchi-Ames. 2012. "Friends in Need: 'Operation Tomodachi' and the Politics of U.S. Military Disaster Relief in Japan." Chap. 12 in *Natural Disaster and Nuclear Crisis in Japan: Response and Recovery after Japan's 3-11*, edited by Jeff Kingston. London: Nissan Monograph Series, Routledge.

Andrews, Molly. 2003. "Grand National Narratives and the Project of Truth Commissions: A Comparative Analysis." *Media, Culture & Society* 25: 45–65.

Anzai, Ikuro. 2011. "An Agenda for Peace Research after 3/11." *Asia-Pacific Journal* 9 (46), no. 1.

Asahi Shimbunsha. 2011. *3.11 go Nippon no Ronten* [Issues facing Japan after 3.11]. Tokyo: Asahi Shimbunsha.

Asō, Iku. 2003. *Jōhō, Kantei ni Tassezu* [Information: Not Getting to the Cabinet]. Tokyo: Shinchō Bunko.

———. 2011. *Mae E! Higashi Nippon Daishinsai to Mumei Senshitachi no Kiroku* [Forward! A record of the anonymous soldiers and the Great Eastern Japan Disaster]. Tokyo: Shinchōsha.

Avenell, Simon. 2012a. "From Fearsome Pollution to Fukushima: Environmental Activism and the Nuclear Blind Spot in Contemporary Japan." *Environmental History* 17: 244–76.

———. 2012b. "From Kobe to Tohoku: The Potential and the Peril of a Volunteer Infrastructure." Chap. 3 in *Natural Disaster and Nuclear Crisis in Japan: Response and Recovery after Japan's 3-11*, edited by Jeff Kingston. London: Nissan Monograph Series, Routledge.

Awata, Yasuo, Yoshihiko Kariya, and Koji Okumura. 1998. "Segmentation of the Surface Ruptures Associated with the 1891 Nobi Earthquake, Central Honshu, Japan, Based on the Paleoseismic Investigations." Research Report of the Active Fault and Earthquake Research Center of the National Institute of Advanced Industrial Science and Technology. Tsukuba. http://unit.aist.go.jp/actfault-eq/english/reports/h10seika/12seika.html.

Ayson, Robert, and Brendan Taylor. 2008. "Carry China's Torch." *Survival* 50 (4): 5–10.

Baumgartner, Frank R., and Bryan D. Jones. 2009. *Agendas and Instability in American Politics*. 2nd ed. Chicago: University of Chicago Press.

Beard, Charles A. 1924. "Goto and the Rebuilding of Tokyo." *Our World*, April, 11–21.

Befu, Harumi. 2001. *Hegemony of Homogeneity: An Anthropological Analysis of "Nihonjinron."* Melbourne, Australia: Trans Pacific Press.

Beinert, Peter. 2006. *The Good Fight: Why Liberals, and Only Liberals, Can Win the War on Terror and Make America Great Again*. New York: HarperCollins.

Benford, Robert D., and David A. Snow. 2000. "Framing Processes and Social Movements: An Overview and Assessment." In *Annual Review of Sociology*, Vol. 26, edited by Karen S. Cook, 625–27. Palo Alto, CA: Annual Reviews.

Birkland, Thomas A. 1997. *After Disaster: Agenda Setting, Public Policy, and Focusing Events*. Washington, DC: Georgetown University Press.

Bōeishō. 2011a. "Higashi Nihon Daishinsai e no Taiō ni Kansuru Kyōkun Jikō no Pointo" [Action items for lessons from the response to the Great Eastern Japan Disaster]. http://www.mod.go.jp/j/approach/defense/saigai/pdf/k_chukan_point.pdf.

———. 2011b. *Nihon no Bōei: Bōei Hakusho* [Japan's defense: Defense white paper]. *Bōeishō*, 2 August.

Boin, Arjen, Allan McConnell, and Paul 't Hart. 2008. "Governing after Crisis." In *Governing after Crisis: The Politics of Investigation, Accountability, and Learning*, edited by Arjen Boin, Allan McConnell, and Paul 't Hart. New York: Cambridge University Press.

Borah, Porismita. 2011. "Conceptual Issues in Framing Theory: A Systematic Examination of a Decade's Literature." *Journal of Communication* 61 (2): 246–63.

Borland, Janet. 2006. "Capitalizing on Catastrophe: Reinvigorating the Japanese State with Moral Values through Education following the 1923 Great Kanto Earthquake." *Modern Asian Studies* 40 (4): 875–907.

Bosner, Leo. 2011. "Japan's Response to a Large-Scale Disaster: Can It Be Improved?" Report to the Maureen and Mike Mansfield Foundation, Washington, DC, 13 July.

Bowers, William J. 2010. "Pakistani Earthquake Relief Operations: Leveraging Humanitarian Missions for Strategic Success." *Prism* 2 (1): 131–44.

Boyd, J. Patrick. 2012. "States of the Nations: Nationalism, Narratives and Normative Change in Postwar Japan." PhD diss., Department of Political Science, Massachusetts Institute of Technology.

Boyd, J. Patrick, and Richard J. Samuels. 2008. "Prosperity's Children: Generational Change and Japan's Future Leadership." *Asia Policy* 6: 15–51.

Brysk, Alison. 1995. "'Hearts and Minds': Bringing Symbolic Politics Back In." *Polity* 27 (4): 559–85.

Bureau of Legislative and Public Affairs. 2006. *Pakistani Earthquake Relief.* Washington, DC: U.S. Agency for International Development.

Busch, Noel F. 1962. *Two Minutes to Noon.* New York: Simon and Schuster.

Capoccia, Giovanni, and R. Daniel Kelemen. 2007. "The Study of Critical Junctures: Theory, Narrative, and Counterfactuals in Historical Institutionalism." *World Politics* 59 (3): 341–69.

Carothers, Thomas. 1999–2000. "Civil Society: Think Again." *Foreign Policy* 117: 18–29.

Center for International and Strategic Studies. 2011. "Partnership for Recovery and a Stronger Future: Standing with Japan after 3-11." Report of a Center for Strategic and International Studies (CSIS) Task Force in Partnership with Keidanren, November.

Chen, Guo, et al. 2010. "The Dragon Strikes: Lessons from the Wenchuan Earthquake." *Anesthesia and Analgesia,* March, 908–15, http://www.anesthesia-analgesia.org/content/110/3/908.

Chong, Dennis, and James N. Druckman. 2007. "Framing Theory." *Annual Review of Political Science* 10: 103–26.

Chūō Bōsai Kaigi Bōsai Taisaku Sokushin Kentō Kaigi. 2012. "Bōsai Taisaku Sokushin Kentō Kaigi Chūkan Hōkoku: Higashi Nippon Daishinsai no Kyōkun wo Ikashi, Yuruginai Nippon no Saikōchiku Wo" [Interim report of the Disaster Policy Study Commission: Living lessons from the Great Eastern Japan Disaster, toward the reconstruction of an unshakeable Japan]. Tokyo: Chūō Bōsai Kaigi, 7 March, http://www.bousai.go.jp/chubou/suishinkaigi/chukan_hontai.pdf.

Chūō Kōron. 2011. "Tomodachi Sakusen no Butaiura" [Behind the scenes of Operation Tomodachi]. *Chūō Kōron,* September, 60–68.

Clancey, Gregory K. 2006a. *Earthquake Nation: The Cultural Politics of Japanese Seismicity, 1868–1930.* Berkeley: University of California Press.

———. 2006b. "The Meiji Earthquake: Nature, Nation, and the Ambiguities of Catastrophe." *Modern Asian Studies* 40 (4): 909–51.

Comfort, L. 2000. "Disaster: Agent of Diplomacy or Change in International Affairs?" *Cambridge Review of International Affairs* 14 (1): 277–94.

Cronin, Patrick. 2011. "Japan's New Deal Opportunity." *Diplomat,* 11 April.

Curtis, Gerald. 2012. "Stop Blaming Fukushima on Japan's Culture." *Financial Times,* 10 July.

Dale, Peter N. 1986. *The Myth of Japanese Uniqueness.* New York: St. Martin's Press.

David Rubens Associates. 2011. "Great Eastern Japan Earthquake, March 11th, 2011: A Preliminary Report on the Japanese Government's Disaster Response Management." David Rubens Associates, London, May.

Davison, Charles. 1931. *The Japanese Earthquake of 1923*. London: Thomas Murby.

De Dilutiis, Guiseppe. 2007. *Il Golpe di Via Fani* [The coup on Via Fani]. Milan: Sperling and Kupfer.

d'Ercole, Marco Mira. 2006. "Income Inequality and Poverty in OECD Countries: How Does Japan Compare?" *Japanese Journal of Social Security Policy* 5 (1): 1–15.

Der Westen. 2010. "Heimatschutz-Dienst statt Bundeswehr?" [Homeland security instead of army service?]. 18 October, http://www.derwesten.de/nachrichten/politik/Heimatschutz-Dienst-statt-Bundeswehr-id3842510.html.

DeWit, Andrew. 2011a. "Fallout from the Fukushima Shock: Japan's Emerging Energy Policy." *Asia-Pacific Journal: Japan Focus* 9 (45), no. 5.

———. 2011b. "Japan's Nuclear Village Wages War on Renewable Energy and the Feed-In Tariff." *Asia-Pacific Journal: Japan Focus* (50).

DeWit, Andrew, Iida Tetsunari, and Kaneko Masaru. 2012. "Fukushima and the Political Economy of Power Policy in Japan." Chap. 9 in *Natural Disaster and Nuclear Crisis in Japan: Response and Recovery after Japan's 3-11*, edited by Jeff Kingston. London: Nissan Monograph Series, Routledge.

Dickie, Mure. 2012. "Beware Post-Crisis 'Made in Japan' Labels." *Financial Times*, 5 July.

Dimmer, Christian. 2011. "Imagining an Alternative Future." JapanEcho.net, 21 June, http://japanecho.net/society/0086/.

Dinmore, Eric Gordon. 2006. "A Small Island Poor in Resources: Natural and Human Resource Anxieties in Transwar Japan." PhD diss., Department of History, Princeton University, Princeton, NJ.

Druckman, James N. 2001. "On the Limits of Framing Effects: Who Can Frame?" *Journal of Politics* 63 (4): 1041–66.

———. 2004. "Political Preference Formation: Competition, Deliberation, and the (Ir)relevance of Framing Effects." *American Political Science Review* 98 (4): 671–86.

Duus, Peter. 2012. "Dealing with Disaster." Chap. 10 in *Natural Disaster and Nuclear Crisis in Japan: Response and Recovery after Japan's 3-11*, edited by Jeff Kingston. London: Nissan Monograph Series, Routledge.

Edelman, Murray J. 1988. *Constructing the Political Spectacle*. Chicago: University of Chicago Press.

Edgington, David W. 2010. *Reconstructing Kobe: The Geography of Crisis and Opportunity*. Vancouver: University of British Columbia Press.

Edgington, David W., Thomas Hutton, and Michael Leaf. 1999. "The Post-Quake Reconstruction of Kobe: Economic, Land Use and Housing Perspectives." *Japan Foundation Newsletter* 27 (1): 13–15, 17.

Energy and Environmental Council. 2011. "Interim Compilation of Discussion Points for the Formulation of 'Innovative Strategy for Energy and the Environment.'" Tokyo, 29 July.

Energy Conservation and Renewable Energy Department, Agency for Natural Resources and Energy. 2010. "Selection of Next Generation Energy and Social Systems Demonstration Areas." Ministry of Economy, Trade, and Industry, Tokyo, April.

Entman, Robert M. 1993. "Framing: Toward Clarification of a Fractured Paradigm." *Journal of Communication* 43 (4): 51–58.

———. 2003. *Projections of Power: Framing News, Public Opinion, and U.S. Foreign Policy*. 1st ed. Chicago: University Of Chicago Press.

Fairley, Peter. 2011. "Japan Faces Post-Fukushima Power Struggle." *IEEE Spectrum*, August, http://spectrum.ieee.org/green-tech/solar/japan-faces-postfukushima -power-struggle.

Feickert, Andrew, and Emma Chanlett-Avery. 2011. *Japan 2011 Earthquake: U.S. Department of Defense (DOD) Response*. Washington, DC: Congressional Research Service.

Fingleton, Eamonn. 2012. "The Myth of Japan's Failure." *New York Times*, 6 January.

Fouse, David. 2011. *Japan Unlikely to Redirect Defense Policy*. Honolulu: PacNet Newsletter.

Freeman, Christopher. 1987. *Technology Policy and Economic Performance*. London: Pinter.

Freeman, Laurie. 2003. "Mobilizing and Demobilizing the Japanese Public Sphere: Mass Media and the Internet in Japan." Chap. 11 in *The State of Civil Society in Japan*, edited by Frank Schwartz and Susan Pharr. New York: Cambridge University Press.

Freeman, Laurie Anne. 2000. *Closing the Shop: Information Cartels and Japan's Mass Media*. Princeton, NJ: Princeton University Press.

Frühstück, Sabine. 2007. *Uneasy Warriors: Gender, Memory, and Popular Culture in the Japanese Army*. Berkeley: University of California Press.

Fujitani, Takashi. 1996. *Splendid Monarchy: Power and Pageantry in Modern Japan*. Berkeley: University of California Press.

Fukao, Mitsuhiro. 2011. "The Great East Japan Earthquake and Japan's Fiscal Consolidation." *Japan Economic Currents* 79 (July), Tokyo: Keizai Kōhō Center.

Fukushima Nuclear Accident Independent Investigation Commission. 2012. "The Official Report of the Fukushima Nuclear Accident Independent Investigation Commission." National Diet of Japan, Tokyo, 5 July. English summary: http:// www.slideshare.net/jikocho/naiic-report-hires.

Fukushima Prefecture. 2011. "Fukushima Ken Fukkō Bijiyon" [Fukushima Prefecture's recovery vision]. Fukushima, August.

Funabashi, Yoichi, and Kay Kitazawa. 2012. "Fukushima in Review: A Complex Disaster, a Disastrous Response." *Bulletin of the Atomic Scientists*, 5 March, http://bos.sagepub.com/content/68/2/9.

Gaillard, Jean-Christophe, Elsa Clavé, and Ilan Kelman. 2008. "Wave of Peace? Tsunami Disaster Diplomacy in Aceh, Indonesia." *Geoforum* 39: 511–26.

Gamson, William A., and Andre Modigliani. 1989. "Media Discourse and Public Opinion on Nuclear Power: A Constructionist Approach." *American Journal of Sociology* 95 (1): 1–37.

Genshiryoku Mirai Kenkyūkai. 2003a. *"Genshiryoku Mirai Kenkyūkai Hōmupeeji"* [Home page of the Future of Nuclear Power Research Group]. http://park.itc.u -tokyo.ac.jp/yamaji/atom/.

———. 2003b. "Rokkasho Saishori: Purojiekuto Ketsudan e no Sentakushi: Deguchi naki Zenshinka, Saisei e no Tettai Ka" [Choices for the resolution of the Rokkasho Reprocessing Project: Going forward without an exit? Retreating toward a rebirth?]. *Genshiryoku Eye* 49 (10): 1–10, http://park.itc.u-tokyo.ac.jp /yamaji/atom/docs/rokkasho.pdf.

Gershenkron, Alexander. 1962. *Economic Backwardness in Historical Perspective: A Book of Essays*. Cambridge: Harvard University Press.

Gourevitch, Peter. *Politics in Hard Times*. Ithaca, NY: Cornell University Press, 1986.

Government of Japan. 2011. "Road to Recovery." Tokyo, September.

———. 2012. "Road to Recovery." Tokyo, March.

Gusfield, Joseph R. 1981. *The Culture of Public Problems: Drinking-Driving and the Symbolic Order*. Chicago: University of Chicago Press.

Hall, Peter A., ed. 1989. *The Political Power of Economic Ideas: Keynesianism Across Nations*. Princeton, NJ: Princeton University Press.

Hammer, Joshua. 2006. *Yokohama Burning: The Deadly 1923 Earthquake and Fire That Helped Forge the Path to World War II*. New York: Free Press.

Handō, Kazutoshi, Hosaka Masayasu, and Mikuriya Takashi. 2011. "Kantō Daishinsai to Higashi Nippon Daijishinsai" [The Great Kanto Disaster and the Great East Japan Disaster]. *Bungei Shunjū*, June, 94–104.

Handō, Kazutoshi, Hosaka Masayasu, and Todaka Kazushige. 2011. "Senkan Yamato to Fukushima Genpatsu: Ano Sensō kara Kawaranai Nihonjin no Jyakuten" [The battleship Yamato and Fukushima nuclear power: The weak points of the Japanese people have not changed since that war]. *Voice*, May, 158–67.

Hart, Janet. 1993. "Cracking the Code: Narrative and Political Mobilization in the Greek Resistance." *Social Science History* 16: 631–68.

Hart, Paul 't. 1993. "Symbols, Rituals, and Power: The Lost Dimensions of Crisis Management." *Journal of Contingencies and Crisis Management* 1: 26–50.

Hasegawa, Koichi. 2004. *Constructing Civil Society in Japan: Voices of Environmental Movements*. Melbourne, Australia: Trans Pacific Press.

Hasegawa, Manabu. 2011. "Sei·Kan·San·Gaku·Mejia wo Torikonda Denryoku Gyōkai" [The political, bureaucratic, industrial, academic, and media worlds entangled in the electric power industry]. *Shūkan Ekonomisuto*, July (special edition), 108–11.

Hasuike, Tōru, and Katsunobu Onda. 2011. "Tōkyō Denryoku to Iu Shakai Mondai" [The social problem known as the Tokyo Electric Power Company]. *Sekai*, August, 232–39.

Hatamura, Yōtarō. 2011. *Mizō to Sōteigai: Higashi Nihon Daishinsai ni Manabu* [Unprecedented and unimagined: Learning from the great eastern Japan earthquake]. Tokyo: Kōdansha.

Hay, Colin. 1996. "Narrating Crisis: The Discursive Construction of the 'Winter of Discontent.'" *Sociology* 30 (2): 253–77.

———. 1999. "Crisis and the Structural Transformation of the State: Interrogating the Process of Change." *British Journal of Politics and International Relations* 1 (3): 317–44.

Hayashi, Toshihiko, and Akihara Masato. 2011. "Shisen Shinsai Fukkō Taikō Shien no Jitsurei" [The facts about partnering support in the recovery from the Sichuan earthquake]. PowerPoint presentation to the 21 Seiki Bunmei Kenkyū Seminaaru 2011, Kobe, 18 November.

Hayashi, Yoshitsugu. 2009. "Chiiki Keizaiken no Kakuritsu ni muketa Dōshūsei no Dōnyū to Gyōsei Kaikaku" [The introduction of a state system that establishes regional economic areas and administrative reform]. 21 Seiki Seisaku Kenkyūjo Kenkyū Purojekuto, Tokyo, March.

Heberle, Rudolf. 1951. *Social Movements: An Introduction to Political Sociology*. New York, Appleton-Century-Crofts.

Higashi Nihon Daishinsai Fukkō Kōsō Kaigi. 2011. *Fukkō e no Teigen: Hisan no Naka no Kibō* [A proposal for reconstruction: Hope from within the misery]. Tokyo: Higashi Nihon Daishinsai Fukkō Taisaku Honbu Jimukyoku.

Higashi Nihon Daishinsai Fukkō Taisaku Honbu Jimukyoku. 2011. "Fukkō Tokku Seido (Kashō) nado no Kentō Jōkyō ni Tsuite" [Concerning the status of the discussion about a Recovery Special Zone System (temporary name)]. Government Commission Report, Tokyo, 23 August.

Hirayama, Yōsuke. 2011. "Kiki wa Kikai na no Ka" [Is the crisis an opportunity?]. *Sekai*, August, 67–75.

Hirose, Takashi. 2011. "Japan's Earthquake-Tsunami-Nuclear DISASTER Syndrome: An Unprecedented Form of Catastrophe." *Asia-Pacific Journal* 9 (39), no. 1.

Hirschman, Albert O. 1991. *The Rhetoric of Reaction: Perversity, Futility, Jeopardy.* Cambridge, MA: Harvard University Press.

Hokutō Kenkyū. 2011. "Higashi Nippon Daishinsai Tokushū" [Great East Japan disaster special edition]. No. 74.

Hood, Christopher P. 2011. *Dealing with Disaster in Japan: Responses to the Flight JL123 Disaster.* London: Routledge.

Horne, Jed. 2006. *Breach of Faith: Hurricane Katrina and the Near-Death of an American City.* New York: Random House.

Hornung, Jeffrey W. 2011a. "The Risks of Disaster Nationalism." *Japan Times*, 4 July.

———. 2011b. "When Disaster Isn't a Zero-Sum Game." *Diplomat*, 28 April.

Hosono, Miwa. 2011. "The Limits of Disaster Diplomacy." *Diplomat*, 17 April, http://the-diplomat.com/china-power/2011/04/17/the-limits-of-disaster-diplomacy/.

Howitt, Arnold M., and Herman B. Leonard, eds. 2009. *Managing Crises: Responses to Large-Scale Emergencies.* Washington, DC: Congressional Quarterly Press.

Huang, Yunong, Linlin Zhou, and Kenan Wei. 2011. "Wenchuan Earthquake Recovery: Government Policies and Non-Governmental Organizations' Participation." *Asia-Pacific Journal of Social Work and Development* 21 (2): 77–91.

Humphreys, Leonard A. 1995. *The Way of the Sword: The Japanese Army in the 1920s.* Stanford, CA: Stanford University Press.

Ido, Toshizō. 2011. *Shin Shin, Ippo Ippo Zoku* [New steps, new steps, continued]. Kobe: Kobe Jyanarusha.

Iida, Tetsunari. 1997. "Bōsō Suru Genshiryoku Mura no Hitobito" [The people of the nuclear power village who are running roughshod]. *Ronza*, February, 25–29.

———. 1999. "Genshiryoku no Unei Taisei no Arikata ni Tsuite" [Concerning the nuclear power plant management system]. Paper for the 5th Roundtable Conference on Nuclear Policy, Tokyo, 21 January.

———. 2011a. "'Genshiryoku Mura' ga Motarashita Hakyokuteki na 'Shūsen no Hi'" [A cataclysmic "day the war ended" brought about by "the nuclear village"]. Foreword to *"Genshiryoku Mura" ni Koete: Posuto Fukushima no Enerugii Seisaku* [Beyond the "nuclear village": A post Fukushima energy policy], edited by Tetsunari Iida, Satō Eisaku, and Kōno Tarō, 5–16. Tokyo: NHK Bukkusu.

———. 2011b. "'Genshiryoku Mura' to Iu Kyokō" [The concoction known as the "nuclear village"]. In *"Genshiryoku Mura" wo Koete: Posuto Fukushima no Enerugii Seisaku* [Beyond the "nuclear village": A post Fukushima energy policy], edited by Tetsunari Iida, Satō Eisaku, and Kōno Tarō, 17–40. Tokyo: NHK Bukkusu.

———. 2011c. "Nihon no Shōrai no Enerugii Seisaku" [Japan's energy policy future]. Presentation to the Keizai Dōyūkaikaiin Seminaa, Tokyo, 28 September.

———. 2011d. "Saiseikanō Enerugii Mazu Shiritai 7tsu no Koto" [The seven things we want to know first about renewable energy]. *Sekai*, November, 109–12.

Immergut, Ellen M. 1998. "The Theoretical Core of the New Institutionalism," *Politics and Society*. 26 (1): 5–34.

Information Economy Division, Commerce and Information Policy Bureau, Ministry of Economy, Trade and Industry. 2011. "Smart Community Initiatives as a New Energy Policy after the Great Japan Earthquake." Slide presentation.

International Atomic Energy Agency. 2011. "Expert Mission to Japan." IAEA Study Mission Report, Vienna, Austria, 1 June.

International Energy Agency. 2012. *Tracking Clean Energy Progress*. Paris: International Energy Agency.

Ishibashi, Katsuhiko. 2011. "Masa ni Genpatsu Shinsai Da" [Certainly this is a nuclear power earthquake disaster]. *Sekai*, May, 127–33.

Ishikawa, Mikiko. 2011. "Hisaichi no Fukkō Keikaku Sakutei no Purosesu no Shiten Kara" [From the point of view of the process of recovery planning in the affected areas]. In *Higashi Nihon Daishinsai no Taiō (Tokushū 1)*. Tokyo: Nihon Gakujitsu Kaigi.

Itagaki, Eiken. 2011. "Kokka no Kiki Taisho wo Ninaeru no wa Chūō Seifu Dake Da" [Only the central government can shoulder the burden of responding to the national crisis]. *Gekiron* 2: 120–25.

Iwate Prefecture. 2011. "Iwateken Fukkō Tokku wo Kōsei Suru 9 no Tokku" [The nine special districts that comprise the Iwate Prefecture Recovery Special Districts]. Prefectural Report. Morioka.

Iyengar, Shanto. 1991. *Is Anyone Responsible? How Television Frames Political Issues*. Chicago: University of Chicago Press.

Izumi, Hiroshi. 2011. "Post-Earthquake Politics: A New Paradigm?" Tokyo Foundation, April 26, http://www.tokyofoundation.org/en/articles/2011/post-quake-politics.

Jacoby, Wade. 2000. *Imitation and Politics: Redesigning Modern Germany*. Ithaca, NY: Cornell University Press.

Jain, Purnendra. 2011. "Japan's Subnational Government: Toward Greater Decentralization and Participatory Democracy." Chap. 9 in *Japanese Politics Today: From Karaoke to Kabuki Democracy*, edited by Takashi Inoguchi and Purnendra Jain. Houndmills, UK: Palgrave Macmillan.

Jennings, M. Kent. 1999. "Political Responses to Pain and Loss," *American Political Science Review* 93 (1): 1–13.

Jobin, Paul. 2011. "Dying for TEPCO? Fukushima's Nuclear Contract Workers." *Asia-Pacific Journal* 9 (18).

Johnson, Chalmers. 1982. *MITI and the Japanese Miracle: The Growth of Industrial Policy, 1925–1975*. Stanford, CA: Stanford University Press.

Johnston, Richard. 1992. "Political Generations and Electoral Change in Canada." *British Journal of Political Science* 22 (1): 93–122.

Jyapan Purattofōmu. 2011. *Chūgoku Shisen Jishin Hisaisha Shien Hōkokusho* [Japan platform summary report on Sichuan earthquake relief]. Tokyo, November.

Kageyama, Yuri, and Justin Pritchard. 2011. "Ties Bind Japan Nuke Sector, Regulators." Associated Press and *Time Magazine*, May 2.

Kamiya, Hideyuki. 2011. "Jichitai Renkei Gannen 2011: Shin Jidai no Makuake, Jichitaikan Shien no Gunsei" [2011 is year one of local government solidarity: A new age begins with the clustering of mutual support among localities]. *Chihō Gyōsei*, 1 September, 1–10.

Kamiya, Matake. 2011. "Don't Underestimate Japan!" *Japan Journal* 8 (1): 14–16.

Kan, Tokusan. 1975. *Kantō Daishinsai* [The great Kanto disaster]. Tokyo: Chūō Kōronsha.

Kapucu, Naim. 2011. "Collaborative Governance in International Disasters: Nargis Cyclone in Myanmar and Sichuan Earthquake in China Cases." *International Journal of Emergency Management* 8 (1): 1–25.

Kashiwagi, Takao. 2012. "Turning Smart Community Products into New Export Items." *Japan Echo Web*, no. 11, April–May, http://www.japanechoweb.jp/wp -content/uploads/downloads/2012/04/jew1112.pdf.

Katzenstein, Peter J. 1996. *Cultural Norms and National Security: Police and Military in Postwar Japan*. Ithaca, NY: Cornell University Press.

Katznelson, Ira. 1997. "Structure and Configuration in Comparative Politics." In *Comparative Politics: Rationality, Culture, and Structure*, edited by Mark Irving Lichbach and Alan S. Zuckerman. Cambridge: Cambridge University Press.

Kawano, Akira. 2011. "Lessons Learned from Our Accident at Fukushima Nuclear Power Stations." Presentation made to GLOBAL2011@Makuhari by Tokyo Electric Power Company, 12 December.

Kawasaki, Akira. 2011. "Nihon no Heiwa Undō ni Mirai wa Aru ka" [Is there a future for Japan's peace movement?]. *Sekai*, September, 79–90.

Kawato, Yuko, Robert Pekkanen, and Yutaka Tsujinaka. 2012. "Civil Society and the Triple Disasters: Revealed Strengths and Weaknesses." Chap. 4 in *Natural Disaster and Nuclear Crisis in Japan: Response and Recovery after Japan's 3-11*, edited by Jeff Kingston. London: Nissan Monograph Series, Routledge.

Keidanren. 1995. "Proposals for the Revitalization of Industry following the Kobe (Hanshin/Awaji Region) Earthquake." Tokyo, 28 March.

———. 2011. "Keidanren Growth Strategy 2011: Accelerating Growth through Private-sector Dynamism." Tokyo, 16 September.

Keidanren Kankyō Honbu. 2011. "Enerugii Seisaku wo meguru Saikin no Dōkō to Keidanren no Torikumi" [Recent directions in energy policy and Keidanren's efforts]. Tokyo, October.

Keizai Kōhō Sentā. 2011a. "Borateia Katsudō ni kansuru Ishiki: Jittai Chōsa Hōkokusho" [Empirical research report on attitudes concerning volunteer activities]. Tokyo, July.

———. 2011b. "Saigai e no Sasae to Taiō ni kansuru Ishiki: Jittai Chōsa Hōkokusho" [Attitudes toward preparation for and coping with disasters: A report of a data-based study]. Tokyo, October.

Kelman, Ilan. 2007. "Hurricane Katrina Disaster Diplomacy." *Disasters* 1 (3): 288–309.

———. 2012. *Disaster Diplomacy: How Disasters Affect Peace and Conflict*. Abingdon, UK: Routledge.

Kelman, Ilan, and Theo Koukis, eds. 2000. "Disaster Diplomacy." *Cambridge Review of International Affairs* 14 (1): 214–94.

Ker-Lindsay, James. 2000. "Greek-Turkish Rapprochement: The Impact of 'Disaster Diplomacy'?" *Cambridge Review of International Affairs* 14 (1): 215–32.

Kershner, Isabel. 2011. "After Soldier Freed, Israelis Reflect on Public Campaign." *International Herald Tribune*, 20 October.

Kido, Atsushi. 1998. "Trends of Nuclear Power Development in Asia." *Energy Policy* 26 (7): 577–82.

Kikkawa, Takeo. 2004. *Nihon Denryokugyō Hatten no Dainamizumu* [The dynamism of Japan's electric power producers]. Nagoya: Nagoya Daigaku Shuppankai.

———. 2011. "Genshiryoku 'Kokusaku Minei' Hōshiki no Hikari to Kage" [The light and shadows of the "national policy, private management" nuclear power formula]. *Gaikō*, July, 36–39.

Kingdon, John W. 1995. *Agendas, Alternatives, and Public Policies*. 2nd ed. Boston: Little, Brown.

Kingston, Jeff. 2004. *Japan's Quiet Transformation: Social Change and Civil Society in the Twenty-first Century*. London: RoutledgeCurzon.

———. 2011. *Contemporary Japan: History, Politics and Social Change since the 1980s*. West Sussex, UK: Blackwell.

———. 2012a. "Mismanaging the Fukushima Nuclear Crisis," *Asia-Pacific Journal* 10 (12), no. 4.

———. 2012b. "The Politics of Disaster, Nuclear Crisis, and Recovery." Chap. 11 in *Natural Disaster and Nuclear Crisis in Japan: Response and Recovery after Japan's 3-11*, edited by Jeff Kingston. London: Nissan Monograph Series, Routledge.

Kinney, Henry. 1924. "Earthquake Days." *Atlantic Monthly*, January.

Kitamura, Jun. 2011. "Beigun [Tomodachi Sakusen] no Seika ni Kakureta Nihon Seifu no Shittai" [The Japanese government's disgraceful obscuring of the success of the U.S. military's "Operation Friendship"]. *Seiron*, June, 157–60.

Klose, Frank, Michael Kofluk, Stephan Lehrke, and Harald Rubner. 2010. "Toward a Distributed Power World: Renewables and Smart Grids Will Reshape the Energy Sector." Boston Consulting Group, June.

Kobayashi, Yoshinori. 2011. *Kokubō Ron* [A theory of national defense]. Tokyo: Shōgakkan.

Koide, Hiroaki. 2011a. *Genpatsu no Uso* [Nuclear power lies]. Tokyo: Fusōsha.

———. 2011b. "Genshiryoku Mura e no Saishū Kankoku" [The final warning to the nuclear village]. In *Genshiryoku Mura no Taizai* [The great crimes of the nuclear village], edited by Koide Hiroaki, Nishio Kanji, Satō Eisaku, Sakurai Katsunobu, Onda Katsunobu, Hoshi Ryōichi, and Genyū Sokyū, 7–42. Tokyo: KK Besutoseraazu.

Koide, Hiroaki, Nishio Kanji, Satō Eisaku, Sakurai Katsunobu, Onda Katsunobu, Hoshi Ryōichi, and Genyū Sokyū, eds. 2011. *Genshiryoku Mura no Taizai* [The great crimes of the nuclear village]. Tokyo: KK Besutoseraazu.

Kokkai Tōkyō Denryoku Fukushima Genshiryoku Hatsuden Jiko Chōsa Iinkai. 2012. "Kokkkai Jikochō" [Diet investigation into the accident]. Tokyo: Kokkai Tōkyō Denryoku Fukushima Genshiryoku Hatsuden Jiko Chōsa Iinkai.

Kokusai Kyōryoku Kikō. 2009. *Chūgoku Seibu Daijishin Higai ni taisuru Kokusai Kinkyū Enjyo Taikyūjo Chiimu-Iryō Chiimu Katsudō Hōkokusho* [Activities report of the International Rapid Relief Assistance Unit and the medical team in responding to the Western China earthquake damages]. Tokyo: Kokusai Kyōryoku Kikō, http://libopac.jica.go.jp/images/report/12004156.pdf.

Komatsu, Yuki. 2011. "Higashi Nippon Daishinsai Hassei wo Uketa Chihō Gyōzaisei Bunya ni okeru Torikumi" [Dealing with local administrative and financial issues resulting from the Great Eastern Japan Disaster]. *Rippō to Chōsa*, no. 317, June, 38–43.

Kōno, Tarō. 2011. "Tōhoku Daishinsai kara Genpatsu Jiko E" [From the Great Tohoku Disaster to the nuclear accident]. In *"Genshiryoku Mura" ni Koete: Posuto*

Fukushima no Enerugii Seisaku [Beyond the "nuclear village": A post-Fukushima energy policy], edited by Tetsunari Iida, Satō Eisaku, and Kōno Tarō, 65–104. Tokyo: NHK Bukkusu.

Krasner, Stephen D. 1984. "Approaches to the State: Alternative Conceptions and Historical Dynamics." *Comparative Politics* 16 (2): 240.

Krauss, Ellis S. 1974. *Japanese Radicals Revisited: Student Protest in Postwar Japan.* Berkeley: University of California Press.

Kubota, Tadae. 2011. "Chaban, Dairenritsu Sōdō ni Sengo Seiji no Byōsō wo Mita" [Farce: Viewing the sickness of postwar politics in the turmoil over building a grand coalition]. *Seiron*, June, 74–81.

Kuhn, Thomas. 1996. *The Structure of Scientific Revolutions.* 3rd ed. Chicago: University of Chicago Press.

Kuznetsov, Sergei, and Yulia Mikhailova. 2008. "Memory and Identity: Japanese POWs in the Soviet Union." In *Japan and Russia: Three Centuries of Mutual Images,* edited by Yulia Mikhailova and M. William Steele, 91–111. Folkestone, UK: Global Oriental.

Lambert, Kathryn Mary. 1993. "Negotiating between State and Non-State Actors: A Structural Analysis of International Hostage Events." PhD thesis, Temple University, Philadelphia PA.

Lane, Robert E. 1962. *Political Ideology.* New York: Free Press of Glencoe.

Lasswell, Harold D. 1930. *Psychopathology and Politics.* Chicago: University of Chicago Press.

Lévi-Strauss, Claude. 1966. *The Savage Mind.* London: Weidenfeld and Nicolson.

Levidis, Andrew. 2011. "Disasters May Help Redefine Japan's Self-Defense Forces." *Jakarta Globe,* 30 May.

Lidsky, Lawrence M., and Marvin M. Miller. 2002. "Nuclear Power and Energy Security: A Revised Strategy for Japan." *Science and Global Security* 10: 127–50.

Lincoln, Edward J. 2011. "The Heisei Economy: Puzzles, Problems, Prospects." *Journal of Japanese Studies* 37 (2): 351–76.

Linde, Charlotte. 1993. *Life Stories: The Creation of Coherence.* New York: Oxford University Press.

Linton, Ralph. 1942. "Age and Sex Categories." *American Sociological Review* 1.7 (5): 589–603.

Locher, James R. 2002. *Victory on the Potomac: The Goldwater-Nichols Act Unifies the Pentagon.* College Station: Texas A&M University Press.

Logan, Justin. 2012. "Japan Still Sleeps." *National Interest,* blog, 9 May, http://nationalinterest.org/blog/the-skeptics/japan-still-sleeps-6903.

Mahoney, James. 2000. "Path Dependence in Historical Sociology." *Theory and Society* 29: 507–48.

Mahoney, James, and Kathleen Thelen. 2010. "A Theory of Gradual Institutional Change." Chap. 1 in *Explaining Institutional Change: Ambuguity, Agency, Power,* edited by James Mahoney and Kathleen Thelen. Cambridge: Cambridge University Press.

Malhotra, Neil, and Alexander Kuo. 2008. "Atrributing Blame: The Public's Response to Hurricane Katrina." *Journal of Politics* 70 (1): 120–35.

Mamiya, Jyūzō. 2011. "Saigai Kyūjo no Minkanjin Bōgotai wo Tsukuri, Jieitai wo 'Kokubō' ni Sennen Saseyo!" [Let's construct a civilian disaster relief corps and have the Self-Defense Forces focus exclusively on national defense!]. *Gekiron* 2: 106–11.

Mann, Michael. 2005. *The Dark Side of Democracy: Explaining Ethnic Cleansing*. New York: Cambridge University Press.

Mannheim, Karl. 1993. "The Problem of Generations." In *From Karl Mannheim*, 2nd ed., edited by K. H. Wolff, 351–95. New Brunswick, NJ: Transaction.

Marcus, George E. 2002. *The Sentimental Citizen: Emotion in Democratic Politics*. University Park: Pennsylvania State University Press.

Marcus, George E., W. Russell Neuman, and Michael MacKuen. 2000. *Affective Intelligence and Political Judgment*. Chicago: University of Chicago Press.

Marcus, George E., John L. Sullivan, Elizabeth Theiss-Morse, and Sandra Wood. 1995. *With Malice toward Some: How People Make Civil Liberties Judgments*. New York: Cambridge University Press.

Martin, Alex. 2011. "Military Wins Hearts, Minds." In *3.11: A Chronicle of Events Following the Great East Japan Earthquake*, 49–50. Tokyo: Japan Times.

Masuda, Hiroya. 2007. "Dōshūsei Koso Chihō Bunken to Jūmin Shuken e no Kirifuda: Shuto, Tōkyō wa Kuni no Chokkatsu Ni" [The state system itself and decentralization are the trump cards toward citizens' sovereignty: The capital and Tokyo come under direct national control]. Chap. 44 in *Nippon no Ronten*, 412–17. Tokyo: Bungei Shunjū.

Matsumoto, Kenichi. 1991. "Sekaishi no Geemu' no Owarasekata" [How to end the "world game"]. *Chūō Kōron* 1269: 180–219.

Matsumura, Masahiro. 2011. "Japan's Earthquake: The Politics of Recovery." *Survival*, June–July, 19–25.

McCarthy, Paul A. 1991. *Operation Sea Angel: A Case Study*. Santa Monica, CA: Rand.

McCloskey, Deirdre Nansen. 2011. "The Rhetoric of the Economy and the Polity." *Annual Review of Political Science* 14: 181–99.

McDermott, Rose. 1992. "Prospect Theory in International Relations: The Iranian Hostage Rescue Mission." *Political Psychology* 13 (2): 237–63.

McGraw, Kathleen M., and Clark Hubbard. 1996. "Some of the People Some of the Time." In *Political Persuasion and Attitude Change*, edited by Diana Carole Mutz, Paul M. Sniderman, and Richard A. Brody. Ann Arbor: University of Michigan Press.

McNeill, David. 2001. *Media Intimidation in Japan: A Close Encounter with Hard Japanese Nationalism (Discussion Paper 1)*. Retrieved from electronic journal of contemporary japanese studies, March, http://www.japanesestudies.org.uk/discussionpapers/McNeill.html.

Midford, Paul. 2011. *Rethinking Japanese Public Opinion and Security: From Pacifism to Realism?* Stanford, CA: Stanford University Press.

———. forthcoming. "The GSDF's Quest for Public Acceptance." In *Japan's Ground Self-Defense Force and Its Search for Legitimacy*, edited by Robert Eldridge, Paul Midford, and Guiseppe Stavale.

Mikuriya, Takashi. 2011a. "Genchi—Genbashugi de Giron" [Debate about the actual place with a bottom-up approach]. *Yomiuri Shimbun*, 29 April.

———. 2011b. "'Sengo' ga Owari, 'Saigo' ga Hajimaru" [The "postwar" is over and the "post-disaster" has begun]. Tokyo: Chikuma Shobō.

Miller, Nathan. 1997. *The U.S. Navy: A History*. Annapolis, MD: Naval Institute Press.

Mine, Yoshiki 2011. "Higashi Nihon Daishinsai to Nicchū no Wakai" [The Great Eastern Japan Disaster and Sino-Japanese rapproachment]. Canon-Ifri Paper Series, Canon Institute for Global Studies, Tokyo, October.

Ministry of Defense. 2011. "Structural Reform of Defense Capability." Report, Tokyo, August.

Ministry of Economy, Trade, and Industry. 2010. "The Strategic Energy Plan of Japan: Meeting Global Challenges and Securing Energy Futures." Tokyo, June.

Miyagi Prefecture. 2011. "Miyagiken Shinsai Fukkō Keikaku" [Miyagi Prefecture plan for disaster decovery]. Miyagi Kenchō, Sendai, September.

Miyazaki, Manabu. 2007. *Kindai Yakuza Kōteiron: Yamaguchi gumi 90-nen no Rekishi* [An affirmative perspective on contemporary Yakuza: The ninety-year history of the Yamaguchi-gumi]. Tokyo: Chikuma Shobō.

Miyazaki, Manabu, and Kunio Suzuki. 2006. "Nani ga Karera o Oitsumeru no Ka" [What are they hunting them down for?]. *Ronza*, November, 30–43.

Mizokami, Kyle. 2011. "Japan's Soft Power Chance." *Diplomat Blogs*, 2 July.

Mizushima, Asaho. 1992. *Kimi wa Sandaabaado wo Shitte Iru Ka* [Are you aware of thunderbird?]. Tokyo: Nihon Hyōronsha.

———. 1995. "Dono Yō na Saigai Kyūjo Soshiki wo Kangaeru Ka" [What sort of disaster relief organization can we imagine?]. *Sekai*, March, 46–51.

———. 1998. "Jieitai no Heiwa Kenpōteki Kaihen Kōsō" [A conception of the conversion of the Self-Defense Forces in conformity to the peace constitution]. In *Kōkyū Sekai Heiwa no tame ni: Nihonkokukenpō kara no Teigen* [In quest for world peace for all time: Proposals based on the constitution of Japan], edited by Fukase Tadakazu, Sugihara Yasuo, Higuchi Yōichi, and Urata Kenji, 589–617. Tokyo: Keisō Shobō.

———. 2005. *Gendai Gunji Hōsei no Kenkyū* [Research on contemporary military law]. Tokyo: Nihon Hyōronsha.

———. 2011a. "Higashi Nippon Daishinsai to Kenpō: Hisaichi de Kangaeta Koto" [The Great Eastern Japan Disaster and the constitution: Thoughts from the affected area]. *Hōritsu Jihō* 83 (8): 1–3.

———. 2011b. "Shijō Saidai no Saigai Haken: Jieitai wo Dō Kaeru Ka" [The largest disaster dispatch in history: How will it change the Self-Defense Forces?]. *Sekai*, July, 112–22.

Mochizuki, Mike. 2008. "U.S.-Japan Alliance Dilemmas Regarding China." In *The Japan-U.S. Alliance and China-Taiwan Relations: Implications for Okinawa*, edited by Akikazu Hashimoto, Mike Mochizuki, and Kurayoshi Takara. Washington, DC: Sigur Center for Asian Studies, George Washington University.

Mōri, Yoshitaka. 2007. "Rokujūnen Ampo wo Meguru Medeia no Seijigaku" [Media politics surrounding the 1960s Japan-U.S. Security Treaty unrest]. *Gendai Shisō* 35 (1): 182–95.

Morinobu, Shigeki. 2011. "Financing Reconstruction with a Solidarity Tax." Tokyo Foundation, April 5, http://www.tokyofoundation.org/en/articles/2011/fi nancing-reconstruction.

Morris-Suzuki, Tessa. 1995. "Sustainability and Ecological Colonialism in Edo Period Japan." *Japanese Studies* 15 (1): 36–48.

Murakami, Akira. 2011. "Nihon no Heiwa Undō ni Mirai wa Aru Ka" [Does the Japanese peace movement have a future?]. *Sekai*, September, 79–90.

Murakami, Yōichirō. 2011. "Fukushima Igo Ikani Anzen wo Kakuritsu Suru Ka?" [How will we ensure our safety after Fukushima?]. *Chūō Kōron*, September, 152–59.

Muramatsu, Michio, and Ellis S. Krauss. 1984. "Bureaucrats and Politicians in Policymaking: The Case of Japan." *American Political Science Review* 78 (1): 126–46.

Murayama, Yūzō. 2011. "Higashi Nihon Dai Shinsai to Dōteki Bōeiryoku" [The Great Eastern Japan Disaster and dynamic defense]. Research Institute for Peace and Security, *RIPS Eye*, no. 135, Tokyo, 22 April.

Nagamatsu, Shingo. 2007. "Economic Problems during Recovery from the 1995 Great Hanshin-Awaji Earthquake." *Journal of Disaster Research* 2 (5): 372–80.

Nagashima, Akihisa. 2011. "Genbatsu Taisho: Nichibei Kyōryoku no Butaiura" [Dealing with nuclear power: Behind the stage of U.S.-Japan cooperation]. *Voice*, July, 134–39.

Naikaku Kanbō Chiiki Kasseika Tōgō Jimukyoku and Naikakufu Chiiki Kasseika Sokushinshitsu, eds. 2011. "Sōgō Tokku Seido ni Tsuite" [Concerning the comprehensive special zone system]. Report, Naikakufu, Tokyo, May.

Naikaku Kanbō Chiiki Seikatsu Tōgō Jimukyoku and Naikakufu Kōzō Kaikaku Tokku Tantōshitsu, eds. 2008. "Kōzō Kaikaku Tokku: Chiiki Tokusei wo Ikashite Miryoku wo Sōshutsu" [Structural reforms special zones: Living in regions with special characteristics and creating attractiveness]. Report, Naikakufu, Tokyo, September.

Naikakufu Kōzō Kaikaku Tokku Tantōshitsu, ed. 2008. "Tokku ni okeru Kōka" [The effectiveness of special zones]. Report, Naikakufu, Tokyo, July.

Nakabayashi, Itsuki. 2009. "Disaster Management System for Wide-Area Support and Collaboration in Japan." *Toshi Kagaku Kenkyū* 3: 73–81.

Nakagawa, Kazuyuki. 2000. "Hanshin Daishinsai kara 5 Nen" [Five years after the Great Hanshin Disaster]. *Chihō Gyōsei*, January.

Nakamura, Akira, and Masao Kikuchi. 2011. "What We Know and What We Have Not Yet Learned: Triple Disasters and the Fukushima Nuclear Fiasco in Japan." *Public Administration Review*, November/December, 893–99.

Nakanishi, Terumasa. 2011. "Nippon no Shukua [Sōteigai] to Sengo Taisei ga Maneku Kokka no Kiki" [Japan's chronic disease (unimagined) and the postwar system invite a national crisis]. *Seiron*, June, 50–61.

Nakasone, Yasuhiro. 2011. "Kan Naoto-kun ni Indō wo Watasu" [Hand Mr. Kan his disimissal notice]. *Bungei Shunjū*, July, 120–29.

Nelson, Thomas E., and Donald R. Kinder 1996. "Issue Frames and Group-Centrism in American Public Opinion." *Journal of Politics* 58 (4): 1055–78.

Neumann, Sigmund. 1939. "The Conflict of Generations in Contemporary Europe from Versailles to Munich." *Vital Speeches of the Day* 5: 623–28.

Nihon Gakujutsu Kaigi. 2011. "Higashi Nihon Shinsai Pearingu Shien" [Eastern Japan Disaster pairing support]. Nihon Gakujitsu Kaigi Kankyōgaku iinkai, Doboku Kōgaku Iinkai, Kenchiku Iinkai. Report, Tokyo, 28 March.

Nihon Genshiryoku Sangyō Kyōkai. 2008. *Genshiryoku Hatsuden ni kakaru Sangyō Dōkō Chōsa, 2008* [A survey of industrial activities related to nuclear power generation, 2008]. Tokyo: Nihon Genshiryoku Sangyō Kyōkai.

Nikolayenko, Olena. 2007. "The Revolt of the Post Soviet Generation: Youth Movements in Serbia, Georgia, and Ukraine." *Comparative Politics* 39 (2): 169–88.

Nippon Keidanren. 2006. "Interim Report on the Integrated Reform of Expenditures and Revenues: Building Streamlined and Well-Muscled Government." Tokyo, 18 April.

————. 2008. "Proposal for Comprehensive Reform of Taxation, Fiscal Policy, and Social Security Programs: Realizing a Secure and Vibrant Economic Society." Tokyo, 2 October.

Nippon Keizai Dantai Rengōkai. 2011a. *Enerugii Seisaku ni kansuru Daiichiji Teigen* [First proposal concerning energy policy]. Tokyo, 14 July.

————. 2011b. *Fukkō/Sōsei Masutaapuran: Futatabi Sekai ni Hokoreru Nippon wo Mezashite* [Reconstruction/creation master plan: Aiming for a Japan once again admired by the world]. Tokyo, 27 May.

Nippon Seisaku Tōshi Ginkō. 2011. "Fukkō Chiikizukuri Kenkyūkai: Chūkan Hōkokusho" [Interim report of the study group on rebuilding the region]. Tokyo: Nippon Seisaku Tōshi Ginkō.

Nishihara, Masashi. 2011. *The Earthquake Has Strengthened the Japan-U.S. Alliance.* AJISS Commentary. Tokyo: Association of Japanese Institutes of Strategic Studies.

Nishio, Kanji. 2011. "Datsu Genpatsu Koso Kokka Eizoku no Michi" [Eliminating nuclear power is the way to preserve our nation]. *WiLL*, July, 44–54.

Noda, Yoshihiko. 2011. "Waga Seiken Kōsō: Ima Koso 'Chūyō' No Seiji wo" [My vision for government: Toward moderate politics]. *Bungei Shunjū*, September, 94–103.

O'Connor, James R. 1987. *The Meaning of Crisis: A Theoretical Introduction.* Oxford: Blackwell.

Ohashi, Hiroshi. 2011. "Think Hard about Renewable Energy." The Association of Japanese Institutes of Strategic Studies, AJISS Commentary No. 133, 7 October, http://www.jiia.or.jp/en_commentary/201110/07-1.html.

Ōhira, Makoto. 2011. "Genpatsu Manee ni Machi wa Shizunda" [Depressed towns with nuclear power money]. In *Tōkyō Denryoku no Taizai* [TEPCO's great crimes], edited by Shūkan Bunshun, 126–31. Special Edition, 27 July. Tokyo: Shūkan Bunshun.

Ōmae, Kenichi. 1995. "Ima Naze Chiji Renmei ga Hitsuyō na no Ka" [Why do we need alliances of governors now?]. *Bungei Shunjū* 73 (4): 197–215.

Ōnishi, Takashi. 2011. "Machi no Saisei, Higaichi Shudō De" [The rebirth of towns through leadership by the disaster areas]. *Nihon Keizai Shimbun (Keizai Kyō-shitsu)*, 11 May.

Onitsuka, Hiroshi. 2012. "Hooked on Nuclear Power: Japanese State-Local Relations and the Vicious Cycle of Nuclear Dependence." *Asia-Pacific Journal* 10 (3), no. 1.

Onuki, Satoko. 2011. "Former Fukushima Governor Sato Eisaku Blasts METI-TEPCO Alliance: Government Must Accept Responsibility for Defrauding the People." *Asia-Pacific Journal* 9 (15).

Ōshika, Yasuaki. 2011. "Tokyo Denryoku wa Kyūsai Sareru: Kekkyoku Futan wa Kokumin ga Ou no Ka" [Tokyo Electric will be rescued: Will the Japanese people bear the burden?]. *Shūkan Aera*, 16 May.

Ōshima, Kenichi. 2010. *Saiseikanō Enerugii no Seijikeizaigaku: Enerugii Seisaku no Guriin Kaikaku ni Mukete* [The political economy of renewable energy: Toward a greening of energy policy]. Tokyo: Tōyō Keizai.

Osnos, Evan. 2011. "The Fallout." *New Yorker*, 17 October, 46–61.

Otabe, Tōru, ed. 2011. *3.11 Higashi Nippon Dai Shinsai Dokyumento: Jieitai Mō Hi-totsu no Saizensen* [3.11 Great Eastern Japan Disaster documentary: One more front line for the Self-Defense Forces]. Tokyo: Mainichi Shimbun.

Ouchi, William G. 1981. *Theory Z: How American Business Can Meet the Japanese Challenge*. Reading, MA: Addison-Wesley.

Ozawa, Ichirō. 1994. *Blueprint for a New Japan: The Rethinking of a Nation*. Tokyo: Kodansha.

Özerdem, Alpaslan, and Tim Jacoby. 2006. *Disaster Management and Civil Society: Earthquake Relief in Japan, Turkey, and India*. London: I. B. Tauris.

Park, Cheol Hee. 2011. "Post-Earthquake Japan-Korea Ties." *Diplomat*, 18 April.

Parshall, Jonathan, and Anthony Tully. 2005. *Shattered Sword: The Untold Story of the Battle of Midway*. Washington, DC: Potomac Books.

Payne, James L. 1968. *Patterns of Conflict in Colombia*. New Haven, CT: Yale University Press.

Pearce, Jenny. 1990. *Colombia: Inside the Labyrinth*. London: Latin America Bureau.

Pekkanen, Robert. 2004. "Japan: Social Capital without Advocacy." In *Civil Society and Political Change in Asia*, edited by Muthiah Alagappa, 223–55. Stanford, CA: Stanford University Press.

———. 2006. *Japan's Dual Civil Society: Members without Advocates*. Stanford, CA: Stanford University Press.

Pempel, T. J. 1982. *Policy and Politics in Japan: Creative Conservatism*. Philadelphia, PA: Temple University Press.

Penney, Matthew. 2011. "Heroes or Victims? The 'Fukushima Fifty.'" *Japan Focus*, 28 March.

———. 2012. "Nuclear Power and Shifts in Japanese Public Opinion." *Asia-Pacific Journal: Japan Focus*, 13 February.

Perlstein, Rick. 2008. *Nixonland: The Rise of a President and the Fracturing of America*. New York: Scribner.

Pierson, Paul. 2000. "Increasing Returns, Path Dependence, and the Study of Politics." *American Political Science Review* 94 (2): 251–68.

———. 2004. *Politics in Time: History, Institutions, and Social Analysis*. Princeton, NJ: Princeton University Press.

Polsky, Andrew. 2000. "When Business Speaks: Political Entrepreneurship, Discourse and Mobilization in American Partisan Regimes." *Journal of Theoretical Politics* 12 (4): 455–76.

Przystup, James J. 2008. "Japan-China Relations: Progress in Building a Strategic Relationship." *Comparative Connections*, July, 1–14, http://csis.org/files/media/csis/pubs/0802qjapan_china.pdf.

Ramseyer, J. Mark. 2011. "Why Power Companies Build Nuclear Reactors on Fault Lines: The Case of Japan." In *Back to the State? Government Investment in Corporations and Reregulation*, Paper presented at the Cegla Center of the Tel Aviv University Buchmann Faculty of Law. Tel Aviv, June.

Reed, Steven R. 1986. *Japanese Prefectures and Policymaking*. Pittsburgh, PA: University of Pittsburgh Press.

Restall, Hugo. 2008. "Shifting the Moral High Ground." *Global Asia* 3 (2): 74–81.

Rheuben, Joel. 2007. "The Rumble in the Regions: Decentralization and a State System for Japan." Research paper, Faculty of Law, University of Sydney, Australia.

———. 2011. "Could the Tohoku Earthquake Lead to Local Government Reform?" *East Asia Forum*, 16 September.

———. 2012. "Earthquake Disaster Could Be Catalyst for Regional Restructure." *Asia Currents*, February.

Riker, William H. 1986. *The Art of Political Manipulation*. New Haven, CT: Yale University Press.

Rochon, Thomas R. 1998. *Culture Moves: Ideas, Activism, and Changing Values*. Princeton, NJ: Princeton University Press.

Rohlen, Thomas P. 1974. *For Harmony and Strength: Japanese White-Collar Organization in Anthropological Perspective*. Berkeley: University of California Press.

Sakamoto, Kazuya. 2011. "Saigo no Jidai no Dōmeiron" [An alliance concept for the postdisaster era]. *Voice*, July, 112–21.

Sakurabayashi, Misa. 2011a. "Daifuntō! Jieitai wa Mukuwareru ka?" [Great struggle! Will the Self-Defense Forces be compensated?]. *Seiron*, June, 90–99.

———. 2011b. "Saigai Shien de Jieitai wo Miru Me wa Kawatta no Ka?" [Have views of the Self-Defense Forces changed with its disaster support?]. *Gekiron* 2: 152–59.

Sakurai, Katsunobu. 2011. "Tōden kara moratta no wa Higai Dake Da!" [All we got from TEPCO was damage!]. In *Genshiryoku Mura no Taizai* [The great crimes of the nuclear village], edited by Koide Hiroaki, Nishio Kanji, Satō Eisaku, Sakurai Katsunobu, Onda Katsunobu, Hoshi Ryōichi, and Genyū Sokyū, 131–45. Tokyo: KK Besutoseraazu.

Sakurai, Yoshiko. 2011. "Gunji Taikoku Chūgoku no Dōkatsu ni Kusshinai Betonamu, Firipin" [Vietnam, Philippines: Do not be intimidated by the great military power China]. *Sapio*, 20 July, 8–11.

Samuels, Richard J. 1983. *The Politics of Regional Policy in Japan: Localities Incorporated?* Princeton, NJ: Princeton University Press.

———. 1987. *The Business of the Japanese State: Energy Markets in Comparative and Historical Perspective*. Ithaca, NY: Cornell University Press.

———. 1994. *"Rich Nation, Strong Army": National Security and the Technological Transformation of Japan*. Ithaca, NY: Cornell University Press.

———. 2003. *Machiavelli's Children: Leaders and Their Legacies in Italy and Japan*. Ithaca, NY: Cornell University Press.

———. 2007. *Securing Japan: Tokyo's Grand Strategy and the Future of East Asia*. Ithaca, NY: Cornell University Press.

Samuels, Richard J., ed., 1977. *Political Generations and Political Development*. Lexington, MA: Lexington Books.

Sano, Toshi. 2011. "Fukushima Jiko de Fureru 'Genpatsu Yushutsu' no Shintenkai wo Saguru" [Nuclear power plant exports shaken by the Fukushima accident: Seeking new development]. *Enerugii Fōramu*, October, 36–37.

Satō Eisaku. 2011. "Honmaru wa Tōkyō Denryoku de wa naku, Keisanshō Da!" [The castle keep is METI not Tokyo Electric!]. In *Genshiryoku Mura no Taizai* [The great crimes of the nuclear village], edited by Koide Hiroaki, Nishio Kanji, Satō Eisaku, Sakurai Katsunobu, Onda Katsunobu, Hoshi Ryōichi, and Genyū Sokyū, 100–130. Tokyo: KK Besutoseraazu.

Satō, Eisaku, and Tamogami Toshio. 2011. "Furusato Fukushima wa Kanarazu Yomigaeru!" [Our home Fukushima will absolutely be rebuilt!]. *Gekiron* 2: 126–35.

Satō, Masahisa. 2011a. "Hontō no Kiki Nihon wa Kokubō wo Suikō Dekiru no Ka?" [Will Japan be able to defend itself in a real crisis?] *Gekiron* 2: 98–105.

———. 2011b. "Saigo ni Tayori ni Naru no wa Jieitai Da" [In the end, it's the Self-Defense Forces we rely on]. *Voice*, May, 62–69.

Sawa, Akihiko. 2011a. "Denryoku Gaisha wa Jiritsuteki na Keiei kaikaku Wo" [Toward a transformation of the electric power companies to independent management]. *Wedge*, November, 47.

———. 2011b. "Enerugii Seisaku no Minaoshi ni Mukete" [Facing a rethinking of energy policy]. Unpublished paper. 21 Seiki Seisaku Kenkyūjo, Tokyo.

———. 2011c. "Hassōden Bunriron Koko ga Okashii"[The debate over separating electric power generation and transmission is strange in these ways]. *Wedge*, November, 14–17.

Scalise, Paul J. 2009. "The Politics of Restructuring: Agendas and Uncertainty in Japan's Electricity Deregulation." Doctoral diss., Department of Politics and International Relations, University of Oxford.

———. 2011a. "Can TEPCO Survive?" In *Tsunami: Japan's Post-Fukushima Future*, edited by Jeff Kingston. London: Foreign Affairs.

———. 2011b. "Japan: Troubled TEPCO Weighs Mounting Damages." Global Strategy Analysis Daily Brief, Oxford Analytica, 1 June.

———. 2012a. "Hard Choices: Japan's Post-Fukushima Energy Policy in the 21st Century." Chap. 8 in *Natural Disaster and Nuclear Crisis in Japan: Response and Recovery after Japan's 3-11*, edited by Jeff Kingston. London: Nissan Monograph Series, Routledge.

———. 2012b. "Japan's Distribution Challenge: Lessons from Abroad." Chap. 6 in *Powering Ahead: Perspectives on Japan's Energy Future*. London: Economist Intelligence Unit, Economist Group.

Schaede, Ulrike. 2008. *Choose and Focus: Japanese Business Strategies for the 21st Century*. Ithaca, NY: Cornell University Press.

Schencking, J. Charles. 2006. "Catastrophe, Opportunism, Contestation: The Fractured Politics of Reconstructing Tokyo following the Great Kantō Earthquake of 1923." *Modern Asian Studies* 40 (4): 833–74.

———. 2008. "The Great Kantō Earthquake and the Culture of Catastrophe and Reconstruction in 1920s Japan." *Journal of Japanese Studies* 34 (2): 295–331.

———. 2009. "1923 Tokyo as a Devastated War and Occupation Zone: The Catastrophe One Confronted in Post Earthquake Japan." *Japanese Studies* 29 (1): 111–29.

Schumpeter, Joseph A. 1942. *Capitalism, Socialism, and Democracy*. New York: Harper.

Segawa, Makiko. 2011. "Fukushima Residents Seek Answers amid Mixed Signals from Media, TEPCO and Government." Report from the Radiation Exclusion Zone. *Asia-Pacific Journal* 9 (16).

———. 2012. "After the Media Has Gone: Fukushima, Suicide, and the Legacy of 3.11." *Asia-Pacific Journal* 10 (19), no. 2.

Seguchi, Kiyoyuki. 2011. "Daishinsai Kokufuku no tame ni Nani wo Subeki Ka?" [What should we do to overcome the disaster?] Memo, *Kyanon Gurōbaru Senryaku Kenkyūjo*, 16 March.

Seidensticker, Edward. 1991. *Tokyo Rising: The City since the Great Earthquake*. Tokyo and Rutland, VT: Tuttle.

Seiple, Christopher. 1996. *The U.S. Military/NGO Relationship in Humanitarian Interventions*. Carlisle, PA: Peacekeeping Institute, U.S. Army War College.

Seligman, Adam B. 1992. *The Idea of Civil Society*. New York: Free Press.

Sheafer, Tamir, and Gadi Wolfsfeld. 2009. "Party Systems and Oppositional Voices in the News Media: A Study of the Contest over Political Waves in the United States and Israel." *International Journal of Press/Politics* 14 (2): 146–65.

Shieh, Shawn, and Guosheng Deng. 2011. "An Emerging Civil Society: The Impact of the 2008 Sichuan Earthquake on Grassroots Associations in China." *China Journal*, January, 181–94.

Shikata, Toshiyuki. 2011. "Seika Ageta Jieitai Muttsu no Tokusei" [Aggregating success: The six special characteristics of the Self-Defense Forces]. In *3.11 Higashi Nippon Dai Shinsai Dokyumento: Jieitai Mō Hitotsu Saizensen* [3.11 Great Eastern Japan Disaster documentary: One more front line for the Self-Defense Forces], edited by Tōru Otabe, 52–53. Tokyo: Mainichi Shimbun.

Shimabukuro, Yumiko. 2012. *Democratization and the Development of Japan's Uneven Welfare State*. Unpublished doctoral diss., Department of Political Science, Massachusetts Institute of Technology.

Shimazu, Naoko. 2012. "The Fukushima Report Hides behind the Cultural Curtain." *Guardian*, 6 July.

Shinoda, Tomohito. forthcoming. *Japanese Politics Then and Now: Institutional Changes and Power Shifts*. New York: Columbia University Press.

Shūkan Bunshun. 2011. *Tōkyō Denryoku no Taizai* [TEPCO's great crimes]. Special edition, 27 July.

Shūkan Taishū. 2011. *Jieitai Shien Katsudō: 100 Nichi Zen Kiseki* [Self-Defense Forces support activities: The entire 100-day trial]. Tokyo, 23 June.

Sieff, Martin. 2011. "Fukushima Disaster Propels Japan Closer to U.S., India." Asia Pacific Defense Forum, 16 September, http://apdforum.com/en_GB/article/rmiap/articles/online/features/2011/09/16/japan-nuclear-disaster.

Simpson, James. 2011. "Competition Rises for SDF Reservist Candidates." *Japan Security Watch*, 25 September, http://newpacificinstitute.org/jsw/?p=8324.

Slater, David H., Keiko Nishimura, and Love Kindstrand. 2012. "Social Media in Disaster Japan." Chap. 5 in *Natural Disaster and Nuclear Crisis in Japan: Response and Recovery after Japan's 3-11*, edited by Jeff Kingston. London: Nissan Monograph Series, Routledge.

Smith, Charles R. 1995. *Angels from the Sea: Relief Operations in Bangladesh, 1991*. Washington, DC: History and Museum Division, U.S. Marine Corps Headquarters.

Smith, Robert J. 1985. *Japanese Society: Tradition, Self, and the Social Order*. Ithaca, NY: Cornell University Press.

Smith, Sheila A. 2006. "Shifting Terrain: The Domestic Politics of the U.S. Military in Asia." East-West Center, Special Report No. 8, Honolulu.

Smits, Gregory. 2006. "Shaking Up Japan: Edo Society and the 1855 Catfish Picture Prints." *Journal of Social History* 39 (4): 1045–78.

Sniderman, Paul M., and Sean M. Theriault. 2004. "The Structure of Political Argument and the Logic of Issue Framing." In *Studies in Public Opinion: Attitudes, Nonattitudes, Measurement Error, and Change*, edited by Willem E. Saris and Paul M. Sniderman. Princeton, NJ: Princeton University Press.

Snow, David A., and Robert D. Benford. 1988. "Ideology, Frame Resonance, and Participant Mobilization," in Bert Klandermans and Hanspeter Kriesi, eds., *International Social Movement Research Across Cultures*. Greenwich, CT: JAI Press, 1988.

Son, Masayoshi, and Andrew DeWit. 2011. "Creating a Solar Belt in East Japan: The Energy Future." *Asia-Pacific Journal* 9 (38), no. 2.

Stackpole, Lt. Gen. Henry, III. 1992. "Angels from the Sea." *Proceedings/Naval Review*, vol. 118, May.

Steiner, Kurt. 1965. *Local Government in Japan*. Stanford, CA: Stanford University Press.

Steiner, Kurt, Scott Flanagan, and Ellis Krauss, eds. 1980. *Local Opposition in Japan: Progressive Local Government, Citizens' Movements, and National Politics*. Princeton, NJ: Princeton University Press.

Stigler, G. J. 1971. "The Theory of Economic Regulation." *Bell Journal of Economic Management* 2 (1): 3–21.

Stone, Deborah A. 1989. "Causal Stories and the Formation of Policy Agendas." *Political Science Quarterly* 104 (2): 281–300.

Stryker, Robin. 1996. "Beyond History versus Theory: Strategic Narrative and Sociological Explanation." *Sociological Methods and Research* 24 (3): 304–52.

Suzuki, Tatsujirō. 2000. "Nuclear Power Generation and Energy Security: The Challenges and Possibilities of Regional Cooperation," Report published by the James A. Baker Institute for Public Policy, Rice University, May.

———. 2011. Testimony before the Kagaku Gijutsu Inobeeshyon Sokushin Tokubetsu Iinkai, April 26.

Suzuki, Tatsujirō, Takeda Tōru, and Mizuno Noriyuki. 2011. "Nihonjin wa Kaku wo Dono yō ni Ronjite Kita no Ka?" [To what extent did the Japanese debate nuclear power?]. *Gaikō Fōramu*, July, 22–31.

Szymkowiak, Kenneth. 2002. *Sokaiya: Extortion, Protection, and the Japanese Corporation*. Armonk, NY: M. E. Sharpe.

Takahashi, Atsushi. 2011. "Mutsu Chūkan Chozō Shisetsu to Genshiryoku Manee no Fukai Kiri" [The deep fog of nuclear power money and the Mutsu City medium-term storage facility]. *Shūkan Tōyō Keizai*, 23 April, 52–55.

Takahashi, Masahito, and Nagata Yutaka. 2011. "Genshiryoku Riyō no Teitai wa Denki Ryōkin ni Dono Teido Eikyō Suru Ka?" [What effect will reduced use of nuclear power have on electric power tariffs?]. Tokyo: Denryoku Chūō Kenkyūjo Shakai Keizai Kenkyūjo Deisukasshonpeepaa.

Takao, Yasuo. 2007. *Reinventing Japan: From Merchant Nation to Civic Nation*. New York: Palgrave Macmillan.

Takarabe, Seiichi. 2008. "Shisen Daijishin: Kyūentai ga motarshita Tainichi Kanjō no Henka" [The Great Sichuan Disaster: Changes in attitudes toward Japan brought about by the Relief Corps]. *Harvey Road Weekly*, no. 585, 16 June, 1–2.

Takeuchi, Kazuhiko. 2011. "Shizen to Kyōsei Dekiru Shakai wo Mezashite" [Toward a society that allows greater symbiosis with nature]. *Kokusai Kōtsū Anzen Gakkaishi* 36 (2): 6–11.

Takubo, Masa. 2011. "Nuclear or Not? The Complex and Uncertain Politics of Japan's Post-Fukushima Energy Policy." *Bulletin of the Atomic Scientists* 67 (5): 19–26.

Takubo, Tadae. 2011. "Gōgan Fuson na Roshia Gaikō ni Taiji Se Yo" [Confront the arrogance of Russian diplomacy]. *Voice*, May, 186–193.

Taleb, Nassim Nicholas. 2010. *The Black Swan: The Impact of the Highly Improbable*. New York: Random House.

Tanabe, Saburō, Kenji Kosugi, and Tadahiro Kyōcho Okano. 1990. *Aikoku Undō Tōshi Retsuden*. Tokyo: Nihon Tosho Senta.

Tanida, Kuniichi. 2011. "Jieitaiwa Shinsai no Kyōkun" [Lessons from the disaster for the Self-Defense Forces]. *Asahi Shimbun*, 30 June.

Tasso, Takuya. 2011. "Kotae wa Genba ni Aru" [The answer lies in the actual locales]. *Sekai*, September, 41–50.

Teet, Jessica C. 2009. "Post-Earthquake Relief and Reconstruction Efforts: The Emergence of Civil Society in China?" *The China Quarterly* 198 (June), 330–47.

Terry, Edith. 1998. "Two Years after the Kobe Earthquake." In *Unlocking the Bureaucrat's Kingdom: Deregulation and the Japanese Economy*, edited by Frank Gibney, 231–42. Washington, DC: Brookings Institution Press.

Tierney, Kathleen, and James D. Goltz. 1997. "Emergency Response: Lessons Learned from the Kobe Earthquake." Preliminary paper no. 260, University of Delaware, Disaster Research Center.

Toba, Futoshi. 2011. *Hisaichi no Hontō no Hanashi wo Shiyō* [Let's have some straight talk about the disaster area]. Tokyo: Wani Bukkusu.

Toichi, Tsutomo. 2003. "Energy Security in Asia and Japanese Policy." *Asia-Pacific Review* 10 (1): 44–51.

Tokyo Electric Power Company. 2011. "Fukushima Nuclear Accident Analysis Report: Interim Report Summary." Tokyo, 2 December, http://www.tepco.co.jp /en/press/corp-com/release/betu11_e/images/111202e13.pdf.

Tomioka, Kōichirō. 2011. "Tennō Kōgō Ryōheika Jyunkō ni Kanrui Shita Nihonjin" [The Japanese people shed tears of gratitude for the Imperial Highnesses' royal tour]. *Gekiron* 2: 92–97.

Toyoda, Masakazu. 2011. "Lessons from Fukushima." PowerPoint presentation, Institute of Energy Economics, Tokyo, 11 October.

Tripartite Core Group. 2008. *Post-Nargis Joint Assessment*. Yangon, Burma: United Nations Information Centre.

Tsuji, Kiyoaki. 1984. *Public Administration in Japan*. Tokyo: University of Tokyo Press.

Uchiyama, Takashi. 2011. "Kindai Sekai no Haiboku to Atarashii Enerugii: Kono Kōsō no Subete wo Toinaose" [The defeat of the modern world and new energy: Question everything about the current structure]. *Sekai*, November, 88–96.

Uchiyama, Yu. 2010. *Koizumi and Japanese Politics: Reform Strategies and Leadership Style*. London: Taylor and Francis.

Umehara, Takeshi. 1983. *Seishin no Hakken* [Discovering (Japan's) spirit]. Tokyo: Shūeisha.

United Nations Centre for Regional Development. 1995. "Comprehensive Study of the Great Hanshin Earthquake." Research Report Series No. 12, Nagoya, October.

U.S. House of Representatives Select Bipartisan Committee to Investigate the Preparation for and Response to Hurricane Katrina. 2006. *A Failure of Initiative*. Washington, DC: U.S. House of Representatives.

Van Oostendorp, Herre. 2001. "Holding onto Established Viewpoints during Processing News Reports." In *New Perspectives on Narrative Perspective*, edited by Willie van Peer and Seymour Benjamin Chatman. SUNY Series, *The Margins of Literature*. Albany: State University of New York Press.

Vogel, Ezra. 1979. *Japan as No. One: Lessons for America*. Cambridge, MA: Harvard University Press.

Von Clausewitz, Carl. 1968. *On War*. London: Penguin Classics.

Washida, Kiyokazu. 2012. *Tōhoku no Shinsai to Sōzōryoku: Wareware wa Nani wo Owasareta no Ka?* [The Tohoku disaster and the power to imagine: What were our responsibilities?]. Tokyo: Kōdansha.

Watabe, Hiro. 2011. "Kinpaku Suru Shōenerugii Seisaku to Saiseikanō Enerugii Katsuyō ni yoru Chōki Chiiki Kasseika" [Strained energy conservation policies and the practical use of renewable energy in long-term regional revitalization]. Presentation to the Okayama-ken Gijitsushikai, September.

Watanabe, Tsuneo. 2011. "An Independent Commission to Explore Japan's Disaster Response." Tokyo Foundation, 16 April, http://www.tokyofoundation.org/en/articles/2011/independent-commission.

Wei, Jiuchang, Dingtao Zhao, and Liang Liang. 2009. "Estimating the Global Responses to China in the Aftermath of the Wenchuang Earthquake." Unpublished paper, http://www.kadinst.hku.hk/PDF_file/PA_Wei,_Zhao%20and%20Liang.pdf.

White, Hayden. 1981. "The Value of Narrativity in the Representation of Reality." In *On Narrative*, 2nd ed., edited by W. J. T. Mitchell. Chicago: University of Chicago Press.

Wike, Richard. 2012. "Does Humanitarian Aid Improve America's Image?" *Pew Global Attitudes Project*, Pew Research Center Publications, Washington, DC, 6 March, http://pewresearch.org/pubs/2213/united-states-humanitarian-aid-disaster-relief-pakistan-indonesia-japan-tsunami-earthquake.

Wilder, Andrew. 2008. *Perceptions of the Pakistan Earthquake Response: Humanitarian Agenda 2015, Pakistan Country Study*. Medford, MA: Feinstein International Center, Tufts University, February.

Williamson, Piers. 2012. "Largest Demonstrations in Half a Century Protest the Restart of Japanese Nuclear Power Plants," *The Asia-Pacific Journal* 10 (27), no.5.

Yamada, Masaki. 2011. "Forces for Good." *Japan Journal* 8 (1): 8–13.

Yamazaki, Shigetaka. 2012. "Daitoshi Seido wo Meguru Giron no Jōkyō Nado ni Tsuite" [Concerning the conditions related to the large city system]. Tokyo: Sōmushō Jichi Gyōseikyoku Gyōseika.

Yokomichi, Kiyotaka. 2010. "New Policies in Wide-Area Administration in Japan." Council of Local Authorities for International Relations, Up-to-Date Documents on Local Autonomy in Japan, No. 6, Tokyo.

———. 2011. "Movement in Decentralization in Japan after the First Decentralization Reform." Council of Local Authorities for International Relations, Up-to-Date Documents on Local Autonomy in Japan, No. 8, Tokyo.

Yokota, Yumiko. 2011. "Geneki Kanryō 83 Nin no Dai Ankeeto" [A large survey of eighty-three current bureaucrats]. *Bungei Shunjū*, May, 374–85.

Yoshikawa, Naohiro. 2010. *Garapagosu Suru Nihon* [Japan as the Galapagos]. Tokyo: Kōdansha.

Yoshitomi, Yūji. 2011. *Hashimoto Tōru: Kaikakusha Ka Kowashiya Ka?* [Hashimoto Tōru: Reformer or destroyer?]. Tokyo: Chūō Kōron Shinsha.

You, Chuanmei, Xunchui Chen, and Lan Yao. 2009. "How China Responded to the May 2008 Earthquake during the Emergency and Rescue Period," *Journal of Public Health Policy* (2009) 30, 379–394.

Zhang, Xiaoling. 2011. "From Totalitarianism to Hegemony: The Reconfiguration of the Party State and the Transformation of Chinese Communication." *Journal of Contemporary China* 20 (68): 103–15.

Zielonka, Ryan. 2011. "Chronology of Operation Tomodachi." Brief, National Bureau of Asian Research, 8 April, http://www.nbr.org/research/activity.aspx?id=121.

Index

Note: Page numbers in *italic* type indicate photographs. Page numbers followed by *t* indicate tables.